Andreas Kehl
Adjunct Islands in English

Studies in Generative Grammar

Editors
Norbert Corver
Harry van der Hulst

Founding editors
Jan Koster
Henk van Riemsdijk

Volume 152

Andreas Kehl

Adjunct Islands in English

Theoretical Perspectives and Experimental Evidence

DE GRUYTER
MOUTON

ISBN 978-3-11-221517-3
e-ISBN (PDF) 978-3-11-109273-7
e-ISBN (EPUB) 978-3-11-109412-0
ISSN 0167-4331

Library of Congress Control Number: 2023936250

Bibliographic information published by the Deutsche Nationalbibliothek
The Deutsche Nationalbibliothek lists this publication in the Deutsche Nationalbibliografie; detailed bibliographic data are available on the Internet at http://dnb.dnb.de.

© 2025 Walter de Gruyter GmbH, Berlin/Boston
This volume is text- and page-identical with the hardback published in 2023.
Printing and binding: CPI books GmbH, Leck

www.degruyter.com

Acknowledgments

This monograph is the revised version of my 2021 University of Tübingen dissertation. I owe special thanks to Susanne Winkler and Sam Featherston, who assisted me throughout this research project with invaluable advice and constructive criticism. Their profound knowledge of the field and experimental techniques had a lasting impact on my own thinking about linguistics and how to systematically approach a phenomenon.

I have benefitted greatly from discussions on this research at various occasions with Peter W. Culicover, Andreas Konietzko, Jutta M. Hartmann, and Jessica Brown. I also thank Hans Kamp, Liliane Haegeman, Katja Jasinskaja, Martin Salzmann, and Michelle Sheehan for valuable comments on talks of the material presented here. The helpful comments of an anonymous reviewer for this volume have encouraged me to clarify the discussion in some points and draw a stronger connection to similar proposals.

All remaining errors and shortcomings are necessarily my own.

The majority of the research for this monograph was carried out during my time at the Collaborative Research Center *SFB 833 – The Construction of Meaning* at the University of Tübingen, funded by the German Research Foundation (Deutsche Forschungsgemeinschaft, DFG, Project-ID 75650358). Among the many colleagues there, I want to thank especially Marion Jäger for being a role model in organizational issues, Robin Hörnig and Edith Scheifele for invaluable assistance in experimental designs and the fundamentals of statistical analysis, as well as Álvaro Cortés Rodríguez and Larissa Specht for always having an open ear when I was stuck at some point.

I also thank the editors of the *Studies in Generative Grammar* series, Norbert Corver and Harry van der Hulst, for considering this monograph for inclusion in the series. At De Gruyter Mouton, I thank Birgit Sievert and Kirstin Börgen for their editorial support throughout the publication process.

The most profound acknowledgment I can make is to my parents, family, and friends, who never ceased to support me. Thank you!

Stuttgart, March 2023
Andreas Kehl

Contents

Acknowledgments —— V

Abbreviations —— XI

List of Figures —— XIII

List of Tables —— XV

1	**Introduction** —— **1**	
1.1	Examples of grammatical extractions from adjuncts —— 3	
1.2	Participle adjuncts and extraction patterns —— 5	
1.3	Empirical scope and focus —— 6	
1.4	Central research question and sketch of the proposal —— 9	
1.5	Conventions —— 13	
1.6	Outline —— 14	
2	**Present participle adjuncts: structure and interpretation** —— **16**	
2.1	Research questions and chapter outline —— 16	
2.2	Towards a syntactic analysis of BPPAs —— 17	
2.2.1	Reduced adverbial clause analysis —— 20	
2.2.2	Converb construction analysis —— 23	
2.2.3	Depictive secondary predicate analysis —— 26	
2.2.4	Interim conclusion —— 29	
2.3	The interpretational space of BPPAs —— 30	
2.3.1	The semantics of depictives —— 31	
2.3.2	Event specification and expansion with co-eventive adjuncts —— 35	
2.3.3	Interpreting complex event structures —— 40	
2.4	Licensing conditions on depictive constructions —— 45	
2.4.1	Licensing conditions on the depictive —— 46	
2.4.2	Licensing conditions on the host predicate —— 50	
2.4.3	Resultative BPPA constructions —— 57	
2.5	Chapter conclusion —— 60	
3	**Previous approaches to extraction from adjuncts** —— **63**	
3.1	Research questions and chapter outline —— 63	
3.2	Syntactic gap-licensing accounts —— 67	
3.2.1	Optional feature sharing (Boeckx 2003; Oseki 2015) —— 67	

3.2.2	Attachment height and forced spell-out (Narita 2014) —— **71**	
3.2.3	Top-down structure building (den Dikken 2018) —— **74**	
3.2.4	Interim conclusion —— **77**	
3.3	Interaction accounts —— **78**	
3.3.1	Reanalysis (Demonte 1988) —— **78**	
3.3.2	Reflexivity (Borgonovo & Neeleman 2000) —— **82**	
3.3.3	Aspectual classes and extraction (Truswell 2007) —— **87**	
3.3.4	Event groupings and agentivity (Truswell 2011) —— **97**	
3.3.5	Semantically conditioned feature inactivity (Ernst 2022) —— **108**	
3.3.6	Spanish gerund complements (París 2003) —— **112**	
3.3.7	Maximal event templates (Fábregas & Jiménez-Fernández 2016a,b) —— **118**	
3.3.8	Pragmatic conditions on extraction (Chaves & Putnam 2020) —— **125**	
3.3.9	Coherence and extraction from adverbial clauses (C. Müller 2019) —— **134**	
3.3.10	Interim conclusion —— **138**	
3.4	An independence approach (Brown 2017) —— **138**	
3.5	Chapter conclusion —— **150**	
4	**Experimental evidence —— 153**	
4.1	Research questions and chapter outline —— **153**	
4.2	Categorical and factorial models of acceptability —— **155**	
4.3	Factors —— **158**	
4.3.1	General factors relevant to extraction from islands —— **158**	
4.3.2	Specific factors for adjunct islands —— **160**	
4.4	Methodology —— **162**	
4.5	Study series 1: Event structure —— **166**	
4.5.1	Experiment 1: Aspectual classes across constructions —— **167**	
4.5.2	Experiment 2: Event structure in declaratives and interrogatives —— **178**	
4.5.3	Experiment 3: Adjunct integration —— **183**	
4.5.4	Interim conclusion for study series 1 —— **188**	
4.6	Study series 2: Grammatical verb type —— **190**	
4.6.1	Experiment 4: Transitives, unaccusatives, and unergatives —— **192**	
4.6.2	Experiment 5: Complex unaccusatives and transitives —— **200**	
4.6.3	Interim conclusion for study series 2 —— **206**	
4.7	Study series 3: *get*-predicates and achievements —— **206**	
4.7.1	Experiment 6: *get*-predicates —— **209**	
4.7.2	Experiment 7: Progressive achievements —— **220**	
4.7.3	Experiment 8: *get*-predicates & achievements —— **228**	

4.7.4	Interim conclusion for study series 3 —— 235
4.8	General discussion and conclusion —— 237
4.8.1	Conclusions for the research questions —— 237
4.8.2	The relation to the islands debate —— 241
4.8.3	Summary of factors —— 244

5 **A factorial acceptability model for present participle adjuncts —— 246**
5.1	Main experimental findings —— 248
5.2	Deriving the factorial acceptability model —— 250
5.2.1	Independence —— 250
5.2.2	Durativity —— 253
5.2.3	Scalar change —— 258
5.2.4	Transitivity —— 264
5.2.5	Description of the final model —— 268
5.3	Predictions and advantages of the factorial model —— 273
5.3.1	Empirical coverage —— 274
5.3.2	Compatibility with CED-style locality conditions —— 277
5.3.3	Activities with directional phrases —— 278
5.3.4	Differences to adjunct licensing in Brown (2017) —— 281
5.3.5	A connection between durativity and scalar change —— 283
5.4	Potential challenges —— 286
5.4.1	Event specification or event expansion —— 286
5.4.2	Perception verbs —— 288
5.4.3	Gap site ambiguity —— 289
5.4.4	The cases of *show up* and *appear* —— 292
5.4.5	V–V linearization —— 293
5.4.6	Informativity —— 296
5.5	Similarities to past participle adjuncts —— 297
5.6	Chapter conclusion —— 300

6 **Conclusion and outlook —— 301**

References —— 307

Index —— 327

Abbreviations

AP	adjective phrase
attach	ATTACHMENT (experimental factor)
B&N	Borgonovo & Neeleman (2000)
BPPA	bare present participle adjunct
CAC	central adverbial clause
CED	Condition on Extraction Domain
CI	confidence interval
CP	complementizer phrase
CS	Conceptual Structure
DAC	Depictive Aspectuality Constraint
DG	Durativity Generalization
DP	determiner phrase
DRS	Discourse Representation Structure
ECM	exceptional case-marking
ESC	Endocentric Structuring Constraint
F&JF	Fábregas & Jiménez-Fernández (2016a)
FAM	Factorial Acceptability Model
FGD	filler–gap dependency
H&SB	Himmelmann & Schultze-Berndt (2005)
id	PARTICIPANT ID (random effect in Experiments 1–8)
IH	Independence Hypothesis
ILP	individual-level predicate
InitP	initiation phrase (Ramchand 2008)
IP	inflection phrase
item	ITEM (random effect in Experiments 1–8)
LDD	long-distance dependency
LF	Logical Form
LI	lexical item
LMEM	linear mixed-effects model
MRC	Manner–Result Complementarity
NP	noun phrase
OOD	object-oriented depictive
PAC	peripheral adverbial clause
PF	Phonetic Form
PP	preposition phrase
ProcP	process phrase (Ramchand 2008)
prog	PROGRESSIVITY (experimental factor)
ResP	result phrase (Ramchand 2008)
RhemeP	rheme phrase (Ramchand 2008)
RUH	Radical Unacceptability Hypothesis
SCG	Scalar Change Generalization
SD	standard deviation
SE	standard error
SEC	Single Event Condition

SEGC	Single Event Grouping Condition
SGC	Spanish gerund construction
SLP	stage-level predicate
SO	syntactic object
SOD	subject-oriented depictive
struc	STRUCTURE (experimental factor)
tela	ADJUNCT TELICITY (experimental factor)
telm	MATRIX TELICITY (experimental factor)
TG	Transitivity Generalization
TP	tense phrase
UDC	unbounded dependency construction
UI	Unintegration
verbtype	VERB TYPE (experimental factor)
*v*P/*v**P	light verb phrase
VP	verb phrase

List of Figures

Fig. 3.1	Gap-licensing accounts —— 64	
Fig. 3.2	Interaction accounts —— 65	
Fig. 3.3	Independence accounts —— 66	
Fig. 4.1	Categorical model of grammaticality —— 155	
Fig. 4.2	Factorial model of acceptability —— 156	
Fig. 4.3	Schematic representation of possible results —— 165	
Fig. 4.4	Results of Experiment 1 —— 171	
Fig. 4.5	Results of Experiment 2 compared to standardized fillers —— 180	
Fig. 4.6	Results of Experiment 3 compared to standardized fillers —— 187	
Fig. 4.7	Results of Experiment 4 compared to standardized fillers —— 195	
Fig. 4.8	Results of Experiment 5 compared to standardized fillers —— 204	
Fig. 4.9	Results of Experiment 6 compared to standardized fillers —— 214	
Fig. 4.10	Results of Experiment 7 compared to standardized fillers —— 224	
Fig. 4.11	Results of Experiment 8 compared to standardized fillers —— 231	
Fig. 5.1	Factorial Acceptability Model for BPPAs —— 247	
Fig. 5.2	Factorial Acceptability Model (extraction) —— 251	
Fig. 5.3	Factorial Acceptability Model (durativity) —— 257	
Fig. 5.4	Factorial Acceptability Model (durativity & scalar change) —— 264	
Fig. 5.5	Factorial Acceptability Model (durativity, scalar change & transitivity) —— 267	
Fig. 5.6	Factorial Acceptability Model for BPPAs (final model) —— 271	
Fig. 5.7	Schematic representation of trivial and non-trivial scalar change —— 284	

List of Tables

Tab. 3.1	Extraction pattern for BPPAs in Truswell (2011) —— 102
Tab. 3.2	Adjunction, licensing, and extraction in Brown (2017) —— 144
Tab. 4.1	Numerical results for Experiment 1 —— 171
Tab. 4.2	Statistical results for Experiment 1 —— 174
Tab. 4.3	Numerical results for Experiment 2 —— 180
Tab. 4.4	Statistical results for Experiment 2 —— 181
Tab. 4.5	Numerical results for Experiment 3 —— 186
Tab. 4.6	Statistical results for Experiment 3 —— 187
Tab. 4.7	Numerical results for Experiment 4 —— 195
Tab. 4.8	Statistical results for Experiment 4 —— 196
Tab. 4.9	Numerical results for Experiment 5 —— 203
Tab. 4.10	Statistical results for Experiment 5 —— 204
Tab. 4.11	Numerical results for Experiment 6 —— 213
Tab. 4.12	Statistical results for Experiment 6 —— 214
Tab. 4.13	Numerical results for Experiment 7 —— 224
Tab. 4.14	Statistical results for Experiment 7 —— 225
Tab. 4.15	Numerical results for Experiment 8 —— 231
Tab. 4.16	Statistical results for Experiment 8 —— 232
Tab. 5.1	Verb classes and the durativity generalization —— 257
Tab. 5.2	Verb classes and the durativity/scalar change generalizations —— 264
Tab. 5.3	Verb classes and transitivity —— 267
Tab. 5.4	Semantic compatibility for different verb classes. —— 268
Tab. 5.5	Overview of the factorial acceptability model —— 270
Tab. 5.6	Effects of telic/atelic PPs —— 280

1 Introduction

Sentences in natural languages are not simply a linear sequence of isolated words like beads on a string. Words and parts of words in one position can influence the form and interpretation of words or elements in another position of the sentence: they encode dependencies between one another in the form of shared properties (Koster 1987: 8–9). There are a variety of such dependencies, including singular–plural agreement, anaphor binding, and case-marking (Koster 1987: 13–14). An important type of dependency surfaces in displacement phenomena, which Corver (2006: 567) considers to be "a core property of human languages". Displacement links an element to another position in the sentence where it is semantically interpreted, even though it does not occur in this position in the surface structure (Chaves & Putnam 2020: 1). Often, dependencies do not apply to elements in linear sequence but rather across other elements; these are called long-distance dependencies (LDDs). In principle, LDDs are not syntactically constrained in the number of constituents or clauses they can span. For example, the sentence in (1a) contains an agreement dependency that stretches across fifteen words, from the plural noun *people* to the plural verb form *are*, indicated here by co-indexation. The *wh*-question in (1b), a filler–gap dependency (FGD), can be formed across multiple CP-boundaries: it links the sentence-initial *wh*-pronoun *what*, the so-called filler, to the complement position of the verb in the most deeply embedded clause. This position where the filler is semantically interpreted is called the gap site, here indicated by an underscore. For ease of reference, FGDs are shown by co-indexing.

(1) a. The people$_i$ who called and wanted to rent your house when you go away next year are$_i$ from California. (see Miller & Chomsky 1963: 430)
   b. [What]$_i$ do you think [the students will say [they believe [the TA claimed [he was trying to do __$_i$]]]]? (Chaves & Putnam 2020: 2)

Dependencies such as these are still subject to non-structural limitations: while there is no theoretical or competence-based limit on the distance for dependency formation, there is a practical, performance-based, one that reflects the finite amount of memory resources available to the parser (Miller & Chomsky 1963; Chomsky 1965; Sprouse & Hornstein 2013; Wagers 2013; Chaves & Putnam 2020). However, there are certain structural domains which apparently do not allow the formation of filler–gap dependencies: these domains are known as *islands* since the landmark dissertation of Ross (1967). Even a comparatively short dependency cannot be established into these domains and the result is considered ungrammatical. Island domains include subjects, complex NPs, relative clauses, and adjuncts; there are also related phenomena such as *wh*-islands, factive, and negative islands, where FGDs cannot be established across elements carrying a specific type of feature. The term "island effect" is used to describe the decreased acceptability of a sentence where a FGD, such as *wh*-extraction, relativization, or topicalization, is established between a filler in the left periphery and a gap inside one of the island domains. Sprouse & Hornstein (2013) do not use the term "island violation" due to its use as an explanatory term in structural or syntactic approaches to islands. The term island effect is more widely applicable in structural as well as non-structural approaches, such as semantic, information-structural or processing approaches because it is an observational term. A violation assumes the presence of a constraint whereas an effect is "agnostic about the source of the unacceptability" (Sprouse & Hornstein 2013: 2, fn. 4).

The main goal of this monograph is to investigate factors that influence the possibility of establishing FGDs into a subset of adjunct islands. Adjuncts are considered to invariably resist extraction in nearly all approaches to islands and are often called strong or absolute islands; in contrast, extraction from weak or selective islands is sensitive to characteristics of the extracted element (Cinque 1990; Szabolcsi 2006). The strong island status of adjuncts is captured in Huang's (1982) *Condition on Extraction Domain* (CED) in (2), which restricts extraction to properly governed categories; governed positions generally refer to complement positions in an X′ phrase structure, excluding specifiers and adjuncts.

(2) Condition on Extraction Domain
    A phrase A may be extracted out of a domain B only if B is properly governed.
    (Huang 1982: 505)

Thus, extraction from adjuncts such as adverbial clauses is illicit, as shown in the examples in (3); gap sites are again indicated by underscores, and square brackets indicate the adverbial clause:

(3) a. *Who did Susan watch TV [while talking to __ on the phone]?
    b. *What did the student read the textbook [without understanding __]?
       (Phillips 2013: 67, 73)

Since the original formulation of the CED, the concepts it is based on have been fundamentally revised and partially become obsolete in the framework of the Minimalist Program (Chomsky 1993, 1995b). However, extractions out of non-properly governed categories, meaning subjects and adjuncts, are still considered ungrammatical by a majority and there have been numerous attempts at a reformulation of the CED using Minimalist concepts; see G. Müller (2010, 2011) or Johnson (2003) for recent proposals, and Stepanov (2007) for an overview of earlier formulations. The categorical failure to establish FGDs into an adjunct constituent as predicted by the CED does not appear to hold up universally, as there are cases where extraction is reported to be possible; these counterexamples to the CED are introduced in the following section.

1.1 Examples of grammatical extractions from adjuncts

Examples of apparently grammatical extractions from adjuncts have been noted in the literature even before the formulation of the CED, for example in Cattell (1976) or Chomsky (1982). However, they do not offer a comprehensive explanation for these exceptions. Chomsky (1982) considers the example in (4b) to show a "fairly high" degree of acceptability, and Cattell (1976) considers the example in (4a) as a potential problem for his restrictive extraction approach.

(4) a. The girl that he bought a book for ... (Cattell 1976: 38, fn. 11)
    b. the article that I went to England without reading c (Chomsky 1982: 72)

There are also more complex examples of grammatical CED violations, such as (5), where the extracted *wh*-phrase is linked simultaneously to a gap inside a subject and an adjunct; this violates both the subject and adjunct clauses of the CED.

(5) [What kinds of books]$_i$ do [the authors of $\_\__i$] argue about royalties [after writing $\_\__i$]? (Chaves & Putnam 2020: 138)

Several attested examples of extraction from adjuncts are collected in Santorini (2019). The sample from these attested examples in (6) shows that extraction out of adjunct constituents occurs naturally despite the fact that this is considered ungrammatical by the CED; square brackets around the adjunct constituent and an underscore as indication for the gap site have been added.

(6) a. a grant application which I spent some money [to get in $\_\_$].
    b. These letters were not at all what he had paid good money [to receive $\_\_$].
    c. a country which adventurous foreigners would think twice [before attacking $\_\_$].
    d. I have this humongous watch that I kick myself [for wearing $\_\_$].
    e. The magazine I spend most of my days [reading $\_\_$].
    f. "This is the game I grew up [watching $\_\_$]," Wilson added.
       (Santorini 2019)

Santorini's list includes mostly extraction from infinitival purpose clauses, but also cases of participial adjuncts with and without prepositions. The two examples in (6a,b) show extraction from a purpose clause introduced by *to* and followed by an infinitive. This is a structure that, although analyzed as an adjunct, is considered to allow extraction quite freely by Huddleston & Pullum (2002: 1093). In the second set of examples in (6c,d), extraction occurs from an adjunct clause headed by a preposition. The two examples in (6e,f) show extraction from an adjunct clause that has no overt preposition heading the adjunct constituent.

The attested example in (7), kindly provided by Peter W. Culicover (p. c.), shows that relativization out of a present participle adjunct occurs even in quality journalism.

(7) Already uncomfortable with the policy — the $ 1.3 trillion legislation includes massive spending hikes that contradict prior GOP complaints about the debt — many Republicans were left dumbfounded by [a process]$_i$ that looked a lot like one they had [won office criticizing __$_i$].

(Washington Post, 22 March 2018[1])

Many of the attested sentences in Santorini (2019) and the examples discussed in the literature share the fact that the extracted phrase leaves a sentence-final gap site, so there is no possibility to indicate the gap by an intonational break (Chaves & Putnam 2020: 2–3); this is not a defining property, however, as it is possible to add sentence-final adverbials like *yesterday* or *at school*. I will largely focus on the types of constructions in (6e,f) and (7), as further described in the next section. Examples like these suggest that the CED may not hold in general; if adjunct constituents are strong islands, then an explanation is needed why there are several examples where extraction from an adjunct occurs in attested sentences. The two possible conclusions are either that such adjuncts are not really adjuncts or that the predictions from the CED need to be re-examined. This monograph will therefore examine the patterns of extraction from adjuncts that have been discussed in the literature and offer experimental evidence about the validity of these claims. The focus of the following chapters is not on the issue of whether or not adjuncts show uniform island behavior compared to extraction from non-islands; rather, I concentrate on the variation that occurs within a subset of adjuncts. Even in nearly minimal pairs, this subset shows different degrees to

---

[1] https://www.washingtonpost.com/powerpost/read-that-bill-some-republicans-now-shout-at-the-their-own-party/2018/03/22/732c83f4-2dee-11e8-8688-e053ba58f1e4_story.html, accessed 3 August 2022.

which extraction is acceptable. In these cases, it is often not the syntactic structure that determines adjunct transparency, but a set of different factors.

1.2 Participle adjuncts and extraction patterns

In most cases, the opacity of adjuncts for extraction operations is illustrated with adverbial clauses, as in the examples in (3) above. The adjunct type that typically exemplifies exceptions to the CED shows three specific characteristics: (i) these adjuncts are syntactically smaller than subordinate or adverbial clauses but larger than single-lexeme adjuncts like adverbials or adjectival depictive secondary predicates; (ii) they are non-finite, subordinate verbal predicates; (iii) they do not have an overt subject but are controlled by an argument of the main verb (Himmelmann & Schultze-Berndt 2005; Fabricius-Hansen & Haug 2012a; Rothstein 2017). The form of the verb under discussion here is in the present participle *-ing*-form, shown in the example in (8a) without extraction. As (8b) shows, this structure is similar to adverbial clauses with an overt subordinator, indicated by italics. I will refer to structures like (8a) as *bare present participle adjuncts* (BPPAs), following the terminology in Truswell (2011: 30).

(8)   a.   John arrived at home [whistling a funny song].   [BPPA]
       b.   John arrived at home [*while* whistling a funny song].   [adverbial clause]

The theoretical and empirical focus here will be on the BPPA construction because of two characteristics: (i) whereas extraction from almost all other types of adjuncts is degraded to some degree, extraction from the BPPA construction can result in almost unmarked interrogatives; and (ii) there is considerable variation in the reported grammaticality of extraction from BPPAs. For example, Truswell (2007) argues that the grammaticality of extraction depends on the aspectual classes of the two predicates in terms of the telic–atelic distinction in Vendler (1957), as in (9); an alternative explanation in terms of the grammatical verb type of the main verb is offered in Borgonovo & Neeleman (2000), seen in (10).

(9)   a.   *What did John work whistling?   [atelic/atelic]
       b.   *What did John work noticing?   [atelic/telic]
       c.   *What did John arrive noticing?   [telic/telic]
       d.   What did John arrive whistling?   [telic/atelic]
           (see Truswell 2007: 1369)

(10) a. *What_i did John dance [imagining t_i]? [unergative]
      b. *Who_i did John finish the portrait [hating t_i]? [transitive]
      c. What_i did John arrive [whistling t_i]? [unaccusative]
         (Borgonovo & Neeleman 2000: 199–200)

These observed grammaticality differences need to be accounted for in an approach to extraction from BPPAs in particular, and from adjuncts in general. In addition to these data patterns, there exist minimal pairs that are not easily captured by these approaches: verbs that belong to the same aspectual class, for example, can still show grammaticality differences in interrogatives. This is seen in (11), where the interrogative is considered grammatical with the achievement predicate *arrive* (11a), but not with the achievement *appear* (11b).

(11) a. What did John arrive [whistling t]?
                                        (Borgonovo & Neeleman 2000: 200)
     b. *What did John appear whistling?   (Truswell 2007: 1370)

Another issue arises with unergative matrix predicates: they typically do not allow extraction. However, adding a particle like *around* or *about* has a positive effect on the grammaticality of extraction, as in (12a) compared to extraction without the particle in (12b).

(12) a. What was John walking about [whistling __]? (Truswell 2011: 156)
     b. *What was John walking [whistling __]?

All these examples show that there is considerable internal variation in the BPPA construction when it comes to the grammaticality of extraction. Empirically, this presents a challenge because the patterns cannot be explained in terms of a strong–weak islands distinction (Cinque 1990; Szabolcsi & Lohndal 2017): it is not the type of extracted element that determines grammaticality, but rather properties of the two verbs in the construction (Ernst 2022). My goal is to provide generalizations that capture the patterns in (9) and (10), and also the challenging cases in (11) and (12).

1.3 Empirical scope and focus

In this monograph, I will largely focus on the extraction asymmetries that are reported for *wh*-extraction from the BPPA construction rather than provide a full picture of different types of adjunct islands across different constructions. The main motivation for this narrow empirical focus is to gain fine-grained insights into the individual factors that influence acceptability by keeping other factors constant. Some of these factors either do not apply to the BPPA construction, or can be integrated into the proposal that will be made in Chapter 5. There is a growing body of literature showing that the uniform predictions of the CED are called into question by variations across (i) different adjunct types and (ii) different extraction operations. I discuss both types of variations briefly in turn.

Adjuncts vary along the three characteristics introduced in the previous section: (a) the syntactic status of the adjunct in terms of phrasal and clausal adjuncts, (b) the presence or absence of finite tense-marking, and (c) the presence or absence of an overt subject that is potentially distinct from the subject of the main clause. Examples of adjuncts contrasting with BPPAs in these characteristics are shown in (13b–d); judgments are omitted for expository purposes, but there is an intuitive decrease in acceptability from (13a) through (13d).

(13) a. What did John arrive [whistling __]? [BPPA]
 b. What did John arrive [after whistling __]? [clausal adjunct]
 c. What did John arrive [after he whistled __]? [tensed adjunct]
 d. What did John arrive [after Mary whistled __]? [distinct subject]

Clausal adjuncts such as the adverbial clause in (13b) are reported to show judgment variations depending on the type of subordinator (Truswell 2011; C. Müller 2019; Nyvad et al. 2022); this is presumably related to the different discourse relations encoded in adverbial clause subordinators, which include temporal, causal, and other complex discourse relations (see also Kehler 2002, 2019). Clausal adjuncts can also show discrete tense-marking, as in (13c); this has been shown to impose additional hurdles for extraction from an adjunct, as shown experimentally in C. Müller (2019), where non-finite adjunct clauses react less severely to extraction than finite adjunct clauses. Clausal adjuncts can also express a subject that is distinct from that of the matrix clause (Fabricius-Hansen & Haug 2012a,b), which adds another discourse referent and thus increases the complexity of the underlying proposition; see Culicover & Winkler (2022).

Among phrasal, untensed adjuncts without an overt subject, past participle adjuncts are close relatives to the BPPA construction. Sentences with past participle adjuncts are reported to show judgment patterns for interrogatives which are similar to those in the BPPA construction, as seen in (14); it seems possible that they can be explained similar to present participle adjuncts.

(14) a. *What$_i$ did John dance [dressed as t$_i$]? [unergative]
 b. *What$_i$ did John finish the portrait [covered in t$_i$]? [transitive]

c. What$_i$ did John come back [addicted to t$_i$]? [unaccusative]
(Borgonovo & Neeleman 2000: 199–200)

In addition to variation across adjunct types, there are also variations across different extraction types, as more recent work has shown (Kush et al. 2018, 2019; Abeillé et al. 2020; Liu et al. 2022). Whereas much of the existing literature has focused on *wh*-extraction, many counterexamples to island constraints appear in other extraction types, such as relativization (Chaves & Putnam 2020). Abeillé et al. (2020) and Liu et al. (2022) argue that the possibility for extraction from an island domain depends in large parts on the information status (focused or backgrounded) of the extractee and the discourse function of the extraction operation (focalizing or non-focalizing). If there is a match between information status and discourse function of extraction, even so-called strong islands often fail to show the characteristic superadditive effect structure of island effects (Sprouse et al. 2012; Sprouse & Hornstein 2013), whereas a mismatch leads to such effects. Other types of focalizing and non-focalizing long-distance dependencies into adjuncts are also discussed in the literature, and they often fail to result in the predicted strong acceptability decrease if A′-operations are considered as a uniform phenomenon; see the examples in (15), which show relativization (15a), clefting (15b), and indirect questions (15c) from an adjunct constituent.

(15) a. This is *the book*$_i$ that John designed his garden [after reading t$_i$].
b. It was *Hey Jude*$_i$ that John arrived [whistling t$_i$].
c. I bet I know *what*$_i$ John drove Mary crazy [trying to fix t$_i$].
(Narita 2014: 123)

As seen in the examples from Cattell (1976) and Chomsky (1982) above and the attested examples in Santorini (2019), reportedly grammatical extractions from adjuncts often occurs with relativization or clefting rather than *wh*-extraction. I will leave these types of extraction and their potential different effects for further research, but assume that the judgment patterns for *wh*-extraction are mirrored to a large degree in other dependency types, as for relativization with unaccusative/telic, unergative/atelic, and transitive matrix predicates in (16), even if these extraction types do not result in an equally strong effect as *wh*-extraction:

(16) a. I liked the song that John arrived [whistling __]. [unaccusative]
b. *I liked the song that John worked [whistling __]. [unergative]
c. *I liked the song that John annoyed Bill [whistling __]. [transitive]

As these additional differences across adjunct types and extraction operations indicate, clausal adjuncts are possibly subject to additional factors that are not directly applicable to the BPPA construction and that have been investigated elsewhere from both theoretical (Truswell 2011) and empirical perspectives (C. Müller 2019; Abeillé et al. 2020; Gibson et al. 2021; Liu et al. 2022; Nyvad et al. 2022). The focus on one type of extraction from one adjunct type allows for a more detailed investigation of the individual factors which influence acceptability, so the goal here is more on the details of a subset of adjunct types and extraction operations rather than on a broad coverage of the entirety of adjunct island phenomena. As the experiments in Chapter 4 will show, there is a considerable degree of acceptability variation even within this narrow empirical scope.

1.4 Central research question and sketch of the proposal

The central research question I will address is formulated in (17).

(17) How strong is the relation between acceptability contrasts in interrogative and declarative BPPA constructions? Are there factors that affect acceptability independently of extraction?

The majority of previous approaches to particple adjunct islands assumes that the extraction needs to be licensed by a specific factor which does not show an effect in the underlying declarative. Their answer to the question in (17) is that the relation between acceptability contrasts in interrogatives and declaratives is very low or zero; this has serious ramifications for the architecture of locality operations, especially when the factors cannot be expressed in syntactic terms, as I will show in Chapter 3. The theoretical discussion in Chapter 2 and the experimental designs in Chapter 4 center around this question and will show that, contrary to the prevailing view on participle adjunct islands, there is a very strong relation between acceptability contrasts in interrogatives and declaratives.

Two major insights concerning (17) arise from the theoretical discussion in Chapters 2 and 3 as well as the experiments reported in Chapter 4: the first is that declarative BPPA constructions are not as unremarkable as the discussions in Truswell (2007, 2011) and Borgonovo & Neeleman (2000) suggest. All experiments reported in Chapter 4 show that the same acceptability differences in interrogatives also surface in the corresponding declaratives; this is in line with the separation of syntactic licensing of the adjunct-internal gap and the licensing conditions on the adjunct predicate first proposed in Brown (2015, 2016, 2017). I will refer to this in the following as the Independence Hypothesis (IH), which I formulate in (18) as an answer to the central research question in (17).

(18) Independence Hypothesis (IH):
The syntactic and semantic licensing conditions on the adjunct predicate are independent of the effects of extraction from the adjunct.

The Independence Hypothesis disassociates the effect of *wh*-extraction and other LDDs from the adjunct constituent and the factors which determine the overall acceptability of the BPPA construction. The result is a two-stage model: in a first step, the acceptability of the declarative BPPA construction is determined, which I will formulate in terms of three generalizations; the next step is the application of *wh*-extraction or another type of extraction, which leads to decreased acceptability in a cumulative, linear-additive fashion. Crucially, the proposed generalizations do not influence the magnitude of the effect of extraction. This has important ramifications for most previous approaches to extraction form adjuncts, which share the assumption that extraction is sensitive to factors which are not operative in declaratives; such a sensitivity results in additional, super-additive effect structures when a single criterion is not met. I will show experimentally that there is no evidence for this view.

The second major insight regarding (17) is that the factors proposed in accounts such as Truswell (2007, 2011) or Borgonovo & Neeleman (2000) fail to capture some contrasts sufficiently. The experiments in Chapter 4 will show that both accounts are largely on the right track and make suitable predictions for contrasts in interrogatives. However, the conditions on extraction they distill are challenged by two facts: (i) there are contrasts which directly contradict their predictions, and (ii) they do not offer precise predictions for other contrasts. In Chapter 5, I will propose three generalizations for the acceptability in declarative BPPA constructions which emerge from the experimental results and the theoretical discussion. Two of these generalizations determine the semantic compatibility between the matrix and adjunct predicate. A high degree of semantic compatibility will lead to increased acceptability of the BPPA construction, whereas sentences with lower semantic compatibility are less acceptable in comparison. These two semantic compatibility generalizations are given in (19) and (20).

(19) Durativity Generalization (DG):
The semantic compatibility between the matrix and adjunct predicate in the BPPA construction is higher if the matrix predicate encodes a durative subevent, either by means of lexical encoding or via event template augmentation.

(20) Scalar Change Generalization (SCG):
The semantic compatibility between the matrix and adjunct predicate in the BPPA construction is higher if the event described by the matrix predicate can be measured against a prominent scale, such as temporal intervals, incremental themes, paths, and property scales.

A suitable test for the Durativity Generalization is compatibility with progressive-marking: it indicates that the predicate's event structure either lexically encodes a durative subevent, or that such a subevent can be added to the event template without incurring excessive coercion costs. The crucial event type here are achievements, which are not by default compatible with the progressive, but can be augmented with a preceding durative subevent that induces a prospective reading (Rothstein 2004b; Truswell 2019b); not all achievements seem to allow this, for example perception verbs like *spot* or *notice*, which are purely punctual.

The Scalar Change Generalization is based on the classification of scalar and non-scalar change structures in Rappaport Hovav (2008) and Rappaport Hovav & Levin (2010), definite and indefinite change in Dowty (1979), as well as the distinction between measuring-out and non-measuring-out verbs in Tenny (1995). Scalar change can be measured against a prominent scale component in the predicate's meaning, which can be of different types: temporal intervals, incremental themes, and property or path scales are the most relevant types of scalar components. Both permanent stative and activity predicates do not encode such a prominent scale and are thus less compatible in the BPPA construction.

Taken together, these two generalizations divide predicates into three groups which show different degrees of semantic compatibility: (i) predicates which meet both generalizations are highly compatible and thus acceptable; (ii) predicates which meet either one of the generalizations show medium compatibility; and (iii) predicates which fail to meet both generalizations are the least compatible in the BPPA construction and are less acceptable than those with medium and high compatibility. The overview in (21) shows the compatibility level of different event types. They are slightly modified compared to the traditional four-fold classification in Vendler (1957) and further differentiate between punctual and non-punctual achievements, as well as permanent and temporary states:

(21) a. High compatibility: achievements, accomplishments, temporary states
  b. Medium compatibility: activities, punctual achievements
  c. Low compatibility: permanent states

In addition to these two semantic compatibility generalizations, I propose the Transitivity Generalization in (22):

(22) Transitivity Generalization (TG):
BPPA constructions are more acceptable if the matrix predicate directly selects only one referentially distinct argument.

Whereas the Durativity Generalization and the Scalar Change Generalization can be conceptualized as semantic compatibility criteria between the two predicates, the Transitivity Generalization is a syntactic complexity factor that increases the processing burden of predicates which select more than one referentially distinct argument. The Transitivity Generalization captures the general preference for BPPA constructions with intransitive matrix predicates, but recognizes possible exceptions for reflexive predicates and resultative constructions.

All three of these generalizations are not intended as inviolable categorical and universal constraints like the CED, but rather as criteria that lead to higher or lower acceptability of the BPPA construction; if they are not met, the sentence will be less acceptable but not entirely impossible. Compared to the decreases in acceptability resulting from extraction, a failure to meet one or more of these generalizations leads to less severe decreases in acceptability.

In Chapter 5, I will combine these three generalizations and the independent effect of extraction into a two-stage factorial model for acceptability in declarative and interrogative BPPA constructions which captures the strong relation between acceptability contrasts in interrogatives and declaratives. The durativity, scalar change, and transitivity generalizations will determine the acceptability of declarative BPPA constructions; as stated in the IH, the negative effect on acceptability of extraction applies in a linear-additive fashion and causes further decreases in acceptability for interrogatives. However, the acceptability contrasts in declaratives remain intact and do not become smaller or larger. The proposed factorial model captures the grammaticality contrasts for interrogatives in (9) and (10); in contrast to most previous approaches, all of these contrasts are predicted to also apply to the corresponding declaratives, as stated in the IH. The factorial model also offers an explanation for the contrasts in (11) and (12), summarized in (23).

(23) a. What did John *appear/√arrive whistling __ ?
 b. What did John *walk/√walk about whistling __ ?

In the case of (23a), there is a grammaticality difference between the predicates *appear* and *arrive*: punctual achievements like *appear* do not easily accept the progressive, except in a slow-motion reading (Rothstein 2004b: 56–58); on the other hand, achievements like *arrive* accept the progressive with a prospective reading. The difference between these two predicates is thus that *arrive* meets the DG while *appear* does not. In (23b), the particle *about* adds a scalar component in the form of a path structure, even if this path does not have an explicit goal; the particle *around* shows similar effects. In this minimal pair, the particle determines whether the SCG is satisfied or not. These two contrasts are difficult to capture in an approach that is limited to a single factor, such as telicity (e.g. Truswell 2007; Brown 2017) or agentivity (e.g. Truswell 2011). In addition to an explanation for these data patterns in the existing literature, the factorial model also makes some novel predictions about a more fine-grained continuum of acceptability in the BPPA construction, the effects of bounded and unbounded prepositional phrases, as well as adjunct constructions with past participles.

1.5 Conventions

Following approaches like Borgonovo & Neeleman (2000) and Truswell (2007, 2011), BPPAs that allow extraction from the adjunct will be called *transparent adjuncts*; when the extraction is considered ungrammatical, the BPPA is called *opaque*. To identify the two predicates in the BPPA construction, I will refer to the verb in the embedding clause as the *matrix predicate* and to the BPPA as the *adjunct predicate*; see (24).

(24) John arrived (at the station) whistling a song.
      _____ _____
           matrix predicate   adjunct predicate

The distinction between the term pairs *(un)grammatical* and *(un)acceptable* along the lines of the competence–performance divide in Chomsky (1965) describes two related but conceptually different notions; ungrammatical sentences cannot be generated by the grammar, but there is no perfect correspondence between grammatical and acceptable sentences on the one hand and ungrammatical and unacceptable ones on the other hand. Grammatical sentences may be unacceptable and, in some cases, sentences that are considered ungrammatical are intuitively acceptable because the grammatical violation can be repaired by the parser. I will reserve the term (un)grammatical for theory-driven sentence judgments about the possibility to generate the construction in question, and will use the term (un)acceptable for judgments based on observed data and distinctions between sentences that are not ruled out by the grammar but are not equally unmarked; sources of unacceptability can stem from semantic or pragmatic oddity, processing difficulty, or other factors (Chomsky 1965; Abrusán 2019; Chaves & Putnam 2020).

In the discussion of aspectual classes, I largely follow the classification in Vendler (1957) into states, activities, achievements, and accomplishments. However, I will assume with Maienborn (2005, 2019) that there is a further distinction between permanent and temporary states, and follow Truswell (2011, 2019b) in differentiating between punctual achievements and achievements which can be extended with a preparatory phase (see also Rothstein 2004b). The *telicity* of an event will be understood as "the boundedness or nonboundedness of its event and time constituents" (Jackendoff 1996: 349), which captures the traditional Vendlerian encoding of a natural endpoint as well as the contribution of event participants; see also Dowty (1991) and Tenny (1994). The term *extraction* is typically used in the sense of *subextraction* (see Corver 2006). This is also indicated by the formulation "extraction from an adjunct" rather than "extraction of an adjunct". Sentences containing FGDs are usually represented in the literature with one of the three notations in (25), all of which have theoretical implications that are not immediately relevant for the present discussion.

(25) a. [Which picture]$_i$ did you see t$_i$? [traces]
 b. [Which picture]$_i$ did you see __$_i$? [gaps]
 c. [Which picture] did you see [which picture]? [deleted copies]

When citing examples from the literature, I will always retain the notation in the original. This leads to some example sets with different notations for filler–gap dependencies, especially when examples from different authors are shown. In constructed examples and annotations of examples from the literature, I will use the gap notation because it offers the highest amount of legibility. Co-indexing of the *wh*-pronoun and the gap is omitted if there is no ambiguity. Annotations to examples from the literature, such as information about clause or extraction types, are added in square brackets at the right margin of the example, as in (25). Judgments for examples from the literature reflect the respective author's judgment and are not necessarily my own. Glosses for foreign languages appear as in the original. In the experimental Chapter 4, the factors of the experimental design are highlighted in SMALL CAPS.

1.6 Outline

This monograph is structured as follows: Chapter 2 examines examine the BPPA construction in more detail, with a focus on its syntactic and semantic properties. I will draw a comparison to reduced adverbial clauses, converb clauses, and depictive secondary predicates. It will be shown that whereas many BPPAs can be analyzed as depictives, this leaves open the question of how the causal reading can be derived. The second major section focuses on the semantic interpretation of BPPAs, especially the interpretation of complex monoclausal events and the distinction between the causal and non-causal reading of BPPAs. I will also discuss the syntactic and semantic licensing conditions on depictives, and how these conditions account for a large part of the reported acceptability pattern for extraction from BPPAs. Chapter 3 reviews the existing literature on extraction from adjunct islands and is divided into three major groups: approaches that propose syntactic mechanisms to establish a gap site inside an adjunct constituent without violating basic principles of syntactic structure-building; the distinction between transparent and opaque adjuncts is for the most part left implicit in these approaches. The approaches in the second group propose more detailed explanations when adjuncts can be transparent, based on syntactic, semantic, and pragmatic factors. The last approach in this chapter is fundamentally different in that it assumes that the observed differences in grammaticality are not related to the application of extraction but represent more general licensing conditions for the adjunct predicate that are also present in declaratives. Chapter 4 presents experimental evidence on the transparency of BPPAs from different angles. These include the aspectual characteristics of the two predicates, the grammatical verb type of the matrix predicate, and the relation to outer aspect marking and argument structure differences. The results will show that the IH in (18) holds because the acceptability differences in interrogatives are also observed in the corresponding declaratives. The last study series also indicates that the licensing conditions for the adjunct predicate do not seem to require a telic matrix predicate, as proposed in Truswell (2007) and Brown (2017). Based on these experimental findings, Chapter 5 re-examines the data pattern for transparent adjuncts in the light of the Independence Hypothesis and the questions about the licensing conditions for the adjunct predicate. I will propose a factorial model for acceptability in the BPPA construction that accounts for the independence of extraction from factors such as telicity or verb type; durativity and the encoding of a scalar change meaning component will emerge as relevant semantic compatibility factors; transitivity of the matrix predicate plays an additional role. It will be shown that this analysis explains the experimental results in Chapter 4, and offers a unified analysis of recalcitrant examples in the previous literature. Chapter 6 concludes and points to further areas of research.

2 Present participle adjuncts: structure and interpretation

2.1 Research questions and chapter outline

This chapter offers an analysis of the BPPA construction in English with a focus on three aspects: (i) the syntactic analysis of BPPAs, (ii) their interpretation, and (iii) their syntactic and semantic licensing conditions. The syntactic analysis centers around the question whether BPPAs can be analyzed as reduced adverbial clauses, converb constructions, or depictive secondary predicates. I will argue that BPPAs are complex depictive secondary predicates because this analysis accounts for the limited range of interpretation in the BPPA construction; both alternative analyses have a much broader range of interpretations which are not attested for BPPAs. However, this syntactic analysis leads to a problem for the possible interpretations of BPPA constructions: it does not account for the possibility of a causal reading in a subset of BPPA constructions. Following Truswell (2007, 2011), I will show that the basic depictive interpretation of temporal overlap can be augmented by a causal interpretation if the matrix predicate is a causative verb which is underspecified for the causal component. Based on the insights which follow from a depictive analysis, I will show that the syntactic and semantic licensing conditions on depictives account for a large set of constraints that have been proposed for *wh*-extraction from the BPPA construction in the previous literature. The following research questions will guide this chapter:

(1)   a.   What is a suitable syntactic analysis of BPPAs?
     b.   How are BPPAs semantically interpreted?
     c.   Which of the constraints proposed for extraction from the BPPA construction can be independently explained by syntactic and semantic licensing conditions on the adjunct predicate?

The main goal of this chapter is to find out which conditions and constraints that follow from a depictive analysis are independent of the application of extraction from the BPPA construction. The literature on depictives agrees that not all types of verbs can host depictives and that depictive predicates need specific aspectual properties. This discussion anticipates the conclusions that will be drawn in the following chapters: the acceptability differences for extraction from BPPAs can also be observed in declaratives and are thus independent of the extraction operation. The observation that acceptability contrasts in interrogative BPPA constructions are related to semantic mismatches in the underlying declaratives was first proposed in Brown (2015, 2016, 2017), and I largely follow this perspective. An analysis of the BPPA construction as an instance of depictive secondary predication along with the licensing conditions on this construction has two advantages: (i) it offers an explanation for a wide range of data observed for extraction from BPPAs, and (ii) it can account for these data patterns without appealing to additional constraints that are specific to locality operations.

This chapter is structured as follows: in Section 2.2, I provide arguments for a depictive analysis of the BPPA construction. Section 2.3 approaches the meaning aspect of the BPPA construction, taking into account the semantic analysis of depictives, and also the interpretation and constraints on the expression of complex events. I will argue that the basic depictive interpretation of the BPPA construction can be enriched to a causal reading if the matrix predicate has a causal structure. In Section 2.4, I discuss conditions and constraints on depictive secondary predicates, including conditions on the depictive itself, but also characteristics of the main verb. The picture that will emerge from this discussion is a set of factors that have an effect on the relative acceptability of depictive constructions which coincide to a considerable degree with factors that have been argued to play a role in the licensing of extraction from the adjunct predicate. Section 2.5 concludes this chapter.

2.2 Towards a syntactic analysis of BPPAs

The existing literature is mostly implicit about the syntactic analysis of the BPPA construction: Borgonovo & Neeleman (2000) use the term "predicative adjunct" to indicate the θ-role assignment to the subject of the matrix predicate; Truswell (2007) distinguishes between causative and depictive secondary predicates to capture the different interpretations. The literature on secondary predication does not recognize a separate class of causatives, only depictives and resultatives. As an additional category, causative secondary predicates raise questions that are beyond the scope of this monograph.

A syntactic analysis of BPPAs needs to capture the following properties of this construction: (i) its syntactic and semantic optionality, (ii) its limited range of interpretation, and (iii) its sensitivity to aspectual properties. In this section, I will discuss three possible syntactic analyses for the BPPA construction in the light of these properties: reduced adverbial clauses, converb constructions, and depictive secondary predicates. I will argue for an analysis as complex secondary predicates because the alternative analyses fail to account for the limited range of interpretation as well as the sensitivity to aspectual classes.

The adjunct status of the participle predicate in the BPPA construction is indicated by its optionality and the fact that it is not semantically selected. Hole (2015) defines the optionality or suppressibility of adjuncts as follows:

(2) Suppressibility of adjuncts
A constituent C of a simple declarative non-negated sentence S is an *adjunct* iff
  i. S is grammatical without C, and
  ii. S without C does not entail the C relation.
  (Hole 2015: 1287)

Since the participle predicate in the BPPA construction can be omitted without affecting the grammaticality status of the sentence, as in (3a), the first sub-clause of (2) is satisfied; the second sub-clause is also met because the information encoded in the BPPA is not entailed if it is omitted (3b,c). Rather, the BPPA acts as a restrictive modifier that further specifies how or why the event encoded in the main verb occurs; see also Ackema (2015: 259) and the concept of "supplement" in Potts (2005). In these examples, ⇏ stands for "does not entail".

(3) a. Peter arrived (whistling a funny song).
   b. Peter arrived. ⇏ Peter arrived whistling a funny song.
   c. Peter drove Mary crazy. ⇏ Peter drove Mary crazy whistling an annoying song.

In fact, an assertion containing a BPPA entails the matrix predication, seen in (4). This is because the BPPA represents a subset of the ways that the event in the matrix clause takes place (Gehrke 2019: 207–208).

(4) a. Peter arrived whistling a funny song. ⇒ Peter arrived.
   b. Peter drove Mary crazy whistling an annoying song. ⇒ Peter drove Mary crazy.

In the light of this evidence from optionality and lack of entailments for the BPPA constituent, the syntactic adjunct status of the present participle seems uncontroversial. All three potential syntactic analyses offer a straightforward explanation for the optionality characteristic because adverbial clauses, converbs, and depictives are all syntactically optional adjunct constructions.

The second property that has to be captured by a structural analysis is that the possible interpretations for the BPPA construction are limited to a simultaneous event, similar to a manner adverbial, and a causal relation (Truswell 2007, 2011).

There is little evidence for additional meanings that can be encoded directly by BPPAs without strong contextual inferences. For example, the sentence in (5) can receive a simultaneous temporal (5a) or causal interpretation (5b), but is unlikely to be interpreted as a posterior temporal (5c) or concessive (5d) adverbial clause. The choice between the temporal or causal interpretation in (5a,b) is in principle indeterminate, but there could be a preference for the causal reading; see Sloman (2005) and Danks (2009) for the argument that the perception of causal relations, if plausible, is "relatively automatic, relatively irresistible" (Danks 2009: 448).

(5) John drove Mary crazy whistling hornpipes. (Truswell 2011: 32)
   interpreted as:
   a. John drove Mary crazy *while* whistling hornpipes. [simultaneous]
   b. John drove Mary crazy *by* whistling hornpipes. [causal]
   c. #John drove Mary crazy *after* whistling hornpipes. [posterior]
   d. #John drove Mary crazy *despite* whistling hornpipes. [concessive]

Whereas the intended meaning of the sentences in (5a) and (5b) can be recovered when *while/by* are not overtly realized, information is lost when *after/despite* is omitted. This shows that participle adjuncts receive a limited set of default interpretations in the absence of overt indicators; see also Behrens et al. (2012) for this distinction between non-finite adjunct predicates and finite adverbial clauses.

The final property in need of an explanation is the sensitivity of the BPPA construction to aspectual properties of the two predicates. Despite his focus on extraction data, Truswell (2007) proposes that the adjunct predicate must be atelic in declaratives as well as interrogatives; the aspectual restrictions on the matrix predicate are considered to be a result of extraction. The requirement for an atelic adjunct is shown in the contrast between the declaratives in (6a) and (6b), but it also seems that not all atelic predicates are acceptable adjunct predicates, as with the state in (6c).

(6) a. John drove Mary crazy whistling an annoying song. [activity adjunct]
   b. ??John drove Mary crazy arriving at the station. [achievement adjunct]
   c. ??John drove Mary crazy being poor. [state adjunct]

In addition to restrictions on the adjunct predicate, Brown (2017) reports acceptability differences between intransitive matrix predicates that depend on their aspectual class. From the examples in (7), the telic intransitive in (7a) is considered more acceptable than the other sentences with atelic intransitives (7b), and both atelic and telic transitives (7c,d); relative judgments between the sentences are added in the right margin.

(7) a. Lucy arrived whistling the national anthem.
    b. Lucy shivered whistling the national anthem.
    c. Mary picked the candidates whistling the national anthem.
    d. Sophie finished sketches whistling the national anthem.
    (Brown 2017: 189–190)

For these examples, it is interesting to note that only (7a) is possible with an indefinite DP like *a woman*; all other sentences require a definite DP. This points to the fact that only (7a) represents a thetic judgment, whereas (7b–d) are categorical in the sense of Kuroda (1972); for the relation between verb classes and theticity, see also Irwin (2020). The acceptability contrasts for the declaratives in (7) indicate that not every verb type is equally suitable in a BPPA construction; a syntactic analysis that captures these differences has an advantage over analyses that do not. The following sections will examine the limited interpretations of the BPPA construction as well as these sensitivities to aspectual classes and argue that an analysis as complex depictives is the most adequate syntactic analysis for BPPAs when adjusted for the possibility of the causal reading. Reduced adverbial clauses and converb constructions fail to account for these properties.

2.2.1 Reduced adverbial clause analysis

A first intuitive structural analysis of the BPPA construction is that they are reduced adverbial clauses with a phonologically zero subordinator, as in (8).

(8) a. Peter arrived [$_{CP}$ [$_C$ ∅$_{while}$] [$_{TP}$ whistling a funny song]].
    b. Peter drove Mary crazy [$_{CP}$ [$_C$ ∅$_{by}$] [$_{TP}$ whistling a funny song]].

Hengeveld (1998: 339) characterizes adverbial verb forms as a "dependent verb form which, apart from being the predicate of the subordinate construction, is used directly as an adverbial modifier"; they are thus forms that cannot occur as main verbs and act as modifiers of the main verb, not a nominal constituent of the clause. The literature on islands often demonstrates the strong island status of adjuncts with examples of extraction from adverbial clauses, where extraction is most often strongly degraded, especially if the adverbial clause is finite. Typical examples are given in (9).

(9) a. *What do you worry [$_{CP}$ if John buys __]?   (Sprouse & Hornstein 2013: 2)
    b. *What were you happy [because John bought __]?   (Newmeyer 2016: 188)

In many cases, extraction is better when the embedded clause is non-finite, as widely noted in the literature (e.g. Chomsky 1986a; Manzini 1992; Truswell 2011; Szabolcsi & Lohndal 2017; Chaves & Putnam 2020) and shown experimentally in C. Müller (2019); Chomsky (1986a), for example, assumes that tensed T acts as an inherent barrier whereas untensed T does not. See the examples in (10) with untensed adjuncts, where extraction is considered grammatical in contrast to the extractions in (9):

(10) a. he is the person who [$_{IP}$ they left [before speaking to *t*]] (before meeting *t*)
(Chomsky 1986a: 32)
b. Who did John get upset [after talking to __]? (Truswell 2011: 129)
c. Which beer did he almost stumble after chugging?
(C. Müller 2019: 121)

BPPA constructions have in common with adverbial clauses that they are dependent on the occurrence of an embedding clause, as seen in (11a,b), and that they are optional in the sense that their absence does not change the grammaticality of the sentence, as in (11c). In addition, (11c) does not entail (11a) because the meaning of the adjunct is not recoverable if it is not explicitly encoded; see Hole (2015) and Hengeveld (1998: 335).

(11) a. John left the room [whistling a funny song].
b. *Whistling a funny song.
c. John left the room.

An analysis of BPPAs as reduced adverbial clauses opens up the question of which types of overtly encoded adverbial clauses they express. This requires a closer look at the possible meanings of BPPAs and the corresponding subordinators in adverbial clauses. Semantically, BPPAs encode meanings that correspond to a simultaneous temporal (*while*) or a causal/instrumental adverbial clause (*by*); see Truswell (2007: 1366). Which of these meanings are available is in part determined by the embedding verb, which do not all allow the causal/instrumental interpretation (12a). When the causal reading is available, it seems to be the default one, but does not completely exclude the temporal reading (12b). A third type of meaning, a manner-like interpretation, is also available but does not correspond to an overt adverbial subordinator (König 1995; Haug et al. 2012).

(12) a. John arrived at the station [while/*by whistling a funny song.]
b. John drove Mary crazy [by/$^?$while whistling an annoying song].

When extraction takes place from constructions like these, the subordinator must be suppressed in some cases and generally has the effect of degrading the structure. Extraction from such prepositional participial adjuncts is discussed in Truswell (2011: 135–145) and is generally considered less acceptable compared to the BPPA construction; see (13) and (14).

(13) a. *What did John arrive [while whistling t]?   (Truswell 2007: 1359)
      b. What did John arrive [whistling t]? (Borgonovo & Neeleman 2000: 200)

(14) a. ?What did John drive Mary crazy [by whistling __]?
      b. What did John drive Mary crazy [whistling __]?

A reduced adverbial clause analysis of the BPPA construction faces three major problems: first, that only a small subset of adverbial clause meanings are represented in BPPAs, mostly temporal overlap and causality. This may be related to the fact that only a set of basic meanings can be expressed in the absence of a clear encoding of a more specific relation between main and subordinate clause (see König 1995: 70). Some BPPA constructions can encode meanings other than simultaneity or causality, like the examples in (15). In (15a), the particle adjunct has a conditional interpretation similar to *when/if* adverbial clauses, and (15b) can be enriched to a concessive interpretation where the matrix event occurs *even though* the adjunct event should prevent this from happening. However, both these interpretations are only accessible through enrichment that is based on contextual information; both sentences still have the more basic simultaneous reading available.

(15) a. I only know Georgian wearing *this* magic hat.   (Truswell 2007: 1362)
      b. Peter got through airport security hiding a gun in his backpack.

The second issue is that adverbial clauses are much less constrained than BPPAs in the combinations of aspectual classes they allow. For example, adverbial clauses with telic adjuncts are completely fine (16a), whereas the BPPA version is slightly degraded in comparison (16b); see Truswell (2007: 1373).

(16) a. Peter arrived at the station before noticing his sister.
      b. ?Peter arrived at the station noticing his sister.

This is related to the possible meanings of the BPPA construction, which are limited to temporal overlap and causality but not other temporal relations such as anteriority or more complex discourse-structuring interpretations. An explanation for this limitation in meaning is not obvious, but would essentially require a generalization that sets the default reading of a zero-subordinator adverbial clause to a temporal relation resulting in simultaneity due to the progressive morphology; the causal reading could then be achieved by pragmatic enrichment that is not directly encoded. For adverbial clauses, there also seems to be no restriction on atelic intransitive matrix predicates (17), which show an effect in the BPPA construction (Brown 2017).

(17)   Peter worked before going to lunch.

The third problem of a reduced adverbial clause analysis is the fact that adverbial clauses can optionally encode tense-marking and an overt subject, which is not possible for the BPPA construction, seen in (18). Limited productivity in terms of tense realizations are thus another argument that the BPPA construction may not fall under the cover term of reduced adverbial clauses.

(18)   a.   Peter arrived while [whistling/he whistled] a funny song.
       b.   Peter arrived [whistling/*he whistled] a funny song.

In spite of the formal similarity of the BPPA construction to adverbial clauses with respect to optionality in the sense of Hole (2015), the limited range of interpretations that is available for BPPAs, the extraction data with overt subordinators in (13) and (14), and the sensitivity of the BPPA construction to aspectual classes suggest that an analysis as reduced adverbial clauses is not feasible.

2.2.2 Converb construction analysis

The term *converb* is not often applied to English, and has been employed more frequently in the typological literature (Haspelmath 1995; Nedjalkov 1998). Like adverbial clauses, converbs modify verbs rather than nouns and are also inherently subordinate forms. Haspelmath (1995) provides the following general definition:

(19)   A converb is defined here as *a nonfinite verb form whose main function is to mark adverbial subordination.* (Haspelmath 1995: 3)

Cross-linguistically, converbs are often a verbal form with specific converb morphology; for this reason, the term has not been widely applied to English because there is no morphological form that is exclusive to a converb form (Haug et al. 2012: 134). However, some cases of subordinate participles share characteristics with converbs and could be classified as such. This also applies to the present participle in the BPPA construction, which shares the following characteristics with converbs, taken from Haspelmath (1995: 4–8):

(20) Converb properties
   a. Converbs are inflectional verb forms rather than independent lexemes.
   b. Converbs do not encode tense, mood, or argument agreement and are nonfinite.
   c. Constructions with converbs are non-argumental, rather acting as modifiers to verbs, clauses, or sentences.
   d. Constructions with converbs are subordinated, but can often be paraphrased by a coordinate construction in English.

Converbs also share similarities with depictive secondary predicates, as the subject is not expressed syntactically and reference is determined by an external controller; the meaning of converbs and copredicates in relation to the main verb is underspecified and determined by context (Haspelmath 1995: 18–19).

In the discussion of converbs in English, the focus is on free adjuncts, as in (21a), or absolute constructions, as in (21b), with a present participle form (Kortmann 1995: 194, 226), but there are some examples of non-detached converb constructions without separating orthography, as in (21c). One of the main properties of converb constructions like (21c) that distinguishes them from absolute constructions such as (21b) is that the subject of the converb is often not encoded overtly, similar to free adjunct constructions like (21a).

(21) a. I checked my diary and rushed off to my 9 am lecture, *managing to skip breakfast*. (Kortmann 1995: 189)
   b. The Dean turned and went out, *his gown billowing darkly behind him*. (Kortmann 1995: 189)
   c. Mary left smiling. (Kortmann 1995: 198)

The meaning of converb constructions varies cross-linguistically and can be divided into three major types: (i) specialized converbs that are morphologically marked for very specific meanings, (ii) contextual converbs whose meaning depends on a variety of different factors, and (iii) narrative converbs that connect events in a coordinative fashion "such that the plot is advanced" (König 1995: 58). Finnish, for example, has several inflections for converb forms as inflected infinitives and can thus be analyzed as a specialized converb language, where a specific inflection corresponds to a specific interpretation. The example in (22) is simplified from Ylikoski (2003) with added glosses for the converb function in square brackets:

(22) *Pekka   tek-i   rikokse-n ...*   (Finnish)
      Pekka   make-PAST.3SG   crime-GEN
      'Pekka committed a crime ...'
   a. ... *juo-malla olut-ta*: by drinking beer.   [means]
   b. ... *juo-matta olut-ta*: without drinking beer.   [lack of circumstance]
   c. ... *juo-dessa-an olut-ta*: while drinking beer.   [temporal]
   d. ... *juo-den olut-ta*: drinking beer.   [manner]
   e. ... *juo-dakse-en olut-ta*: in order to drink beer. [purpose]
   f. ... *juo-tua-an olut-ta*: after drinking beer.   [temporal]
      (see Ylikoski 2003: 203–204)

English converbs, on the other hand, are of the contextual type, where a basic meaning is fleshed out by contextual information such as the aspectual class of the host verb and pragmatic inferences, for example about causality (König 1995: 73, 84). Especially in the absence of a subordinator that is characteristic for adverbial clauses, converb constructions allow different meanings depending on the context. König (1995: 73) argues that the basic interpretation of contextual converbs is similar to a coordinate structure, which can be enriched with information from the surrounding syntactic environment.

Three types of enriched contextual meaning are especially common: (i) causal or instrumental readings provide additional information on the causal structure of the event described in the main verb and thus form a close connection between the two verbal forms. (ii) Manner readings of converbs elaborate on the unspecified manner component of the main verb, and are thus descriptions of a single event expressed in two predicates. In contrast to manner readings, (iii) attendant circumstance describes two independent events that are still closely related to each other and thus more informative than simple coordination; this is described as "perceptual unity" (König 1995: 66) since they overlap spatio-temporally. Examples of all three types are given in (23): (23a) exemplifies the instrumental reading, (23b) shows a manner meaning, where *stammering* elaborates on the speaking event, and (23c) shows the attendant circumstance meaning, with two independent events that form a perceptual unit.

(23) a. Using a sharp knife he cut the bread into four pieces.   (König 1995: 66)
      b. Thanks, he said stammering.   (Haug et al. 2012: 161)
      c. He walked to the station thinking of the girl he had just left.
                                                                   (Haug et al. 2012: 169)

Not all of these readings are available in all languages with contextual converb constructions: German is understood as a language that prefers the attendant circumstance meaning, and imposes other restrictions on converbs, such as a limit on complexity; converb clauses with internal complexity are marked compared to single-lexeme converbs, as seen in (24), where the addition of a complement to the converb *pfeifend* 'whistling' leads to decreased grammaticality (König 1995: 73).

(24) Hans kam   (? ein Lied) pfeifend in   die Küche
      Hans came   a   song   whistling into the kitchen
      'Hans came into the kitchen, whistling (a tune).'   (König 1995: 73)

As also noted in Kortmann (1995: 231, note 11), complex converb-like constructions such as (24) may not be fully productive in German. This lack of productivity in German receives support from experimental work in Brown (2017), who finds that complex constructions as in (24) are not very acceptable, and that extraction from complements to such participles is highly degraded. The cross-linguistic difference in productivity will also be discussed below in Section 2.4.1 from the angle of depictive secondary predicates, with potential counterexamples to König's (1995) claim about limited productivity in German.

Since converbs are by definition optional constituents, they easily fulfill the optionality characteristic of the BPPA construction. With respect to the second characteristic, a limited range of interpretation, the results are less clear because converbs can encode a wide variety of meanings depending on additional cues from their environment. As the BPPA construction does not have an overt subordinator like adverbial clauses, this wide range of interpretations may not be available, except when the relevant information comes from other sources, like the aspectual class of the main verb. Here, the basic meaning of the converb could be enriched from a fuzzy temporal relation to a causal reading when the causal component is not specified in the lexical content of the main verb. It is thus possible that the limited range of interpretations for the BPPA construction is a result of the limited information that is available from its environment; extra-sentential context could provide the information required for a more specific interpretation of the BPPA. As far as the sensitivity to verb type is concerned, the literature on converbs does not clearly identify the patterns that are observed for BPPAs. Thus, it does not seem that a converb analysis provides a fully satisfactory explanation for all characteristics of the BPPA construction.

2.2.3 Depictive secondary predicate analysis

A wide variety of typologically unrelated languages allows the encoding of an additional predication relation in a sentence under the cover term *secondary pred-*

ication (see Halliday 1967a; Rothstein 1985, 2017; Winkler 1997; Rapoport 1999, 2019; Himmelmann & Schultze-Berndt 2005; Simpson 2005). Williams (1980, 1983) argues that this form of predication is an instance of a more general predication relation, where a nominal constituent c-commands a predicate and the two bear the same index. Secondary predication does not violate the theta-criterion (Chomsky 1981) because the nominal, such as *John* in (25a), receives the two θ-roles from two different argument complexes (Williams 1983: 301). This contrasts with a small-clause analysis of secondary predication involving a PRO structure with control, as in (25b).

(25) a. John$_i$ [arrived$_i$ dead$_i$]$_{VP_i}$ (Williams 1983: 301)
 b. John [ate the meat]$_{VP}$ [PRO raw]$_S$ (Williams 1983: 296)

Secondary predicates are differentiated into resultatives, as in (26), and depictives, as in (27). The latter are further subdivided by their referent or controller in transitive sentences, which can be either the subject in subject-oriented depictives (SODs) as in (27a) or the object in object-oriented depictives (OODs) such as (27b). In each of these cases, the secondary predicate attributes a property to its controller, which is either that of result or a property attribution during the interval of the main verb (Rothstein 2017: 3873).

(26) John hammered the metal$_i$ flat$_i$. [resultative]

(27) a. John$_i$ arrived at the party drunk$_i$. [SOD]
 b. Mary ate the meat$_i$ raw$_i$. [OOD]

The main difference between depictives and the broad class of adverbials is that depictives are participant-oriented rather than event-oriented, and that they are always in the potential focus domain of a sentence (Schultze-Berndt & Himmelmann 2004; Himmelmann & Schultze-Berndt 2005). Depictives are typically exemplified with simple adjectival secondary predicates as in (27) above, but there are also depictives from other categories, such as PPs (28a) or DPs (28b); see Rothstein (2017) for an overview.

(28) a. She reached the house *out of breath*.
 b. He left the hospital *a shade of his former self*.
 (Rothstein 2017: 3874)

Participles can also be used as depictives, as in (27a); however, the focus of discussion is mostly limited to simple deadjectival participles, and excludes complex participles which take a complement and are thus used verbally. The strong position in the literature that there "appear to be no VP secondary predicates" (Rothstein 2006: 211) has been called into question, and it has become more widely acknowledged that complex participles like in (29) can be analyzed as depictives; this is also based on cross-linguistic comparisons, as there are differences in which categories can function as depictives (Schultze-Berndt & Himmelmann 2004; Himmelmann & Schultze-Berndt 2005; Simpson 2005; Rothstein 2017; Hatav 2020).

(29) a. She walked down the street *searching for her wallet*.
 (Rothstein 2017: 3874)
 b. John$_i$ fixed the car whistling a happy tune$_i$. (Farrell 2019: 100)

Schultze-Berndt & Himmelmann (2004: 99) note that when simple participles are accepted as depictives, then there is no reason to exclude complex participles with a complement. Himmelmann & Schultze-Berndt (2005), in the following abbreviated as H&SB, go a step further and include other types of subordinate clauses, depending on whether they meet the defining criteria for depictives, such as non-finiteness, cotemporality, and participant-orientation.

Often, the line drawn between adverbials and depictives is thin, especially considering the cross-linguistic variation in what can act as a depictive. One way of differentiating between the two groups in English is with paraphrases. The depictive construction allows a paraphrase where the depictive predicate acts as the main predicate of the sentence; the main predicate of the depictive construction can then be optionally expressed in an adverbial *when*-clause that emphasizes the simultaneity of the matrix event and depictive state (H&SB 2005: 11); see (30) for a simple adjectival depictive and (31) for a possible VP depictive.

(30) a. George bought the carrots **fresh**. (H&SB 2005: 1)
 b. The carrots were fresh (when George bought them). (H&SB 2005: 11)

(31) a. John arrived at the station whistling a funny song.
 b. John whistled a funny song (when he arrived at the station).

The *when*-paraphrase is unproblematic for extraction of the complement of *whistle* since it is not inside an adjunct. However, the *when*-paraphrase is not possible for all types of BPPA. In cases where the adjunct elaborates on the causal structure of the matrix predicate, as in the intuitive interpretation of (32a), the paraphrase in (32b) changes the meaning: the two events are no longer necessarily interpreted as standing in a causal relationship.

(32) a. John drove Mary crazy whistling an annoying song.
 b. John whistled an annoying song (when he drove Mary crazy).

This difference in the availability of meaning-preserving paraphrases indicates that non-causal and causal BPPAs may not be identical in terms of their semantics, even though they share a common morphosyntactic form (see H&SB 2005: 3; Rapoport 1993b: 166). It seems at least possible that causal adjuncts are reduced adverbial clauses whereas non-causal BPPAs can be analyzed as depictives. Such a differentiated syntactic analysis results in differences regarding which part of the main clause is modified: depictives are defined as participant-oriented adjuncts (H&SB 2005), whereas adverbial clauses modify the verb (Hengeveld 1998). This makes sense inasmuch as a causal BPPA can be analyzed as being part of the main verb's event or argument structure and is thus not directly oriented towards its controller. I will argue in Section 2.3 that the causal meaning can be derived for BPPAs without abandoning a depictive analysis.

Among the alternatives discussed in this section, a depictive analysis for the BPPA construction is the only one that makes predictions about the sensitivity to the aspectual class of the main verb. As widely noted in the literature on depictives and further discussed in Section 2.4.2 (e.g. Winkler 1997; Simpson 2005; H&SB 2005; Rapoport 2019), depictives do not work equally well with different verb types. A depictive analysis also captures the intuition that the two events have to overlap spatio-temporally and share a participant (Rothstein 2003). At least this is the case for non-causal BPPAs: causal adjunct participles are more compatible with a reduced *by*-adverbial clause analysis, as the additional causal meaning component and the re-ordering facts in (32) indicate. So either the two types of BPPAs are morphosyntactically identical manifestations of two separate syntactico-semantic constructions (H&SB 2005), or they are both depictives with an additional inference of the causal meaning by pragmatic principles. The possibilities how both interpretations can be derived compositionally via complex event formation are discussed below in Section 2.3.2. Since the analysis of the BPPA construction captures the optionality and restricted meaning characteristics, it has an advantage over the reduced adverbial clause and converb analyses, which predict more possible meanings than are attested in the construction.

2.2.4 Interim conclusion

In the remainder of this chapter, I will adopt the complex depictive analysis of the BPPA construction. The discussion in this section has shown that while all three analyses considered capture the optionality of the BPPA, reduced adverbial clauses and converbs have problems with the limited range of interpretation as well as the sensitivity to aspectual classes. The depictive analysis is able to account for optionality as well as some of the aspectual restrictions. A major issue for a depictive analysis is the availability of readings that go beyond the temporal overlap relation that is characteristic for depictives. Whereas adverbial clauses and converb constructions generate meanings that are not attested in the BPPA construction, a depictive analysis undergenerates because it does not account for the causal interpretation of the BPPA. The rest of this chapter will focus on these problematic aspects of a depictive analysis for BPPAs: Section 2.3 will show that it is possible to derive the causal interpretation of the BPPA in addition to the depictive overlap reading, and Section 2.4 will examine how the syntactic and semantic licensing conditions on depictives can account for the sensitivity to aspectual classes seen in the BPPA construction.

2.3 The interpretational space of BPPAs

This section focuses on the possible interpretations of the BPPA construction in the light of a syntactic analysis as depictive secondary predicates. I will argue that the depictive analysis is justified by the limited range of interpretation of the BPPA construction; the causal interpretation of a subset of BPPAs is not necessarily encoded directly, but can be derived by discourse-pragmatic means which enhances the basic depictive overlap reading by a specification relation between two assertions. In a first turn, Section 2.3.1 will survey the most common semantic analyses of depictives, which provide a good initial fit for the interpretational range of many BPPAs, namely the relation of temporal overlap holding between the two events. However, this analysis has shortcomings because the BPPA construction can also be interpreted as a causal relation between the two predicates, which is not directly available in a depictive analysis. The following two Sections 2.3.2 and 2.3.3 draw on approaches to the interpretation of complex events that enrich a basic depictive reading and allow for a causal interpretation for a subset of configurations; it will be shown that there are ways to account for the causal reading of some BPPAs while excluding other readings that are too complex to be expressed in a monoclausal structure. This reverses the empirical problem which the reduced adverbial clause or converb construction analyses face: instead of having to restrict the wide range of possible interpretations for these constructions, a depictive analysis of the BPPA construction needs to account for the additional causal reading that is available for a subset of BPPAs.

2.3.1 The semantics of depictives

Introducing depictives into a syntactic structure raises the question of how this additional predication relation is interpreted and which constituent it modifies. The characterization in Halliday (1967a: 62) asserts that attributive predicates like depictives ascribe a property to a participant in relation to an event. In (33a), the complex assertion can be separated into the two assertions A_1 and A_2 in (33b,c), plus some relation between the two simple assertions (33d). A similar situation is found in the BPPA construction, which can also be separated into two assertions.

(33) a. Peter arrived [drunk/whistling a song].
    b. A_1: Peter arrived.
    c. A_2: Peter is [drunk/whistling a song].
    d. $R(A_1, A_2) = ?$

There are several formalizations of the meaning of depictives, which largely focus on the temporal relations of the two predicates. One formalization that imposes strict temporal relations between depictive and main verb is proposed in McNally (1994), who considers depictives to be temporal modifiers that require the two predicates to have coextensive, identical intervals (McNally 1994: 568–569):

(34) $[\![[V'\ XP[PRED]_i]_{VP}]\!] = \{< e, x > \mid$ there is an $e', e'' \leq e$ such that
    $V'(e', x)$, $\mathbf{XP[PRED]}_i(e'')$, and $\tau(e) = \tau(e') = \tau(e'')\}$ (McNally 1994: 568)

The interval of the VP (e) is composed of two subevents e' and e'' which have identical intervals among each other and in relation to e. Thus, (35a) is analyzed as in (35b), which requires that the lying in bed and the state of being awake have identical intervals as long as the sentence is considered true. Identical intervals mean that the two events happen simultaneously and that the overlap is complete, i.e. there is no interval during which only one but not the other event holds. In (35b), 'c' is the variable for *child* and 'τ' stands for the interval of the event.

(35) a. The child lay in bed awake.
    b. $\{e \mid$ there is an $e', e'' \leq e$ such that $\mathbf{lay}(e', c)$, $\mathbf{awake}(e'', c)$,
    and $\tau(e) = \tau(e') = \tau(e'')\}$
    (McNally 1994: 568)

For Rothstein (2003), depictive secondary predicates are interpreted by means of an *event summing* operation '⊔', where two events e_1 and e_2 are summed to denote a singular event *e*. The single-event character of the summed event *e* is denoted by the superscript 'S' in (36b).

(36) a. John drove the car drunk.
 b. $\exists e \exists e_1 \exists e_2 [e = {}^S(e_1 \sqcup e_2) \wedge \text{DROVE}(e_1) \wedge \text{Ag}(e_1) = \text{JOHN} \wedge \text{Th}(e_1) = \text{THE CAR} \wedge \text{DRUNK}(e_2) \wedge \text{Arg}(e_2) = \text{JOHN}]$
 (Rothstein 2003: 561, 563)

The two events of driving and being drunk are each predicated of the common argument *John* and unified to denote an event where both predications hold, similar to coextensiveness in McNally (1994). As in the predication theory of Williams (1980, 1983), the argument *John* is identified as the referent of the two predicates *drive* and *drunk*. The important contribution in Rothstein (2003) is the formulation of the relation that holds between these two instances of predication. For a successful summing operation to a singular event, two conditions need to be satisfied, which define the "time–participant connectedness" (TPCONNECT) of the two events:

(37) TPCONNECT(e_1,e_2,y) iff:
 i. $\tau(e_1) = \tau(e_2)$ (i.e. the run time of e_1 is the same as the run time of e_2);
 ii. e_1 and e_2 share a participant y.
 (Rothstein 2003: 568)

This imposes the requirement for a common argument, and also that the intervals of the two predicates need to be identical. Strictly speaking, the two events are not independent and the termination of one entails the termination of the summed event *e*.

Geuder (2004: 138–141) criticizes the strict identity relation between the two events for depictives as formulated in Rothstein (2003) because such a strict condition seems unwarranted. Instead, he proposes a semantics for the depictive construction building on a weakened overlap relation 'o'; this relation merely requires that the intervals of the matrix event and the depictive state "have some part in common" (Geuder 2004: 138). This allows for a more flexible temporal relation between the two predicates than a strict identity relation as in Rothstein (2003). A semantic analysis is given in (38), where the state of being tired can easily be understood to start before and continue after the eating event. The sentence in (38a) is still understood in a way where the state of being tired holds during the entire eating event, possibly because the main verb denotes a bounded event.

(38) a. We had eaten tired.
  b. $\lambda x[\exists e[eat(e, x)\ \&\ \exists s[tired(s, x)\ \&\ s \circ e]\ \&\ t = \text{AFTER}(e)]]$
  (Geuder 2004: 137)

Compared to the strict identity relation in Rothstein (2003), this analysis captures the intuition that the intervals during which the two predicates hold are to some degree independent. This can account for the accessibility of punctual predicates with depictives, which are difficult to explain when the punctual nature of the main verb restricts the interval of the depictive to hold of just that moment; (39) illustrates the oddity of a depictive with an achievement predicate under the interpretation that the depictive holds just for the instant of the achievement.

(39) #The guests arrived drunk.
  (intended reading: the guests are only drunk at the moment of arrival)

Geuder (2000) assumes that depictives carry constructional meaning by establishing the overlap relation between the event of the main verb and the state of the depictive; together, they express a complex situation (Geuder 2000: 190).

The liberal temporal overlap relation from Geuder (2004) is adapted in Pylkkänen's (2008) analysis of depictives, but in contrast to Geuder she does not assume that depictives have constructional meaning (Pylkkänen 2008: 23). Rather, she postulates a syntactic head that introduces the depictive and is responsible for interpretation. This allows the depictive to contribute compositionally to the meaning of the sentence and simultaneously limits the possible attachment sites, which have to be of the right type for the depictive (<e,<s,t>>; see Pylkkänen 2008: 23). The semantics of the depictive head are given in (40):

(40) $\lambda f_{<e,<s,t>>}.\lambda x.\lambda e\ (\exists s)\ f(s, x)\ \&\ e \circ s$ (Pylkkänen 2008: 23)

Pylkkänen (2008: 22–23) departs from the analysis of depictives as participant-oriented modifiers postulated in H&SB (2005) and rather considers them as adverbials modifying the event. As noted above, for a characterization of the BPPA construction it is necessary to decide whether the adjunct predicate modifies the participant, the event, or both, as the different possible structural analyses differ in this respect. A similar interpretation of the depictive with respect to a liberal overlap relation is adopted in Fortmann (2015), who notes that the intersection of the intervals of the main verb, the depictive, and the reference time of the main verb must be non-empty (Fortmann 2015: 231).

The precise nature of the overlap relation is studied from a cross-linguistic perspective in Irimia (2012): she finds seven logically possible realizations that are not always fully available in a given language. These realizations range from coextensive (as in McNally 1994 and Rothstein 2003) to realizations where only parts of the two intervals overlap (Irimia 2012: 155–160). This allows for a flexible interpretation of the depictive with respect to the matrix predicate, and can also explain cases that are more difficult to capture when the relation is strict. For example, (41a) could be analyzed as a "terminative overlap" relation, where the whistling terminates together with the point of dying. The sentence in (41b) is flexible in the possible relations because the whistling can start long before the point of coming home and continue afterwards; the precise interpretation has to be determined by additional means.

(41) a. John died [whistling *Ode to Joy*].
b. 'Dad, I came home whistling the *Marseillaise* today.'
(Truswell 2011: 152)

Whether the adjunct event stops with the culmination in cases like (41) is also determined by the semantics of the main verb (Truswell 2011: 152–153): dying precludes the possibility to continue whistling, whereas coming home does not.

This section has shown that a temporal overlap relation together with the modification of a participant in the event of the main verb is the characteristic interpretation of depictives. For a large subset of BPPA constructions, namely those with achievement matrix predicates, the depictive analysis results in an appropriate interpretation; however, there is no explanation for the availability of a causal reading with some matrix predicates, like *drive crazy*. Identification as a causal component in the semantics of the matrix predicate and the morphological encoding as a progressive form requires an overlap relation just as with other matrix predicates. The availability of the causal reading depends on whether there is a plausible connection between the activity in the BPPA and the result in the matrix predicate; it is just as possible that in the absence of such a connection, the BPPA is interpreted as a depictive (see Truswell 2011: 163). It is an important question whether the causal interpretation can be compositionally derived without abandoning the underlying syntactic analysis as a depictive secondary predicate. In the next section, I will discuss possible ways to semantically enrich the basic depictive overlap interpretation to a causal reading. Such a division of labor between the basic meaning encoded in the depictive and the semantic enrichment to a causal interpretation obviates the need to postulate a third type of secondary predicates, which Truswell (2007) implicitly introduces under the term causatives. I do not exclude the theoretical possibility of a third type of secondary predicates, which explicitly encodes the causal reading; following the semantic principle of compositionality, causatives should syntactically differ from other secondary predicates, just as depictives and resultatives differ syntactically (see Winkler 1997).

2.3.2 Event specification and expansion with co-eventive adjuncts

As discussed in the previous section, the interpretation of depictives is limited to spatio-temporal overlap relations and the linking of the depictive to an argument of the main verb. One of the reasons for this is the limitation of the discussion to a small set of depictive predicates, typically single-lexeme adjectives (Rothstein 2006, 2017). Verbal adjuncts, regardless of whether they should be considered as depictives or not, have received comparatively little attention. They are to a certain degree considered in Schultze-Berndt & Himmelmann (2004) and Himmelmann & Schultze-Berndt (2005). Non-finite verbal adjuncts are surveyed in detail in Fabricius-Hansen & Haug (2012a,b) under the term "co-eventive adjuncts". Based on these insights, Haug et al. (2012) develop a compositional semantic derivation for participial adjuncts without an introducing subordinator. The results are almost identical to the interpretational space of the BPPA construction, i.e. the temporal overlap and the causal reading. This compositional semantics for present participle adjunct predicates takes into account both the aspectual characteristics of the participle adjunct and the event- and argument-structure of the matrix predicate. Whereas depictives typically introduce stative adjuncts and are characterized by temporal overlap relations, participle co-events can introduce non-stative, eventive predicates with a richer variety of possible relations that are not exclusively temporal (Haug et al. 2012: 131–132). Following Bary & Haug (2011), Haug et al. (2012) propose that co-eventive adjuncts like BPPAs are linked to the main verb by an *elaboration* (ELAB) discourse relation that establishes a closer semantic and pragmatic link between the two predicates on the level of Discourse Representation Structure (DRS), indicated by the DRS merge operator '⊕'; it is conceptualized as a form of constructional meaning that allows a compositional semantics for eventive adjuncts. This relation, given in (42), forces the participle to use the event time of the matrix event by merging the adjunct predicate Q with the interval of the main predicate P (Haug et al. 2012: 156).

(42) ELAB: $\lambda P \lambda Q \lambda e [P(\tau(e)) \oplus Q(e)]$ (Bary & Haug 2011: 38)

A second operator, *independent rheme* (INDRHEME), is used for detached/free adjuncts that constitute an independent intonation unit and represent coordinated events instead of subordination (Bary & Haug 2011: 42). The choice between these two operators correlates with adjunction sites: high adjuncts are interpreted by

INDRHEME, whereas low adjuncts are interpreted by ELAB. I will not discuss IN-DRHEME further here, but the distinction between these operators is relevant in Experiment 3 in the experimental Chapter 4.

Participles linked by an ELAB relation instantiate new information that stands in a subordinate discourse relation to the main verb and depends temporally on the main verb (Bary & Haug 2011: 17). Based on a definition of the English -*ing*-form as compatible with both perfective and imperfective readings in the form of a general overlap relation (Haug et al. 2012: 156) and the ELAB relation in (42) as the meaning of the adjunct participle construction, a depictive construction like (43a) receives the basic semantic representation in (43b); BPPA constructions can be analyzed in the same way, for example by replacing *smiling* with *singing a song*. This formula establishes a simple overlap relation, represented by 'o', between the intervals of the two events *e* and *e'* and additionally identifies the subject as a common agent. This basic interpretation is very similar to the TPCONNECT operation from Rothstein (2003) and Geuder's (2004) overlap relation.

(43) a. Peter left *smiling*.
　　 b. $\lambda t.[e, e', t1, x \mid t \supseteq \tau(e)$, leave($e$), peter($x$), Agent($x$)($e$), $\tau(e) \circ \tau(e')$, smile(e'), Agent(x)(e')]
　　　 (Haug et al. 2012: 162)

As Haug et al. (2012: 162) note, this representation ignores possible relations between the two events that may hold in addition to temporal overlap and participant-sharing. To capture the possible semantic relations more accurately, they use the concepts of *event specification* for cause and manner relations and *event expansion* for a looser connection that is still more complex than simple overlap. These two concepts adequately characterize the range of possible meanings of the BPPA construction.

The event specification relation provides additional information that is left implicit in the lexical semantics of the main verb. When the main verb is causative but does not specify the cause component, this slot can be filled by the participle adjunct. That many accomplishments can be analyzed as causatives without an explicitly given cause is already observed in Dowty (1979):

(44) a. John dissolved the Alka Seltzer.　　　　　　　　　　[implicit cause]
　　 b. John dissolved the Alka Seltzer by doing something.　[explicit cause]
　　　 (Dowty 1979: 92)

Haug et al. (2012) provide the following analysis for the manner-neutral causative *repair* in (45a). In a first step (45b), the participle is introduced in the formula without an explicit linking to the cause slot, represented by 'e' =?'. If the participle qualifies as a possible cause, which is determined by world knowledge, the linking to the causing event is made explicit by identifying the participle event with the causing event, seen in (45c): e' becomes e_2, the cause component of e_1. The semantic representation is simplified by this identification process because it reduces the number of events from three to two.

(45) Event specification with manner-neutral causatives
   a. Experts restored the canvas *repairing the boot*.
   b. $\lambda e.[e_1, e_2, e' \mid \text{Become}(\text{restored})(\text{canv})(e_1), \text{Cause}(e_1)(e_2), e_1 \leq e,$
      $e_2 \leq e, \text{repair\_boot}(e'), \tau(e') \supseteq \tau(e), e' = ?]$
   c. $\lambda e.[e_1, e_2 \mid \text{Become}(\text{restored})(\text{canv})(e_1), \text{Cause}(e_1)(e_2),$
      $\text{repair\_boot}(e_2), e_1 \leq e, e_2 \leq e, \tau(e_2) \supseteq \tau(e)]$
      (Haug et al. 2012: 165, 167)

When the main verb is not causative, as in (46a), the participle can specify the manner in which the event occurs. Similar to causatives, the initial semantic representation does not make the link obvious (46b). Since the main verb does not have an open position in its argument structure, the link between main verb and participle has to be made by introducing a linking event. In the example, *stammering* is one of the possible ways that the manner-neutral verb *say* can be expressed; the underspecification of the precise realization is indicated by the linking event *articulate*(e_a), which adds a manner component to the representation. The intermediate formula in (46c), similar to (45b) above, introduces all required events but leaves out the precise linking; if the participle qualifies as a possible manner of the main verb, the link is made (e' becomes e_a), as in (46d). Here, the final representation is more complex than with manner-neutral causatives because an additional event position has to be introduced in the form of the linking event.

(46) Event specification with manner adjuncts
   a. Thanks, he said *stammering*.
   b. $\lambda e[e' \mid \text{say\_thanks}(e), \tau(e) \circ \tau(e'), \text{stammer}(e'), e' = ?]$
   c. $\lambda e.[e_a e' \mid \text{say\_thanks}(e), \text{articulate}(e_a), e_a \leq e, \tau(e) \circ \tau(e'),$
      $\text{stammer}(e'), e' = ?]$
   d. $\lambda e[e_a e' \mid \text{say\_thanks}(e), \text{articulate}(e_a), e_a \leq e, \tau(e) \circ \tau(e_a),$
      $\text{stammer}(e_a)]$
      (Haug et al. 2012: 164–167)

These two examples show that a participle adjunct can be fitted into the semantic interpretation if one of two conditions is met: the participle has to be identified either with the implicit cause or manner component. If these slots are already filled in the lexical semantic representation of the main verb or if they are implausible or contradictory, the linking fails; see (47), where '#' stands for pragmatic oddness. This introduces a degree of flexibility in interpretation that incorporates world knowledge. Examples like these also indicate that there is a minimum of semantic selection in the BPPA construction; see also Himmelmann & Schultze-Berndt (2005), Travis (2010), and Graf (2015) for semantic selection with adjunct predicates.

(47)   a. #Experts restored the canvas ruining the painting.
       b. #Thanks, he screamed whispering.

The semantic representations so far all allow the participle to be identified with an implicit position in the lexical semantics of the main verb, either cause or manner. This is not possible for all cases of event elaboration: when the participle qualifies neither as a plausible cause nor manner, a different mechanism needs to be involved, which is called event expansion. This mechanism can be seen as a last resort option when the linking to a semantic component is not feasible. It works similar to the introduction of the manner subevent in (46c) above in that it introduces an additional event into the representation. Compare the two possibilities in (48b,c) as representations of the sentence in (48a). The relation between the two events of walking and thinking are interpreted in a temporal overlap relation in (48b); this is the basic interpretation introduced by the ELAB relation in (43) above. In contrast, they are interpreted as parts of a newly introduced complex event e^* which subsumes the two events e and e' in (48c).

(48)   Event expansion
       a. He walked to the station *thinking of the girl he had just left*.
       b. $\lambda t.[ee' \mid \text{walk\_to\_station}(e), \tau(e) \subseteq t, \text{think\_of\_girl}(e') \& \tau(e) \circ \tau(e')]$
       c. $\lambda t.[ee'e^* \mid \text{walk\_to\_station}(e), e \leq e^*, \tau(e) \subseteq t, \text{think\_of\_girl}(e')$
          $\& \tau(e) \circ \tau(e') \& e \leq e^*]$
          (Haug et al. 2012: 169–170)

The difference between two representations in (48b) and (48c) is the strength of conceptual linking that takes place between the two events; events can happen simultaneously but do not have to be related in another way. They can also be interpreted as parts of a larger event structure that is characterized by temporal overlap and a notion of "perceptual unity" (König 1995: 66). They do not have to "describe two aspects or dimensions of only one event" (König 1995: 65), a relation that is for example present in the manner adjuncts in (46) above. Haug et al. (2012: 169–170) suggest that the accommodation of a big event e^* instead of a simple overlap relation primarily happens with animate behavior like motion and articulation because animates can be occupied by more than one action at the same time. Event expansion offers the possibility to express complex states of affairs that are not lexicalized in a single verb.

The semantic representation of complex events with participial adjunct predicates in Haug et al. (2012) captures precisely the interpretations that are available for BPPA constructions. One of the challenges in interpreting these complex structures is that the present participle in English appears to be aspectually underspecified, which precludes a precise way that it is interpreted compositionally with the main event (see Haug et al. 2012: 132). The notion of a "big event" $e*$ in Haug et al. (2012) is similar to that of an "event grouping" in Truswell (2011), even though there are differences in the precise implementations of the concept. Event groupings are more restrictive because they allow at most one agentive event and are primarily introduced to explain patterns in *wh*-extraction from BPPAs. Haug et al.'s (2012) analysis is not tied to extraction and thus a more general approach to the interpretation of complex events with participial adjuncts. Haug et al. (2012) do not explicitly link the availability of either of the three possible interpretations to aspectual classes as done in Truswell (2007, 2011). They do note, however, that the interpretation of a complex construction with a participle event is influenced by "pragmatic reasoning based on the Aktionsart of the event descriptions" (Haug et al. 2012: 132), but the focus is on the influence of perfective and imperfective aspect and how the two events are temporally related. An event specification relation is limited to main predicates that are underspecified for either a causal or a manner component, so they will typically be accomplishments like *restore* in (45) and activities with a more general meaning such as *say* in (46); for verbs where no such underspecified meaning slot is available, the event expansion relation is an alternative option, conditioned by the possibility to construe both predicates as the description of a single event.

The idea of linking events together compositionally can be seen as an extension of less formalized approaches to such relations, as for example proposed in Hobbs (1979, 1990) and Kehler (2002, 2019) under the term of *discourse relations*. Coherence relations are a way of linking separate sentences together and explaining how a narrative sequence is structured. The approach to co-eventive adjuncts presented in Bary & Haug (2011) and Haug et al. (2012) operates on a more local level by establishing linking relations between a main verb and an adjunct predicate within a single sentence. As shown in Kehler (2002), discourse coherence relations have an effect on syntactic operations such as pronoun resolution and extraction. Thus, the concept of event elaboration can offer insights into the possible interpretations of the BPPA construction, and also about the possibility for extraction. As will be shown in the Chapter 3, discourse coherence relations have been employed to explain data patterns for extraction from BPPA constructions in C. Müller (2019).

In conclusion, the concepts of event specification and expansion are a suitable semantic representation of the interpretational range of the BPPA construction. They offer a solution to the question of why participial adjuncts can receive a causal reading and are not limited to the temporal overlap relation of a depictive analysis. The basic depictive reading is augmented on the level of DRS by the ELAB relation and does not need to be encoded directly in the depictive semantics. The restrictions on temporal relations between events with an aspectually underspecified participle can also be used as an explanation for the limited range of interpretations compared to reduced adverbial clauses.

2.3.3 Interpreting complex event structures

In this section, I discuss two further approaches to the interpretation of complex events which focus on the lexical semantics of predicates instead of the discourse-level integration of complex events as in Haug et al. (2012). The first is the approach developed by Rappaport Hovav & Levin on the distinction between manner and result verbs, which can be extended to explain some of the aspectual restrictions of the BPPA construction; the second approach is the frame–satellite typology by Talmy (1985, 2000), which imposes similar restrictions on the type of events which can co-occur in a monoclausal structure. I will show that both approaches offer insights for the BPPA construction in two aspects: (i) how the complex meaning of the BPPA construction is derived, and (ii) which restrictions on the types of events follow from these approaches.

One generalization about transparent adjuncts in Truswell (2007: 1369), discussed in the following chapter, is that the two predicates in the BPPA construction need to stand in a relation that mirrors a possible event structure of a lexical verb. For example, since no lexical verb encodes a relation between two culminations, the combination of two telic predicates in the BPPA construction disallows extraction. Essentially, adjunct transparency is linked to the question of how complex the event description of the matrix and adjunct predicate can be without requiring a multiple-event reading. Constraints on the complexity of verbal meanings are the subject of several works by Rappaport Hovav & Levin, especially Rappaport Hovav (2014), Rappaport Hovav & Levin (1998, 2010), and Levin & Rappaport Hovav (2013, 2014, 2019), under the term *Manner–Result Complementarity* (MRC).

The basic principle behind MRC is that a lexical verb can either express a manner component or a result component, but not both simultaneously.² There is a correlation between the classification of a predicate as either manner or result and its verb type: unergatives are typically manner verbs and describe the manner in which an event happens, whereas unaccusatives are mostly result verbs which describe a change of state. An example is given in (49).

(49) a. unergative (e.g. *run, work*) → typically MANNER verbs
      b. unaccusative (e.g. *arrive, break*) → typically RESULT verbs

MRC predicts that when one of the two meaning components is expressed in the verb, the other meaning component can be expressed outside of the verb in another constituent, such as result or goal phrases (Rappaport Hovav & Levin 2010: 22); see (50).³

(50) a. Peter [wiped the table]$_{manner}$ [clean]$_{result}$
      b. Sarah [ran]$_{manner}$ [to the store]$_{result}$

The MRC restriction on possible verb meanings is related to the issue of which meanings can be expressed in complex events. This can also be applied to the BPPA construction with some modifications, and makes predictions that limit the possible combinations of different predicate types. However, MRC cannot be directly transferred to explain restrictions on the BPPA construction because it is designed to constrain the meaning of individual lexical verbs, not of constructions with multiple predicates. Still, there are similarities in the restrictions of the MRC and the data pattern observed for BPPAs. If, as Truswell (2007) proposes, the transparency of the BPPA really depends on whether the sentence does not exceed the maximum meaning of a lexical verb, then the BPPA construction should likewise show effects that resemble MRC: it should be impossible for two manner or result verbs to occur in the construction simultaneously. On a first pass, this prediction is met in the BPPA examples in (51): sentences where the BPPA encodes an identical

---

2 See also Mateu & Acedo-Matellán (2012) for a syntactic formulation of MRC, where manner and result occupy different syntactic positions.

3 Intuitively, the incremental theme verb *wipe the table* encodes a result, namely that the table is wiped; however, as argued in Rappaport Hovav (2008), Rappaport Hovav & Levin (2010), and Kennedy (2012), such verbs do not lexically encode measure-of-change functions because the attainment of a result is defeasible (Rappaport Hovav & Levin 2010: 22). This measure-of-change function can be contributed by a resultative secondary predicate, as in (50a); without the resultative, *wipe the table* is a MANNER verb.

meaning component as the main verb are intuitively slightly worse than those where the two predicates encode different components.[4]

(51) a. Peter [arrived]_result [whistling a funny song]_manner
 b. ?Peter [arrived]_result [noticing his brother]_result
 c. Peter [ran]_manner [noticing his brother]_result
 d. ?Peter [ran]_manner [whistling a funny song]_manner

However, MRC does not offer an immediate explanation for the fact that compared to (51a), the reverse combination of meaning components in (51c) does not seem to be equally acceptable, as proposed in Truswell (2007). This is probably a reflex of the progressive morphology on the perception verb *notice*, which strongly resists progressive formation (Rothstein 2004b: 42). There should thus be a three-way difference between these sentences, caused by two independent factors: (51b,d) are less acceptable than (51a,c) due to MRC, and (51c) is less acceptable than (51a) due to specific characteristics of *notice*. These predictions from MRC are surprisingly similar to the pattern for extraction proposed in Truswell (2007), but can be obtained without resorting to specific constraints on the applicability of extraction operations because these restrictions also show an effect in declaratives; it is an open question whether the potential acceptability differences in declaratives are equally strong as those reported for interrogatives. Note that the pattern predicted for interrogatives in Truswell (2007) differs from that predicted by MRC in that Truswell (2007) considers (51b,c,d) degraded in interrogatives in a two-way distinction, based on the dual requirement that the matrix predicate needs to be telic and the BPPA atelic to allow extraction. The fact that this pattern can be derived for declaratives under MRC in a more nuanced pattern will be shown to have serious ramifications for Truswell's (2007) approach in the following chapter.

A second approach to the interpretation of complex events is presented in Talmy (1985, 1991, 2000), who proposes limitations on the types of meaning that a single event can express. Talmy's work is rooted in the cognitive semantics tradition, but is not without influence in generative approaches; see, for example, the adaptation in Acedo-Matellán (2016). The initial observations in Talmy (1985) constrain the meaning components expressed in motion verbs, which is later

---

[4] It could be possible to capture the unaccusative behavior of unergatives like *run* with prepositional phrases as a shift from a MANNER to a RESULT interpretation (Levin & Rappaport Hovav 1995; Borgonovo & Neeleman 2000); this would allow the BPPA construction to encode both MANNER and RESULT in a single sentence, with RESULT in the matrix clause and MANNER in the BPPA:

(i) a. Sarah [ran]_manner [to the store]_result → Sarah [ran to the store]_result
 b. Sarah [ran to the store]_result [whistling a funny song]_manner

extended to verbs encoding change in a more general way in Talmy (1991). In the following, I will show that this approach makes predictions about the combinations of predicates in the BPPA construction. Similar to Rappaport Hovav & Levin's MRC, Talmy argues that a lexical verb can only encode one of two components of motion: MANNER or PATH. If one of these components is expressed in the verb, then the other one cannot also be expressed in the verb but can be expressed in another constituent. This additional constituent is called the "satellite" and can for example be realized as particles, affixes, or other material such as the PP in (52a). Languages differ in the constituent that primarily encodes PATH; the two prototypical cases are verb-framed (V-framed) and satellite-framed (S-framed) languages, where framing determines which constituent encodes the PATH component. While this idealization holds up surprisingly well cross-linguistically, it is not without counterexamples, for example from languages that allow both framing alternatives (see Levin & Rappaport Hovav 2019: 405–409). There is also a third option, where the verb lexicalizes neither MANNER nor PATH, but simply the fact of movement, as in (52b). In these cases, both MANNER and PATH can be lexicalized outside the verb, as in (52c); see Beavers et al. (2010: 362).

(52) a. John [ran]$_{manner}$ [out of the room]$_{path}$.
      b. John moved.
      c. John moved [stealthily]$_{manner}$ [out of the room]$_{path}$.

The data patterns from the different framing options for motion predicates are important with respect to the discussion of the interpretation of BPPAs in at least two aspects: first, the framing options delimit the way in which complex event descriptions are formed cross-linguistically and where meanings that are too complex cannot be considered as a single event; and second, because the different framing options show correlations between whether the main verb encodes MANNER or PATH and its grammatical or aspectual type. The following set of examples in (53/54) from English, which is typically S-framed but V-framed with verbs borrowed from Romance, and strictly V-framed Spanish illustrates how the two meaning components can be distributed in a sentence with a BPPA construction.

(53) Verb-framed alternate (verb encodes PATH):
      a. The bottle entered the cave floating.
      b. *La botella entró   a la   cueva (flotando)*
         the bottle MOVED-in to the cave   (floating)
         'The bottle floated into the cave'   (Talmy 2000: 49)

(54) Satellite-framed alternate (verb encodes MANNER):
  a. The bottle floated into the cave.
  b. ??*La botella flotó a la cueva.*
     the bottle floated to the cave
     'The bottle floated to the cave' (Beavers et al. 2010: 341)

While English allows both framing options (53a/54a), the S-framed alternate is degraded in Spanish (54b).[5] The reason that English is more flexible than Spanish in this regard is the relatively high number of motion verbs that derive from the Romance languages (Acedo-Matellán 2016: 73; Levin & Rappaport Hovav 2019: 401). In his original framework, Talmy (2000) imposes restrictions on which constituents can function as satellites: particles, prefixes, and other categories that are not NP or PP complements. In addition, only sisters to verbs can be satellites (Talmy 2000: 102). This position is discussed in Beavers et al. (2010), who conclude that adjuncts to V also qualify as satellites (Beavers et al. 2010: 339), which allows BPPAs to function as satellites. If the main verb in the BPPA construction encodes either MANNER or PATH, the BPPA can express the other meaning component, but not the same as the main verb; this restricts the possible combinations of predicates to verbs encoding non-identical meaning components, as does MRC.

Talmy (1991, 2000: chapter 3) argues that there are several ways that two simple events can be integrated to form a "macro-event". There are two idealized options on a continuum of event integration: (i) either the macro-event consists of two events plus a relation between them, typically expressed in a two-clause structure with an optional overt linking word; or (ii) the two events are fused together to form an event that can be expressed by a single clause (Talmy 2000: 213). Of the two events, the one that is more dominant is termed the "framing event", which provides the general event schema of the macro-event; often, the framing event is of an abstract nature, whereas the subordinate event, the so-called "co-event", is "more substantive or perceptually palpable" (Talmy 2000: 219). Among the several possible support relations between the subordinate and the framing event, Talmy (2000: 220) notes that cause and manner relations are the most common ones, which mirrors the readings found in BPPAs.

In English, both the BPPA construction and a variety of adverbial clauses can be analyzed in terms of event integration and support relations. For example, the

---

5 Croft et al. (2010: 211) note that Spanish allows the S-framed option only when "the path expression is atelic" and does not entail that the goal is reached:

(i) *El libro deslizó hasta el suelo.*
    the book slide.3.SG.PST towards the floor
    'The book slid down to the floor' (Croft et al. 2010: 211, originally from Aske 1989: 3)

adverbial clauses in (55) stand in a specific support relation to the main clause, and the combination can still be interpreted as one event. The BPPA construction is special in this case because it does not clearly separate the framing event from the co-event in a two-clause structure as with adverbial clauses. It also does not overtly encode one of the support relations; the relation remains implicit and can thus be expected to default to one of the most prominent relations, i.e. cause or manner; see the example in (56).

(55)   a.   Peter traveled to England (in order) to paint the queen.   [purpose]
       b.   Peter arrived at the station while/without whistling a song.   [manner]
       c.   Peter drove Mary crazy by whistling a song.   [cause]

(56)   Peter drove Mary crazy whistling a song.   [BPPA]

MRC and Talmy's typology agree on the terminology for the MANNER component but differ in the classification of RESULT and PATH; in Chapter 5, I will argue that both belong to the same group of scalar meaning components and can thus receive a unified explanation that takes into account their similar aspectual behavior. The discussion of MRC and Talmy's (2000) approach to complex events shows that several restrictions on English BPPA constructions can be explained by the distribution of meaning components in complex event descriptions. The restrictions on the meaning components that can be encoded in a complex sentence rule out a considerable subset of BPPA constructions without interference from extraction. Three main insights follow from this discussion: (i) a monoclausal structure can express only one result; (ii) additional verbal forms typically contribute manner or cause meanings; and (iii) the relative distribution of result and manner/cause follows language-specific preferences.

2.4 Licensing conditions on depictive constructions

This section examines syntactic and semantic conditions on depictive secondary predicates; the goal is to find out whether these conditions mirror the reported data pattern for extraction from BPPAs. Since the literature on depictives is substantial, only a subset that is relevant to the research questions for this chapter will be discussed. Particularly, this includes approaches to depictives that impose category and semantic restrictions on the depictive itself in Section 2.4.1 and the types of main verbs that can host depictives in Section 2.4.2. It will be seen that these conditions already narrow down possible depictive configurations, and that similar restrictions apply to the BPPA construction. In Section 2.4.3, I will focus on BPPA constructions with resultative secondary predicates in the matrix clause and show that this can explain transparency characteristics of a subset of BPPAs with two arguments.

2.4.1 Licensing conditions on the depictive

There is substantial cross-linguistic literature on what qualifies as a depictive secondary predicate; see for example Schultze-Berndt & Himmelmann (2004), Himmelmann & Schultze-Berndt (2005), and Simpson (2005), among many others. The discussion focuses on two property sets that are required for a depictive: syntactic category restrictions and semantic restrictions.

Regarding the syntactic category restrictions, the focus is on single-lexeme adjectival depictives, including adjectival uses of present and past participles. In addition, some PP and DP depictives are considered to be possible (Rothstein 2017: 3874; Rapoport 2019: 432). Opinions differ on whether more complex constituents can function as depictives, which also depends on the exact definition of the term. For Schultze-Berndt & Himmelmann (2004: 77–78), optionality, obligatory control, independence, and non-finiteness are among the characteristic features of depictives. This allows for more verbal categories to act as depictives than a focus on adjectives and prepositional or nominal categories; under this definition, it is possible to include not only adjectival participles, but also clauses headed by a participle in the group of potential depictives as long as they are obligatorily controlled by a participant of the main predication (Schultze-Berndt & Himmelmann 2004: 98–107). As noted in Section 2.2.3, the acceptance of complex verbal depictives such as participles with a complement is not universal but finds increasing support, also from a cross-linguistic perspective; see Rothstein (2017) for a more conservative view. While depictives of the form in (57a) are uncontroversial, the same cannot be said for (57b).

(57) a. John$_i$ came home drunk$_i$.   [adjectival participle depictive]
      b. John$_i$ came home [whistling a song]$_i$.
                                                        [complex participle depictive (?)]

It is possible that this issue is subject to cross-linguistic variation, where English occupies a position where some instances like (57b) can be analyzed as depictives, but the data are not as clear as for other languages (see Simpson 2005). For example, König (1995) argues that participle adjuncts in German such as (58) degrade when the participle takes a complement due to complexity restrictions:

(58)   Hans kam (? ein Lied) pfeifend   in   die Küche.
       Hans came a   song   whistling into the kitchen
       'Hans came into the kitchen, whistling (a tune).'   (König 1995: 73)

However, it seems possible to add further material to the participle adjunct without further degradation; see (59), where the complex participle adjunct is indicated by square brackets. It is thus unclear whether König's (1995) argument is empirically valid; see also (61)–(62) below.

(59) a. Hans kam [laut   vor   sich hin   pfeifend] in   die Küche.
          Hans came loudly before self along whistling into the kitchen
          'Hans came into the kitchen, whistling along loudly.'
      b. Hans kam [einen neu   komponierten Schlager pfeifend] in
          Hans came a   newly composed   hit-song whistling into
          die Küche.
          the kitchen
          'Hans came into the kitchen, whistling a newly composed hit-song.'
          (Susanne Winkler, p. c.)

In principle, there is no reason to limit verbal depictives to single-lexeme constituents because there are clear instances of more complex PP/DP depictives:

(60) a. She reached the house *out of breath*.
      b. He left the hospital *a shade of his former self*.
          (Rothstein 2017: 3874)

The same applies to participle depictives in German, which are discussed in Fortmann (2015) with several examples of complex argument-taking participles. Two examples are given in (61) and (62); italics indicate the complex participle depictive and bold typeface the nominal referent.

(61) **der** [_AP_ [*mit   den Zähnen   klappernd*] ins   Fegefeuer eintretende]
      the   with the teeth   chattering   into purgatory entering
      Eremit errötete.
      hermit   blushed
      'The hermit entering purgatory with chattering teeth blushed.'
                                                             (Fortmann 2015: 223)

(62) *Einen derben Fluch ausstoßend* glotzte **der Eremit** den Teufel an.
      exclaiming a rough curse   gawked the hermit the devil at
                                                              (Fortmann 2015: 232)

There are some crucial differences to depictives in English, which are typically postverbal and follow non-subject arguments of the verb. In these two German cases, (61) is embedded in an adjectival constituent that stands in an attributive function to the subject (Fortmann 2015: 223); (62) represents a sentence-initial depictive, which is also possible in English but bears closer similarity to free adjunct constructions instead of depictives. The grammaticality status of non-initial orderings as in (63) are intuitively slightly worse compared to (62) under the intended reading where the depictive is not analyzed as a parenthetical comment. Both examples are, however, completely acceptable as free adjunct constructions (Stump 1985), where the highlighted material is pronounced with intonational breaks preceding and following it, as in (63c).

(63) a. ?Der Eremit glotzte *einen derben Fluch ausstoßend* den Teufel an.
          the hermit gawked exclaiming a rough curse   the devil at
      b. ??Der Eremit glotzte den Teufel *einen derben Fluch ausstoßend* an.
          the hermit gawked the devil   exclaiming a rough curse   at
      c. Der Eremit glotzte – *einen derben Fluch ausstoßend* – den Teufel an.
          the hermit gawked   exclaiming a rough curse   the devil at
          (adapted from Fortmann 2015: 232)

The extensive use of particle verbs is certainly a complicating factor in German because the complex depictive considerably increases the distance between the lexical verb *glotzen* 'gawk' and the particle *an* 'at'.

In addition to the category restrictions, there is also a semantic restriction on the depictive: for adjectival depictives, the adjective has to denote a non-permanent property (Rothstein 1985; Winkler 1997; Simpson 2005). This distinction is typically formulated in terms of Carlson's (1977) individual-level (ILP) and stage-level (SLP) contrast. Thus, a temporary depictive like (64a) is fine, whereas a depictive that encodes a permanent property is not (64b). Geuder (2000: 190) relates this to the fact that ILP secondary predicates lead to a trivial overlap relation between the two predicates, which is not considered informative; as ILP are permanent properties, the interval of the main verb will always overlap with it.

(64) a. John arrived drunk.
      b. *John arrived tall.

Rapoport (1993a: 171–173) summarizes this contrast in Davidsonian (1967) terms because only SLP have an event position that can be identified with the event position of the main predicate. ILP, which lack the event argument *e* (see Kratzer 1995), fail to satisfy a semantic licensing principle, which requires that all phrases need to be licensed by linking to a position in the argument or event structure of the main verb (Rapoport 1993a: 159, 173–174). For potential complex participle depictives, this should apply in the same way. Indeed, sentences with ILP adjuncts (65a) are degraded compared to SLP adjuncts (65b):

(65) a. ?John hurt himself having a neatly mown lawn. [ILP depictive]
 b. John made himself angry trying to fix the radiator. [SLP depictive]
 (Truswell 2007: 1371)

In (65a), it is implausible that the event of John hurting himself is connected to or caused by the fact of having a neatly mown lawn; the depictive fails to be licensed because it is not connected to the argument structure of the main verb and cannot be linked to its event structure because it does not have an event argument. For (65b), it is easier to establish a causal argument structure link between the two events. Past participle depictives are predicted to be possible because they express a result state after a change of state and are thus SLP rather than ILP; see (66).

(66) John came back [addicted to chocolate].
 (Borgonovo & Neeleman 2000: 200)

Irimia (2012: 218) points out an additional semantic condition on the licensing of depictives with unergative main verbs: citing data from Bolinger (1972: 77), she argues that the depictive needs to encode a scalar meaning. This does not apply to other types of main verbs; her explanation is based on "sortal" congruence between the two predicates, where different types of main verbs impose different requirements. A similar restriction on OODs is proposed in Farrell (2019). These conditions that are based on the interplay of the main verb and the depictive are discussed in Section 2.4.2.

Following the depictive analysis of BPPAs, both the category and semantic restrictions on the possible form of depictives narrow down the possible adjunct predicates. Verbal predicates that qualify as ILP should not be possible; this rules out permanent stative BPPAs. In addition to these properties of the depictive, there are also restrictions on the main verb, which will be discussed in the next section.

2.4.2 Licensing conditions on the host predicate

Not all types of verbs are equally compatible with depictive modification: some verb types generally fail to host depictives, others allow only a specific orientation to one of the participants of the main verb. These restrictions have been analyzed as a sort of "weak selectional restrictions" (Himmelmann & Schultze-Berndt 2005: 24), which blurs the line between depictives and predicative complements (see also Simpson 2005). I will first sketch some fundamental observations about these restrictions before turning to more recent analyses. This discussion largely follows data from Rapoport (2019), who agrees with the data reported in Simpson (2005: 99–104); dissenting views are discussed where they occur.

The verb types that are accessible for depictives are defined more in terms of event structure and aspectual class rather than their syntactic form. This is due to the fact that verbs which differ in aspectual class but have the same syntactic surface structure behave differently with respect to depictives. One of the fundamental conditions is that the main verb in a depictive construction cannot be stative; this can again be formulated in terms of the SLP–ILP distinction. The contrast is clearly seen in (67), where the permanent stative *own* (ILP) is degraded with the OOD (67a); replacing *own* with an activity predicate like *cook* (SLP) yields a grammatical sentence (67b).

(67)   a. *Noa owns chickens$_i$ young$_i$.
       b. Noa cooks chickens$_i$ young$_i$.
       (Rapoport 1993a: 172)

Like the requirement for depictives to be SLPs, this contrast can be explained with the presence or absence of an event variable in non-statives and statives, respectively (Rapoport 1993a: 173). There are a few cases where ILP statives are well-formed with a stative secondary predicate like (68), but there is disagreement whether this is the same construction as (67b); see also Winkler (1997: 368).

(68)   Jones prefers her coffee black.   (Rapoport 1999: 654, fn. 2)

It has to be kept in mind that not all stative predicates are necessarily permanent, as evidence from posture verbs and other non-permanent statives shows (Dowty 1979; Maienborn 2005); this has an immediate effect on depictive accessibility (Rapoport 2019: 438). The predictions are that depictives should be more acceptable with non-permanent statives than with permanent ones, as recognized in the literature (Winkler 1997; Simpson 2005; Rapoport 2019) and shown in (69).

(69) a. Many linguists were intelligible drunk. (Simpson 2005: 101)
 b. Peter lay in bed drunk.

The remaining verb classes mostly accept SODs but are restrictive with respect to OODs (Simpson 2005; Irimia 2012; Rapoport 2019); see also Demonte (1988) for similar observations in Spanish, where OODs in transitives appear to be more restricted than in English. In transitive sentences, SODs are possible (70a,b), but OODs are only possible when the transitive encodes an accomplishment (70a) and not an activity (70b).

(70) a. Jones$_i$ bought the dog$_j$ sick$_{i/j}$. [accomplishment]
 b. I$_i$ kicked John$_j$ depressed$_{i/*j}$. [activity]
 (Rapoport 2019: 434)

Rapoport (1993b) links the availability of the OOD reading to the encoding of a change of state or location in the object. Since the OOD reading is only available for transitive accomplishments, there is an asymmetry in the resolution of possible orientation ambiguities. The orientation of the depictive has to be determined in the accomplishment case but is fixed to the subject with activities. This results in a potential processing disadvantage for accomplishments because the parser cannot rely exclusively on information drawn from the aspectual class of the main verb. Plausibility criteria and contextual information act as sources for disambiguation.

The pattern for achievements is split into those that do not accept the subject-oriented depictive (71a) and those that do (71b); note that (71a) is acceptable under a resultative reading. The split seems to go along the line of degree and punctual achievements (Rapoport 2019: 435). As the discussion in Chapter 4 will show, degree achievements are more appropriately analyzed as abstract accomplishments because they share the same temporal profile and also have argument-structural similarities (Rothstein 2004b). Another point is that cases like (71a) can be analyzed as the anticausative form of the causative alternation, which is not possible for non-alternating achievements like (71b). This is seen in the causative alternates of these two sentences in (72).

(71) a. *The potatoes$_i$ fried raw$_i$. [degree achievement]
 b. Willa$_i$ arrived breathless$_i$. [punctual achievement]
 (see Rapoport 2019: 435, 449)

(72) a. Jones boiled the potatoes raw. (Rapoport 2019: 435)
 b. *Peter arrived Willa breathless.

Sentences like (72a) allow both a depictive and a resultative reading of the adjective under the condition that the adjective qualifies as a possible resultative state: compare (73), where either the pasta were already dry when John began to cook them, or they became dry as a result of the cooking (Horrocks & Stavrou 2007: 617). This is not plausible for the combination of *boil* and *raw*.

(73)   John cooked the pasta dry.   (Horrocks & Stavrou 2007: 617)

From this limited set of data it is not clear whether the properties of gradual and punctual change or the possibility of the causative alternation are the only determinants of depictive accessibility.

The pattern for activity main verbs is more intricate and receives different judgments in the literature. A differentiated pattern is sketched in Rapoport (2019: 434–435). She notes several grammatical examples such as (74a,b,d), but also degraded cases like (74c). It is not only the semantic content of the verb that appears to have an influence on depictive accessibility, but also the presence of delimiting arguments as in (74d), which do not necessarily induce telicity. The example in (74d) is better analyzed as a transitive activity, where the SOD reading is generally possible; see (70b) above.

(74)   a.   Jones ran barefoot/sick/tired that day.
       b.   Jones danced/lectured drunk.
       c.   *Jane laughed/drew drunk.
       d.   Jane drew pictures drunk.
            (Rapoport 2019: 434–435)

A particular strict perspective on activity verbs with depictives is presented in Irimia (2012), who approaches the restrictions on depictive hosts not in event-structural terms, but rather starts at grammatical verb types and modifies the restrictions in terms that are neither fully syntactic nor event-structural. Irimia (2012) considers unergative activities to be degraded with depictives (75a) unless they are further modified by a quantifier (75b) ore are otherwise placed in focus (Irimia 2012: 204).

(75)   a.   ??/*Cliff$_i$ laughed *happy$_i$*.
       b.   Cliff$_i$ laughed *all happy$_i$/giddy$_i$*.
            (Irimia 2012: 206)

Irimia's (2012) main proposal is that complex predicate formation of main verb and depictive is only possible under predicate–predicate linking, which requires that the two predicates match in aspectual types and sortal types. Sortal types or roles are a notion that crosscuts aspectual classes and has the effect of ruling out pure statives and unergatives from depictive modification. Irimia (2012: 213–215) proposes four sortal types: STAT for undifferentiated events like permanent statives, WHOLE for events without stages like *consider*-type verbs, STAGE for events with accessible stages, and DELIMITED WHOLE for events with stages that are constructed from repeated wholes like *love*. A fundamental distinction among sortal types is whether a situation is considered as undifferentiated without subevents or as containing differentiated stages (Irimia 2012: 213). This analysis is similar to the notion of scalar and non-scalar change in Rappaport Hovav & Levin (2010), which also singles out permanent statives and activities, but in event-structural terms. Sortal matching is a reflex of the semantics of the depictive, which requires an overlap relation to hold between the two predicates (Geuder 2000; Rothstein 2003; Pylkkänen 2008); an overlap relation is difficult to establish when one of the predicates is of a different sortal type or completely unspecified with respect to aspectual characteristics. Irimia's (2012) matching hypothesis of the sortal status of the two predicates also bears similarities to the proposals in Rapoport (1993a) and Winkler (1997) that the predicates need to match in their ILP/SLP type. This explains why SLP main verbs require SLP depictives and *vice versa* (Irimia 2012: 209).

Like pure statives, unergatives are typically sortally unspecified in that they are not further differentiated into subevents, hence the difficulty in accepting depictives. When the depictive is further sortally specified by delimiting or gradual information, as in (75b), this characteristic is assumed to percolate to the main verb and facilitate the sortal matching (Irimia 2012: 216–217). It is thus this additional information that is required to coerce an unergative predicate into one that is compatible with the sortal type of depictives. This analysis of unergatives agrees with Tenny's (1995) claim about the non-measuring-out status of isolated unergatives and the experimental findings in Lukassek et al. (2017). In isolation, then, the three grammatical verb types are accessible to depictives to different degrees, as formulated in the accessibility hierarchy for SODs in (76):

(76) Accessibility hierarchy for SODs:
 unaccusative > transitive > unergative (> more accessible)
(Irimia 2012: 206)

The depictive is thus only licensed when the overlap relation can be established because the two predicates already match in sortal status, or when additional material resolves the mismatch by shifting a predicate's sortal type.

The approach to depictive modification with unergative main verbs in Irimia (2012) provides a first step towards the grammaticality judgments in (74) above. The grammatical examples in (74a,b,d) are delimited in a way and can thus be assigned to a sortal category, unlike the cases in (74c), which are not delimited in the same way. As (74d) shows, delimitation can occur in the absence of telicity. Following the analysis of unergatives as verbs derived from a nominal root in Hale & Keyser (1993, 2002, 2005) as shown in (77), the delimitation can be traced back to boundedness characteristics of the presumably underlying noun.

(77)
```
      V
     / \
    V   N
        |
      laugh
```
(Hale & Keyser 2002: 15)

Focusing on the intransitive cases in (74a–c), there is a difference between *run/dance/lecture* on the one hand and *laugh/draw* on the other hand. The former are possible in a dummy *do* construction, whereas the latter are very odd (see Harley 2005: 50). This is shown in (78).

(78)   a.   Do a run/dance/lecture
       b.   #Do a laugh/draw[ing]

The verbalizations in (78a) sound natural, and it is clearly understood what is meant by these sentences: they refer to a performance of the event referred to by the noun. These three examples represent nouns that are understood as taking a specific time. A run is usually a specific form of exercise with a fixed course and hence a temporal delimitation; the same goes for a dance, where delimitation depends on the type of dance. Lastly, a lecture is often limited to a specific time slot or at least follows a script that is delimited. In contrast, the examples in (78b) sound odd, especially since it is not clear what should happen morphologically to *draw*. These examples seem odd in the *do*-paraphrase for different reasons: in the case of *laugh*, the indeterminacy of a semelfactive or iterative reading; for *draw*, it is the fact that this is an incremental theme verb which needs a complement to be delimited. In a sense, then, *laugh* may be too restricted and *draw* too unrestricted compared to the examples in (78a), which are delimited by world knowledge about the nominal root.

Irimia's (2012) focus is on the licensing of SODs; licensing conditions for OODs are examined in Farrell (2019). He proposes that the licensing of an OOD requires two properties: durativity and telicity. This requirement is expressed in the *Depictive Aspectuality Constraint* (DAC) in (79):

(79) Depictive Aspectuality Constraint:
For Object-Oriented depictives, the verb-object-depictive complex must be aspectually compatible with durativity and telicity.   (Farrell 2019: 109)

Durativity as temporal spread and telicity as the encoding of a culmination are the two main characteristics of verbs in the aspectual classification of Vendler (1957). For example, activities lack telicity and achievements lack durativity. Accomplishments have both of these properties. Crucially, Farrell (2019) claims that these properties do not have to be encoded in the host verb alone, but can also be contributed by the depictive: the DAC has to be satisfied by the host–OOD complex. For main verbs that miss either durativity or telicity, i.e. activities and achievements, the depictive has to contribute the missing respective properties to meet the DAC. Since adjectival depictives have a variety of semantic characteristics with respect to durativity and boundedness in the form of absolute and relative, open and closed scales, there are several configurations where the requirements of the DAC can be fulfilled. As an example, consider (80a), where the achievement main verb *find* lacks durativity, which is contributed by the depictive *broken* with durative but not telic properties. On the other hand, with an activity main verb like *carry* in (80b), which lacks telicity, the depictive is not licensed because the overall VP complex lacks the telicity property.[6]

(80) a. She found the bag$_i$ broken$_i$.
　　 b. ??She carried the bag$_i$ broken$_i$.
　　　　(Farrell 2019: 109)

A condition like the DAC can also account for the productivity of depictives with activity matrix predicates, as discussed above for the examples in (74). Telicity and durativity can be added to the predicate complex by incorporating world knowledge information, such as the fact that running, dancing, and lecturing are typically an activity with a delimited runtime; likewise, drawing pictures is an iteration of several bounded but durative events. While these script-like events are bounded in a certain sense, their boundaries are not delimited by a clearly defined and inherent culmination, as in the cases of prototypical achievements like *arrive* or *find*. This point will be further examined in Chapter 5. In cases like (74c), however, there are potential problems: laughing can be analyzed as a semelfactive, lacking durativity. Drawing in the absence of a delimitation qualifies as atelic. Thus, these

---

[6] The feature specifications for durativity and telicity according to Farrell (2019) are as follows: *find* [+telic/−durative]; *carry* [−telic/+durative]; *broken* [−telic/+durative].

two examples are problematic for the DAC, leading to reduced acceptability. This brief discussion indicates that a condition like the DAC can be fruitfully employed to explain a variety of data patterns regarding the productivity of depictives.

The ability of different event types to host depictives thus shows a largely uniform picture in different approaches, with only minor differences. Modification of activity predicates by depictives is the most controversial aspect, as the data pattern is not obvious and has received different judgments in the literature. The question then is whether the reported grammaticality judgments in the literature on extraction from participle adjuncts can be at least partially accounted for by considering the ability of different verb types to host SODs. An important aspect is the unclear status of activities with SODs: while Irimia (2012) claims that unergatives are not easily accessible for depictives, Rapoport (2019: 434–435) gives several examples that are judged grammatical. The role of intransitive activities is thus one of the points that is highly relevant for an evaluation of the approaches to transparent adjuncts discussed in Chapter 3.

These differences in the possibility for verb types to host depictives offers an explanation for at least part of the extraction patterns proposed for the BPPA construction: as not all activities host depictives with equal success, it is no surprise that extraction degrades acceptability even further, as in (81a). A similar situation holds for stative main verbs as in (81b), which allow depictives in even less cases.

(81)   a. *What does John work [thinking about __]?   (Truswell 2011: 155)
         b. *What is John blond whistling __ ?

Thus, a depictive analysis of the BPPA construction already rules out some configurations that have been discussed as ungrammatical when extraction takes places from the adjunct. It also indicates that BPPA constructions with activity main predicates require more research into the distinction which allow depictive modification without problems and which do not. So far, the depictive analysis does not explain the entire range of data patterns reported in the literature, but it provides a first step towards such a comprehensive analysis. In the discussion in Chapter 5, I will propose adjustments to this initial analysis.

The discussion of depictives in this section has shown that there are a variety of conditions on depictives that have similarities with constraints proposed for extraction from the BPPA construction. Especially the insight that not all types of verbs accept depictives to the same degree leads to a hierarchy of depictive accessibility that identifies a similar set of verb types that are less accessible for depictives and that appear to disallow extraction from the adjunct. This provides additional evidence in favor of a depictive analysis of many BPPA constructions. Before concluding this chapter, I will turn to a subtype of BPPA constructions that has received controversial judgments in the literature on extraction from adjunct islands and that has syntactic and event-semantic properties which have not been thoroughly examined in the existing literature: BPPAs with a resultative in the main clause.

2.4.3 Resultative BPPA constructions

In this section, I focus on a complex subtype of BPPA constructions where the main verb can be interpreted as an instance of resultative secondary predication, as shown in (82).

(82) John$_i$ drove Mary$_j$ crazy$_j$ [whistling an annoying song]$_i$.
                    resultative   *depictive*

This subtype shows two characteristics which distinguish them from other types of BPPA: (i) the matrix clause looks like a transitive predication on the surface but differs in the way the non-subject argument receives its θ-role; (ii) this type appears to be more transparent to extraction than other syntactic encodings of an accomplishment event structure. I will argue that the resultative analysis of this subtype of BPPA construction explains the higher transparency of this construction compared to other accomplishment BPPAs.

As noted in Rothstein (2017: 3875) and Rapoport (2019: 429), a sentence can contain more than one depictive, a resultative plus one or more depictives, but only one resultative secondary predicate. In (82), the adjective *crazy* is interpreted as a resultative modifying *Mary*, and the BPPA *whistling an annoying song* is a depictive. Subject-orientation of the resultative is typically considered to be impossible (Simpson 1983), so that the it can only refer to the object.[7] Since a depictive in accomplishments can in principle refer either to the subject or the object, the orientation of the BPPA is less clear. A closer examination of the θ-role assignment in sentences like (82) suggests that the BPPA can only be subject-oriented, resulting in the indexing in (83):

(83) John$_i$ drove Mary$_j$ crazy$_j$ [whistling an annoying song]$_{i/*j}$.

---

[7] This claim, known as the *Direct Object Restriction*, is not entirely uncontested, as there are some counterexamples, especially with unergatives (Levin & Rappaport Hovav 1995; Rappaport Hovav & Levin 2001; Wechsler 2005). However, there appear to be no such counterexamples in which the subject is interpreted as an AGENT, so resultative BPPA constructions should only allow the object-oriented reading of the resultative.

Rothstein (2017: 3875–3876) argues that the non-subject argument in such resultative constructions does not receive its θ-role directly from the main verb, but rather from the resultative secondary predicate; see also Rapoport (1993a: 160). For this reason, I will prefer the term "non-subject argument" over "object" to refer to these arguments. Carrier & Randall (1992) use the term "intransitive resultatives" for this type of construction, which emphasizes the difference to prototypical transitives where the main verb directly selects two arguments. This is seen in (84a), where the verb selects both *the gardener* and *the tulips*; in this case, the resultative is entirely optional. In (84b), on the other hand, the verb does not select *the Nikes*, and this argument is only licensed in the presence of the resultative.

(84)   a.   The gardener watered the tulips$_i$ (flat$_i$).   [transitive resultative]
       b.   The joggers ran their Nikes$_i$ *(threadbare$_i$).   [intransitive resultative]
           (see Carrier & Randall 1992: 173)

Like Rothstein, Carrier & Randall (1992) assume that the resultative assigns a θ-role to the non-subject argument in intransitive resultatives, not the verb; see also Kratzer (2005). Winkler (1997) argues that for intransitive resultatives, "the resultative predicate introduces the internal argument into the theta structure of the verb and thus increases the valency of the intransitive verb" (Winkler 1997: 349). This process is analyzed in terms of the event composition of the resultative construction. See also Hu (2018: 56–57) for a similar event-based licensing of intransitive resultatives. In the absence of the resultative, *Mary* cannot be licensed, as shown in (85a), at least under the intended reading of *drive*; the same applies to resultatives like *make happy* in (85b).

(85)   a.   *John drove Mary.
       b.   John made his wife *(happy).

With resultative accomplishments like *drive crazy* or *make happy*, the result encoded in the adjective is often subject to semantic selectional restrictions and the sentence is often idiomatic. Although this idiomatic character of many resultatives has to be acknowledged, there are also other resultatives such as (86) and (87), which are less idiomatic but still indicate a close connection between the verb and the resultative; this can be seen as an argument for a complex predicate analysis (see Winkler 1997).

(86)   John sang the baby *(asleep).   (see Rothstein 2017: 3876)

(87) The football team drank the bar *(empty) [ordering one round of beer after another].

An additional effect of the resultative in transitive sentences like (88) is a shift from an activity to an accomplishment reading (Rothstein 2004a); an activity reading in the absence of the resultative is not possible for (85)–(87) because the non-subject argument does fulfill the semantic subcategorization properties of the main predicate.

(88) a. The gardener watered the tulips. [activity]
b. The gardener watered the tulips flat. [accomplishment]
(see Carrier & Randall 1992: 173)

In contrast to resultatives such as (83), (86), and (87), the non-subject argument in other accomplishment constructions such as (89a) directly receive their θ-role from the verb, as shown by the grammaticality of (89b). These are prototypical transitive constructions because the non-subject argument is directly selected by the verb as a direct object.

(89) a. John$_i$ hurt Bill$_j$ [trying to fix the roof]$_{i/j}$.
(see Borgonovo & Neeleman 2000: 200)
b. John hurt Bill.

As a result, both the SOD and OOD readings are available. Plausibly, a preference for the SOD reading arises in (89a) because this allows a causal interpretation of the depictive, which is not available with the OOD reading. These examples show that resultative BPPA constructions differ syntactically from transitive accomplishments in the way θ-roles are assigned in the sentence. The precise implementation is not immediately relevant for the present discussion, but it has become clear that resultative accomplishments show different argument-selection characteristics compared to transitive predicates, and that this has ramifications for the available orientations of a BPPA in these constructions.

The second characteristic of resultative BPPA constructions is that extraction from the adjunct is considered grammatical in some of the literature on adjunct islands. For example, (90a) is considered grammatical in Truswell (2007, 2011), whereas Borgonovo & Neeleman (2000: 212) consider such extractions ungrammatical. In contrast to this, the literature largely agrees that transitive BPPA constructions like (90b) are typically opaque for extraction.

(90) a. What did John drive Mary crazy [whistling __]?   (Truswell 2011: 30)
b. *What$_i$ did John hurt Bill [trying to fix t$_i$]?
(Borgonovo & Neeleman 2000: 200)

It could be the case that extraction over the non-thematic argument is grammatical just in this particular configuration because the resultative forms a complex predicate with an idiomatic character (Carrier & Randall 1992; Winkler 1997). Most of the examples given in the literature for transparent adjuncts with transitive accomplishment matrix predicates can be analyzed as resultatives with a nonthematic argument, such as (91a); there are almost no instances of two-argument accomplishments that cannot be analyzed in this way, as for example (91b):

(91) a. What did John turn the house upside down [looking for __]?
(Truswell 2011: 155)
b. What did John enrage his neighbours [whistling t]?
(Truswell 2007: 1357)

A resultative analysis can also be applied to sentences as in (92), which have *get* as the main verb with an adjectival complement, followed by a BPPA.

(92) Peter got scared watching a horror movie.

The adjectival complement of *get* has a resultative reading similar to *drive crazy* in (90a) above. A major difference is that the resultative adjective in (92) does not license a non-thematic argument. This sentence type will be discussed in more detail in Chapter 4; I will show in Chapter 5 that the question whether the main verb directly licenses one or two arguments is a relevant factor in determining the acceptability of the BPPA construction. Both the resultative BPPA construction and sentences like (92) are two possible ways to express an accomplishment event structure, along with reflexive and non-reflexive transitives; in Chapter 5, I will argue that accomplishments are in principle good candidates for extraction from the BPPA, but that the type and number of arguments selected by the main verb is an additional complicating factor.

2.5 Chapter conclusion

The discussion in this chapter was guided by the research questions in (93), repeated from above.

(93) a. What is a suitable syntactic analysis of BPPAs?
 b. How are BPPAs semantically interpreted?
 c. Which of the constraints proposed for extraction from the BPPA construction can be independently explained by syntactic and semantic licensing conditions on the adjunct predicate?

Section 2.2 proposed three structural analyses for the BPPA construction: (i) zero-headed adverbial clauses, (ii) converb constructions, and (iii) depictive secondary predicates. These analyses all offer a straightforward explanation for the optionality of the BPPA; however, they capture the limited interpretations of BPPA constructions and their sensitivity to the main predicate with different success. The possible interpretations of adverbial clauses and converb constructions are not restrictive enough to account for the limited range of interpretation of the BPPA construction; depictives, however, are too constrained because they do not typically encode a causal reading. For the final characteristic, sensitivity to the main predicate, the depictive analysis comes closest to the observations about similar restrictions in the BPPA construction.

The research question in (93b) was the main topic of Section 2.3, which focused on the possible interpretations for the BPPA construction in the light of the potential structural analyses. Considering the BPPA to be a type of depictive secondary predicate derives the interpretation where the two events encoded in the main verb and the BPPA stand in an overlap relation. However, the causal reading for some BPPA constructions, especially with underspecified accomplishment main verbs and *get*-predicates, is not covered under a depictive analysis and requires additional consideration. As argued in Section 2.3.2, it is possible to derive the causal reading of BPPA constructions with accomplishment main predicates compositionally via a discourse-level operator that merges the two events and allows for more precise relations between the two predicates rather than simple temporal overlap; both the argument structure and the event structure of the main verb have an effect on the availability of the causal reading. This section also considered approaches to the possible forms and interpretations of complex event structures in different frameworks. Both the literature on Manner–Result Complementarity (Rappaport Hovav & Levin 2010) and verb–satellite framing (Talmy 2000) show that there are constraints on the expression of complex event interpretations that show similar patterns as those proposed for extraction from the BPPA construction.

The discussion of the final research question in (93c) is an attempt to trace back as many of the restrictions on extraction from the BPPA construction as possible to independent licensing or felicity conditions on depictives that have been discussed in the existing literature (Section 2.4). Not only are there limitations to which constituents can act as depictives, there are also constraints that narrow down the range of main verbs that can host depictives. Stative and some activity main verbs were shown to be problematic with depictive modification, whereas other verb types are more accessible. The discussion has shown that many of the restrictions proposed for extraction from the BPPA construction can be derived from independent syntactic and semantic licensing conditions on depictives and that it is not a strict necessity to assume that locality operations are sensitive to these characteristics because they already show effects in declaratives, as proposed in Brown (2017). In Chapter 3, I will discuss previous approaches to extraction from adjunct islands in general and the BPPA construction in particular; it will be shown that approaches which assume this sensitivity of locality operations are the majority view, but also that this is not entirely uncontested.

3 Previous approaches to extraction from adjuncts

3.1 Research questions and chapter outline

This chapter reviews previous approaches to apparently grammatical extractions from adjunct constituents and how these exceptions to strict CED-style approaches affect the overall architecture of the grammar, especially the application of locality operations. The main research questions for this chapter are as follows:

(1) a. How can extraction from adjunct constituents be syntactically licensed?
 b. Which factors are relevant for the distinction between transparent and opaque adjuncts? Are these factors syntactic, semantic, or pragmatic?
 c. Which consequences for the architecture of locality follow from the different approaches?

The first research question in (1a) focuses on how extractions from constituents that are traditionally analyzed as adjuncts can be licensed in a syntactic framework; I will concentrate on approaches in the generative–transformational tradition, as currently employed in the Minimalist Program (Chomsky 1995b). As the discussion will show, there are various ways of syntactically licensing an adjunct-internal gap using the machinery of Minimalist syntax; the main shortcoming of such accounts is that they are typically unspecific about when the conditions proposed for transparency are met and when not. To explain this, recourse to other modules of the grammar is often required.

The influence of these factors is investigated in research question (1b); in addition to pure gap-licensing accounts, there are different proposals that offer explanations for the grammaticality differences for extractions from different adjunct configurations. In the typical case, these proposals formulate conditions under which extraction from an adjunct is permitted; when these conditions are not met, the result of the extraction is not grammatical.

The final research question in (1c) takes stock of the theoretical conclusions that the different approaches to transparent adjuncts make with respect to the overall organization of the grammar, more specifically the interplay of adjunction, extraction, and the application of locality constraints. This research question is also the basis for the organization of the rest of this chapter. I will organize previous accounts of extraction from adjuncts into three groups: (i) syntactic gap-licensing accounts in Section 3.2, (ii) interaction accounts in Section 3.3, and (iii) independence accounts in Section 3.4. The main distinction between them is whether the factors they propose can be captured in core-syntactic terms or whether other, non-structural factors are involved in the licensing of extraction.

Syntactic gap-licensing accounts
Syntactic gap-licensing accounts focus on a syntactic derivation of the gap inside the adjunct that does not violate fundamental syntactic rules; most of these approaches are couched within the framework of the Minimalist Program and use concepts such as Agree, Spell-Out, and Phases to derive adjunct-internal gaps. This section centers around the research question in (1a). Gap-licensing approaches are mostly implicit about the factors that divide transparent and opaque adjuncts and do not commit to the formulation of more precise predictions. Their focus is on the licensing methods of adjunct-internal gaps and not the formulation of predictions which combinations of main verb and adjunct allow extraction and which do not. Figure 3.1 shows a schematic representation of gap-licensing accounts, which function similar to CED-type locality conditions in that they differentiate whether a given declarative meets the structural criteria for extraction, such as Agree relations or the correct attachment site. This is indicated by the presence of two declaratives A and B, where A does not meet the structural criteria for extraction but B does. The extraction operation examines the structural properties of the declaratives, shown by the two-way arrows. If the criteria are met, indicated by the check mark, extraction is grammatical; if they are not met, shown with the lightning bolt, extraction is ungrammatical.

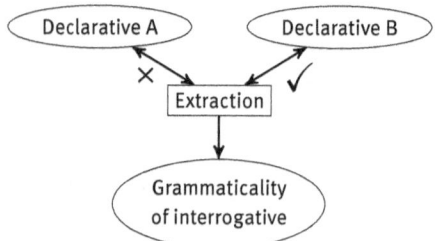

Fig. 3.1: Schematic representation of gap-licensing accounts.

Interaction accounts
Interaction accounts complement gap-licensing accounts in being more explicit about the factors which influence whether an adjunct allows extraction or not. They propose sets of factors from different components of the grammar, such as syntax, semantics, or pragmatics. Their goal is to find ways to distinguish between configurations that allow for extraction from an adjunct and those that do not. Most of these approaches assume that there are properties of the matrix–adjunct predicate configuration, such as the aspectual classes of the two predicates or their argument structure, that determine how strongly *wh*-extraction or other types of A′-movement affect grammaticality. When the criteria are met, *wh*-extraction from

an adjunct is fully grammatical or only slightly degraded, while the extraction leads to full ungrammaticality when the criteria are not met. In addition, these approaches typically assume that the same properties that determine the severity of *wh*-extraction are tied to extraction and do not have a noticeable influence in the declarative counterparts. Therefore, I will use the term *interaction accounts* to refer to these approaches in the following and formulate their basic assumption as the *Interaction Hypothesis* in (2).

(2) Interaction Hypothesis:
Properties of the matrix and adjunct predicates determine the strength of the effect of *wh*-extraction, for example their aspectual classes, argument structure, or the semantic relation between the two predicates.

Figure 3.2 shows schematically how most interaction accounts work: in principle, all adjuncts are a barrier for extraction, but this barrier can be lifted if the declarative meets specific criteria. In interaction accounts, an often non-structural property of the declarative input is evaluated whether it can lift the barrier status or not, shown by the two-way arrow between extraction and the relevant property of the declarative. The grammaticality of extraction depends on this property rather than structural differences between the declarative input. The main difference of interaction accounts to gap-licensing accounts is that they are more explicit about when the conditions for extraction are met and offer falsifiable predictions, which is often not the case in gap-licensing accounts.

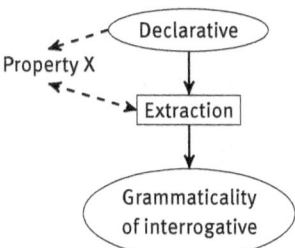

Fig. 3.2: Schematic representation of interaction accounts.

Independence accounts
The account presented in Section 3.4 takes a radically different approach than the interaction accounts: it distinguishes between semantic licensing conditions on the adjunct predicate, which results in acceptability differences in declaratives, and syntactic licensing conditions for the adjunct-internal gap. These independent licensing conditions allow for gradient acceptability in declaratives and interroga-

tives that depends on which licensing conditions are satisfied or violated. I will refer to this type of approach as *independence approaches* and use the following hypothesis to capture their fundamental assumption:

(3) Independence Hypothesis (IH):
The syntactic and semantic licensing conditions on the adjunct predicate are independent of the effects of extraction from the adjunct.

Figure 3.3 shows a schematic representation of independence accounts, which differ from interaction accounts in that they differentiate between declaratives that permit extraction and declaratives that do not, while allowing for acceptability variations in those declaratives that allow extraction.

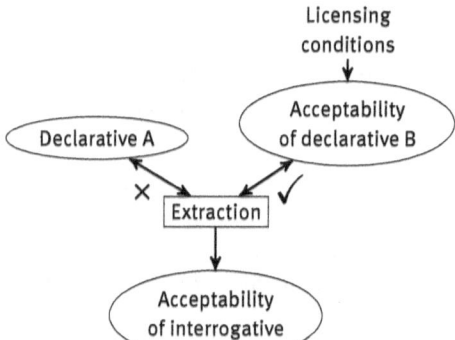

Fig. 3.3: Schematic representation of independence accounts.

The specific formulation of an independence account in Brown (2017) shares certain characteristics with gap-licensing accounts because there are attachment sites for the adjunct that do not meet the structural criteria for well-formed extractions, again shown by the distinction between a check mark on declarative B and a lightning bolt on declarative A. Low adjuncts to VP, i.e. those that meet the structural criteria for extraction, are subject to local licensing conditions at their attachment site, which can lead to negative effects on acceptability in declaratives. The effect of extraction operates on this input and further decreases acceptability when the structural criteria for extraction are not met. Crucially, extraction is only sensitive to the structural differences between declaratives A and B. This model derives the multi-level outcomes of extraction in Brown (2017), who differentiates between felicitous or infelicitous but well-formed extractions, and ill-formed extractions when the adjunct is merged in the wrong position. Independence accounts thus provide a way to account for the data patterns in both gap-licensing accounts and interaction accounts without the need for extraction to be sensitive to non-structural properties of declaratives.

Interaction and independence accounts make very different assumptions about the nature of extraction from an adjunct constituent and the ramifications that apparently transparent adjuncts have for the organization of the grammar. For interaction accounts, it is difficult to find a formulation that respects the autonomy of syntax (Chomsky 1957; Koster 1987; Adger 2018) because extraction is sensitive to characteristics that are not usually expressed in structural terms, as noted in the criticism in Brown (2015). The different predictions of interaction and independence accounts will be the main focus of the experiments in Chapter 4. Supported by the results there, I will subscribe to an independence approach and develop a factorial model for extraction from the BPPA construction in Chapter 5.

3.2 Syntactic gap-licensing accounts

The first set of approaches to transparent adjuncts focuses on how a gap can be licensed inside an adjunct constituent in terms of the Minimalist Program (Chomsky 1995b). They show that under specific circumstances, this gap does not lead to a violation of independently required constraints and is thus grammatical. This is in opposition to the traditional formulation of the island status of adjuncts in the CED (Huang 1982), and takes advantage of recent developments in Minimalist syntax, such as the notions of Agreement (e.g. Boeckx 2008a) and Phases (Chomsky 2001, 2008). The major insight of these approaches is that there is a distinction between adjuncts that merge high or low in the verbal domain, i.e. to phasal vP or non-phasal VP, respectively. However, there is little explanation for when precisely an adjunct merges high or low; the circular argument that an adjunct merges low when it allows for extraction is not satisfactory. By no means all recent approaches consider the transparency of some adjuncts possible and are rather strict with respect to apparent exceptions to this rule; for example, Hunter (2011) presents a unified account to adjunct island, freezing, and subject island effects without taking into account the numerous counterexamples to the adjunct clause of the CED that have been discussed over the years.

3.2.1 Optional feature sharing (Boeckx 2003; Oseki 2015)

Adjuncts receive special treatment in the framework of the Minimalist Program. Most importantly, they enter the derivation by a merge mechanism that is different from the one that applies to arguments: Pair-Merge and Set-Merge, respectively (e.g. Chomsky 2004: 117–118). The distinction between the two Merge operations is not uncontroversial: Boeckx (2008b: 99–101) proposes that adjunction should be analyzed as Set-Merge because it is mere conjunction of constituents that do not involve Agree operations. More recent proposals argue that arguments and adjuncts are distinguished by a different application of the Labeling algorithm (Chomsky 2013, 2015); see, for example, Hornstein & Nunes (2008) and Hornstein (2009). Set-Merge creates an unordered set out of the two merged elements (4a), whereas Pair-Merge results in an ordered pair that is translated to an unordered set by the SIMPL (Simplify) operation (4b).

(4)   a.   Set-merge (for complements and specifiers):
$\quad\quad$ Merge(α, β) = {α, β} $\quad\quad$ (see Chomsky 2004: 108; Boeckx 2015: 27)
     b.   Pair-merge (for adjuncts):
$\quad\quad$ Merge(α, β) = <α, β> $\stackrel{\text{SIMPL}}{=}$ {α, β}
$\quad\quad\quad\quad\quad\quad\quad\quad\quad\quad\quad$ (see Chomsky 2004: 118; Boeckx 2008b: 99)

This difference in the way that adjuncts enter the derivation can serve as an explanation for why adjoined constituents are typically opaque for syntactic operations like the formation of filler–gap dependencies. One example of this type of approach to the islandhood of adjuncts is presented in Boeckx (2003), who claims that adjuncts are impenetrable to syntactic operations because they do not participate in Agree relations, which are necessary for these operations; see Boeckx (2003: 100) and Rackowski & Richards (2005) for a similar Agree-based approach to CED-effects. A similar position is taken in Chomsky (2008: 146–147), who argues that adjuncts are not in the search domain for probes precisely because they are merged by a different mechanism than other constituents. When no Agree relations can be established between a c-commanding probe and material inside the adjunct, this derives the islandhood of adjuncts without further stipulations.

The relevant question is not how to explain the islandhood of adjuncts, but rather why some adjuncts allow grammatical subextractions, as widely noted in the literature. Oseki (2015) takes these counterexamples as the motivation to develop an alternative approach to the merging of adjuncts, which is also able to offer an explanation for the counterexamples where extraction out of the adjunct is grammatical. Instead of Pair-Merging and later simplifying adjunction structures, Oseki (2015) proposes that adjunction involves the symmetric merger of two phrases XP and YP where the result remains without a label since the labeling algorithm cannot unambiguously determine the label for the XP–YP structure. However, when the adjunction structure is merged with another head, the labeling algorithm detects the head of the phrase to be merged with the adjunction structure as the new head. This results in a "two-peaked" or multidominance structure (see Epstein et al. 2012; Citko 2005, 2011a,b; van Riemsdijk 2006). This two-peaked structure is shown in (5), where YP is adjoined to XP; XP is dominated both by ZP and the unlabeled result of adjunction.

(5)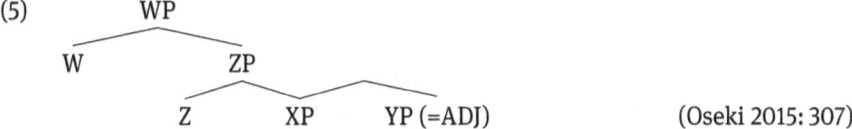

(Oseki 2015: 307)

The derivation of the adjunct condition follows from the assumption that part of the adjunction structure has to undergo Transfer for the derivation to continue successfully. This means that it will no longer be accessible to further operations like extraction because the landing site is not yet present in the structure when Transfer applies. The explanation for adjunct island effects is thus similar to that for subject islands in Epstein et al. (2012). See also Johnson (2003) and Boeckx (2015) for the argument that adjuncts are transferred and spelled out as soon as they are merged and are thus inaccessible to further operations.

Assuming the default opacity of adjuncts, Oseki (2015) argues that the apparent counterexamples to the adjunct condition can be derived by introducing a mechanism of feature sharing into the derivation that keeps adjuncts from transferring early. Feature sharing can assist the labeling algorithm if both phrases in an {XP, YP} configuration contain a common prominent feature, which can then serve as the common label for the so far unlabeled node; relevant features may be the interrogative feature Q or φ-features (Chomsky 2013: 45–46). This is shown in (6), which also contains the XP–YP configuration as in (5), but the output is labeled as FP because XP and YP share the common strong feature F; as a result, Z can merge with FP in a binary structure that avoids the two-peak structure above and hence does not trigger Transfer.

(6)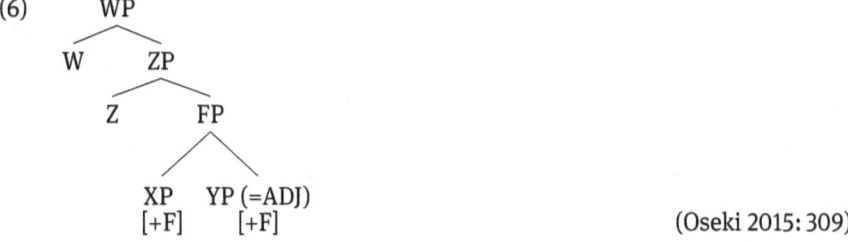

(Oseki 2015: 309)

Feature sharing lifts the special status of the adjunct and integrates it into the main clausal spine, which results in transparency of the adjunct constituent for relations and operations such as binding and extraction. This account makes it clear that feature sharing need not apply to all adjuncts and that some can remain on the far side of the two-peaked structure, as unlabeled nodes are not seen as problematic for spell-out since they are transferred early. In effect, feature sharing boils down to an Agreement relation, which is often taken to be unavailable for adjuncts, as in Boeckx (2003):

(7) Agree cannot target adjuncts, as adjuncts have inert Φ-features. Nor can it target anything inside adjuncts, as no material contained inside adjuncts ever triggers agreement outside them. ... Agree is restricted to selected domains (arguments). (Boeckx 2003: 100)

Oseki (2015) does not go into details what the relevant features are that allow feature sharing, which in principle allows a number of ways in which grammatical extractions from adjunct constituents can be formulated. If it is indeed the case that "constraints on extraction are mainly reflexes of constraints on agreement" (Boeckx 2003: 67), then the availability of specific mechanisms that allow a participle adjunct to share a common feature with the matrix predicate in a BPPA construction can be restricted to derive those cases that hold up to this generalization in experimental investigations. One of the possible ways this can be formalized, which will also be discussed in later chapters, is to permit feature sharing only in those cases where the matrix and adjunct predicate can be construed as a plausible extension of the basic event described in the matrix predicate, either by means of event specification or event expansion (Haug et al. 2012), without constituting a separate event. Whether the matrix predicate allows this elaboration mechanism or not could be the key to define when feature sharing will be available and thus result in an adjunct predicate that allows further subextraction.

A similar explanation for transparent adjuncts along with parasitic gap constructions is suggested in Graf (2015), who distinguishes between two types of adjuncts: (i) adjuncts that are both syntactically and semantically optional, and (ii) adjuncts that are syntactically optional constituents but are semantically selected by the main predication; semantically selected adjuncts are similar to argument-adjuncts discussed in Grimshaw (1990) in relation to *by*-phrases in passive constructions. If a syntactic adjunct is semantically selected, this results in a type of Agree relation between the phrases, and the adjunct can then be targeted by further operations. Randall (2010) likewise draws a distinction between peripheral adjuncts that are not linked to the main predicate's argument structure and Conceptual Structure (CS) as well as fusing adjuncts that are represented in the CS; so-called fusing adjuncts thus have a tighter bond with the main predicate and show weak selectional restrictions (Randall 2010: 131). The formulation of optional Agree relations or feature sharing can be seen as a Minimalist formalization of such approaches to a differentiated class of syntactically optional constituents and thus explain *why* some adjuncts can be transparent for extraction; they do not, however, provide detailed criteria as to *which* adjuncts allow such tight relations to the main predication.

3.2.2 Attachment height and forced spell-out (Narita 2014)

A fundamentally minimalist approach to the contrast between transparent and opaque adjuncts is proposed in Narita (2014). This conception of the syntactic component abandons the Projection Principle (Chomsky 1986b) and is centered around the Merge operation, which is constrained by the underlying fundamental principle of Minimal Computation. Endocentricity effects that are attributed to heads in X′-syntax are derived by interpretive prominence of a lexical item (LI) with respect to a Minimal Search algorithm. To facilitate this algorithm at Spell-Out, syntactic objects (SOs) have to be constructed in conformity to the template {H, α}, with H being the head LI and α another SO. This principle is formulated as the *Endocentric Structuring Constraint* (ESC):

(8) Endocentric Structuring Constraint (ESC):
Merge can only generate SOs whose head LI H is immediately detectable via minimal search at Interpret/Spell-Out. (Narita 2014: 77)

The ESC poses a problem for the merger of phrasal adjuncts because head detection fails in a symmetrical XP–YP configuration; see also the discussion in Chomsky (2013: 43–46). To solve this problem, one of the phrases has to undergo Transfer and is simplified to a LI, and material inside the adjunct is opaque for further operations; this derives CED effects for adjuncts. If the adjunct is not reduced, the ESC would not be able to determine the head of the resulting XP–YP merge structure and the derivation would crash at a later stage. The crucial difference between adjuncts that show CED effects and those that do not is that the former are high adjuncts above v/v^* and the latter are low adjuncts below v/v^* (Narita 2014: 124). Similar to Truswell (2011), Narita (2014) includes bare and PP gerundives as well as purpose clauses in the group of transparent adjuncts. The following examples are used to illustrate these different adjunct types:

(9) a. *This is *the girl$_i$* that John failed the test [because he was thinking about t_i].
b. *Which book$_i$* did John design his garden [after reading t_i]?
(Narita 2014: 122, 123)

In (9a), the problem is that high adjuncts attach above v^*; the potential adjunction sites have an unvalued case feature on the subject that is only checked after the C head is introduced and thus cannot be reduced to a LI. Consequently, it is the adjunct that needs to be reduced and thus cannot be targeted by further operations (Narita 2014: 125–126). For non-finite adjuncts like the participle adjunct in (9b), low adjunction under the scope of v^* is possible. In this case, it is the complement of the main verb, *his garden*, that is reduced to a LI; the adjunct can remain syntactically active and move the *wh*-item to its edge for further operations. This occupied edge position keeps the phrase active and precludes reduction (Narita 2014: 124–125).

The concept of enforced Spell-Out for high adjuncts because they would otherwise fail to comply with the ESC is similar to the concept of Renumeration in Johnson (2003): this operation returns SOs constructed by Merge back into the Numeration N for further applications of Merge. When this happens, the SO that is renumerated is spelled-out, making it only accessible to Merge as a unit and without access to its individual components. This derives subject and adjunct island effects under the assumption that both have to be assembled separately and are then renumerated because otherwise the derivation cannot continue.

Narita (2014: 38) argues that semantic constraints on syntactic operations are problematic in general because semantic tampering with narrow syntactic operations is not independently motivated by Minimal Computation. The main argument for a syntactic rather than event-semantic characterization for transparent adjunct island effects comes from the contrasts in (10), where the type of matrix clause determines whether the adjunct allows extraction or not.

(10) a. ?*Which trial$_i$ did the DA prove [the suspect to have been at the scene of the crime] [in order to conclude t_i]?
   b. Which trial$_i$ did the DA prove [that the suspect was at the scene of the crime] [in order to conclude t_i]?
   c. Which trial$_i$ did the DA decide [to call the suspect for psychiatric examination] [in order to conclude t_i]?
   (Narita 2014: 127)

The degraded extraction in (10a) differs from the more acceptable extractions in (10b,c) in that the exceptional case-marking (ECM) infinitive construction in (10a) is a TP and cannot constitute a phase and thus trigger Spell-Out; in contrast, the finite *that*-clause in (10b) and the infinitival control CP in (10c) are phases and thus reduced by Spell-Out. The raising subject in (10a) still has an unvalued case feature that keeps the phrase active and thus blocks *wh*-extraction out of the purpose clause adjunct because the subcategorized complement clause cannot be reduced to a LI. This contrast can be shown schematically as in (11), where the boxed constituent undergoes reduction when the adjunct is merged; in (11a), the adjunct has to undergo reduction because the complement clause still has unvalued features, indicated by 'uF'. In (11b), the complement clause does not have unvalued features, indicated by the checkmark, and thus can undergo reduction:

(11) a. *wh [matrix clause] [$_{uF}$ complement clause] [adjunct t]

b. wh [matrix clause] [√ complement clause] [adjunct t]

The examples in (10) show that the distinction between convergent and incomplete complement clauses have an effect on the transparency of the adjunct. Crucially, Narita (2014: 127–128) argues that (10a,b) are "virtually identical in their semantic interpretations" and both describe single events in terms of Truswell (2011); the fact that there are differences in transparency of the adjunct that can be explained in syntactic terms but fail to be differentiated semantically is problematic for Truswell's explanation. Narita (2014) turns the argument upside down and proposes that his approach of phase-based successive cyclicity is the reason that derives single event readings of main verb–adjunct predicate configurations in the first place. Two proposals with similar assumptions about the possibility of either the adjunct or the host XP undergoing Spell-Out when an adjunct is merged are presented in Johnson (2003) as well as Sheehan (2013), who considers the possibility of late or early adjunction in terms of Lebeaux (1988) to explain some of the contrasts between transparent and opaque adjuncts.

There are two unresolved issues with this account: first, Narita (2014) mostly focuses on properties of the adjunct that determine whether it is forced to be reduced or can remain active for extraction; the only case Narita discusses where low adjunction does not result in a grammatical structure is the ECM structure in (10a) above. Here the unvalued case feature of the ECM subject has to keep the phase active and thus extraction from the adjunct is impossible (Narita 2014: 126). This raises potential problems for other verb types with unvalued case features, namely unaccusative and passive predicates: in contrast to the object of transitive predicates, surface subjects of these predicates are not assigned accusative case but rather nominative case by C after raising to T. Thus the VP part of the verbal domain is incomplete and presumably has to remain active, which enforces the reduction of low adjuncts. In contrast, the VP of transitive predicates is complete because the subject is introduced by the $vP/v*P$ (Kratzer 1996). Narita (2014) notes that unaccusative and passive vP cannot constitute a phase because the VP still has this unvalued case feature, in contrast to transitive $v*P$. This mean that transparent adjuncts are never possible for unaccusative and passive predicates, which runs counter to the observations in the existing literature that lists numerous examples where transparent adjuncts modify unaccusative predicates, most notably Borgonovo & Neeleman (2000). The possibility of transparent adjuncts with unaccusatives is not clearly formulated in Narita (2014) and deserves closer investigation.

The second issue with this account is that its predictions are limited: the issue of single event effects on extraction (Truswell 2007, 2011) is re-formulated as a high or low adjunction account, similar to the argumentation about possible Agree relations in Boeckx (2003) or Oseki (2015). While the possibility of a theoretical derivation of transparent adjunct constituents is a definite requirement for a comprehensive explanation, the identification of the remaining factors is often less clear. To avoid the circular argument that an adjunct merges low when it is transparent, more has to be said about the availability of the low adjunction position, also in relation to different verb types. The availability of a single event reading as a prerequisite for low adjunction could be one of the possibilities, even though this raises further unresolved issues and can be expected to be subject to variation.

In conclusion, Narita (2014) shows that a phase-based theory of Merge and feature valuation can allow transparent adjuncts, and also draw a distinction between transparent and opaque adjuncts. Even though the details of the decision when an adjunct merges high or low needs some refinement to cover the observed data, this theoretical foundation opens the possibility for a principled account based on empirical data.

3.2.3 Top-down structure building (den Dikken 2018)

Den Dikken (2018) presents an approach to constraints on FGDs in a top-down structure-building mechanism (see also Chesi 2015; Bianchi & Chesi 2014). Such a framework requires a radical re-thinking of FGDs because, in contrast to other approaches, they are not triggered by movement of a constituent to a structurally higher position in order to satisfy an uninterpretable feature. The situation is exactly the opposite: in a top-down approach, the [WH] feature is satisfied early by the presence of a *wh*-element, but other features of the *wh*-element like θ-, φ-, or case-features, cannot be locally interpreted and trigger the search for an element that satisfies these features. The mechanism for FGDs works as follows (see den Dikken 2018: 104–108): an element that cannot be fully interpreted in its overt position is (i) *uploaded* onto a buffer, (ii) *downloaded* at the edge of the next predication structure, and (iii) linked to a suitable trace position if it cannot be interpreted in the download position. This last step establishes the FGD. The upload–download procedure is impossible in two contexts: (i) opaque domains or absolute islands, where the downloaded filler cannot be linked directly to a gap site, and (ii) intervention islands, where an intervening filler has similar feature characteristics than the uploaded filler. Opaque domains are essentially constituents where no Agree relation can be established between the head of the constituent that hosts the downloaded filler and the domain that contains the gap site. This is defined as in (12), where α stands for the downloaded filler and β for the trace:

(12) *opaque domain*
 in [α ... π ... [$_\Delta$ ... β ...]], Δ is an *opaque domain* for a relation between α and β iff:
 (a) Δ dominates β and excludes α, and
 (b) Δ is not in an Agree relation with an asymmetrically c-commanding head π
 (den Dikken 2018: 107)

This definition of opaque domains presents a syntactic derivation of the CED (Huang 1982): Agreement fails when an opaque domain is encountered during the search for a trace where the downloaded filler can be integrated (den Dikken 2018: 111). It correctly rules in FGDs between a filler and a trace in complement position and rules out FGDs between a filler and traces inside subjects and adjuncts.

Adjuncts to verbal projections are absolute islands because they systematically fail to establish an Agree relation with their c-commanding verb. In order to account for the examples of adjuncts that allow the establishment of FGDs, den Dikken (2018) argues for an optional Agree relation when the adjunct is low enough in the structure. There are two possibilities that can trigger Agreement between the verb and an adjunct: Agree for aspect and Agree for case. The first option is a syntactic formulation of the event-structural condition on extraction in Truswell (2011), discussed in Section 3.3.4. An aspectual feature on *v* can form an Agree relation with an adjunct to VP, a position that is asymmetrically c-commanded by *v*; higher adjuncts to *v*P do not allow this Agree relation because the condition on asymmetric c-command in (12) is not met. There are several factors that influence the acceptability of extraction from a temporal adjunct clause: (i) the difference between DP/PP extraction that is typical of weak islands (Cinque 1990; Abrusán 2014; Szabolcsi & Lohndal 2017), seen in the contrasts between (13a/14a) and (13c/14c); (ii) the transitivity of the matrix predicate and the possibility of a parasitic gap reading, as in (13b/14b) compared against (13c/14c); (iii) and the question whether the matrix verb and the temporal adjunct clause can be construed as a "natural course of events" (den Dikken 2018: 128) and thus a single event in terms of Truswell (2011), which is seen in the contrast between (13c) and (14c).

(13) a. *he is the person to whom they left before speaking __ [PP extraction]
　　 b. he is the person who they left __ before speaking to __ [parasitic gap]
　　 c. ⁇he is the person who they left town before speaking to __
　　　　　　　　　　　　　　　　　　　　　　　　　　　　　[DP extraction]
　　　(den Dikken 2018: 127)

(14) a. *he is the person to whom they left after speaking __ [PP extraction]
　　 b. he is the person who they left __ after speaking to __ [parasitic gap]
　　 c. he is the person who they left town after speaking to __ [DP extraction]
　　　(den Dikken 2018: 128)

With respect to Agree for aspect, the contrast between (13c) and (14c) is of interest because this minimal pair manipulates the plausibility of a single event construal: it is more plausible to leave after speaking to someone than it is to leave before doing so. As a result, (13c) is pragmatically infelicitous rather than grammatically marked (den Dikken 2018: 130). This adjustment does not improve the PP extraction in (14a). This is what den Dikken (2018) offers as an explanation for the possible Agree for aspect relations: the contrasts are related to attachment height on the syntactic side, and the pragmatics of single event construal on the other side, without a more detailed explanation when this construal is possible and whether it depends on the type of matrix predicate. The contrast between (13c) and (14c) is problematic for a uniform account of adverbial clauses in terms of attachment height, such as Narita (2014): the plausibility effects are not captured in this account. The approach to the opacity of adverbial clauses in Brown (2017) faces the same problem. From a phase perspective, participle adjunct predicates headed by *before* and *after* should have identical sets of unvalued case features.

The second option for an Agree relation between the main verb and the adjunct is Agree for case; den Dikken (2018) provides examples from Hungarian, Icelandic, Russian, Finnish, and Korean to show that some adjuncts receive case-marking, which indicates an Agree relation between the adjunct and the c-commanding verb. Accusative-marked adverbials are analyzed as merging low in the verbal domain, similar to transparent adverbials in English, so Agree for case is also related to attachment height and aspectual characteristics (see den Dikken 2018: 138).

A similar mechanism for opaque and transparent adjuncts from a computational perspective is presented in Shafiei & Graf (2020): an intervening adjunct category blocks the linking of the filler and the gap site. The blocking adjunct category works like the opaque domains in den Dikken (2018), and the "intervention effect" of adjuncts can be lifted by excluding certain categories that define transparent adjuncts, for example non-finite adjuncts, from the list of items that are not allowed between a filler and the gap.

Summarizing the argumentation in den Dikken (2018), a top-down approach to structure-building provides similar distinctions between transparent and opaque adjuncts as bottom-up approaches. It is only the direction of the computation that is reversed, where a filler that cannot be interpreted in its surface position is kept in memory until a suitable trace position is encountered. Despite the only superficial characterization of when Agree for aspect can take place, this approach is in principle compatible with much of the attested data and is also equipped to further differentiate between temporal adverbials that are glossed over in purely syntactic approaches such as Narita (2014) or Brown (2017).

3.2.4 Interim conclusion

The gap-licensing accounts presented in this section show the following characteristics: an opposition between high and low attachment of the adjunct to phasal *v*P or non-phasal VP and height effects on transparency of the adjunct; the possibility or unavailability of Agree relations between the adjunct and the main predicate; forced Spell-Out for some adjuncts but not others, as well as late or early adjunction and timing effects. Often, these features are combined: for example, the availability of Agree relations is tied to attachment height in den Dikken (2018). Narita (2014) distinguishes between an active adjunct and adjuncts that must be spelled out in terms of attachment height.

References to transparent adjuncts are also found in other works that do not focus on this phenomenon, which I do not discuss here for reason of space; these accounts include G. Müller (1995), who explains the higher transparency of untensed adjuncts with the stipulation that extraction here crosses fewer barriers than with tensed adjuncts, and Weisser (2015), who draws a connection between transparency and adjuncts as so-called "medial" converb constructions.

The accounts of extraction from adjuncts discussed in this section provide the theoretical machinery to derive gaps in adjunct constituents without violating core syntactic principles. Despite the strong predictions of the CED, there are ways to make adjuncts available for extraction. However, most approaches are not explicit about when a specific adjunct will be grouped with transparent adjuncts and when it will remain opaque. The following section discuss approaches to transparent adjuncts that make more precise predictions about the transparent–opaque distinction based on a variety of different factors.

3.3 Interaction accounts

In this section, I will present accounts which provide further explanations for the observed variability of extraction patterns. They share the assumption that the strength of degradation in the presence of *wh*-extraction or other A′-operations depends on characteristics of the matrix or adjunct predicate, or both; they can be classified as interaction approaches because they are based on a specific formulation of the Interaction Hypothesis. Extraction needs to be licensed by a factor that does not affect grammaticality in declaratives at all or not to the same degree. These accounts differ in the type of property they consider relevant, including syntactic, semantic, information-structural, and pragmatic characteristics. Syntactic interaction accounts share many properties with gap-licensing accounts. One of the main advantages of such accounts is that they are more explicit about the conditions that allow extraction from adjuncts; the syntactic gap-licensing accounts typically leave these properties implicit or vague. A more problematic characteristic of these accounts is that they often require the sensitivity of locality operations to non-structural properties, which should not be possible in an autonomous syntactic component.

Sections 3.3.1 and 3.3.2 discuss accounts which propose a syntactic condition on extraction from adjuncts; Sections 3.3.3 through 3.3.7 focus on accounts which introduce semantic criteria; Sections 3.3.8 through 3.3.9 introduce accounts that incorporate information-structural and pragmatic factors.

3.3.1 Reanalysis (Demonte 1988)

The discussion of secondary predicates in Demonte (1988) is one of the earliest principled accounts of extraction from non-subcategorized adjunct constituents. But the possibility to extract from secondary predicates is not the only topic of Demonte (1988): it is also a discussion of the productivity of depictive secondary predicates and the difference between secondary predicates and sentence adverbials like MANNER or INSTRUMENT (Demonte 1988: 14, Demonte 1992). This section first discusses depictive productivity in Spanish, then the extraction patterns, and lastly the explanation why some extractions are possible and not others.

The productivity of adjectival depictives modifying the subject (SOD) is relatively unconstrained in that an adjectival depictive can modify the subject of unergative, unaccusative, as well as transitive sentences; the only restriction is that the subject needs to be a THEME or AGENT, but cannot be an EXPERIENCER (Demonte 1988: 2–3, 6). Depictives modifying an object (OOD) are reported to be much more constrained, being limited to a small set of transitives (Demonte 1988: 7).

Demonte (1988) assumes different attachment heights for SODs and OODs: SODs are attached high, at the level of IP, whereas OODs attach within the VP, as sisters to V' (see also McNally 1997, Winkler 1997). This means that OODs are syntactically and semantically closer to their referents than SODs (Demonte 1988: 25), which has effects on the mobility and transparency of the depictive. See the structural representations in (15a) for SODs and in (15b) for OODs.

(15) a. SOD   b. OOD

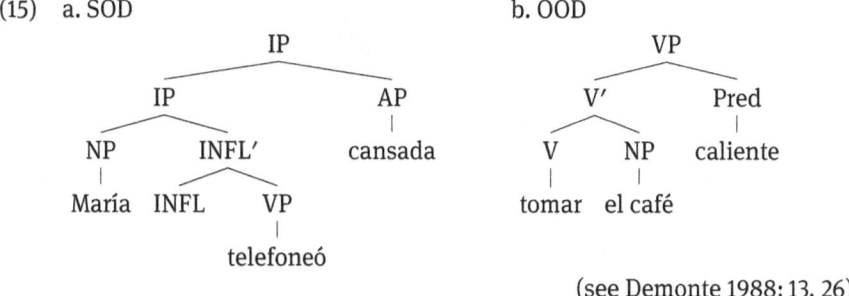

(see Demonte 1988: 13, 26)

As far as extraction of and from the depictive is concerned, there is a clear difference between SODs and OODs: whereas SODs consistently refuse to be extracted and do not subextraction, OODs are much more liberal in this respect. In single-clause sentences, extraction of the depictive is ungrammatical for SODs (16a), but fine for OODs (16b); subjects of unaccusative main verbs pattern with OODs rather than SODs in allowing extraction (16c). The Unaccusative Hypothesis (Perlmutter 1978) offers a straightforward explanation for this because surface subjects of unaccusatives are considered structural objects of the main verb (Demonte 1988: 23).

(16) a. *Cuán entusiasmada compró Lola el coche e   [transitive SOD]
        'How enthusiastic did Lola buy the car?'
     b. Cuán caliente toma Pepe el café e   [transitive OOD]
        'How hot does Pepe drink the coffee?'
     c. Cuán satisfecha volvió Rosa e de Ginebra   [unaccusative SOD]
        'How content did Rosa come back from Geneva?'
        (Demonte 1988: 20)

A similar situation holds for extraction from depictives in embedded clauses, from depictives in *wh*-islands, and subextraction from the depictive in *wh*-islands. The SOD never yields grammatical results, but OODs and unaccusative SODs are not strongly degraded (Demonte 1988: 20–22). The most interesting extraction pattern surfaces when subextraction takes place from within the depictive. Here, subextraction from SODs leads to ungrammaticality (17a), OODs of transitive predicates are intermediate (17b), and SODs of unaccusative main verbs allow the extraction without degradation (17c):

(17) a. *Con qué novio no sabes [si Lola compró el coche [enfadada e]]
'At which boyfriend don't you know whether Lola bought the car mad?'
b. ?Con qué novia no sabes [si Maria encontró a Pepe [enfadado e]]
'At which girlfriend don't you know whether Maria found Pepe mad?'
c. De qué novia no sabes [si Pepe volvió [harto e]]
'From which girlfriend don't you know whether Pepe came back fed up?'
(Demonte 1988: 22)

The question now is why secondary predicates to structural objects should allow extraction and subextraction in Spanish, considering the fact that English does not allow extraction of SODs or OODs; this is shown in (18). See Halliday (1967a: 64) as well as Winkler (1997: 82–83) for an overview of judgments in the literature.

(18) a. *How angry$_i$ did John leave the room e_i? [SOD]
b. *How raw$_i$ did John eat the meat e_i? [OOD]
(Demonte 1988: 23)

The situation in English is taken to be the cross-linguistic default one, meaning that in general, extraction of or from secondary predicates is ungrammatical, unless the structure is modified in such a way that makes extraction grammatical (Demonte 1988: 23–24). Demonte's solution is to propose a reanalysis process that can affect OODs but not SODs. Reanalysis here refers to a process that moves the secondary predicate into the V′ projection, which leads to a thematic restructuring: the OOD is then part of the argument structure of the main verb and no longer considered an adjunct (Demonte 1988: 27). The reanalysis process is considered to be a subtype of a more general incorporation operation proposed in Baker (1988). This is shown in (19), where the secondary predicate moves inside the V′ projection and incorporates with the main verb to form a complex predicate designated V*.

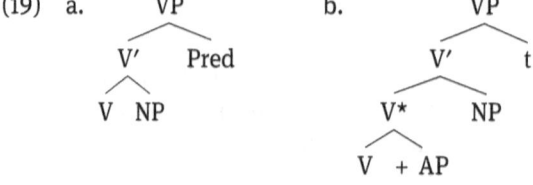

(Demonte 1988: 34)

One reason that reanalysis and thus extraction is only possible for OODs but not SODs lies in the structural difference between them, as shown in (15) above. SODs are attached too high in the structure to allow reanalysis to a complex predicate, as OODs do. The reanalysis process for OODs is taken to be (i) language-specific (Demonte 1988: 27) and (ii) lexically conditioned, meaning that it cannot apply to any combination of verb and secondary predicate. Specifically, the generalization is that the resulting V + AP string needs to be interpretable as "a unit from a semantic point of view" (Demonte 1988: 30). Interpretation as a unit is possible when there is a predictable relation between the adjective and the verb, i.e. when the meaning of the adjective can be integrated into the semantic structure of the main verb. This plausibility criterion distinguishes the grammatical cases where reanalysis can apply in (16b,c) and (17c) above from those cases where reanalysis cannot apply because the meaning of the adjective is not part of the semantic structure of the main verb, as in (20). Since the main verb and the secondary predicate undergo an incorporation process, this explains why extraction is more acceptable when the two occur in adjacent linear order (Demonte 1988: 33), which is also noted in Fábregas & Jiménez-Fernández (2016a).

(20) a. ??*Cómo de roto$_i$ escondió mi hija el regalo* e$_i$
'How broken did my daughter hide the present?'
b. **Cómo de furiosa$_i$ alojé a mi prima italiana* e$_i$
'How furious did I lodge my Italian cousin?'
(Demonte 1988: 29)

Despite the fact that Demonte (1988) focuses on adjectival secondary predicates, there are several aspects that are relevant for the present discussion: (i) depictive productivity is not entirely free. OODs occur only with a restricted set of transitive predicates; SODs are relatively unconstrained as long as they are stative (Demonte 1988: 5). (ii) Subextraction is better when it takes place from secondary predicates that modify underlying objects rather than subjects. This predicts that subextraction from secondary predicates to subjects of unaccusatives and to objects of transitives should be better than from secondary predicates to unergative and transitive subjects. (iii) The semantic compatibility of OODs determines the grammaticality of extractions because the availability of the reanalysis process hinges on this factor. The predictions are that when the secondary predicate fits into the argument structure of the main verb, reanalysis can apply and the secondary predicate becomes accessible for extraction and subextraction because the barrier status of the adjunct is lifted by the structural manipulation.

3.3.2 Reflexivity (Borgonovo & Neeleman 2000)

One of the most detailed accounts of transparent adjuncts in English is presented in Borgonovo & Neeleman (2000), henceforth abbreviated as B&N. B&N formulate a syntactic criterion for removing a predicative adjunct's barrier status, which is then transparent for subextraction. They discuss the possibility of subextraction from predicative adjuncts, which depends on the verb type of the embedding predicate. Predicative adjuncts are adjuncts that are predicated of another adjunct-external DP; this means that a θ-role is assigned across the adjunct boundary from the adjunct to the DP (B&N 2000: 199, fn. 1). The DP will then discharge θ-roles from both the verb and the adjunct predicate. Predicative adjuncts include participant-oriented adjuncts like depictives, but not event-oriented adjuncts such as manner, temporal, or locative adjuncts (Borgonovo & Neeleman 2000: 199); see also Himmelmann & Schultze-Berndt (2005). This distinction is similar to that in Demonte (1988), who also does not consider manner and instrumental adjuncts.

The status as a participant-oriented predicative adjunct is, however, not a sufficient condition for extraction from the adjunct. The type of embedding predicate also plays a role: unergative (21a) and most transitive (21b) matrix predicates do not allow subextraction from predicative adjuncts, while unaccusatives do (21c).

(21) a. *What$_i$ did John dance [imagining t$_i$]? [unergative]
      b. *What$_i$ did John finish the portrait [covered in t$_i$]? [transitive]
      c. What$_i$ did John arrive [whistling t$_i$]? [unaccusative]
      (B&N 2000: 199–200)

The following set of minimal pairs in (22) shows that for single-argument verbs, the distinction between unaccusatives and unergatives determines whether extraction is grammatical or not; B&N assume that the directional element *home* is an adverbial and not an argument. Motion predicates with a directional element behave as unaccusatives rather than unergatives; see also Hoekstra & Mulder (1990) and Levin & Rappaport Hovav (1995). This is why extraction from the unergative in (22b) is ungrammatical, but grammatical in the unaccusative version (22d). Note that in this and the following example, there are only grammaticality differences in interrogatives but not declaratives.

(22) a. The athlete ran [singing Carmen].
      b. *What$_i$ did the athlete run [singing t$_i$]?
      c. The athlete ran home [singing Carmen].
      d. What$_i$ did the athlete run home [singing t$_i$]?
      (B&N 2000: 200)

For transitives, as in (23), the factor determining adjunct transparency is syntactic reflexivity in terms of Reinhart & Reuland (1993): reflexivity obtains when two arguments are co-referential. When the object of the matrix clause is an anaphor co-referential with the matrix clause subject, as in (23a,b), extraction is grammatical; when the object is not co-referential, as in (23c,d), it is ungrammatical.

(23) a. John hurt himself [trying to fix the roof].
 b. What$_i$ did John hurt himself [trying to fix t$_i$]?
 c. John hurt Bill [trying to fix the roof].
 d. *What$_i$ did John hurt Bill [trying to fix t$_i$]?
 (B&N 2000: 200)

As B&N (2000) show, the two patterns in (22) and (23) can be accounted for by the same principle of reflexivity and the availability of L-marking in the presence of reflexivity. What is most interesting about these patterns is that they are prototypical examples of an interaction account to islands: declaratives are entirely insensitive to manipulations that yield a sharp grammaticality contrast when extraction takes place from the adjunct.

The adjunct is not limited to present participle activities, as there are also examples of grammatical extractions with past participle adjuncts. In this construction, the same criteria can be met: the past participle adjunct can discharge a θ-role to the subject DP of the matrix clause, and can be L-marked when the matrix predicate allows reflexive marking. See the example with a past participle in (24). In fact, B&N (2000) do not impose any type of constraint on the adjunct predicate, all the requirements apply exclusively to the matrix predicate.

(24) What$_j$ did John come back [addicted to t$_j$]? (B&N 2000: 203)

The explanation for the extraction patterns and the conditions that determine transparency in B&N (2000) has essentially two components: the first is the requirement that all transparent adjuncts need to be predicative in the sense noted above, because only predicative adjuncts can enter into the θ-structure of the sentence; this is a prerequisite for L-marking. Another structural aspect is the projection to which the adjunct is merged: B&N (2000) propose that there are different attachment sites for predicative and non-predicative adjuncts. Predicative adjuncts can be merged in the V' projection, allowing for θ-marking and thus L-marking (B&N 2000: 205). Non-predicative adjuncts, on the other side, without θ-role assignment, are merged at the VP level. This makes them opaque for extraction because they cannot be L-marked. The attachment to VP is taken to be the default case, with the ensuing island status of depictive adjuncts (B&N 2000: 213).

The depictive is integrated into the verb's θ-structure as follows: the DP binds the θ-role of the adjunct XP as well as of the main verb V. This means that the adjunct's and the verb's θ-role have the same index, which allows L-marking because the verb can bind the adjunct predicate under transitivity of coindexation (B&N 2000: 203–204). For a sentence like (25), the assignment of θ-roles in the verbal projection is as shown in (26): first the V' internal DP binds the XP under predication (26a), and also binds the internal θ-role of the verb (26b); as both the verb and the XP share the same index, transitivity of coindexation obtains and both bear the same index (26c). In this configuration, the XP is bound by the verb and counts as L-marked; this lifts the barrier status of the XP and makes it transparent for extraction (Chomsky 1986a).

(25)   [$_{DP}$ John]$_i$ [$_V$ died θ$_i$] [$_{XP}$ thinking about his unpublished papers θ$_i$].
(see B&N 2000: 203)

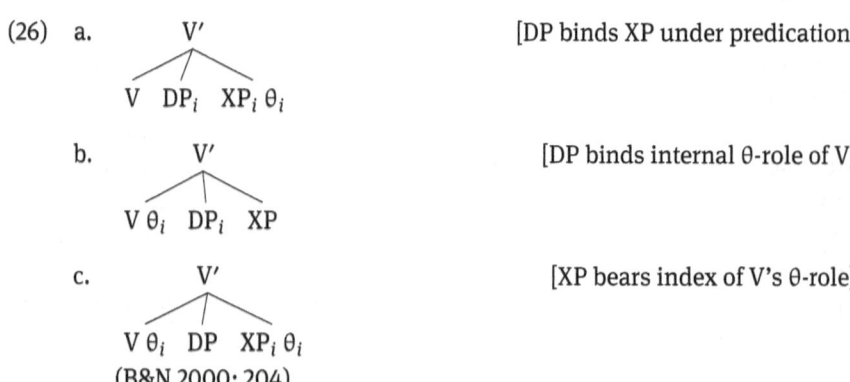

(26)   a.   V'   [DP binds XP under predication]
            V DP$_i$ XP$_i$ θ$_i$

       b.   V'   [DP binds internal θ-role of V]
            V θ$_i$ DP$_i$ XP

       c.   V'   [XP bears index of V's θ-role]
            V θ$_i$ DP XP$_i$ θ$_i$
            (B&N 2000: 204)

In a next step, B&N (2000) show that reflexivity is another defining characteristic of predicates that can host transparent adjuncts because they readily allow L-marking of the adjunct. A syntactically reflexive construction involves the "coindexation between two arguments within the domain of a single predicate" (B&N 2000: 205) and leads to the situation where the adjunct is structurally similar to a complement of the predicate. This boils down to two conditions on transparency: (i) the adjunct has to bind a θ-role of the verb, as in (26c) above, and (ii) it has to be contained within the intermediate projection to allow binding and thus reflexive-marking (B&N 2000: 207). The resulting structure takes the form of ternary branching because in this configuration, the distribution of θ-roles between the verb, the DP and the adjunct XP happens in the same predicative domain. Subextraction from an L-marked predicative adjunct takes the form in (27):

(27) Wh$_j$ ...

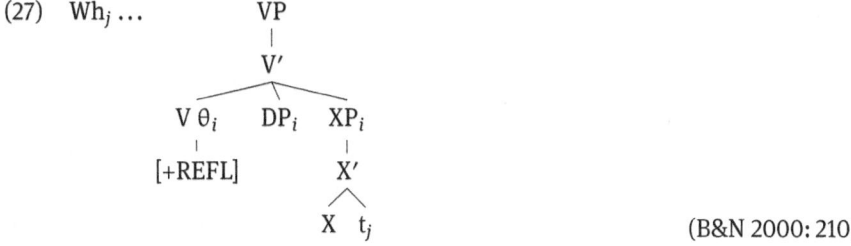

(B&N 2000: 210)

The pattern observed with respect to matrix predicate classes that allow extraction from the adjunct is explained by the default reflexive status of unaccusative predicates, which can be analyzed as structures where the transitive causative variant has been reflexivized and a reduction of the verb's argument structure has taken place (see Reinhart 2002: 239; Reinhart 2016; Reinhart & Siloni 2005). As the subject of unaccusatives is considered to be an underlying internal argument of the verb (Perlmutter 1978; Burzio 1986), it is by default in the right structural position for reflexive-marking.

However, reflexivity cannot be the only requirement, as not all one-place predicates expressing an inherently reflexive activity allow extraction, as the examples in (28) show. Inherently reflexives that are expressed with an unergative syntax do not project an object argument and thus by hypothesis no intermediate bar-level that is required for L-marking (B&N 2000: 212–213).

(28) a. *What$_i$ did John shave [whistling t$_i$]?
 b. *What$_i$ did John shower [thinking of t$_i$]?
   (B&N 2000: 212)

This derives the third requirement on transparent adjuncts, namely that only predicates which project a complement allow for subextraction from the adjunct. When the structural conditions for predicative adjuncts are met, i.e. the adjunct XP can be projected within V' and is co-referential with the subject DP, then subextraction from the adjunct XP is licensed because it counts as L-marked.

Like Truswell (2007), B&N (2000) represent an approach to transparent adjuncts that derives the distinction into transparent and opaque adjuncts from conditions that are able to lift the barrier status of the adjunct. It is thus an approach that largely adheres to the CED but argues that in certain environments, predicative adjuncts behave like L-marked and thus transparent constituents. In this approach, transparency is contingent on the right level of adjunction and integration into the θ-grid of the matrix predicate via the common DP argument. The theoretical apparatus employed to cover the proposed pattern of transparent adjuncts in B&N (2000) is in some points no longer up-to-date with current approaches to syntactic structures. This includes the issue of ternary branching, which is required here to get the adjunct XP close enough to the main predicate and its subject, which is solved by a reanalysis step in Demonte (1988). Also, the notion of L-marking and Subjacency-based derivational constraints have received substantially less attention since the shift to Minimalism (see G. Müller 2011).

This account makes a series of predictions that differ from those postulated in Truswell (2007, 2011), especially for transitive matrix predicates. Consider the two examples in (29), which are similar to canonical examples of transparent BPPA constructions with accomplishment matrix predicates in Truswell (2007, 2011). However, they do not qualify as reflexive in the sense of B&N (2000) and thus do not allow the extraction.

(29) a. *What$_i$ did John hurt Bill [trying to fix t$_i$]?
 b. *What$_i$ did John drive Mary crazy [talking about t$_i$]?
 (B&N 2000: 211, 212)

The judgments for these types of transitive matrix predicates differ categorically in Truswell (2007, 2011), who considers both these extractions grammatical, and the ungrammatical judgments in B&N (2000). Crucially, neither of the two approaches predicts a strong degradation of the corresponding declaratives; the reflexivity status of the embedding verb is the factor that determines whether the adjunct will turn out transparent or opaque in B&N (2000). As far as the distinction in single-argument predicates is concerned, B&N (2000) and Truswell (2007, 2011) make largely identical predictions, even though they are derived by different means: telic unaccusative matrix predicates are better candidates for subextraction from the adjunct than atelic unergatives.

There seem to be grammaticality contrasts in interrogatives that cannot be explained with a reflexivity analysis; this includes agentive predicates with an optional argument, such as in (30) and (31). The presence of an object seems to ameliorate the extraction, but the structure still fails to be reflexive because the subject of the adjunct predicate is outside the V'-projection. This is unlike the addition of path phrases to unergative manner-of-motion predicates, which are shifted to an unaccusative analysis (Levin & Rappaport Hovav 1995; Irwin 2012, 2018, 2020).

(30) a. *What does John dance screaming __?
 b. What does John dance the YMCA screaming __?
 (see Brown 2017: 54, 55)

(31) a. *What did Susan work whistling __?
    b. What did Susan work on her thesis whistling __?

These contrasts do not receive a straightforward analysis in B&N's reflexivity framework. In both cases, the adjunct predicate should be a VP adjunct and occur outside the V'-projection because it cannot be predicated of the direct object.

The approach to transparent adjuncts in B&N (2000) attempts to explain the apparent exceptions to the CED with an analysis that allows L-marking for adjuncts in specific environments; as L-marking is one of the ways that an empty category can be licensed (Chomsky 1986a; Lasnik & Saito 1984), predicative adjuncts that are in the θ-grid of the main verb do not fall under the CED. The main advantage of this specific interaction account over others in this group is that it is a syntactic interaction account, meaning that the factors to which extraction is sensitive are all represented in the syntax and need no mediation from semantics, pragmatics, or information structure. Even if the necessity of ternary branching is suspicious from a strictly Minimalist perspective, this account does not require a substantial reformulation of locality operations.

3.3.3 Aspectual classes and extraction (Truswell 2007)

The first approach classified as a semantic interaction account is the influential event-structural approach to transparent participle adjuncts presented in Truswell (2007). Even though the theoretical apparatus receives considerable alterations in later work (Truswell 2011), this paper and its examples are most often cited in the general literature on islands and exceptions to the CED (e.g. Phillips 2013). The main claim is that the transparency of the adjunct predicate depends on the aspectual classes of both the matrix and adjunct predicates in terms of Vendler (1957), as well as the meaning relation between the two predicates. Truswell's semantic account is motivated by the fact that narrow syntactic approaches are better at explaining the strong island status of adjuncts than at offering insights into exceptional cases where the extraction is reported to be grammatical (Truswell 2007: 1356). Some generalizations can be captured by a syntactic account, for example that matrix predicates which do not project an internal argument disallow extraction (Truswell 2007: 1357–1358). The examples in (32) illustrate this contrast with the unergative *dance*, the unaccusative *arrive*, and the transitive *drive crazy*. Truswell (2007: 1357) explicitly classifies (32c) as transitive, but its status as a resultative construction is noted in Brown (2017: 24); see also the discussion in Chapter 2. As unergatives are the only verb type which do not project an internal argument, this grammaticality contrast can be captured in syntactic terms.

(32) a. *What does John dance [whistling t]? [unergative]
 b. What$_i$ did John$_j$ arrive t$_j$ [whistling t$_i$]? [unaccusative]
 c. What did John drive Mary crazy [whistling t]? [transitive]
 (Truswell 2007: 1357)

This is close to one of the generalizations in Borgonovo & Neeleman (2000), who also consider extractions like (32b) grammatical, but not those like (32c). In contrast to this account based on the grammatical verb type of the matrix predicate alone, Truswell (2007) develops a generalization in terms of aspectual classes; there are correlations between these two notions, but the overlap is not perfect (see Dowty 1991: 607). Truswell's decision for a semantic account is motivated by the fact that in some cases, locality principles make the wrong predictions: the contrast in (33) shows that extraction is grammatical in the more complex biclausal adjunct predicate (33a), compared to the ungrammatical extraction from the monoclausal adjunct (33b). Syntactic locality principles would, however, predict that the addition of material between the *wh*-filler and the gap should make the extraction harder instead of easier (Truswell 2007: 1358).

(33) a. What did John drive Mary crazy [trying to fix t]?
 b. *What did John drive Mary crazy [fixing t]?
 (Truswell 2007: 1358)

The judgments for (32c) and (33a) are in opposition to the analysis in Borgonovo & Neeleman (2000), who would consider both extractions ungrammatical because the sentences fail to satisfy their conditions for reflexivity. Truswell (2007) takes a semantic perspective and proposes a unified analysis for the restrictions on the type of matrix predicate as well as properties of the adjunct predicate. The condition that governs the possibility to extract from the adjunct is stated in (34):

(34) Extraction from Adjunct Secondary Predicates:
 Extraction of a complement from a secondary predicate is permitted only if the event denoted by the secondary predicate is identified with an event position in the matrix predicate. (Truswell 2007: 1359)

Two requirements follow from this condition: (i) the matrix predicate must have at least two event positions or subevents; (ii) one of these event positions needs to be lexically unspecified so that the adjunct predicate can fill this open position, for which the term "identification" is used. If the matrix predicate has only one subevent, then there is no open event position which the adjunct can fill. Taken together, these requirements lead to the generalization that subextraction from the adjunct is only possible if the relation between matrix and adjunct predicate "parallels the event structure of a possible lexical verb" (Truswell 2007: 1369), i.e. that the matrix–adjunct predicate complex does not exceed the meaning components of a verb with complex event structure. Throughout his discussion, Truswell assumes the traditional classification of verbs in Vendler (1957) with minor modifications, and the decompositional aspectual calculus of Dowty (1979); the notion of telicity corresponds to the presence or absence of Dowty's BECOME operator (Truswell 2007: 1368). It follows from this that only accomplishments and achievements should be able to qualify as suitable host predicates for transparent adjuncts because only they can be decomposed into two subevents; in contrast, states and activities are simple event structures with only one subevent. Truswell (2007: 1366) analyzes accomplishments as a causal relation between two subevents, where one causes the other, and most achievements as a relation of temporal succession, which is conceptualized as a change of state. Not all achievements can encode temporal succession, which is why the extraction condition in (34) cannot be satisfied for a subtype of achievements. Achievements are often so-called telic pairs, which encode a transition from a state $\neg\varphi$ to the opposite state φ (see Higginbotham 2009). Typically, the interval preceding the actual change of state is not part of the event (Helland & Pitz 2012: 116). The subevent structures of accomplishments and most achievements are defined as in (35):

(35) Subevent structure for telic verb classes:
    a. Accomplishments: e_1 CAUSE e_2
    b. Many achievements: e_1 THEN e_2
    (Truswell 2007: 1366)

This exhausts the maximal structure of subevents in the two telic aspectual classes. Atelic predicates without a BECOME operator like activities and states are considered to consist only of one subevent, which is either unbounded for states or bounded but monotonous for activities. In a next step, a connection is drawn between these subevent structures and the interpretational range of the BPPA construction, which can either encode a causative or a depictive relation with respect to the matrix predicate. The causative and depictive interpretations of BPPAs are defined as in (36) with examples in (37); the subscripts "secondary" and "matrix" refer to the adjunct and matrix predicate in the BPPA construction, respectively. At this point, Truswell (2007) is unspecific about the precise relation between the matrix and secondary predicates in the depictive BPPA construction and simply refers to it by the relation R.

(36) Interpretations of the BPPA construction:
   a. Causative: $e_{secondary}$ CAUSE e_{matrix}
   b. Depictive: $e_{secondary}$ R e_{matrix}
   (Truswell 2007: 1366)

(37) a. John [drove Mary crazy]$_{matrix}$ [trying to fix the sink]$_{secondary}$ [causative]
   b. John [arrived at the station]$_{matrix}$ [whistling a funny song]$_{secondary}$ [depictive]

The causative interpretation of BPPAs in (36a) corresponds to the subevent structure for accomplishments in (35a): the secondary adjunct event is the cause of the matrix event. Provided that the causal semantics of the matrix predicate is unspecified, the adjunct predicate can be identified with the causing subevent. Another condition is that the adjunct predicate needs the proper aspectual characteristics of a causing event: typically, only activities qualify as such causing subevents when human subjects are involved; see Dowty (1979: 124–125). Causative adjunct predicates hosted by causally unspecified accomplishment matrix predicates are thus predicted to be transparent for extraction because the condition in (34) is met.

For achievement matrix predicates, the correspondence is less clear than for accomplishments: depictives are typically characterized by a temporal overlap relation, which does not provide a good fit for the telic pair reading of achievements encoded by the THEN operator (Rothstein 1985, 2004b, 2017; Winkler 1997; McNally 1997; Geuder 2004; Pylkkänen 2008). Truswell (2007) approaches the initial mismatch between the semantics of achievements in (35b) and the interpretation of the BPPA in (36b) by assuming that the adjunct predicate stands in a depictive relation to a so-called "preparatory phase" of the matrix predicate which precedes the the achievement's culmination; see Moens & Steedman (1988) for a similar use of this term. For many achievement predicates such as *arrive*, this preparatory phase can be linked to a path component or even a causal structure, which makes the distinction between achievements and accomplishments less clear.

The conditions on event identification in the sense of (34) are thus different for accomplishments and achievements: (i) for accomplishments, the causing subevent of the matrix predicate must be unspecified so that the BPPA can fill this position; (ii) for achievements, the culmination point needs to be extended by a preparatory phase that can be modified by the BPPA. This further narrows down the verbs which allow extraction from the adjunct, as seen in the examples in (38).

(38) a. *What does [John work] [whistling ~~what~~]?
   b. *What did [John write the cheque] [complaining about ~~what~~]?
   c. What did [John arrive] [whistling ~~what~~]?

d. What did [John drive Mary crazy] [complaining about ~~what~~]?
   (S. Müller 2011: 156)

An activity modifying an activity, as in (38a), is ungrammatical because this type of matrix predicate does not have any open event position that could be targeted by the adjunct; likewise, a fully specified accomplishment like (38b) does not allow a transparent adjunct. The writing process encodes the activity and the DP *the cheque* encodes the resultant state of the accomplishment: *the cheque* comes into existence by the writing process, which is a fully specified causal structure. There is no open position for the BPPA. In contrast to these two cases, achievements that can be extended with a preparatory phase (38c) and accomplishments with an underspecified causal component (38d) allow for extraction from the adjunct because the adjunct fills the underspecified event position of the matrix predicate. In the case of (38c), the whistling activity modifies the phase preceding the actual arrival event; in (38d), the BPPA specifies the cause that leads to the event described in the matrix predicate, which is left implicit in the absence of the adjunct.

These observations about the event structures of different verb types and the possibilities for the adjunct predicate to identify with an underspecified event position of the matrix predicate lead Truswell (2007) to propose the generalization about the possibility to extract from the participle adjunct as stated in (39).

(39) All transparent secondary predicates must be atelic, and must modify telic predicates. (Truswell 2007: 1369)

The secondary predicate has to be atelic because only these predicates can specify the causing subevent for accomplishments and the preparatory phase of achievements; the matrix predicate must be telic because only telic predicates consist of two subevents, one of which can be unspecified and provide an open event position for the adjunct predicate. The maximal resulting event structure is thus similar to that of an accomplishment, where an activity precedes a culmination; see Dowty (1979). This also satisfies the condition that the BPPA construction is limited to the maximally complex event structure of a lexical verb. From this, it follows that the adjunct predicate event, identified with e_1 in (35), must be simplex and thus atelic (Truswell 2007: 1369). The generalization in (39) and the possible event structures of complex events result in the extraction pattern shown in (40). The adjunct only allows extraction in the right combination of telic and atelic predicates in the BPPA construction.

(40) a. *What did John work whistling?   [atelic/atelic]
     b. *What did John work noticing?   [atelic/telic]

c. *What did John arrive noticing? [telic/telic]
d. What did John arrive whistling? [telic/atelic]
   (see Truswell 2007: 1369)

The requirement that the BPPA construction has to be compatible with the event structure of a possible lexical verb further excludes stative adjunct predicates. There are two reasons why stative adjuncts do not allow extraction: (i) statives cannot be interpreted as the causing subevent of accomplishments, as seen in (41a); and (ii) they are generally excluded as depictives because of their classification as ILPs (Rothstein 1985; Winkler 1997; Simpson 2005), seen in (41b), where extraction is ungrammatical even though the generalization about aspectual classes in (39) is met. This singles out activity adjuncts as the best candidates for transparency.

(41) a. *What did John hurt himself having/owning? (Truswell 2007: 1372)
     b. *What did John arrive at the station having/owning?

In addition to the event-structural characteristics that the adjunct predicate needs to qualify as a causing subevent or a depictive, there is another, independent reason why atelic activities are preferred: the progressive-marking on the adjunct is not easily compatible with all predicate types, especially achievements and states (Rothstein 2004b; Croft 2012).

The generalization in (39) is further constrained by the requirement that the adjunct has to fulfill one of the two relations to the matrix event as noted in (36) above. This rules out non-causative accomplishments and achievements that cannot be augmented by a preparatory phase; this group includes many perception verbs and verbs like *appear*; examples of ungrammatical extractions from these types of predicates are shown in (42).

(42) a. *What did John appear whistling?
     b. *What$_j$ did John$_i$ [notice his brother] [looking through t$_j$]$_i$?
        (Truswell 2007: 1370)

The achievements that are singled out by not allowing extraction are also the achievements that strongly resist progressive-marking (Rothstein 2004b). The tripartite classification of achievement predicates in Truswell (2019b: 7) offers an explanation for this distinction: purely punctual achievements like *appear* are classified as "points" and do not allow the encoding of a process component; thus, there is no open event position for the adjunct. In contrast, the group which Truswell (2019b) classifies as "other achievements", which includes predicates like *arrive*, can encode a preparatory phase with which the adjunct can identify.

Truswell (2007) concludes that not all combinations of aspectual classes in the BPPA construction satisfy the criteria to form a complex event structure similar to those encoded by accomplishments or achievements with a depictive. Extraction is only grammatical when these event-structural conditions are met.

Truswell (2007: 1373–1374) briefly discusses participle adjuncts in declarative constructions and concludes that not all requirements of the telicity generalization in (39) apply there. Crucially, it is the application of *wh*-extraction that reveals the contrasts between transparent and opaque adjuncts: "The assumption has been that *wh*-movement out of the secondary predicate is responsible for the necessity of the cluster of interpretive properties described above" (Truswell 2007: 1373). In declaratives, two observations are crucial: (i) the preference for atelic adjunct predicates also applies here, but (ii) the telicity of the matrix predicate is not relevant: "declaratives with atelic matrix verbs are quite unremarkable" (Truswell 2007: 1373). So, while extraction from an adjunct modifying an activity is ungrammatical (43b), the corresponding declarative structure is completely fine (43a) and not constrained by the telicity of the matrix predicate or the identification with an unspecified position in the matrix predicate's event structure. Likewise, perception verbs in declaratives are grammatical with an adjunct predicate (44a), but extraction results in ungrammaticality (44b). The same applies to declarative BPPA constructions with stative main predicates, as in (45).

(43) a. I work listening to music.
      b. *What do you work [listening to t]?
          (Truswell 2007: 1373)

(44) a. John noticed the heavy traffic coming back from the shops.
      b. *What$_i$ did John$_j$ [notice the heavy traffic] [coming back from t$_i$]$_j$?
          (Truswell 2007: 1374)

(45) a. I only know Georgian wearing *this* magic hat.
      b. *Which of your magic hats do you know Georgian [wearing t]?
          (Truswell 2007: 1362)

The consequence of these observations is that the application of syntactic extraction operations is sensitive to the aspectual characteristics in the BPPA construction: whereas declarative BPPA constructions are unconstrained in the type of matrix predicate they allow, extraction only results in a grammatical sentence when the generalization in (39) is satisfied. This claim leads to the requirement for adjustments to locality theory, which is considered to be sensitive to event-semantic factors in this approach. If extraction can only operate on a subset of event-structural configurations, this means that the syntactic component requires access to semantic features like telicity and causality.

The approach in Truswell (2007) explains grammatical extractions from the BPPA construction in terms of the event-structural characteristics of the two predicates.[8] There are, however, cases where the telicity generalization in (39) does not make the right predictions about adjunct transparency, as well as consequences for the architecture of grammar that require justification. I will discuss four of these issues in the remainder of this section.

First, the observations about a missing effect of the telic–atelic contrast in matrix predicates is dismissed based on a small set of examples, such as (46a). It is not difficult to construct similar examples that feel slightly marked even in the absence of extraction, as in (46b,c).

(46) a. I work listening to music. (Truswell 2007: 1373)
 b. ?John worked whistling a funny song.
 c. ?Mary walked listening to music.

Since the major theoretical claim of this approach is that interrogatives are subject to conditions that are inoperative in declaratives and that syntactic operations are sensitive to non-syntactic properties, a more detailed discussion of the relation between declaratives and interrogatives is required. This account makes strong predictions about locality operations which require substantial revisions to these syntactic operations; Truswell (2007: 1375) explicitly states that a phrase-structural, geometric approach to the data pattern he discovers is highly difficult to formulate, if not impossible. As shown in the discussion of syntactic gap-licensing approaches above, there are in fact several possible ways of deriving an adjunct-internal gap without violating fundamental locality principles. The main issue left open by most gap-licensing accounts is the distinction between high or low adjuncts, or when an Agree relation is possible. The generalization in Truswell (2007) can be seen as one possibility to draw such distinctions.

Second, there are contrasts which cannot be reduced to the telicity of the matrix predicate, such as in (47). In these examples, extraction is ungrammatical if the activity verbs *prance* and *jump* occur in isolation; extraction becomes grammatical

---

[8] Miyamoto (2012) proposes that adjuncts can become transparent in Japanese if there is an Agree relation between the nominal referent of a floating quantifier and a specified quantity feature in an aspectual projection; this account shares several points with Truswell (2007) in the importance of event structure for extraction, but differs in two fundamental ways: (i) the relevance of specified quantity over telicity, and (ii) the observation that this property also shows effects in the absence of extraction. For reasons of space, I do not discuss this approach in detail here.

when the particles *around/about* are added, which change the verb class from unergative to unaccusative (Hoekstra & Mulder 1990; Levin & Rappaport Hovav 1995; Borgonovo & Neeleman 2000; Irwin 2020). In both cases, the sentence remains atelic and thus does not conform to the predictions from Truswell's telicity generalization. Adding the particle does not change the fact that both predicates do not have an open event position which the adjunct predicate can modify; the improved grammaticality in the presence of the particles receives no principled explanation in the aspectual classes framework.

(47) a. Who are you prancing *(about) [trying to impress t]?
    b. What did she jump *(around) [singing t]?
    (Truswell 2007: 1361)

Truswell interprets this as evidence for the relevance of agentivity: extraction is much improved if there is an asymmetry in agentivity between the two predicates, which can be induced by augmenting an activity with a particle that removes the entailment of deliberate action (Truswell 2007: 1361); see also McIntyre (2004). Contrasts like these indicate that an approach based on aspectual properties and interpretations alone is not able to account for a larger set of patterns and that other factors also play a role. I will argue in Chapter 5 that the opacity of BPPA constructions with punctual achievements in (42) and the effects of directional elements seen in (47) can receive a uniform analysis in terms of characteristics of the matrix predicate that are not linked to telicity alone, but rather to scalar meaning components like paths: in both cases, the presence or absence of a path structure seems to influence transparency, as shown in (48):

(48) a. *What did John walk whistling __?   [−path]
    b. What did John walk around whistling __?   [+path]
    c. *What did John appear whistling __?   [−path]
    d. What did John arrive whistling __?   [+path]

I will show that Truswell's (2007) concept of telicity is too narrow for extraction from BPPAs, and that a more general notion of boundedness that also includes spatial intervals and property degrees offers a more unified explanation for the cases in (48); see Champollion (2017) and Gawron (2005, 2009) for similar extensions of boundedness. This more general concept also accounts for the distinction between transitory (49a) and permanent (49b) states.

(49) a. What is John sitting there [eating t]? (Truswell 2007: 1360)
b. *Which of your magic hats do you know Georgian [wearing t]?
(Truswell 2007: 1362)

The third issue is that Truswell's telicity generalization makes predictions that differ from Borgonovo & Neeleman (2000). The accounts agree in their predictions about the advantage of achievements/unaccusatives over intransitive activities/unergatives in interrogatives, but crucially differ in their predictions about the class of transitive predicates, which include activities and accomplishments in event-structural terms and reflexive/non-reflexive predicates in syntactic terms. The examples in (50) illustrate these different predictions: the first judgments are those by B&N, the second those by Truswell (2007). Truswell (2007) considers all these examples grammatical because the matrix predicate is a telic accomplishment, whereas B&N consider (50a,b) ungrammatical because the matrix predicate is not reflexive. Both accounts agree on the grammatical status of the reflexive transitive in (50c), but for fundamentally different reasons.

(50) a. */√ What did John enrage his neighbours [whistling t]?
(Truswell 2007: 1357)
b. */√ What$_j$ did John hurt Bill [trying to fix t$_j$]? (B&N 2000: 200)
c. √/√ What$_j$ did John hurt himself [trying to fix t$_j$]? (B&N 2000: 200)

The final issue with this account is the requirement for adjustments to locality theory. Truswell (2007) claims that extraction from participle adjuncts is only grammatical under specific conditions, as formulated in the telicity generalization in (39). Since declaratives are not as tightly constrained as interrogatives, this predicts a sensitivity of extraction operations to event-semantic properties that cannot be captured in purely syntactic terms. Unlike reflexivity in Borgonovo & Neeleman (2000), the distinction between transitive accomplishments and transitive activities cannot be reduced to structural differences, so that information about the type of event structure is needed in determining the grammatical status of extraction. For example, there is no fundamental syntactic difference between the accomplishment *John built a house* and the activity *John built houses*. The majority of the intuitive judgments for interrogatives in Truswell (2007) appear to be accurate, but the architectural conclusions require more rigid justification than the approach offers. The independence of syntax is called into question without a serious examination of declaratives and the relation between the two sentence types. It is left unanswered why declaratives should not also be sensitive to similar or even identical conditions that show an effect in interrogatives; after all, the formation of complex predicates is not totally free, as the discussion of depictives in Chapter 2 has shown. This approach is substantially modified in later work (Truswell 2011), which is discussed in the following section.

3.3.4 Event groupings and agentivity (Truswell 2011)

The updated approach to Truswell (2007) presented in Truswell (2011) extends the empirical coverage to include more adjunct constructions and develops the theoretical approach with a different focus. The architectural conclusions remain the same: there are event-semantic factors which determine the grammaticality of extraction from specific adjunct predicate configurations. Declaratives are still considered to be relatively unconstrained in terms of event-structural properties.

In addition to the BPPA construction, Truswell (2011) also considers the following constructions: infinitival purpose clauses (51a) as well as a variety of adverbial clauses under the term "prepositional adjuncts" (51b). Prepositional adjuncts include temporal adverbial clauses, instrumental *by*-adjuncts, and adjuncts headed by *without*.

(51) a. What did you come round [to work on __]? [rationale clause]
     b. Who did John get upset [after talking to __]? [prepositional adjunct]
     (Truswell 2011: 129)

The extraction conditions and telicity generalization from Truswell (2007) do not readily cover these extensions, so a more general condition for extraction from adjuncts is proposed. Truswell's (2011) initial formulation of the extraction condition is similar to the condition in Truswell (2007: 1359). It is called the *Single Event Condition* (SEC):

(52) The Single Event Condition (first approximation):
An instance of *wh*-movement is legitimate only if the minimal constituent containing the head and the foot of the chain can be construed as describing a single event. (Truswell 2011: 121)

The constituent which contains the head and foot of the movement chain includes both matrix and adjunct predicate and so their combination has to qualify as the description of a single event rather than a conjunction of two independent events. The matrix and adjunct predicate together qualify as a single event if they can be construed as two subevents of a more complex event (Truswell 2011: 38). Linking two predicates to a single event description is mediated by so-called "contingent relations", which are conceptually similar to the discourse coherence relations in Hobbs (1979, 1990) or Kehler (2002, 2019), but on a more local, clause-internal level. There is also a close analogy to the perception of two verbal elements as describing facets of a single event, as in the event elaboration framework of Haug et al. (2012), Manner–Result Complementarity (Rappaport Hovav & Levin 2010), or the frame–satellite typology (Talmy 1985, 2000). For Truswell (2011), the relevant contingent relations that allow two predicates to be interpreted as a single event are direct causation and enablement (Truswell 2011: 125). A causal contingent relation holds, for example, for prepositional adjuncts headed by the preposition *by*, which encodes the cause or means by which the event described in the matrix predicate is achieved; see (53a), which is considered grammatical but shows speaker variation, indicated by the '%'-marking. Causality can also be encoded in BPPAs, as in (53b).

(53) a. %Which item of furniture did John upset his hosts [by eating __]?
(Truswell 2011: 136)
b. What did John drive Mary crazy [whistling __]? (Truswell 2011: 155)

Enablement is a similar relation holding between the two predicates, but the causal chain is in the reverse order. Typically, purpose or rationale clauses encode an event in the matrix predicate that enables the adjunct predicate, as in (54).

(54) What did Christ die [to save us from __]? (Truswell 2011: 131)

This covers two of the three constructions considered by Truswell (2011); the BPPA construction is subject to slightly different conditions on single-event formation, but the case of accomplishment matrix predicates as in (53b) shows the possibility of a temporally contingent relation plus an identification of the adjunct with an unspecified causal component in the event structure of the matrix predicate, which can be considered as an enriched and pragmatically determined contingent relation. The same holds for prepositional adjuncts headed by *before/after* as in (51b), which can also receive a causal interpretation in addition to temporal contingency. Achievement matrix predicates as in (55a) are a special case because they cannot be enriched by a causal relation but nonetheless allow extraction in many cases. This is one of the motivations for proposing a revised version of the SEC.

(55) What did John arrive [whistling __]? (Truswell 2011: 155)

Throughout the discussion, Truswell (2011) assumes that non-syntactic factors determine the acceptability of extraction from the adjunct predicate. This is partially motivated by a comparison to the corresponding declarative constructions. Here the pattern is different for the three types of adjunct under consideration: for rationale clauses, extraction is reported to be possible for all grammatical declaratives (Truswell 2011: 29–30). As there are independent conditions on the grammaticality of rationale clauses, for example that an enabling action has to precede the intended effect, the pattern from interrogatives is also seen in declaratives; this means that the strength of the degradation under extraction does not depend on semantic factors in the declarative, but on the grammaticality contrasts that obtain there. This is also what Brown (2017) claims for the BPPA construction. Adjuncts introduced with *by* are tightly constrained in the declarative, which bears resemblance to the condition in Truswell (2007) that transparent BPPA constructions must not exceed the maximal event structure template of a possible lexical verb (Truswell 2011: 136–137). When this condition is met in the declarative, then the extraction is not strongly degraded. Since prepositional adjuncts with temporal prepositions like *before/after* are flexible in declaratives, also with respect to admissible aspectual classes, no deeper insights into declaratives are offered here. However, for grammatical extractions, the temporal overlap relation needs to be enriched to yield a contingent relation (Truswell 2011: 137–138).

For BPPAs, almost no constraints on declaratives are considered, except that state predicates cannot host adjunct predicates (Truswell 2011: 30, fn. 12). There are, however, differences in possible interpretations that depend on the aspectual class of the matrix predicate. Two possible interpretations are available in declarative BPPA constructions: a reading where the two events are interpreted as two conjoined events whose intervals overlap; and a reading where both are interpreted as forming a single event (Truswell 2011: 148). The availability of these readings depends on the aspectual class of the matrix predicate: BPPA constructions with telic matrix predicates allow both readings, whereas constructions with atelic matrix predicates allow only the conjoined reading, (Truswell 2011: 150). This contrast is shown in (56), where (56a) with an atelic matrix predicate has only the conjoined reading; (56b) with a telic matrix predicate allows both the conjoined and the single-event readings, but prefers the latter.

(56)   a.   John works [listening to music].   [conjoined]
        b.   John drove Mary crazy [whistling the *Marseillaise*].   [single-event]
            (Truswell 2011: 148)

From these observations, the following prediction with respect to the SEC can be derived: since extraction is only possible in the non-conjoined, single-event reading, BPPA constructions with activity matrix predicate will not allow grammatical extraction from the adjunct predicate. For accomplishment matrix predicates, the possibility of a causal reading of the adjunct, which modifies a matrix predicate whose causal component is unspecified, allows the single-event interpretation. The formation of a single-event reading for achievement matrix predicates is less clear, but Truswell (2011: 154) assumes that the reading is available because achievements regularly allow the extraction.

A set of problematic cases for the SEC is given in (57), which do not conform to it because an atelic matrix predicate hosts the adjunct; the only available reading here should be that of temporally overlapping but independent core events and thus extraction should not be possible. Still, the extractions are considered grammatical. Truswell (2011) analyzes all these predicates as activities; for the posture verb *lie* in (57a), this is not the only option advanced in the literature. Posture verbs with human subjects are classified as agentive statives in Dowty (1979: 184), which is not easily compatible with Truswell's (2011) analysis as a less agentive activity.

(57) a. What did John lie around [reading __] all day?
      b. Which chair did John eat his breakfast [sitting on __]?
      c. What was John walking about [whistling __]?
          (Truswell 2011: 155)

To accommodate these grammatical extractions as well as BPPAs to achievement matrix predicates, Truswell (2011) revises the condition on extraction from adjunct predicates. Whereas the SEC refers to one complex event (as in Truswell 2007), the larger notion of "event grouping" is introduced, which allows for a larger set of matrix–adjunct predicate combinations, including activity matrix predicates. The final statement of this updated extraction condition is given in the *Single Event Grouping Condition* (SEGC) in (58).

(58) The Single Event Grouping Condition
      An instance of *wh*-movement is legitimate only if the minimal constituent containing the head and the foot of the chain can be construed as describing a single *event grouping*.   (Truswell 2011: 157)

One crucial aspect of this condition is carried over from the extraction condition formulated in Truswell (2007): the possibility for extraction from the adjunct depends on event-semantic characteristics of the construction, i.e. it is a condition that incorporates interpretational, non-structural factors into the theory of locality. In other aspects, the SEGC differs substantially from the approach in Truswell (2007); this can be seen in the definition of "event grouping", which imposes less strict constraints on the interpretation of the BPPA construction. Instead of limiting the meaning of the matrix–adjunct predicate complex to the meaning of a possible verb, a certain degree of independence is acknowledged: the two predicates are only constrained by an overlap requirement and a restriction related to agentivity. Truswell (2011) defines the notion of an event grouping as in (59).

(59) An *event grouping* $\mathcal{E}$ is a set of core events and/or extended events $\{e_1, \ldots e_n\}$ such that:
  a. Every two events e_1, $e_2 \in \mathcal{E}$ overlap spatiotemporally;
  b. A maximum of one (maximal) event $e \in \mathcal{E}$ is agentive.
  (Truswell 2011: 157)

The requirement of a spatio-temporal overlap relation between the two events is not formalized, but can take a variety of different precise implementations, similar to general depictive overlap relations; see Irimia (2012). Agentivity is defined as assignment of an AGENT role to one participant in atomic events or the initial subevent of a complex event (Truswell 2011: 158). Observations about the preference for agentive adjuncts and a non-agentive subject of the matrix predicate are also made in Borgonovo & Neeleman (2000: 210, fn. 6, 215). An asymmetry between the two predicates in terms of agentivity of the subject is discussed as a criterion for extraction in Truswell (2007: 1360), where it follows from the possible event structure of complex events, which cannot naturally encode an event that consists of two agentive subevents. This is also related to data from activity matrix predicates that are modified by "non-agentive" particles like *around*. The SEGC makes several predictions that differ from the condition on extraction from Truswell (2007). For one, the telicity of the adjunct predicate is no longer considered as a relevant factor for extraction because there are independent reasons for a preference for atelic adjunct based on considerations about the morphological -*ing*-marking (Truswell 2011: 150). Provided that the SEGC is satisfied and no more than one event is agentive, some agentive and atelic matrix predicates are allowed.

Truswell (2011: 162–165) shows the predictions of the SEGC with the examples given in (60). The only two ungrammatical cases are accomplishment matrix predicates with an agentive adjunct that does not stand in a causal relation to the matrix predicate (60d), and activity matrix predicates with an agentive adjunct (60i).

(60) a. What did John arrive whistling?
  b. What did John arrive wearing?
  c. What did John drive Mary crazy whistling?   (causal reading)
  d. *What did John drive Mary crazy whistling? (no causal relation)
  e. What did John drive Mary crazy wearing?
  f. Which chair did John eat his breakfast sitting on?
  g. Which book did John lie around reading?
  h. What did John wait around sitting on?

i. *What does John dance screaming?
   (Truswell 2011: 162–165)

The properties which are relevant for the SEGC are shown schematically in Table 3.1, which includes the presence or absence of a culmination in the matrix predicate, as well as the agentivity of the two predicates. The letters in parentheses refer to the examples in (60); ungrammatical combinations are marked with an asterisk. The most interesting cases are those that would be considered ungrammatical in the approach in Truswell (2007) but are grammatical under the SEGC; these are the cases in (60f), (60g), and (60h), shown by bold typeface in Table 3.1.

Tab. 3.1: Extraction pattern for BPPAs in Truswell (2011), based on the examples in (60a–i).

Matrix predicate		Adjunct predicate	
culmination	agentivity	agentive	non-agentive
culminated	non-agentive	(60a)	(60b)
culminated	agentive	(60c), *(60d)	(60e)
non-culminated	non-agentive	**(60g)**	**(60h)**
non-culminated	agentive	*(60i)	**(60f)**

The SEGC allows extraction from BPPA constructions that are predicted to be ungrammatical by the SEC but which feel intuitively acceptable. As I will point out below, however, the shift from aspectual classes to agentivity is not the only possible way to explain the exceptions to the SEC. The SEGC also captures the case of two agentive events, for example an accomplishment matrix predicate with an activity adjunct predicate, by re-stating the requirement on a causal interpretation where the adjunct is identified with the causal activity component of the matrix predicate (see Truswell 2007). As with (57b) above, the examples in (60f,h) represent extractions from a prepositional complement instead of extraction of a direct object argument. They are thus more similar to the examples on preposition stranding in Sheehan (2013), who notes that measure, locative, rationale, and temporal PPs often allow subextraction, in contrast to opaque manner or extent PPs. According to Sheehan (2013), the discourse function of the PP has an effect on transparency. In addition, it is possible that preposition-stranding in these configurations provides the parser with support for finding the true gap site.

There are a few conceptual points of the theory that are described in more detail compared to Truswell (2007): for example, the SEC is described as a semantic condition that filters out multi-event readings in interrogatives, whereas the interpretational possibilities are less constrained in declaratives (Truswell 2011: 124);

when the BPPA construction is hosted by an atelic matrix predicate, however, only a multi-event reading is available, and thus the interrogative is filtered out as ungrammatical because this reading is not allowed by the SEC. Extraction is permitted to operate with relative freedom. Ultimately, Truswell (2011) considers a processing-based explanation for the the SEGC in terms of Dependency Locality Theory (Gibson 1998, 2000): in the configurations that violate the SEGC either in terms of aspectual classes or agentivity, the dependency crosses more discourse referents in the form of events than in configurations that obey the SEGC. One of the motivations for a processing-based account is the reported variability in speaker judgments about most of the constructions discussed in Truswell (2011: 233); in addition, the availability of a single-event reading is sometimes not straightforward in BPPA constructions. The role of plausibility and coercion for extraction are also part of the approaches developed in Demonte (1988: 30) and G. Müller (1995: 40–41).

Kohrt et al. (2018) report on two experiments that examine the predictions from Truswell (2011). They use an acceptability judgment task with a 2 × 2 design that includes the factors ±WH and ±EXTRACTABLE, i.e. whether the matrix predicate is predicted to allow extraction from the adjunct or not. Achievements and states are considered as permitting extraction because they are non-agentive and thus do not violate Truswell's (2011) SEGC; accomplishments and activities are used as non-extractable conditions. Their design is shown in (61), where (61a) corresponds to the –WH conditions and (61b) to +WH; *worked* exemplifies –EXTRACTABLE verbs and *arrived* +EXTRACTABLE.

(61) a. John wondered whether his best friend $\left\{\begin{array}{c}\text{worked}\\\text{arrived}\end{array}\right\}$ at the office drinking some coffee late this afternoon.

b. John wondered which coffee his best friend $\left\{\begin{array}{c}\text{worked}\\\text{arrived}\end{array}\right\}$ at the office drinking __ late this afternoon.
(Kohrt et al. 2018)

The results show a main effect of extraction, but no main effect of verb type and no significant interaction between the two factors. This is unexpected in the account of Truswell (2011) because there are no differences between non-agentive and agentive matrix predicates. The SEGC predicts that there should be a degrading effect when extraction takes place from an adjunct in a sentence with two agentive predicates. These results thus cast doubt on the validity of agentivity as a factor determining adjunct transparency. In a second experiment, Kohrt et al. (2018) manipulate the plausibility of interrogatives to investigate the effect of the matrix predicate in an online plausibility mismatch experiment. The experimental paradigm is shown in (62), with (62a) being +PLAUSIBLE and (62b) −PLAUSIBLE.

(62) a. John wondered which coffee his best friend $\begin{Bmatrix} \text{worked} \\ \text{arrived} \end{Bmatrix}$ at the office drinking ___ late this afternoon.

b. John wondered which report his best friend $\begin{Bmatrix} \text{worked} \\ \text{arrived} \end{Bmatrix}$ at the office drinking ___ late this afternoon.
(Kohrt et al. 2018)

Their hypothesis is that plausibility should only have an effect on reading times in the +EXTRACTABLE conditions (e.g. *arrived*), but not in conditions where the matrix predicate does not qualify as extractable (e.g. *worked*). Kohrt et al. (2018) find a marginal main effect for PLAUSIBILITY, no main effect for EXTRACTABLE, and no significant interaction. A closer analysis of the verb types used in this experiment (achievements, states, and accomplishments) reveals that only achievements show a plausibility effect, but states and accomplishments do not. Thus, the plausibility of the filler as a complement of the adjunct predicate is only relevant for a subset of matrix predicates, which can be taken as evidence that plausibility is not evaluated when the matrix predicate counts as non-extractable. Overall, the results in Kohrt et al. (2018) show that the influence of the matrix predicate is not as predicted by the agentivity-based account in Truswell (2011). While there is a marginal advantage of achievements, the results are less clear than predicted theoretically. See also Kohrt et al. (2020) for an ERP study with similar items as in (62).

As with the telicity-based approach in Truswell (2007), the main architectural issue with this account is that core-syntactic operations like *wh*-extraction are sensitive to non-syntactic factors. Even if the SEGC is conceptualized as a semantic filter on the output of extraction, the major aim of Truswell (2011) is to show that there are semantic effects on the grammaticality of interrogatives that cannot be explained in core-syntactic terms. In the following, I want to point out four major issues with this account: (i) unclear predictions about declaratives with activity matrix predicates and (ii) unclear relations to declaratives in general, (iii) sentences where the agentivity restriction does not make the right predictions, and (iv) an alternative analysis of locational particles with activity main predicates that does not rely on agentivity.

(i) A common assumption in Truswell (2007) and Truswell (2011) is that declarative BPPA constructions with atelic activity matrix predicates are fully grammatical and are more liberal in their possible interpretations. One important difference between BPPAs hosted by atelic and telic matrix predicates is that the former, especially atelic activities, appear to be highly sensitive to tense and result in different readings. Compare the following, where (63a) is taken from Truswell (2011):

(63) a. John works [listening to music]. (Truswell 2011: 148)
 b. ?John worked [listening to music].
 c. John arrived [listening to music].

Compared to (63a), the past tense version (63b) seems to be slightly less felicitous. A major difference between these two sentences is that the simple present version results in a habitual reading, whereas the past tense favors a reading that singles out a single instance of an event in the past. There, the habitual reading depends on additional cues, such as the adverbial *always*, which can also modify the simple present version and enforce the habitual reading. No habitual reading is available for achievement matrix predicates such as (63c), where the habitual reading only arises in the present tense with adverbial support. If it is indeed the case that BPPAs to past tense activity matrix predicates are less acceptable, then this suggests that declarative BPPA constructions with activity matrix predicates are not as unconstrained as Truswell (2007, 2011) proposes.

(ii) In general, the relation to declarative BPPA constructions receives by far less detailed attention than the other types of construction discussed in Truswell (2011): for rationale clauses and *by*-adjuncts, Truswell compares declaratives with different types of aspectual class combinations and finds that they are not all fully grammatical. Examples for marked and ungrammatical declarative rationale clauses and *by*-adjuncts are given in (64) and (65). In these cases, the aspectual classes of the two predicates are the reason for the markedness.

(64) a. ??John arrived at base camp [to reach the summit in a few days].
 b. #John noticed the typo [to help the copyeditor].
   (Truswell 2011: 132–133)

(65) a. *John drove Mary crazy [by reaching the summit].
 b. ??John works on the project [by building a prototype].
   (Truswell 2011: 136)

Extraction from a rationale clause is predicted to be possible if the declarative is grammatical (Truswell 2011: 29–30); a similar point is raised for *by*-adjuncts (Truswell 2011: 136–137). In these cases, grammaticality of *wh*-extraction is a reflection of these independent licensing conditions for rationale clauses and prepositional adjuncts. For the BPPA construction, most constraints only concern the interpretation of the relation between the two predicates. In fact, the only event-structural condition is that the adjunct predicate needs to be atelic due to the progressive nature of the present participle morphology (Truswell 2011: 150). All other effects are related to interpretation, such as the unavailability of a single-event reading when the matrix predicate is atelic, whereas both single-event and conjoined readings are possible when the matrix predicate is telic. In declaratives, there is also no restriction for accomplishment matrix predicates that the adjunct needs to be identified with the cause component; since the conjoined reading is possible, the adjunct can express an independent event without leading to ungrammaticality (see Truswell 2011: 151). As noted above, Truswell (2011) does not see grammaticality distinctions for declarative BPPAs with atelic adjunct predicates that depend on aspectual classes, which emphasizes the nature of the SEGC as a semantic condition on the output of extraction, where multi-event readings of BPPAs are filtered out as semantically infelicitous.

(iii) The generalizations of the SEGC do not find complete empirical support, as there are constructions where the grammaticality of extraction does not appear to depend on the number of agentive events. In (66), the addition of a direct object for the matrix predicate licenses the extraction. Brown (2015: 11) attributes this effect to the disambiguation of the true gap site (see Fodor 1978).

(66) a. *What does John dance screaming?
 b. What did John dance the YMCA screaming?
 (see Brown 2017: 54–55)

Disambiguation of the gap site is not the only effect that the addition of the object has: it also introduces an incremental theme that measures out the duration of the dancing event, namely the progression of the dancing through the song. This allows for a close identification of the intervals of the adjunct and matrix predicates; Brown (2017: 75) calls this "amalgamated" scales. The SEGC also fails to make the right predictions in cases where the matrix predicate encodes a non-voluntary bodily action, as shown in (67). Shivering is not under the control of the subject and should thus not be considered as an agentive verb. Nonetheless, it does not matter whether the adjunct predicate is agentive (67a) or not (67b): the extraction is degraded in both configurations. Verbs in this group show unergative behavior despite their non-agentive character, as shown in Levin & Rappaport Hovav (1995: 137). Verbs like *shiver* can also be analyzed as semelfactives, but it seems that the adjunct induces an atelic, iterative reading.

(67) a. *Which tune did Mary shiver whistling?
 b. *Which chair did Mary shiver sitting on?
 (see Brown 2017: 55)

(iv) A similar point can be raised about the exceptional cases with activity matrix predicates that motivate the transition from the SEC to the SEGC: whereas activities are typically unbounded events, the three examples in (69) as well as Brown's (2017) example in (66b) encode events that can be considered bounded because there is either reference to an object that measures out the duration or progression of the event, or the matrix predicate describes a non-permanent stative event. A similar point has already been made in the discussion of Truswell (2007) for the examples in (47) above, repeated here for convenience.

(68) a. Who are you prancing *(about) [trying to impress t]?
 b. What did she jump *(around) [singing t]?
 (Truswell 2007: 1361)

I will suggest in Chapter 5 that these examples receive a unified analysis in terms of bounded eventualities that refer to a prominent scalar structure. Scalar structures come in different varieties, for example in incremental themes, property, or interval scales (Rappaport Hovav 2008; Rappaport Hovav & Levin 2010). I illustrate this point with the following examples from Truswell (2011):

(69) a. Which chair did John eat his breakfast sitting on?
 b. Which book did John lie around reading?
 c. What did John wait around sitting on?
 (Truswell 2011: 164–165)

In (69a), *his breakfast* measures out the duration of the event via the incremental theme, and the particle *around* in (69b,c) highlights a temporal scale, which emphasizes the temporary character of the stative predicate. Similarly, *around/about* in (68) add a path scale to the typically unbounded activity (see Levin & Rappaport Hovav 1995; Borgonovo & Neeleman 2000). The grammatical cases of extraction thus appear to depend on the boundedness of the matrix predicate, or at least on reference to a prominent scalar structure. An analysis that treats particles like *around/about* as removing agentivity is thus not the only possible way to explain these cases. Agentivity is certainly involved in these cases, but it may be a technical aspect that is not independently necessary to describe the data pattern. In addition to these cases, a boundedness and scale requirement analysis also has the potential to account for the oddness of punctual matrix predicates like perception verbs and *appear*, as well as the semelfactives in (67). A second requirement could be that the matrix predicate encodes an event that can be construed as involving a scale with more than two points. One way to test this is by applying the progressivity test to Vendler-type achievements, which seems to be compatible with achievements which can be augmented to include more points on a temporal scale than a telic pair, such as punctual predicates and probably also semelfactives. Truswell (2011: 59) acknowledges this distinction between purely punctual point predicates which only encode a culmination, and achievements that can encode an additional preparatory phase. This distinction is considered relevant for rationale clauses and *by*-adjuncts, but not explicitly for the BPPA construction.

Despite certain weak points in the discussion of the acceptability of declarative BPPA constructions and the empirical challenges of the SEGC, most of the points about aspectual classes and the nature of complex events encoded in the BPPA construction seem to be on the right track. Especially the revised Vendlerian aspectual classes that incorporate a distinction among achievement predicates deserves closer attention, as the compatibility of many but not all achievements with the progressive shows. While this issue is not further discussed with respect to extraction, the intuition from Truswell (2007) carries over that punctual achievements which resist the progressive disallow extraction. In continuation of the approach presented in Truswell (2007), this account represents a typical interaction account where declaratives are relatively unconstrained, and the contrasts observed in interrogatives are considered a direct result of extraction. Even if the SEGC can be successfully formulated as a processing condition on the output of extraction, it remains unclear why this condition makes predictions that appear to be opposite to the intuitive pattern, as the examples in (66) and (67) above show. Also, the discussion of (68) shows that, similar to the issues raised with Truswell (2007), agentivity may not be the only possible factor to cover the observed pattern under extraction.

3.3.5 Semantically conditioned feature inactivity (Ernst 2022)

Ernst (2022) integrates the SEGC from Truswell (2011) into a feature-based syntactic account of grammatical extractions from a wide range of adjuncts, cross-linguistic variation, and the possibility of island-repair by sluicing. Ernst (2022) criticizes previous approaches to adjunct islands which categorically ban all extractions from adjuncts for three reasons: they (i) fail to account for the observed extraction asymmetries, (ii) do not explain that sluicing can repair island violations if extraction is blocked in the first place, and (iii) ignore the fundamental properties of adjuncts as peripheral elements (Ernst 2022: 106–109). Accounts that allow some extractions but not others and draw a connection between attachment height and adjunct transparency, such as Narita (2014) or Brown (2017), face similar problems because they do not account for sluicing, and ultimately require some condition like the

SEGC to explain whether an adjunct merges high or low; the focus on attachment height is redundant if the SEGC is independently required (Ernst 2022: 110–111).

Syntactically, adjuncts differ from subcategorized constituents in their lower integration with the main clause; this is captured by a *Unintegration* (UI) feature on the adjunct. This feature leads to the different behavior of adjuncts in Logical Form (LF) and Phonetic Form (PF), where they behave similar to independent clauses. If extraction takes place, the UI feature creates a full chain from the lowest copy of the *wh*-item to the specifier of the adjunct, defined in (70); an additional copy is later made in the left-peripheral specifier of the matrix clause.

(70) When UI is active on a phase head, an A-bar chain link within that phase is realized according to the default for full chains. (Ernst 2022: 115)

The UI feature can be turned inactive at LF and PF, which allows grammatical extractions and explains island-repair by sluicing. Whether UI is active at the interfaces or not is relegated to the event-semantic SEGC. Ernst (2022: 87) adopts Truswell's (2011) definition of the SEGC and its conditions on macro-event formation. As encoded in the SEGC, whether an adjunct is transparent or opaque for extraction does not solely depend on characteristics of one of the predicates, but on the semantic combination of both predicates in context (Ernst 2022: 103). This condition on rendering UI inactive is formulated in (71).

(71) If the SEGC is respected, UI is inactive. (Ernst 2022: 116)

The different behavior of the UI feature at LF is illustrated in (72), where (72a) does not conform to the SEGC because it has two agentive events, and (72b) respects the SEGC.

(72) a. *What did you go home [after you bought __]?
b. What did Carol arrive [whistling __]
(Ernst 2022: 116)

In (72a), the SEGC is not respected, and thus the UI feature survives at LF, where copies of *wh*-items are converted to operators *Op* and the lowest copy to a variable *x*. If UI is active at LF, this leads to the conversion of the *wh*-item in the adjunct phase's specifier to a second operator, seen in (73b). This structure is illegitimate at LF and leads to ungrammaticality, as predicted by the CED. In contrast to the CED, however, extraction is not banned altogether; in this configuration, it simply leads to a crash at LF after it has taken place. The effects observed in Huang (1982) and later formulations of the CED are thus explained in terms of illegitimate LF representations instead of a categorical ban on extraction.

(73) a. **What** did you go home **what** after [UI] you bought **what**
    b. **OP** did you go home **OP** after [UI] you bought **x**
    (adapted from Ernst 2022: 116)

On the other hand, if the SEGC is respected, as in (72b), the intermediate copy of *what* can be deleted and is not converted to a second operator. The derivation along this line is shown in (74):

(74) a. **What** did John arrive **what** PRO [UI] whistling **what**
    b. **OP** did John arrive PRO [UI] whistling **x**
    (adapted from Ernst 2022: 117)

Grammatical extractions from adjuncts are thus explained in terms of a semantic condition like the SEGC that renders a potentially problematic feature inactive at the interface to LF; this avoids illegitimate LF representations but does not block extraction entirely.

The syntactic output of extraction can pose a problem if UI is active at PF. An active UI enforces a copy of the *wh*-item on the phase head of the matrix clause and one on the phase head of the adjunct (75a), which is a problem for linearization because there are two overt copies, resulting in conflicting statements about linear precedence because only the lowest copy of *what* is deleted (75b).

(75) a. **What$_1$** did you go home [$_{PP}$ **what$_2$** after you bought **what$_3$**]?
    b. **What$_1$** did you go home [$_{PP}$ **what$_2$** after you bought ~~**what$_3$**~~]?
    (Ernst 2022: 117)

If the UI feature is inactive at PF, the offending intermediate *wh*-item *what$_2$* in (76a) can be deleted because there is no requirement at PF to keep this copy; see (76b), which is a legitimate PF representation.

(76) a. **What** did John arrive **what** PRO [UI] whistling **what**
    b. **What** did John arrive ~~**what**~~ PRO [UI] whistling ~~**what**~~
    (adapted from Ernst 2022: 118)

This account also incorporates evidence for the possibility of extraction from adjunct islands because they can be repaired by sluicing (Ross 1969; Merchant 2001), seen in the sluiced version (77b) of the ungrammatical (77a).

(77) a. *I don't know what she went home after she bought.
　　b. She went home after she bought something, but I don't know what ~~she went home after she bought~~.
　　　(Ernst 2022: 120)

Following Boeckx (2012), Ernst (2022: 86) assumes that island repair by sluicing is only possible if extraction has occurred and has not been blocked in the syntax. The case of an opaque adjunct in (77a) is ungrammatical in its non-sluiced version because the intermediate copy of the *wh*-item is not deleted at LF; the relevant structure is seen in (78a). Repair of this structure by sluicing is possible even if UI is active at PF because then the spellout of this item is not required.

(78) a. *…know [**what**₁ she went home [ₚₚ **what**₂ after she bought **what**₃]
　　b. …know [**what**₁ ~~she went home [ₚₚ **what**₂ after she bought **what**₃~~]?
　　　(Ernst 2022: 120, strikethrough in b adjusted)

Ernst (2022: 90–91) also points towards the large degree in cross-linguistic variation in the possibility to extract from adjuncts. This variation is linked to language-specific conditions on how macro-events are formed, the strength of the UI feature, as well as the possibility for preposition stranding, which is only available in a small set of languages (Ernst 2022: 102); see also Truswell (2008) for the connection between transparent adjuncts and preposition stranding. The absence of many island effects in languages without overt *wh*-movement in interrogatives fall under the same explanation: in these languages, Ernst (2022: 120–121) argues that the main difference lies in the question which part of the chain is overtly realized, but underlyingly the same principles as in English apply.

　　This account bears resemblance to the syntactic gap-licensing accounts discussed at the beginning of this chapter, but extends these purely structural approaches with the event-semantic condition on the contextual interpretation of the two predicates in the BPPA construction. Ernst (2022: 122) points out that semantic properties also differentiate adverbials in their potential for topichood and result in effects at LF and PF, so that the influence of semantics on syntactic operations is not problematic. The advantage of this proposal is that it is able to capture a large part of the patterns observed for extraction from different adjunct types, repair by sluicing, and cross-linguistic variation. Like many other interaction accounts, Ernst (2022) considers the effects of the SEGC as a condition on extraction. In the light of experimental evidence that not all extraction types result in island effects for adjuncts, such as Kush et al. (2019), Abeillé et al. (2020), and Liu et al. (2022), it remains to be evaluated how well this account is able to incorporate these observations.

112 — 3 Previous approaches to extraction from adjuncts

3.3.6 Spanish gerund complements (París 2003)

The detailed survey of Spanish gerund structures in París (2003) offers a varied range of data points with different verb types combined with a characterization of the relation between main verb and gerund; it also makes observations about subextraction from gerunds that partly overlap with and partially contradict generalizations in the literature on adjunct islands. In the Spanish gerund construction (SGC), a non-finite gerund form appears in the same clause as an inflected verb (79); this is similar to the English BPPA construction (80).[9]

(79) *Todos los estudiantes salieron de la clase llevando un afiche.*
All the students exited from the classroom carrying a flyer
'Every student left the classroom carrying a flyer' (París 2003: 2)

(80) John arrived at the station whistling a song.

París (2003) is not primarily concerned with extraction from this construction, but the possibility of subextraction is used as an argument for the proposal that some gerund constructions in Spanish behave like complements, despite their syntactic optionality. París (2003: 22) subscribes to a CED-perspective in that he considers extraction to be possible only from complement domains; since extraction is possible from some SGCs, they have to be complements. The focus of París (2003) is on the different kinds of relations that hold between the gerund and the main verb, such as common arguments, causal relations, spatio-temporal overlap and information-structural focus–background partitions. In this section, I will focus on the extraction data and their relevance to a formulation of which factors determine whether extraction from a gerund is allowed or not. Notably, París (2003) offers a broad discussion of declarative constructions with gerunds, and shows that the sensitivity to lexical properties of the main verb is not exclusive to interrogatives.

París (2003) develops a typology of gerund modifiers in Spanish that differentiates between their status as complements and adjuncts, as well as between the interpretations they can receive. SGCs that are adjuncts roughly correspond

---

9 The examples in this section are taken directly from París (2003), with minor corrections of obvious spelling errors. The English translation of the examples is not very consistent: some adjuncts are translated as subordinate clauses introduced by subordinators like *while* or *by* and sometimes the linear order of the adjunct and matrix predicate is reversed in both declaratives and interrogatives. This practice is especially interesting because it avoids extraction from the adjunct and rather extracts from the complement of the main verb. Examples of this can be seen in (82), (85b), (86b), (89), and (90).

to absolute and free adjuncts in English. SGCs that are complements are further differentiated by their controller, i.e. the subject or object of the main verb, if there is an object. SGCs that refer to the subject of the main verb come in two varieties that differ in their interpretations, namely Circumstance and Means. Means SGCs have a further subtype that encodes Cause relations. The example in (81a) shows the Circumstance relation, (81b) the Means relation, and (81c) the Cause relation.

(81) a. *Las niñas fueron a Toronto cantando Manuelita todo el viaje.*
 the girls went to Toronto singing Manuelita all the trip
 'The girls went to Toronto singing Manuelita the whole way'
 (París 2003: 6)
 b. *Todos los estudiantes salieron de la clase llevando un afiche.*
 all the students exited from the classroom carrying a flyer
 'Every student left the classroom carrying a flyer' (París 2003: 2)
 c. *Este tipo asustó al niño gritando.*
 this guy scared to-the kid screaming
 'This guy scared the kid by screaming' (París 2003: 5)

These three classes of SGCs have a number of different characteristics: Means gerunds show temporal overlap relations for the two predicates along with the sharing of a subevent that is common to both predicates, whereas Circumstance gerunds only encode a shared spatio-temporal circumstance for a common participant without the sharing of subevents (París 2003: 5–6). There is thus a difference whether the sentence contains two aspects of one event, or two separate events.

Before focusing on the extraction data, I turn to some observations about the grammaticality of gerunds in declaratives. París (2003) gives grammatical examples of gerunds modifying almost all types of matrix predicate: this includes telic achievement and accomplishment predicates, as in (81) as well as atelic activities, as in (82).

(82) *Juan caminó rengueando por el parque.* [activity]
 Juan walked limping in the park
 'Juan was limping while walking in the park' (París 2003: 140)

Stative main verbs are usually degraded with modifying gerunds; individual-level predicates are mostly odd with gerunds (83a), but some cases of stage-level predicates accept the gerund (83b):

(83) a. #*Mi   tío   odia   el   Otoño   barriendo   las   hojas.*   [ILP]
         M[y] uncle hates the Fall   raking   the   leaves
         'M[y] uncle hates Fall while he is raking the leaves'
    b. *El   paciente parecía   triste contando   su   historia.*   [SLP]
         the patient   seemed-IMP   sad   telling   her/his story
         'The patient looked sad while telling his story'
         (París 2003: 99)

Another contrast in declaratives comes from change-of-state predicates that differ in felicity when modified by a gerund. The gerund degrades the structure when the main verb encodes a punctual change, but when the verb encodes a change that progresses gradually along a path component, the gerund is felicitous:

(84) a. #*El   policía   se   cayó   fumando.*   [punctual]
         the   policeman REF   fell   smoking
         'The policeman fell while smoking'
    b. *El   gato   cayó del   segundo piso   aullando.*   [gradual]
         the cat   fell from-the second   floor   howling
         'The cat fell from the second floor howling'
         (París 2003: 101–102)

París (2003: 101–102) proposes that the predicates in the SGC may require not only dynamicity, which rules out ILPs, but also durativity, ruling out inherently punctual predicates. He argues that the difference between reflexive *caerse* 'fall-REF' and non-reflexive *caer* 'fall' is that the latter encodes the totality of the path that is traversed, whereas the former focuses on the punctual nature of the event.[10] This contrast corresponds to the apparent distinction between *appear/arrive* in English, where the path component is lexically accessible only for *arrive* but not for *appear*, possibly because of the different deictic center; Truswell (2007: 1369–1370) also notes this contrast in relation to extraction but does not consider possible effects in declaratives. Despite the differences between English and Spanish, this similarity suggests that durativity may be an independent requirement on participle gerund adjunct constructions.

Turning to the patterns of extraction from the gerund construction, París (2003) observes the general tendency that extraction from gerunds modifying transitive predicates are generally ungrammatical, irrespective of whether the gerund stands in a causal relation to the main verb (85a) or not (85b).

---

[10] This difference is also noted in Fábregas & Jiménez-Fernández (2016a: 1318, fn. 6).

(85) a. *¿Qué sorprendió al   público (el potro) saltando?
         what surprised to-the public (the stallion) jumping-over
         'What did the stallion jump over surprising the spectator?' (intended
         meaning)   (París 2003: 47)
      b. *¿Qué construyó la casa cantando __ ?
         what built   the house singing
         'What did he sing while building the house?'   (París 2003: 49)

For intransitive main verbs, París (2003) proposes that the division between grammatical and ungrammatical extractions from the gerunds is drawn along the lines of the unergative–unaccusative distinction: unaccusatives allow the extraction (86a) but not unergatives (86b). This pattern is similar to that observed for English in Borgonovo & Neeleman (2000), though París (2003: 50–51) notes that reflexivity does not appear to be the relevant factor in Spanish.

(86) a. ¿Qué volvió   Pedro gritando?   [unaccusative]
          what came.back Pedro screaming
          'What did Pedro come back screaming?'   (París 2003: 22)
      b. ?/*¿Qué lloró recitando __ ?   [unergative]
          what cried reciting
          'What did he recite (while) crying?'   (París 2003: 49)

This pattern leads to the hierarchy of extraction from gerunds summarized in (87); crucially, all these verb types allow gerunds in declaratives, meaning that extraction is sensitive to properties of the main verb and affects the verb types to a different degree.

(87) Extraction hierarchy for SGCs:
      achievements > $^?$activities > *accomplishments

The discussion in París (2003) initially suggests that the grammaticality of extraction depends on the type of SGC that differentiates between Cause, Means, and Circumstance relations. As noted above, the three subject-oriented gerunds differ in the strength of the relation that holds between the two predicates. However, as París (2003: 49) points out, not all SGC$_C$ Circumstance allow subextraction from the adjunct. This indicates that the relations between the predicates are independent of transparency. It rather seems that the possibility for extraction is "sensitive to the lexical properties of the (main) verb" (París 2003: 49).

The lexical properties that París (2003) identifies as facilitating extraction from the gerund are (i) intransitivity, (ii) motion, and (iii) telicity (París 2003: 234).

These properties predict that intransitive verbs of inherently direction motion are privileged for extraction, but also that extraction may be possible if not all conditions are met. One of the reasons that extraction is facilitated by these properties is that the gerund can stand in a harmonic relation with the main verb, namely in a description of the manner component of the main verb. The result is a tight semantic connection between the two verbs because the gerund provides further information "about the way in which the Path was traversed" (París 2003: 52).

This leads to the formulation of two additional generalizations about extraction: first, it appears that extraction from the gerund is most acceptable when the semantic roles of the common subject contrast in the two predicates, e.g. if the subject is an UNDERGOER in the main verb and an ACTOR in the gerund (París 2003: 53). This could reduce to a ban on the subject distributing the same θ-role twice, in accordance with an extended version of the θ-criterion.

Second, there is a semantic or information-structural requirement that determines which main verb–gerund constructions qualify as felicitous: the gerund has to be more informative than the main verb in relation to the shared subevent (París 2003: 11, 199). This is exemplified with gerunds modifying motion verbs. Typically, Spanish motion predicates imply a default, unspecified manner of motion, so that it does not have to be mentioned separately; if a specific manner is nonetheless specified, this cancels out the standard implication of a default manner and places the asserted manner of motion in the focus (París 2003: 227–228). See the examples in (88), where the gerund adjunct in (88a) further specifies the manner in which Juan enters his office. In the absence of the gerund, as in (88b), a default, unspecified manner of motion is understood.

(88) a. *Juan entró a su oficina caminando.*
Juan entered to his office walking
'Juan walked into his office'
b. *Juan entró a su oficina.*
Juan entered to his office
'Juan entered his office'
(París 2003: 228)

In terms of Haug et al. (2012), the gerund in (88a) stands in an event specification relation to the main verb, where the manner is not specified; the gerund is thus more informative, which is a prerequisite for focusability. If the gerund carries the highest informational load in the sentence, it acts as the default focus; the default focus structure of a sentence can also be overridden by additional focus marking (París 2003: 199); see also Johnson (2003). The relation of relative information load and the resulting focus structure seems to be fully compatible with a focus theory of extraction along the lines of Erteschik-Shir (1973) or Goldberg (2006, 2013), as well as a semantic–pragmatic approach such as Chaves & Putnam (2020).

Some cases of extraction from the gerund in Spanish do not agree with the data reported for English in Truswell (2007, 2011) and Spanish in Fábregas & Jiménez-Fernández (2016a). For example, there are instances of activity main verbs that still allow extraction from the gerund:

(89) ¿Qué   caminó leyendo __ ?
      what walked reading
      'What did [he] read while walking?'   (París 2003: 51)

These cases are apparently subject to speaker variation (París 2003: 51); a potential contrast that emerges between the ungrammatical cases with activity main verbs as in (86a) and those that allow the extraction for some speakers (89) could be related to the presence or absence of a path component, similar to the distinction between punctual achievements and durative change-of-state verbs in (84).

The example in (90) is potentially problematic for the generalization in Truswell (2007) because it seems to have a telic gerund *romper* 'break'; however, as noted in París (2003: 55), the gerund morphology would cancel the implicature of a culmination with lexically telic predicates and leave the process component, quite similar to the function of the progressive in English (see Kamp & Reyle 1993; van Lambalgen & Hamm 2005; de Swart 2012). However, it is also possible that *romper* 'break' is interpreted as an atelic activity in (90), so there would not be a problem with Truswell's generalization.

(90) ¿Qué   entró   rompiendo Juan?
      what entered breaking   Juan
      'What was Juan breaking coming in?'   (París 2003: 38)

To a large extent, the pattern for extraction from SGC coincides with Truswell's (2007) proposal for English. There are some notable differences, mostly in the behavior of transitive accomplishments, which appear to allow extraction under a causal reading of the adjunct in English but are ungrammatical in Spanish. In important aspects, however, the two accounts make similar predictions, especially for the distinction with intransitives between unergative activities and unaccusative achievements. The similarities in predictions include the generalization that telic main verbs combined with atelic gerunds are most felicitous under extraction (París 2003: 139), which results in the preference for telic intransitive main verbs and the morphological constraints imposed by the gerund morphology.

Despite the differences between English and Spanish, there are several correspondences in the pattern of modification by a non-finite predicate form. París (2003) uses extraction from the gerund as a diagnostic for the complement nature of some gerunds, which is at odds with their syntactic and semantic optionality. The extraction pattern is slightly more restrictive than for English, disallowing extraction from gerunds that are interpreted as causal components of transitive accomplishment predicates. Importantly, there are contrasts in the felicity of gerund modification in Spanish that depend on properties of the main verb. Especially the observation that a gerund adjunct is not possible with all types of main verb is relevant: it shows that there are reasons independent of extraction that have an influence on grammaticality of SGCs. Purely punctual and permanent stative matrix predicates are less compatible with the gerund construction, and not all contrasts are the result of extraction.

3.3.7 Maximal event templates (Fábregas & Jiménez-Fernández 2016a,b)

Fábregas & Jiménez-Fernández (2016a,b), henceforth abbreviated as F&JF, examine extraction from adjunct predicates in Spanish and English. Like París (2003), their focus is on gerund adjuncts in Spanish, the translation equivalent of the English BPPA construction. They argue for an event-structural explanation of an intricate pattern of extraction from such gerunds: gerunds that are semantically integrated into the maximal aspectual structure of a decomposed verbal domain in terms of Ramchand (2008) are transparent, whereas gerunds that cannot be integrated into the aspectual structure of the main verb have to be introduced as adjuncts and disallow extraction, as predicted by the CED. Transparent gerunds do not fall under the CED because they are merged in complement position.

F&JF (2016a) report on a large-scale experimental study with 200 participants which analyzes extraction from gerund adjunct constructions in Spanish. Participants judged question–answer pairs on a 10-point Likert scale; no further details about the number of items and conditions are provided, but it seems that they only tested interrogative conditions without declarative conditions to control for extraction-independent effects of their restrictions. They identify three restrictions on extraction from the gerund: first, the transparency of the adjunct predicate is sensitive to the aspectual class of the main verb. Spanish allows extraction only from gerunds that modify achievement predicates (F&JF 2016a: 1312–1314), as in (91a). Conditions with activities (91b), accomplishments (91c), and states (91d) are significantly less acceptable. This contrasts slightly with English, where extraction is reported to be possible from adjuncts modifying a certain subset of accomplishments, activities, and statives (Truswell 2011).

(91) a. ¿Qué llegó [silbando qué] María? [achievement]
what arrived-3SG whistling María?
'What did María arrive whistling?' (F&JF 2016a: 1308)
b. *¿Qué rodaba [perdiendo qué] el tonel? [activity]
what rolled-3SG losing the barrel?
'What was the barrel rolling down the hill losing?' (F&JF 2016a: 1313)
c. *¿Qué adelgazó [comiendo qué] Juan? [accomplishment]
what slimmed-3SG eating Juan
'What did Juan lose three kilos eating?' (F&JF 2016a: 1312)
d. *¿Qué esperaba leyendo María? [state]
what waited-3SG reading María?
'What did María wait reading?' (F&JF 2016a: 1314)

The second restriction is that the gerund adjunct has to immediately follow the matrix predicate: the subject cannot intervene between the two predicates, seen in (92). Sentences like these are significantly less acceptable than those where the main predicate and the gerund are adjacent, as in (91a).

(92) *¿Qué llegó María [silbando qué]?
what arrived-3SG María whistling
'What did María arrive whistling?' (F&JF 2016a: 1315)

While this condition is confirmed in their experimental study, París (2003) includes examples of transparent gerunds that do not obey it:

(93) ¿Qué volvió Pedro gritando?
what came.back Pedro screaming
'What did Pedro come back screaming?' (París 2003: 22)

F&JF report a moderate effect size in their experimental results, so it is possible that this condition is subject to speaker variation. For Talmy (2000: 224), there is a syntactic difference between the V–gerund–subject and the V–subject–gerund word orders in Spanish: the former word order qualifies for a monoclausal macro-event interpretation where the gerund expresses a satellite. In the latter, the gerund is more likely to be interpreted as a subordinate adverbial clause, which constitutes a separate event; in this case, there is no satellite in the sentence. Speakers may be sensitive to this possible distinction to different degrees.

The third restriction is that Spanish disallows overt result phrases, for example locations, as in (94); this is related to the adjacency requirement for the main predicate and the gerund because the result phrase also intervenes between the two predicates. Such result phrases are unproblematic in English, as seen in (95). This is explained by different characteristics of result phrases in Spanish and English, which depend on the main verb in Spanish but can be independently introduced in English (F&JF 2016a: 1347–1348).

(94) ¿Qué llegó   (*a casa) [silbando qué] (*a casa) María?
      what arrived-3SG to home whistling   to home María
      'What did María arrive (at home) whistling?'   (see F&JF 2016a: 1317)

(95) What did John come home whistling?   (Truswell 2007: 1362)

F&JF (2016a) agree with Demonte (1988) that gerunds only allow subextraction when they modify an internal argument. This is the fourth condition they propose; it is not backed up experimentally due to its uncontroversial status in Spanish (F&JF 2016a: 1318). Demonte (1988) has shown that this condition explains a large part of the pattern found for extraction from depictive secondary predicates, which is only grammatical for OODs and depictives that modify the surface subject of unaccusatives. While this condition holds robustly for Spanish, this point is more controversial in English, where extraction from at least a subclass of predicates modifying external arguments appears possible, e.g. in *What did John drive Mary crazy whistling?*. This difference is not considered in detail in F&JF (2016a) but seems important, as most approaches to transparent adjuncts make largely different predictions about the extraction behavior of transitive accomplishments.

The main goal of F&JF's approach is to derive a syntactic explanation of extraction from gerunds that incorporates the semantic generalizations discussed in Truswell (2007), with which they agree in almost all aspects. As a result, these two approaches have a substantial list of similarities; most importantly, F&JF argue that extraction from gerunds is only possible when they are introduced as one of the semantic heads making up the verbal domain and are thus "in the same verbal structural space as the finite verb" (F&JF 2016a: 1324). This is only possible under specific conditions, which mostly determine how the verbal domain is structured and whether the position required for transparent gerunds is already filled by material that is selected by the main verb. There are obvious parallels with the concept of filling a slot in the event structure of the main verb and single-event groupings in Truswell (2007, 2011). The derivation of the extraction patterns are, however, derived in fundamentally different ways: Truswell (2011) uses a semantic filter that operates on the output of extraction in the syntactic component, whereas F&JF (2016a) only allow extraction to take place from gerunds that are introduced as a specific type of complement and not as adjuncts.

F&JF employ the decompositional approach to the verbal domain in Ramchand (2008) to incorporate event semantic properties into syntactic structure. Ramchand's (2008) approach is based on the idea that a VP can be decomposed into a series of semantic heads which are based on the primitive predicates of decompositional semantic approaches to aspectual classes (e.g. Dowty 1979). Similar frameworks have been proposed, among others, in Ritter & Rosen (1998, 2000), Borer (2005), MacDonald (2008, 2009), and Travis (2010). They share the assumption that event-structural notions such as telicity and durativity are syntactically encoded and thus legible by derivational processes. The verbal domain is decomposed into three main event projections by Ramchand (2008), shown in (96) and visualized in (97):

(96) a. InitP: initiation/causation of an event
b. ProcP: process component
c. ResP: result component
(see Ramchand 2008: 39–40)

(97)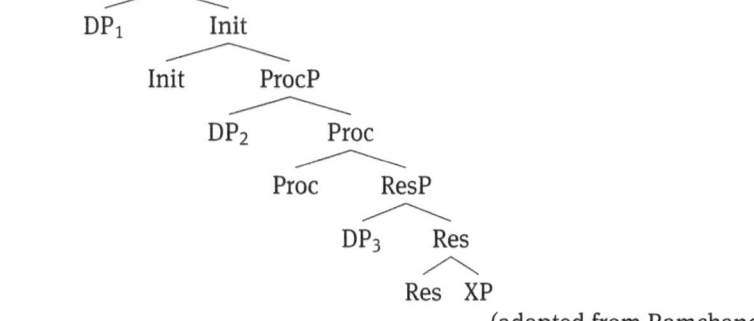

(adapted from Ramchand 2008: 39)

The DP arguments in the specifiers of these projections are interpreted as follows: the specifier DP_1 of InitP acts as the INITIATOR of an event, the specifier DP_2 of ProcP as the UNDERGOER of an event, and the specifier DP_3 of ResP as the RESULTEE argument that is affected by a resulting state; one and the same discourse entity can, but need not, occupy more than one of these specifier positions. Lexical verbs differ in the types of eventive heads they lexicalize: for example, atelic verbs lack a ResP, and non-agentive verbs lack an InitP. ProcP can select a further, optional, head: this is called RhemeP and acts as a modifier of the event in ProcP. The term is not identical to the information-structural *theme–rheme* partitioning, as for example in Halliday (1967b). A Rheme in Ramchand's terms further describes the event introduced by the Proc head and does not introduce a separate event

(Ramchand 2008: 46). Typically, Rhemes are spelled out as path structures, but DPs and adjectival scales can also be used to modify the internal structure of the process component (F&JF 2016a: 1327; Ramchand 2008: 47). F&JF (2016a: 1331–1334) argue that Spanish gerunds such as *gritando* 'screaming' in (93) and the BPPA construction in English can be analyzed as RhemePs: they are interpreted together with the main verb as one verbal structure and not as adjuncts. They thus occupy a position in the event structure of the main verb. This captures the event-semantic generalization from Truswell (2007) syntactically.

The acceptability contrasts for extraction from adjuncts to different types of matrix predicates are explained as follows: if the gerund or BPPA is to be spelled out as RhemeP in the extended verbal domain, then the main verb must lack RhemeP. Otherwise, there is no space for the gerund to integrate into the event structure, which forces projection as a structural adjunct (F&JF 2016a: 1331). The extraction pattern in Spanish is reduced to the fact that achievements are the only aspectual class that do not spell out RhemeP independently. Activities and accomplishments require a RhemeP in the form of a path structure to "define the internal development of the event" (F&JF 2016a: 1331). Statives are assumed to lack ProcP altogether, which means that no RhemeP can be projected (Ramchand 2008: 106); this explains why statives in Spanish do not allow modification by gerunds, not even in declaratives (F&JF 2016a: 1313). The pattern is illustrated in (98) with the four aspectual classes as main verbs and an activity gerund predicate:[11]

(98) a. ¿Qué llegó [silbando __] María? [achievement]
'What did María arrive whistling __ ?'
b. *¿Qué adelgazó [comiendo __] Juan? [accomplishment]
'What did Juan lose weight eating __ ?'
c. *¿Qué corría [escuchando __] María? [activity]
'What did María run listening to __ ?'
d. *¿Qué esperaba [leyendo __] María? [state]
'What did María wait reading __ ?'
(see F&JF 2016a: 1308, 1312–1314)

Accomplishment and activity main verbs by hypothesis already encode a RhemeP because they have to specify the internal structure of the event: losing weight can

---

[11] Note that extraction from the translation equivalent of the state main verb in (98d) is reported to be grammatical in English, which may be explained by the fact that *wait* differs from other states: it can receive a temporally bound interpretation (see Maienborn 2005) and may thus encode a ProcP component. This issue is addressed only briefly because the structural differences between statives are not clear (F&JF 2016a: 1350).

be measured along a property scale of weight in (98b), whereas running necessarily implies a path that is traversed in (98c). As a result, achievements are the only aspectual class that spell out ProcP but not RhemeP, which are thus the only type of main verb that allows extraction from a modifying gerund in Spanish.

Maximal event structures in Ramchand (2008) and F&JF (2016a) are characterized by a sequence of at most three aspectual projections as in (96) above plus the optional RhemeP selected by ProcP. An additional constraint on event structures that are interpretable as single verbal domains is that there can only be one instance of an eventive projection, i.e. at most one ProcP and at most one ResP; see F&JF (2016a: 1324). The double projection of a head violates conditions on maximal event structures and enforces multiple event readings, if the structure can be licensed in the first place. This is captured in the following condition:

(99) For two verbs to integrate in one single syntactic space, the combination of the projections of both constituents must not exceed the maximal structural space of a single verbal event structure. (F&JF 2016a: 1340)

This condition has obvious similarities to Truswell's (2007) generalization that the adjunct predicate in a BPPA construction has to fill an empty position in the event structure of the matrix predicate and that the resulting event structure has to mirror that of a lexical verb. The major difference is that F&JF provide a fully structural explanation for the transparency differences they observe in Spanish.

When the main verb does not spell out RhemeP and the other conditions are met as well, the gerund constituent occupies a position in the tree structure that is not classified as an adjunct. Despite the similarity of minimal pairs that differ only in the choice of the main verb, the differences in event structure result in distinct structural analyses. In many cases, this seems unintuitive and requires justification. There is a long tradition of incorporating insights from aspectual properties into the structural configuration of the sentence and when two verbs differ in their event-structural properties, it is not unthinkable that they also differ in their syntactic configuration; see Ritter & Rosen (1998, 2000), Borer (2005), and Travis (2010). One question concerning this issue that is not discussed in F&JF (2016a) is whether the projection of the gerund as either Rheme or an adjunct might also have observable effects in declaratives. The only relevant contrast is discussed for stative main verbs, which do not accept gerunds at all in Spanish. For the remaining verb types, no relative differences in grammaticality are reported for declaratives.

This approach is based on the assumption that there are syntactic correlates of event structure in the form of dedicated projections for the individual subevents of a complex event, such as initiation and result. A clear empirical advantage is that the transparency or opacity of a gerund predicate can be explained in terms of its status either as part of the complex event in RhemeP or as a structural adjunct. Despite the fact that the gerund is an optional constituent, this does not entail that it is a structural adjunct. Whether a gerund qualifies as a Rheme or structural adjunct is determined by the event-structural properties of the main verb and its lexical semantics, for example the question whether RhemeP is already encoded in the meaning of the main verb.

As an explanation for the restriction on overt result phrases with achievement verbs as in (100), F&JF propose that the ResP hosting such phrases is not projected in these cases (F&JF 2016a: 1347–1348). Even if it were projected, the gerund in the RhemeP would intervene between the ProcP and the ResP, preventing the association of the main verb with this projection because this process is only possible for adjacent projections. In English, result phrases as in (101) are allowed because they are licensed independently of the main verb, similar to resultative secondary predicates (F&JF 2016a: 1347).

(100) *¿Qué llegaste [silbando qué] a casa?
what arrived-2SG whistling to home
'What did you arrive home whistling?' (F&JF 2016a: 1347)

(101) What did John arrive home whistling __ ?

While the predictions following from this approach are relatively clear for the Spanish extraction data, it is less clear if they carry over to English. One of the major differences between English and Spanish is that English allows some extractions from adjuncts modifying accomplishments, which is impossible in Spanish. F&JF (2016a: 1350) explain this with the different structural layout of the gerund phrase in the two languages: in English, the gerund is an NP, whereas it is a PathP in Spanish. By hypothesis, the causing component in an accomplishment predicate is realized by a SOURCE preposition. The English gerund is not already headed by a preposition, so it can function as SOURCE; the same is not possible in Spanish because the gerund cannot be headed by two prepositions.

A second issue arises with the examples of extraction from adjuncts modifying certain statives and activities in English, as in (102).

(102) a. What did John lie around [reading __] all day?
b. What was John walking about [whistling __]?
(Truswell 2011: 156)

The problem with statives as in (102a) is difficult to accommodate in Spanish because gerunds modifying states are not permitted according to F&JF (2016a: 1313–1314). Apparently, the distinction between temporary and permanent states does not make a difference here: neither the permanent state verb *odiar* 'hate' nor the temporary state verb *esperar* 'wait' allow modification by a gerund. París (2003: 98–99) disagrees with this judgment and considers modification of statives by gerunds possible if the stative verb has a dynamic component, i.e. if it is a stage-level instead of an individual-level predicate (Carlson 1977). It is unclear what could explain the apparently grammatical extraction in (102b) because the activity predicate *walk* would need to spell out a path RhemeP, which may actually be realized by *about* in this case; it is thus unclear how the adjunct could be introduced as Rheme if this projection is already projected by the main verb and potentially occupied. However, as the data for English are not yet supported by experimental investigations, this point is difficult to assess and deserves further investigation.

The account presented in F&JF (2016a) offers a detailed description of extraction from gerunds in Spanish, including several new data patterns. Their experimental investigation reveals constraints on extraction from gerunds in Spanish that are similar to those proposed for English in Truswell (2007): the aspectual class of the matrix predicate is an important factor, but not the only one. Adjacency in linear order and the absence of constituents that spell out a RhemeP are further conditions. A problem with this account is that the cross-linguistic comparison between Spanish and English requires additional assumptions that are at times difficult to assess because a limited toolkit of syntactic tests is available for these contrasts. Many of the contrasts between these two languages are in areas where the empirical data on English is largely confined to intuitive judgments; this includes the modification of stative main verbs and transitive verbs in English. Especially transitives are a crucial verb class because they yield experimental judgments (see Brown 2017; Kohrt et al. 2018) that are not fully compatible with the data reported in Truswell (2007, 2011) or Borgonovo & Neeleman (2000).

3.3.8 Pragmatic conditions on extraction (Chaves & Putnam 2020)

In addition to the syntactic and semantic interaction accounts discussed so far, there are also approaches which draw a connection between the possibility of extraction and the pragmatic or information-structural status of the extraction domain. The empirical coverage of such accounts applies to extraction operations in general and is not specific to a single island type. Examples for such general extraction constraints in information-structural and pragmatic terms are found, among others, in Erteschik-Shir (1973) and Erteschik-Shir & Lappin (1979), who restrict extraction to "dominant" constituents; see (103).

(103) Extraction can only occur out of clauses or phrases which can be considered dominant in some context. (Erteschik-Shir 1973: 27)

In information-structural terms, a constituent can be considered dominant when it is in the potential focus domain of the sentence (Erteschik-Shir 1973, 2007). Goldberg (2006, 2013) similarly argues that constituents which are neither part of the primary topic nor the focus domain of the sentence cannot be extracted because they are backgrounded, which corresponds to a lack of dominance in Erteschik-Shir (1973) and Erteschik-Shir & Lappin (1979). Proposals in a similar direction are made in Van Valin (2005: 277), who proposes that extraction is only possible if the extracted constituent can be interpreted as part of the focus domain of the sentence, as well as Matić (2014), who argues that the possibility to extract from an adjunct depends on the "questionability of certain clausal elements, their potential for interrogative interpretation" (Matić 2014: 130). Since adjuncts are often presupposed, they count as backgrounded and resist extraction (Goldberg 2013). In the light of the acceptability patterns for adjunct islands reported in the literature, specifically the BPPA construction, this opens up the question whether there are construction-internal differences in whether the adjunct counts as backgrounded or dominant.

In a broad survey of unbounded dependency constructions (UDCs) and different island types, Chaves & Putnam (2020) propose that the majority of island effects, including acceptability differences within specific island configurations, can be explained in general semantic–pragmatic terms centering around Kuno's (1987) topichood condition, which is given in (104):

(104) *Topichood Condition for Extraction:*
Only those constituents in a sentence that qualify as the topic of the sentence can undergo extraction processes (i.e., *Wh*-Q Movement, *Wh*-Relative Movement, Topicalization, and *It*-Clefting). (Kuno 1987: 23)

With few exceptions, such as the Left Branch Condition or factive islands, the majority of island domains can be captured by semantic–pragmatic relevance criteria and are grouped together as *Relevance Islands* in Chaves & Putnam (2020); they share the common condition that only material can be extracted which is "sufficiently relevant to the main action that the utterance describes" (Chaves & Putnam 2020: 203). Chaves & Putnam (2020: 63) understand "relevance" in terms of Lambrecht (1994: 53), who defines the relevant constituent of an utterance as the "center of current interest"; this roughly corresponds to the concepts of topic in Kuno (1987), dominant constituents in Erteschik-Shir (1973) and Erteschik-Shir & Lappin (1979), salience in Deane (1991), as well as non-backgrounded constituents in Goldberg (2006, 2013). Relevance is thus an information-structural notion which relates to the contribution of information in a given utterance and the way this information is distributed across the utterance; see also Chafe's (1976) concept of "information packaging". The question is how it is determined whether a constituent counts as relevant in a given context.

Chaves & Putnam (2020: 204–206) argue that verbs activate specific sets of entities that are relevant for the event and that the relevance of a constituent is determined by the general world knowledge about the participants in that event. Following Deane (1992), this set of world knowledge is called a "frame". Schank & Abelson (1977) use the similar concept of "scripts" to describe the knowledge background that is activated by the use of verbs. For example, the verb *read* activates an entity doing the reading as well as something that is being read. The arguments which are syntactically required by the use of a given verb are activated by default, but non-core arguments can also be activated. Based on this concept of frames, Chaves & Putnam (2020) define salience or relevance relative to the verb as follows:

(105) Event participant salience condition:
event participants that are part of the conventionalized world knowledge directly or indirectly evoked by the main action that the sentence describes are salient and, by definition, relevant for the utterance (though not necessarily equally relevant). (Chaves & Putnam 2020: 206)

This definition cuts across the argument–adjunct distinction because adjunct constituents and other syntactically non-obligatory elements can also contribute information that is relevant for the utterance (Chaves & Putnam 2020: 35–36); take for example goal phrases of motion verbs, which are syntactically optional but indirectly evoked by a verb like *walk*.

The salience of an event participant in the frame evoked by a verb has pragmatic effects when a sentence is used in a specific discourse context, especially if it instantiates a non-canonical structure such as an interrogative. These pragmatic effects can affect acceptability if there is a mismatch between sentence form and the information-structural status of the extractee; see also Abeillé et al. (2020). As each utterance is intended to contribute to the discourse, its content has to be relevant to the preceding context and connect to it in a meaningful way; see Roberts (1996) and Stalnaker (2002, 2014). As non-canonical and partially non-assertive syntactic structures, UDCs fulfill more specific communicative functions than declaratives:

they draw the attention of the addressee towards a specific event participant. This can take the form of an information-seeking *wh*-phrase in an interrogative, but also a highlighted constituent as in topicalization and extraposition. Based on the definition of relevance in terms of activation in a background frame, Chaves & Putnam (2020) formulate the following pragmatic condition on extraction:

(106) Relevance presupposition condition:
the referent that is singled out for extraction in a UDC must be highly relevant (e.g. part of the evoked conventionalized world knowledge) relative to the main action that the sentence describes. Otherwise, extraction makes no sense from a Gricean perspective, as there is no reason for the speaker to draw attention to a referent that is irrelevant for the main contribution of the sentence to the discourse.　　　　(Chaves & Putnam 2020: 206)

Failure to meet the condition in (106) results in violations of Grice's (1975) Maxims of Quantity and Manner. If a comparatively unimportant constituent is targeted by extraction, the relevance of the utterance to the discourse is not clear because there is a mismatch between the pragmatic function of the UDC and the information-structural status of the targeted constituent. It is seen as a pragmatically infelicitous discourse move to draw the addressee's attention to a referent that is not relevant for the purpose of the utterance (Chaves & Putnam 2020: 62); see also Van Valin (2005: 288) for a similar argument. This pragmatic condition on the felicity of UDCs connects the lexical semantics of a verb and the expectations about the event described in a verb to the way a sentence contributes to the discourse situation: lexical semantics and the event participants evoked in the background frame can be seen as factors which determine the relevance of individual event participants.[12]

Effects of relevance as formulated in (105) are not exclusive to the relevance condition on UDCs in (106). However, the effects differ in their impact on sentence acceptability. Simple declarative sentences which introduce an entity that is neither directly nor indirectly evoked by the semantic frame of the main verb do not suffer acceptability differences, but are rather subject to pragmatic infelicity. They pose problems from a Gricean relevance perspective because irrelevant information is supplied. Consider the pair in (107), which do not seem to show clear acceptability contrasts, but differ in their pragmatic felicity (indicated by the '#' judgment).

---

[12] Jin (2015) goes in a similar direction by linking the transparency of adverbial clauses to the type of discourse coherence relation (Kehler 2002, 2019; Van Valin 2005) holding between the main clause and the adverbial clause. Jin (2015) argues that extraction from MANNER and CAUSE adverbial clauses is more acceptable from adverbial clauses establishing a PARALLEL relation. For reasons of space, I do not discuss this approach in detail.

(107) a. I read a book about chemistry.
    b. #I dropped a book about chemistry.
        (Chaves & Putnam 2020: 207, judgment added)

Chaves & Putnam (2020: 205–207) argue that the topic of the book is indirectly evoked by general world knowledge about reading events, but not for dropping events.[13] Thus, it is pragmatically felicitous to refer to the topic of the book in a reading event, but not a dropping event. Even in the absence of extraction, specific constructions are sensitive to relevance and show different degrees of acceptability, even if the difference may not be too strong. In (108), for example, the preposing of a plausible book topic is more acceptable when a topic is evoked by the main verb; see also Kuno (1987: 121).

(108) a. Speaking of Napoleon, I just read a book about him.
    b. ?Speaking of Napoleon, I just dropped a book about him.
        (Chaves & Putnam 2020: 205)

In extraction sentences such as (109), a failure to meet the relevance condition in (106) leads to a sharp acceptability contrast. If the element targeted for extraction is not relevant for the event denoted in the main predicate, it resists extraction; the contrast in (109) and the relation to relevance are also noted in Cattell (1976: 39–40).

(109) a. What did you read a book about?
    b. *What did you drop a book about?
        (Chaves & Putnam 2020: 207)

The assumption behind the patterns in (107)–(109) is that differences in pragmatic felicity can have effects on acceptability in UDCs, whereas there are no clear acceptability differences in the absence of a dependency. This is similar to the telicity and agentivity approaches in Truswell (2007, 2011), who also diagnoses different event-semantic interpretations which are present in declaratives but only have an effect on acceptability in interrogatives.

For adjunct islands, mainly adverbial clauses, Chaves & Putnam (2020) propose that typical examples such as (110a) are unacceptable because there is no obvious connection between the two events; hence, the adjunct constituent does not contribute relevant information to the event described in the main verb and

---

[13] The book's topic is activated only indirectly because not all things that qualify for reading center around a specific topic. The activation chain is as follows: *read* → information source → topic.

constitutes not-at-issue content, which does not allow extraction. Nothing in the background frame of watching TV activates a phone call, so the two events are conceptualized as separate, even though they occur simultaneously; see Truswell (2011) for similar arguments. Importantly, the sentence is grammatical as a yes–no question (110b), and the corresponding declarative should be unproblematic as well (Chaves & Putnam 2020: 86).

(110)   a.   *[Who]$_i$ did Susan watch TV [while talking to __$_i$ on the phone]?
        b.   Did Susan watch TV while talking to Kim on the phone?
            (Chaves & Putnam 2020: 86)

In acceptable extractions from adjuncts, the adjunct contributes relevant information for the main verb and can be a target for extraction; see (111), originally from Truswell (2011: 175, fn. 1), where the adjunct contributes information about what caused the event in the main verb. An event of getting upset typically activates a circumstance or event that is interpreted as the cause, and thus the event in the adverbial clause is indirectly activated.

(111)   This is the watch$_i$ that I got upset when I lost __$_i$.
                                                     (Chaves & Putnam 2020: 87)

This example is especially problematic for Truswell's (2011) account based on event groupings because the independent tense-marking on the adjunct should preclude the formation of an event grouping (Chaves & Putnam 2020: 87). The contrast between the examples in (110a) and (111) raises the question under which conditions an adjunct describes relevant information, and whether this is only possible for adjuncts that can be interpreted as the causal component of the event encoded in the matrix predicate. The second question is easily answered to the negative, as there are other types of adjuncts which are reported to allow extraction, such as those in (112). Here the adjunct provides information that is syntactically optional but seems to carry relevant information, as the absence of the adjunct leads to pragmatically odd or uninformative sentences; see (113) and the discussion of these examples in Sheehan (2013).

(112)   a.   Which room does Julius teach his class [in __]?
                                                     (Pollard & Sag 1994: 191)
        b.   What temperature should I [wash my jeans [at __]]?   (Chaves 2013: 292)

(113)   a.   Julius teaches his class #(in room 304).
        b.   I wash my jeans #(at 40 °C).

These examples show that adjuncts can encode information that is at the center of attention, and that the adjunct need not encode a causal component. The Relevance Presupposition Condition in (106) thus accounts for cases like (111), where the adjunct bears a clear causal relation to the main verb, and cases such as (112), where the adjunct provides other relevant information. It is more difficult, however, to account for the reported acceptability of examples like (114), where the adjunct encodes information that has no clear connection to the main verb and should thus be circumstantial not-at-issue information that resists extraction.

(114)   What did John arrive whistling __ ?   (Borgonovo & Neeleman 2000: 200)

Chaves & Putnam (2020) do not discuss examples like these, but their relevance condition can be applied as follows. Since the constituent from which extraction takes places has to be highly relevant "relative to the main action", informationally light main verbs facilitate extraction; this is the bridge-verb phenomenon which is also discussed for other island types (Chaves & Putnam 2020: 92). If achievement verbs like *arrive* are informationally lighter than verbs with agentive subjects because they are semantically more abstract than activities or accomplishments, then this informativity asymmetry can rule in extractions like (114) because the adjunct carries more information weight than the matrix predicate and is thus more informative from a pragmatic perspective; see Chaves & Putnam (2020: 81).

It should be pointed out that (114) may still not be the ideal question to obtain the requested information, as there are interrogatives which have the same assertive content *{John arrived}* and evoke the same alternative set *{What did John whistle?}*, namely the interrogative in (115).

(115)   What did John whistle __ when he arrived?

From this perspective of alternative, non-island-violating interrogatives, it should be expected that sentences like (114) will always be degraded compared to sentences such as (115); the latter always conforms to the Relevance Presupposition Condition because the target of movement is the complement of the main clause, whereas in the former, the extraction can only be pragmatically felicitous if the main verb is considered to be backgrounded.

Following experiments in Chaves & Dery (2019), Chaves & Putnam (2020) report on experiments investigating extraction from subject NPs and clausal subjects, subextraction from objects, as well as non-finite and different types of finite adverbials. Examples for their adverbial experiments are given in (116).

(116) a. Just a few years ago, Mosul was a city which terrorists would have thought twice before attacking. [untensed adverbial]
b. Who did Sue blush when/because/if she saw? [tensed adverbials]
(Chaves & Putnam 2020: 230, 236)

The main experimental results are two-fold: first, there is evidence that acceptability of island-violating extractions increases with enough repeated exposure, so that in some cases there remain no significant differences to non-island-violating control conditions at the end of the experiment; second, the acceptability of extraction shows considerable variation within individual island types. Specifically for untensed adverbials as in (116a), they observe that acceptability of island-violating conditions increases with a significant number of exposures, whereas non-island-violating conditions do not improve. For different types of tensed adverbials as in (116b), the results are especially interesting because of the considerable variation in acceptability for individual items, and the fact that acceptability of interrogatives is not predicted by acceptability in the corresponding declaratives (Chaves & Putnam 2020: 237). The relevance of the adverbial for the main verb's background frame depends on the type of adverbial, for example temporal, causal, and conditional adverbials in (116b); conditional adverbials received more favorable judgments than temporal adverbials, which in turn are more acceptable than causal adverbials.[14] The experimental results are consistent with their overall conclusion that extraction from adverbials is "contingent on the proposition itself, rather than strictly on its syntax" (Chaves & Putnam 2020: 230): different types of adjunct constituents show different degrees of relevance for the main event and thus react differently to extraction.

I see two unresolved issues of this approach. First, there is the question whether the differences in declaratives are really simply related to pragmatic felicity or whether they have subtle effects on acceptability. From the discussion, it is not immediately clear whether Chaves & Putnam (2020) can be classified as an interaction account. Their formulation of the Relevance Presupposition Condition in (106) suggests that acceptability is only affected under extraction, and they claim that "extractability ... is contingent on the proposition itself" (Chaves & Putnam 2020: 230). Similar to approaches like Erteschik-Shir (1973) or Goldberg (2006), the focus is on the pragmatic and information-structural prerequisites on the acceptability of a non-canonical sentence structure, rather than on the relation between pragmatic felicity and acceptability in declaratives without a UDC. This

---

[14] The low acceptability of causal adverbials is surprising because a causal component would be expected to constitute relevant information; similar results are, however, reported in C. Müller (2017, 2019).

suggests that the effect of relevance and the resulting pragmatic felicity affects acceptability to different degrees, as also seen in the examples in (107)–(109) above: there are only pragmatic felicity differences in equally acceptable declaratives, but in non-canonical sentences such as the *speaking of* topic construction, differences in felicity result in acceptability differences, which are more pronounced in the non-canonical interrogative UDC.[15]

Second, there are acceptability contrasts for different verb types that fail to activate the event participants of the adjunct predicate. The concept of background frame activation offers a reasonable explanation for BPPA constructions which encode a causal relation between the two predicates, as the cause can be indirectly activated by the frame of the matrix predicate. However, it is not clear how to account for the different acceptability patterns for BPPA constructions where the adjunct does not stand in a causal relation to the matrix predicate; this should mean that the adjunct's arguments are not activated and thus cannot be extracted. This is problematic for the acceptability contrast in (117), where the adjunct does not seem to be activated by the background frame of either matrix predicate.

(117) a. *What did John walk whistling __ ?
       b. What did John arrive whistling __ ?

In both cases, the adjunct stands in an indirect relation to the event of the matrix predicate, which can be formulated as *And what else did John do when he walked/arrived?*. There is, however, an important contrast in these examples: in (117a), John is the AGENT of both predicates, whereas in (117b), he is a THEME for the matrix predicate and an AGENT for the adjunct predicate. As argued in Chaves & Putnam

---

15 An anonymous reviewer likewise raises the question whether the approach in Chaves & Putnam (2020) really qualifies as an interaction account. I agree with the reviewer that the influence of pragmatic effects in their model are less interactional in nature than is the case with the other accounts discussed in this section because they are also operative in declaratives; the formulation of UDCs in a non-movement based framework and the more general discourse-pragmatic Gricean relevance effects are to a certain degree independent. In contrast to the other interaction accounts in this section, their extraction condition seems to fall more on the performance side than on competence in terms of Chomsky (1965). The main reason that I have chosen to classify Chaves & Putnam (2020) as an interaction account is based on two points: (i) their explicit formulation of the Relevance Presupposition Condition as a pragmatic condition on extractability, which fits the definition of interaction accounts assumed in this chapter, and (ii) their argument that acceptability differences are only attested in UDCs but are absent in declaratives, where minimal pairs may differ in pragmatic felicity but are still considered to be highly acceptable (cf. their discussion of the sentence pair *Kayla booked/cancelled a trip to Paris*; Chaves & Putnam 2020: 207). These diverging effects of pragmatic felicity on acceptability in different sentence forms fit minimally better with the definition of interaction accounts in this chapter than with independence accounts.

(2020: 206), AGENTS constitute more relevant event participants than THEMES/ PATIENTS, which are in turn more relevant than non-core components such as MANNER or TIME (see also Chaves & Putnam 2020: 81). It could be argued that the agentive adjunct constitutes the more relevant information in the sentence when the matrix predicate is non-agentive, whereas there is a relevance competition when both are agentive. This is related to the discussion of agentivity effects in Truswell (2011).

Chaves & Putnam (2020) provide a unified approach to almost all island constructions, centering around the pragmatic concept of relevance. The reliance on generalized world knowledge in the form of event participants which are activated by a verb's background frame can be seen either as an unspecified and murky intervening variable, or as a principled approach to the large degree of lexical variability and speaker variation. The strongest point in their account is that extractability can be reduced to the communicative function of UDCs, which fail to conform to Gricean maxims if a constituent with low relevance is targeted for extraction. In contrast to many other interaction accounts, it is not postulated that the extraction operation is limited by non-syntactic factors and unacceptable for this reason, but rather that the result of extraction may simply turn out to be so pragmatically infelicitous that it becomes unacceptable. This is immediately related to accounts which explain acceptability differences of extraction in terms of coherence relations between the two predicates, which are discussed in the following section. Capturing the island-internal variation of the BPPA construction along these lines is a tempting avenue for further research.

3.3.9 Coherence and extraction from adverbial clauses (C. Müller 2019)

The Scandinavian languages have the tendency to be more liberal with extraction from constituents that typically resist extraction in other languages (see Engdahl 1980; Sprouse & Hornstein 2013). C. Müller (2017, 2019) investigates extractions from different types of adverbial clauses in Swedish and English; she proposes that the transparency of the adverbial clause depends on three factors: (i) the degree of semantic coherence between the adverbial and the host clauses; (ii) the degree of syntactic integration of the adverbial clause; (iii) the grammatical function as argument or adjunct of the extractee (C. Müller 2019: 104). The degree of semantic coherence is operationalized as a causal relation between the adverbial clause and the main verb; the less coherent relation is a simple temporal succession relation. Syntactic integration of the adverbial clause is modeled as the distinction between central adverbial clauses (CACs) and peripheral adverbial clauses (PACs) in terms of Haegeman (2010, 2012), which are considered to be attached to different levels of the structure: CP for PACs and TP or *v*P for CACs. A central hypothesis is that extraction from event-modifying CACs is more acceptable than extraction from discourse-structuring PACs. C. Müller (2019: 123) also finds an area of crosslinguistic variation: Swedish is insensitive to the finiteness of the adverbial clause, whereas English shows an effect in the coherent conditions.

C. Müller's (2019) conclusions are based on a set of four experiments on extraction from adverbial clauses, two for Swedish and two for English. An informal grammaticality judgment experiment on extraction from adverbial clauses in Swedish, originally from C. Müller (2017), reveals that there are acceptability contrasts between the different types of adverbial clauses. She compares extractions from a variety of CACs and PACs configurations, including purpose clauses, temporal, conditional, result, as well as causal adverbial clauses, which can for the most part be either analyzed exclusively as CAC or PAC; only conditional and causal adverbial clauses have both structural realizations. Contrary to her predictions, these contrasts cannot be reduced to differences in the degree of syntactic integration along the CAC–PAC distinction, or semantic integration in terms of coherence: for example, causal adverbial clauses yield very low ratings despite being classified as CAC. C. Müller (2017: 78–80) explains this with the more complex syntax of these clauses in Swedish, which increase difficulty for extraction.

Two formal acceptability studies examine the factors COHERENCE and FINITENESS in Swedish and English; a causal relation between adjunct and matrix predicate is considered a coherent relation, whereas a non-causal temporal relation is considered non-coherent. It has to be noted that COHERENCE is implemented as the distinction between telic and atelic matrix predicates; it is thus difficult to judge whether there are clear coherence effects or whether these contrasts can be reduced to telicity. The sample item in (118) shows the experimental design for the English experiment; the items for Swedish are translation equivalents (C. Müller 2019: 114). The COHERENT conditions include main verbs such as *almost stumble*, where the adverbial clause can establish a causal relation; NON-COHERENT conditions with verbs such as *stroll a little* have no such connection and describe causally unconnected event. FINITENESS in the adverbial clause is modeled as a tensed verb and a present participle.

(118) Which beer did he { almost stumble / stroll a little } after { chugging / he chugged } ?

(C. Müller 2019: 121)

In both experiments, coherent conditions are judged as more acceptable than non-coherent conditions. However, Swedish and English behave differently with respect to the factor FINITENESS: Swedish does not show a significant effect of this factor, and also no interaction with COHERENCE (C. Müller 2019: 118–119). For English, both factors show significant main effects and a significant interaction: only coherent conditions are negatively affected by finiteness, but not the non-coherent conditions, which are both equally less acceptable than coherent conditions (C. Müller 2019: 124). In a reading time experiment on English, C. Müller (2019: 172–173) also finds that coherent relations with telic intransitives have a positive effect on reading times compared to non-coherent relations with atelic intransitives.

Some aspects of these experiments deserve closer attention. For example, a comparison of the extraction conditions with declaratives is not made in the experiments, which does not allow conclusions about how strongly degraded the extractions are or whether the coherent condition is less strongly affected by extraction than the non-coherent one. C. Müller (2019: 115) notes that all declarative conditions for the Swedish experiment were considered acceptable by two native speakers, so it is possible that there are no observable differences in the declarative conditions. There is, however, the possibility that both coherence and finiteness may be factors that are independent of extraction (C. Müller 2019: 173). For the extraction conditions, the judgments in the controlled rating studies are in general quite low and do not reach the middle of the 7-point Likert scale.

It is not clear if these two experiments actually test for a coherence contrast. As seen in the example from the English experimental items in (118), this contrast is operationalized by different aspectual classes of the matrix predicate: achievement matrix predicates induce a strongly coherent causal reading, whereas activity matrix predicates only show a temporal relation, which is less strongly coherent than causality (see also Kehler 2019). She assumes that the availability of a causal reading is modulated by the choice of matrix predicate (C. Müller 2019: 114–115), but this contrast could also be related to other factors, such as the syntactic structure of achievements compared to activity predicates (Perlmutter 1978; Levin & Rappaport Hovav 1995). Manipulating one factor without also affecting another one is a difficult matter, especially when it concerns aspects of a verb's meaning. The same applies in the opposite direction: changes in verb type often also affect the coherence relation between the predicates.

It is unclear whether the contrast observed for coherent and non-coherent conditions depends only on the presence or absence of a causal coherence relation or the type of matrix predicate. A closer look at the data reported in the literature suggests that coherence relations may not be able to account for all contrasts. Consider the data in (119) for English participle adjuncts.

(119)   a.   What did John drive Mary crazy whistling __ ?   [causal]
          b.   What did John arrive at the station whistling __ ?   [non-causal]

c. *What does John dance whistling __ ? [non-causal]
     (see Truswell 2007: 1357)

The sentence in (119a) implies a causal relation between the adjunct and the matrix predicate, the other two examples do not allow a causal interpretation. In terms of Hobbs (1990), the causal relation in (119a) can be classified as an Explanation relation because the adjunct provides a cause for the event described in the matrix clause. The relations in (119b,c) are better analyzed as Elaboration or Parallel relations (see Kehler 2019: 600). However, the grammaticality contrast does not depend on the presence or absence of a causal relation; rather, the contrast is drawn along the line of the aspectual class of the matrix predicate. It is true that matrix predicates with different aspectual classes already anticipate whether a possible adjunct stands in a strongly coherent relation with the matrix predicate or not. Verbs with a complex argument structure, such as accomplishments, have more potential slots than unergatives or unaccusatives.

The conclusions drawn from the experimental results are that (i) the tightness of syntactic integration matters: CACs behave more like weak islands, whereas PACs remain strong islands (C. Müller 2019: 190, 195); (ii) extractions from weak CAC islands can deteriorate when they violate interface conditions such as coherence (C. Müller 2019: 193). C. Müller (2019) proposes to extend the definition of weak islands to account for her experimental data. Traditionally, weak islands are defined based on the type of element that can be extracted (Cinque 1990; Abrusán 2014; Szabolcsi & Lohndal 2017); in an extended definition of weak islands, grammaticality is not only based on properties of the extractee, but also on properties of the domain from which extraction takes place (C. Müller 2019: 190). This definition also allows properties such as finiteness of the adjunct and the coherence relation between the two predicates to have an influence on the grammaticality of extraction. The result is a composite approach to the different degrees of observed grammaticality. For example, PACs can still be considered strong islands because they hardly allow extraction from an adjunct. CACs, on the other hand, are more liberal and sensitive to features such as finiteness and the coherence relation holding between the adjunct and the matrix predicate.

A remaining question concerning the theoretical conclusions in C. Müller (2019) is whether the coherence and aspectual class differences that she finds in her experiments are unique to extraction or whether they can be traced back to the declarative counterparts. As such, it is difficult to evaluate this account in relation to the interaction–independence discussion; the problem is mentioned but not fully addressed in C. Müller (2019: 173).

3.3.10 Interim conclusion

All accounts in this section share the fundamental assumption that the grammaticality of extraction from an adjunct depends on a factor that shows no effect or at most a much weaker effect in the corresponding declaratives. The factors identified in these approaches are located in different components of the grammar: the argument structure of the embedding verb, the event-semantics of the adjunct construction, as well as the information-structural status of the two predicates. From a conservative generative perspective, the grammaticality of syntactic operations like extraction should be blind to non-structural factors; this presents a problem for the semantic and information-structural approaches in this section because these factors should not have an effect on the application of extraction. If factors like these do have an effect on extraction, then semantics and/or information structure interact with the syntactic component in a way that is not accounted for in a narrow syntactic theory. The syntactic interaction account presented in Borgonovo & Neeleman (2000) can at least be reduced to structural factors without the need for such an interaction with other components of the grammar. These architectural considerations lead Brown (2017) to propose an alternative approach to extraction from adjuncts that maintains the separation of syntax and semantics, and that accounts for a wider range of acceptability contrasts in both declarative and interrogative adjunct constructions.

3.4 An independence approach (Brown 2017)

This last section discusses an approach to extraction from adjuncts which differs fundamentally from the interaction accounts in the previous section. The main claim in Brown (2017) is that acceptability contrasts in interrogative adjunct constructions are the result of two different mechanisms: (i) the syntactic licensing of the adjunct-internal gap; and (ii) the semantic licensing of the adjunct in its merge position (Brown 2017: 63). Brown thus combines elements of gap-licensing accounts with non-structural factors that affect acceptability independently of extraction. As a result of this division of labor between semantic licensing and syntactic locality operations, the latter do not need to be sensitive to properties of the former, which are independently operative in interrogatives and declaratives (Brown 2017: 73). I have formulated this claim as the Independence Hypothesis in the introduction to this chapter (see p. 66): extraction is not sensitive to factors such as transitivity or telicity of the matrix predicate, but these factors determine how acceptable the declarative counterparts are because they invoke different licensing mechanisms when the adjunct is merged. For example, the observation that

(120a) is more acceptable than (120b) is related to the fact that a similar contrast is observed in the declaratives in (121).

(120) a. Which tune did Monica arrive whistling?   > more acceptable than
 b. Which tune did Julia pick the candidates whistling?
 (Brown 2017: 119)

(121) a. Lucy arrived whistling the national anthem.   > more acceptable than
 b. Mary picked the candidates whistling the national anthem.
 (Brown 2017: 119)

In this section, I will first focus on Brown's (2017) syntactic derivation of the gap inside the adjunct before turning to the semantic licensing conditions and the resulting two-stage approach to extraction from adjuncts.

The core of Brown's proposal for the syntactic licensing of the adjunct-internal gap is that the gap can only be licensed when the adjunct is in the c-command domain of the phase-head v. By hypothesis, the v-head contains an uninterpretable wh-feature that needs to be checked before the phase is completed; the presence of this [wh:_] feature on v is motivated by percolation of unvalued versions of all features in the current phase on the phase head (Brown 2017: 70). Uninterpretable features are checked by corresponding interpretable features that c-command the uninterpretable feature, either from their in-situ position or after being raised to the phase edge. This second option requires the interpretable feature to be in the c-command domain of the uninterpretable feature.

Event modifiers can adjoin to two projections: phasal vP and non-phasal VP; Brown (2017: 63) suggests that the position of adjunction as high or low is determined by the semantics of the adjunct, i.e. whether it acts as an event-internal modifier in the sense of Ernst (2002) or not. An additional assumption is that all event-related adjuncts are PPs, which are either introduced by an overt preposition or conjunction, or a phonetically null P; see also Emonds (2009) for a similar assumption. This approach explains the transparency of event-internal modifiers such as BPPAs (122a), pseudocoordination (122b), and prepositional adjuncts (122c), as well as the opacity of event-external modifiers such as temporal adverbial clauses (122d).

(122) a. What did John arrive whistling? [VP adjunct]
 b. Which car did I go and buy? [VP adjunct]
 c. What temperature should I wash my jeans at? [VP adjunct]
 d. *Which celebrity did Mary eat an ice cream before she saw? [vP adjunct]
 (see Brown 2017: 2–3)

The adjuncts in (122a)–(122c) qualify as internal event modifiers because they modify the manner (122a), purpose (122b), and measure domain (122c) of the event in the VP (see Ernst 2002: 257; Sheehan 2013); the result is a single event reading. On the other hand, the adjunct in (122d) does not modify an internal aspect of the event and is thus merged high to vP. As the semantics of these adjunct constructions require different attachment heights, the extraction is syntactically well-formed for event-internal adjuncts (122a–c), but ill-formed for event-external modifiers (122d). The phrase-structural distribution of transparent and opaque adjuncts is shown schematically in (123). PP_1 is a low adjunct to non-phasal VP, while PP_2 is a high adjunct to phasal vP. The phase head v is indicated by the subscript 'ϕ'; all phase heads in the derivation are assumed to share the same set of uninterpretable features (Brown 2017: 66). Examples and schematic underlying structures for extraction from VP-adjoined PP_1 and vP-adjoined PP_2 are given in (124) and (125), respectively. In these structures, I ignore the first-merge position of the subjects, which Brown (2017) all locates in the specifier of vP.

(123)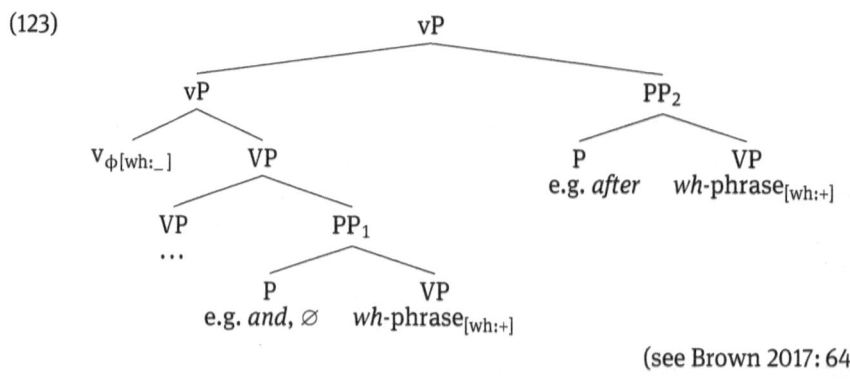

(see Brown 2017: 64)

(124) a. What did John arrive whistling? (see Brown 2017: 68)
b.
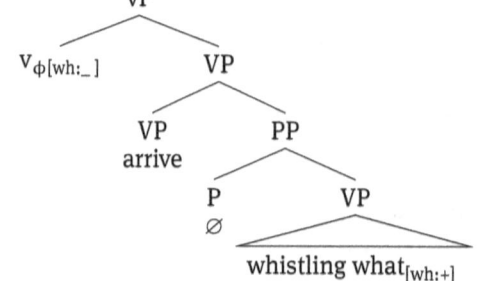

(125) a. *What did Mary eat an ice cream before whistling?

(see Brown 2017: 67)

b.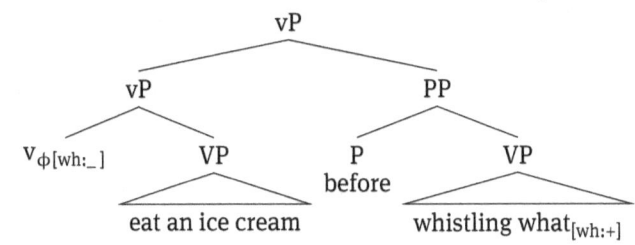

Brown (2017: 66) employs a definition of Agreement or valuation between interpretable and uninterpretable features where the interpretable feature can check uninterpretable features in its c-command domain. If no suitable interpretable feature c-commands the phase head with the uninterpretable feature, a constituent in the c-command domain of the phase head can be moved to the phase edge to allow feature checking ex-situ. The uninterpretable [wh: _] feature is located on the v-head; in this configuration, there is no interpretable [wh:+] feature on a node that c-commands v and could check v's [wh:_] feature in situ. Neither the [wh:+] feature in PP_1 nor PP_2 c-command the unvalued feature in situ. This leaves the possibility of moving a constituent with an appropriate feature to the phase edge. This is not possible for the [wh:+] feature on PP_2 because it is not c-commanded by v. High vP adjuncts as in (125) are not in the c-command domain of the phase head and can thus not move to the phase edge to value the [wh:_] feature on v. On the other hand, the interpretable [wh:+] feature inside PP_1, a low VP adjunct seen in (124), is in the c-command domain of v and thus a candidate for movement to the phase edge, where it can check the [wh:_] feature and keep the interpretable [wh:+] active for further feature checking by C (Brown 2017: 66). The difference between transparent VP adjuncts and opaque vP adjuncts is thus the geometric possibility of raising to the phase edge when in-situ Agreement fails.

This derives the contrast between opaque high vP and transparent low VP adjuncts that is also proposed in Boeckx (2003) and Narita (2014). These approaches can be classified as configurational approaches to gap-licensing because the well-formedness of extraction can be explained in phrase-structural terms. The advantage of Brown's (2017) approach is that the transparency–opacity distinction can be made without the need to assume early or late merger of adjuncts (Lebeaux 1988; Stepanov 2001, 2007; Sheehan 2013), enforced early Spell-Out of the adjunct (Nunes & Uriagereka 2000; Johnson 2003), or a different merger operation for adjuncts (Chomsky 1995a, 2004; Åfarli 2010).

The major innovation over other configurational gap-licensing approaches is that Brown formulates criteria which determine (i) whether an adjunct is merged high or low, and (ii) whether the adjunct can be semantically licensed and felicitously interpreted in its merge position (Brown 2017: 73). Syntactically, adjuncts are freely merged; this free insertion is balanced by semantic licensing or felicity conditions, which result in lower acceptability due to semantic infelicity when an adjunct fails to be semantically licensed in its merge position (Brown 2017: 63). Certain types of adjuncts merge in high position to *v*P by default, for example tensed adverbial clauses such as in (126a); in this structural position, they never meet the geometric criteria for extraction. Untensed adjuncts, such as BPPAs, on the other hand, can be merged low to VP, as in (126b); see Brown (2017: 60). Other event-internal modifiers, for example those in (122b) and (122c), also merge to VP.

(126) a. Who did John [*v*P [*v*P [VP cry]] [PP after Mary hit]]?
      b. What did John [VP [VP arrive] [PP whistling]]?

Licensing in low position to VP is considered to be only possible when the two predicates can be interpreted as a single event, similar to Truswell (2007); for this, the event denoted in the participial adjunct predicate stands in a relation to the event denoted in the matrix predicate which qualifies as a background description (Brown 2017: 74–75). Such a background description holds when the interval of the matrix predicate is a proper subset of the interval introduced by the matrix predicate; as a result, the event described by the matrix predicate will occur while the event in the adjunct predicate is going on. Formally, this is implemented by a progressive operator in the P shell of the adjunct predicate, which is phonologically null in BPPA constructions (Brown 2017: 63–64). This is illustrated with (127a), where the culmination encoded in the matrix predicate, an instantaneous point in time rather than an extended interval, is properly included in the temporal interval of the adjunct predicate, which can be informally expressed as in (127b), where 'τ' stands for an interval and '⊂' indicates proper inclusion.

(127) a. Mary arrived whistling the national anthem.   (Brown 2017: 75)
      b. τ(arrive) ⊂ τ(whistle)

The low adjunction operation to VP is analyzed as a so-called "amalgamation" of the two intervals encoded in the matrix and adjunct predicate; the result is a composite interval where the two predicates can be interpreted felicitously as part of one composite event (Brown 2017: 75); this is conceptually similar to the SEC in Truswell (2011) and the event expansion relation in Haug et al. (2012). Brown refers to these temporal intervals as "scales", which are understood as either unbounded atelic temporal scales or bounded telic temporal scales. Brown (2017) does not go into detail about the amalgamation process with other types of matrix predicates, especially those cases where the mechanism fails to construct a composite single-event reading. However, these are the interesting cases, because they require a coercion mechanism that is not explicitly spelled out in Brown (2017); she refers to de Swart (1998), who defines coercion operators which repair aspectual mismatches between a predicate and other elements in the sentence (de Swart 1998: 360). An example is progressive-formation on achievement predicates as in (128), which requires event template augmentation so that the event has a preceding phase that can be targeted by the progressive (see Vendler 1957; Zucchi 1998; Rothstein 2004b; Bott 2010).

(128) ?John is arriving at the party.

Specific cases of coercion are not discussed, but the example in (129) illustrates the situation where both the matrix and adjunct predicate have temporally unbounded intervals. In these cases, the amalgamation mechanism is problematic because the precise relation of the intervals cannot be determined (see Irimia 2012); the interval of the matrix predicate cannot be subsumed in the interval of the adjunct predicate as in (127). It is thus not clear whether the adjunct qualifies as a background description of the matrix predicate.

(129) a. #Mary worked whistling the national anthem.
   b. τ(work) ? τ(whistle)

In such cases, the adjunct cannot be licensed by amalgamation in its adjunction position to VP, and aspectual coercion has to apply to the matrix predicate to allow this process; the result is semantically infelicitous, indicated by the hash mark judgment in (129a).

Brown (2017) extends her account to explain extraction from pseudocoordination in addition to the BPPA construction. In pseudocoordination, the aspectual requirements differ from the BPPA construction: either the second conjunct contains the culmination point, as in (130a), or two unbounded temporal scales can be amalgamated, as in (130b). Especially the second option is not possible for BPPAs.

(130) a. Mary went and got a newspaper.
   b. Mary sits and reads.
   (Brown 2017: 75)

Taken together, the adjunction site, the licensing conditions for VP adjuncts, and the well-formedness of extraction result in a three-way distinction (Brown 2017: 63, fn. 5); this is shown in Table 3.2 on the following page. The distinction between felicitous semantic licensing via amalgamation and semantic licensing through coercion is not categorical: it allows for a graded continuum between these two extremes that depends on the amount of coercion required to obtain a single-event reading. For high vP adjuncts, this distinction is not relevant because the extraction is ill-formed and coercion cannot repair such structures (Brown 2017: 63).

Tab. 3.2: Adjunction, adjunct-licensing, and extraction in Brown (2017).

Adjunction to...	Adjunct licensing	Extraction	Result
non-phasal VP	amalgamation	well-formed	felicitous/well-formed
non-phasal VP	coercion	well-formed	infelicitous/well-formed
phasal vP	possible	ill-formed	ill-formed

One consequence of the amalgamation mechanism is that it leads to a requirement that the matrix predicate should encode a culmination point; other conditions on the amalgamation process are considered a possibility but are not mentioned explicitly (Brown 2017: 77). Thus, Brown's (2017) approach to adjunct-licensing is much closer to the event-structural analysis of transparent adjuncts in Truswell (2007) than to the agentivity-based approach in Truswell (2011). The focus on telicity instead of agentivity is motivated by two empirical issues with the agentivity approach: first, interrogative BPPA constructions with two agentive predicates, such as those in (131), show grammaticality contrasts which depend on whether the matrix predicate encodes a telic culmination point or not, not on the agentivity of the predicates:

(131)   a.   *What does John dance screaming?
         b.   What does John dance the YMCA screaming?
            (see Brown 2017: 54–55)

The addition of a complement in the matrix clause shifts the atelic activity predicate *dance* in (131a) to a telic accomplishment reading in (131b); both sentences still contain two agentive predicates. This contrast is elusive in a purely agentivity-based approach such as Truswell (2011). Second, there are non-agentive predicates which are ungrammatical in interrogative BPPA constructions regardless of whether the adjunct predicate is agentive or not, seen in (132).

(132)   a.   *Which tune did Mary shiver whistling?   [agentive adjunct]
         b.   *Which chair did Mary shiver sitting on?   [non-agentive adjunct]
            (see Brown 2017: 55)

Here the matrix predicates can be analyzed as non-agentive because they are involuntary and not under the control of the subject. Thus, they should pose no problem for Truswell's (2011) agentivity constraint on extraction; however, the extraction is ungrammatical with both agentive (132a) and non-agentive (132b) adjunct predicates. Again, this is left unexplained in an agentivity-based approach.

Brown (2017) conducts three experiments on extraction from present participle adjuncts in English, German, and Norwegian to examine the effects of telicity, transitivity, and extraction. Items are presented as auditory stimuli to avoid a free adjunct interpretation, and participants used a 6-point Likert scale. She manipulates the three factors EXTRACTION (±WH), TELICITY (±CUL), and TRANSITIVITY (±DP), resulting in a 2 × 2 × 2 factorial design. A sample item from her experimental design for the English sub-experiments given in (133); the German and Norwegian experiments use translated versions of these items.

(133) a. Mary picked the candidates whistling the national anthem.
 [+CUL, +DP, −WH]
 b. Which tune did Julia pick the candidates whistling?
 [+CUL, +DP, +WH]
 c. Lucy arrived whistling the national anthem. [+CUL, −DP, −WH]
 d. Which tune did Monica arrive whistling? [+CUL, −DP, +WH]
 e. Sophie finished sketches whistling the national anthem.
 [−CUL, +DP, −WH]
 f. Which tune did Sophie finish sketches whistling? [−CUL, +DP, +WH]
 g. Lucy shivered whistling the national anthem. [−CUL, −DP, −WH]
 h. Which tune did Sophie shiver whistling? [−CUL, −DP, +WH]
 (Brown 2017: 119)

For English, Brown (2017) finds significant effects for the factors EXTRACTION and TRANSITIVITY, but not for TELICITY. Instead, there is a significant interaction between TRANSITIVITY and TELICITY: telicity only has an influence for intransitive predicates, where telic intransitives are more acceptable than atelic intransitives (Brown 2017: 123). For German and Norwegian, only EXTRACTION shows a significant main effect, the other factors and their interactions are not significant (Brown 2017: 135, 142). These results show three major insights: (i) there is a connection between acceptability in declaratives and interrogatives; (ii) transitivity has a stronger effect than telicity; and (iii) there is cross-linguistic variation in the general acceptability of the BPPA construction across the three examined Germanic languages. The observation that the EXTRACTION factor does not interact with the other factors indicates that extraction is not sensitive to TELICITY or TRANSITIVITY, even if they have an overall effect on acceptability. This provides experimental support for the relation between acceptability contrasts in declaratives and interrogatives, as formulated in the Independence Hypothesis.

The independence approach to extraction from adjuncts in Brown (2017) has the advantage that the conditions on extraction can be formulated in entirely syntactic terms without a sensitivity to non-syntactic factors. Rather, Brown (2017) draws a distinction between extraction operations that cannot be licensed in the syntax and interrogatives that are syntactically well-formed but which differ in acceptability depending on how well the semantic licensing conditions are met. The result is a division of labor between semantic licensing and syntactic operations that does not require these components to interact with each other. This conception of architectural aspects of extraction is considerably simpler than that of interaction accounts. It is an elegant approach to the wide spectrum of reported acceptability in the BPPA construction which is difficult to capture in interaction accounts. It also draws attention to the distinction between perceived unacceptability as a result of syntactic factors, i.e. the distinction between adjuncts that are structurally transparent and opaque, and unacceptability that arises due to semantic mismatches, i.e. the semantic licensing of the adjunct in its merge position.

However, this account is not without problems. I will discuss four issues with this approach in the remainder of this section. I begin the discussion with three types of matrix predicate which are not compatible with Brown's culmination requirement for the amalgamation process: punctual achievements, temporary states, and degree achievements; I then show that extraction from adverbial clauses shows internal variation and is not categorically ill-formed, as the syntactic gap-licensing in Brown (2017) claims; in the final two issues, I concentrate on alternatives to Brown's telicity requirement and the failure to confirm her predictions for transitives experimentally.

First, there are problems with Brown's telicity requirement for adjunct licensing: not all telic matrix predicates automatically result in good extractions, and there are predicate types which are not telic but seem to allow extraction. Punctual achievements like *appear* and perception verbs like *notice* are clearly telic but are reported to be ungrammatical in interrogatives. Truswell (2007) draws a distinction between achievements that can be augmented by a preparatory phase which can be identified with the adjunct predicate (134a), and those achievements that resist the augmentation and are purely punctual (134b,c).

(134)   a.   What did John arrive [whistling t]?
            b.   *What did John appear whistling?
            c.   *What$_j$ did John$_i$ [notice his brother] [looking through t$_j$]$_i$?
               (Truswell 2007: 1356, 1370)

If the requirement is only that the matrix predicate must encode a culmination point, these apparent contrasts fail to receive a principled explanation: they should be equally acceptable because both types of achievement encode a culmination point. Thus, it appears that the requirement for a culmination is either not the correct or not the only generalization that is needed. To my knowledge, the contrast between punctual and extendable achievements has not been experimentally investigated so far, also because the distinction is not always clear-cut. A second group of predicates that are problematic for the culmination requirement are the examples of non-agentive activities which resemble stative predicates. They are one of the motivations to turn from event-structure conditions to agentivity conditions in Truswell (2011). The examples in (135) illustrate:

(135)   a. What is John sitting there [eating t]?
           b. What was John lying in bed [reading t] all day?
             (Truswell 2007: 1360)

These predicates do not encode a culmination in their semantics, but seem intuitively acceptable in interrogatives. Likewise, the corresponding declaratives are not marked:

(136)   a. John is sitting there eating a sandwich.
           b. John was lying in bed reading *The Lord of the Rings* all day.

Truswell (2007) considers these matrix predicates to be non-agentive activities which come close to a stative interpretation; this is not the only analysis available in the literature. For example, Dowty (1979: 184) considers predicates like *stand*, *lie* to be temporary statives, i.e. states that are temporally delimited; see also Maienborn's (2005) distinction between Davidsonian and Kimian states. These matrix predicates are an empirical challenge for the proposed licensing conditions on depictives in Brown (2017), just as they are a problem for Truswell's (2007) event-structural approach. A final issue with a culmination requirement is that there is a verb class that is compatible with both telic and atelic interpretations. This is the class of so-called degree achievements (Dowty 1979; Hay et al. 1999; Rothstein 2004b, 2008; Kennedy & McNally 2005; Kennedy & Levin 2008; Kennedy 2012), which are compatible with both telic *in*- and atelic *for*-adverbials and other markers that imply a total or an incomplete change. This class of matrix predicate differs from verbs typically analyzed as degree achievements, which are often deadjectival verbs like *harden* or *widen*. Semantically, however, they are very similar, as both constructions imply a certain degree along a property scale without making a commitment that a final culmination is reached. Consider the example in (137), where both the declarative and the interrogative seem acceptable.

(137) a. John got scared watching a horror movie.
       b. What did John get scared watching __ ?

These predicate types are unlikely to be captured entirely in terms of a culmination point encoded in the matrix predicate. Depictive licensing appears to depend on a property that includes a culmination point, but is not identical to it. I will return to this issue in Chapters 4 and 5.

The second problem with Brown's account is that she predicts extraction from adverbial clauses to be uniformly ill-formed because adverbial clauses are high adjuncts to phasal *v*P; the adjunct-internal gap cannot be syntactically licensed in this position. If extraction from adverbial clauses is always ill-formed, there should be no acceptability differences in structurally similar adverbial clauses (Brown 2017: 63). However, there are observations about different degrees of acceptability in the extraction from adverbial clauses that differ only minimally. These observations include the influence of tense and coherence relations in C. Müller (2019) discussed in Section 3.3.9 and the following cases in den Dikken (2018):

(138) a. $^{??}$ he is the person who they left town before speaking to __
       b. he is the person who they left town after speaking to __
           (den Dikken 2018: 127–128)

Regardless of whether the adverbial clause is headed by *before* or *after*, it should adjoin to *v*P and thus the gap cannot be licensed. However, den Dikken (2018) detects an acceptability contrast in these extractions that is based on the pragmatic plausibility of the situation described in the sentence: intuitively, (138b) describes a situation that is more plausible than (138a). The acceptability contrast is thus not one of well-formed or ill-formed extraction, but rather one of pragmatic oddity. The pragmatically marked sentence (138a) can be ameliorated by additional contextual licensing which turns it into a plausible scenario:

(139) Peter and Mary visited their hometown and tried to catch up with their friends. They talked to everyone except Sam before they had to leave in a hurry. *He was the only friend who they left town before speaking to.*

A context that removes the pragmatic oddity seems to improve the extraction. This speaks against a uniform analysis of adverbial clauses as opaque domains.

The third point of criticism concerns Brown's focus on temporal scales or intervals to explain the semantic licensing of the adjunct predicate during the amalgamation process. This focus results in the problematic predictions noted in the preceding paragraphs, and imposes requirements on adjunct licensing which seem too strict. For example, a telicity requirement leaves the following apparently grammatical extractions unexplained:

(140) a. Who are you prancing *(about) [trying to impress t]?
                                                         (Truswell 2007: 1361)
      b. What was John walking about [whistling __]?   (Truswell 2011: 155)

As pointed out in Section 3.3.4, agentivity is not the only way to approach these sentences. The particle can also be interpreted as supplying a prominent scale in terms of Rappaport Hovav & Levin (2010) that encodes a path that is traversed by the typically unbounded and spatially indeterminate manner-of-motion predicate (Tenny 1995). If the presence or absence of such particles really determines how acceptable the extraction is, then an alternative analysis in terms of scalar structures encoded in the matrix predicates is possible.

I suggest that the encoding of a culmination point in the matrix predicate is one of the possibilities that can lead to scale amalgamation and thus to coercion-free licensing. One plausible way to extend the licensing conditions to also cover the cases above is to extend the notion of scales that allow amalgamation. Scales come not only in the shape of temporal intervals, but in a variety of forms (see Rappaport Hovav 2008): spatial paths, property ascriptions, and incremental themes also supply a scalar component, and as a result, verbs encoding these scales show interesting similarities (see Rappaport Hovav 2008; Hay et al. 1999; Kennedy & McNally 2005; Kennedy 2012). Degree achievements as in (137) above are easily analyzed in terms of a property scale, even though they do not necessarily encode a culmination point but rather a progression along a property scale. That means that they do not encode a simple transition but rather an extended directed change. I will discuss this in more detail in Chapter 5.

The last issue concerns the prediction that the BPPA construction and extraction from it should be acceptable with more transitive matrix predicates than assumed in other accounts (Brown 2017: 76–77). This prediction is not verified in Brown's experimental studies. Sentences with transitive matrix predicates, both telic and atelic, are less acceptable than conditions with intransitive matrix predicates. For example, the interrogative of the transitive sentence in (141) is expected to be acceptable; this is not reflected in Brown's results.

(141) Which tune did Julia pick the candidates whistling?   (Brown 2017: 119)

In sentences with telic matrix predicates like this, the scale amalgamation should work because the culmination point of the matrix predicate can be subsumed as a proper subinterval of the adjunct predicate's unbounded interval. The fact that sentences like (141) and their corresponding declaratives are not judged very acceptable is problematic for the predictions about transitives. This lack of experimental validation indicates that there are further factors at work which do not follow from Brown's phrase-structural approach to adjunct licensing and the derivation of the adjunct-internal gap. There are good reasons to believe that amalgamation succeeds for telic matrix predicates where the adjunct serves as a background description, but it seems that a strict telicity requirement is neither a necessary nor a sufficient factor that plays a role.

The major innovation of this approach is the fundamental disassociation of semantic licensing conditions for the adjunct and syntactic licensing conditions of the adjunct-internal gap site, which is conceptually attractive. Whereas a violation of the adjunct licensing conditions results in decreased acceptability because coercion is required, a violation of the syntactic gap-licensing conditions can result in a crash of the syntactic derivation. This approach allows for more predictable variation in interrogatives without incorporating semantic properties into the syntax. Extraction operations still operate blindly when they can be syntactically licensed, but the acceptability of an interrogative will also reflect the coercion effects that infelicitous adjunction of the BPPA incurs. As such, the approach presented in Brown (2017) and the Independence Hypothesis that can be formulated based on it stand out in the current literature on transparent adjuncts. As the experiments in Chapter 4 will show, the Independence Hypothesis receives substantial experimental support; since there are several technical possibilities to derive grammatical extractions from adjuncts, the semantic licensing conditions on the adjunct deserve closer theoretical investigation.

3.5 Chapter conclusion

This chapter has provided a review of the existing literature on extraction from adjunct constituents. I have followed three main strands of investigation: (i) pure gap-licensing accounts which provide mechanisms to derive adjunct-internal gaps without syntactic violations; (ii) interaction accounts which propose more nuanced criteria to determine whether a given adjunct is be transparent or not; and (iii) an independence approach which traces back apparent acceptability differences in interrogatives to semantic licensing conditions of the adjunct in declaratives. The main research questions addressed in this chapter are repeated in (142):

(142) a. How can extraction from adjunct constituents be syntactically licensed?
   b. Which factors are relevant for the distinction between transparent and opaque adjuncts? Are these factors syntactic, semantic, or pragmatic?
   c. Which consequences for the architecture of locality follow from the different approaches?

The research question in (142a) was addressed in Section 3.2, which sketched current syntactic approaches to how an adjunct-internal gap can be derived without violating core syntactic principles. This is complemented by the phrase-structural approach proposed in Brown (2017) as discussed in Section 3.4. It was shown that the approaches differ in the tools they use: (i) an optional Agree relation between the main verb and the adjunct predicate, for example in event-structural terms; (ii) unchecked features that keep the phase including the adjunct active for further operations by preventing early Spell-Out; and (iii) and a purely geometric approach where only specific nodes in the BPPA structure are accessible to a probing *wh*-feature and can thus undergo movement. A common characteristic of these approaches is that they derive a distinction between transparent and opaque adjuncts but do not offer extensive details about the conditions that determine which verb–adjunct combinations will belong to which one of these groups. On the positive side, these approaches are more flexible than the strict CED (Huang 1982), which does not allow any extraction from adjuncts. They allow for some adjuncts to be transparent, while others remain opaque; this derives at least a binary distinction that accommodates the counterexamples to the CED that have surfaced in the existing literature.

The second research question in (142b) was addressed in Section 3.3. It has been shown that there are a variety of approaches which offer more detailed explanations and predictions about which BPPA configurations will allow extraction from the adjunct and which will not. I have largely focused on accounts that take syntactic, semantic, and pragmatic perspectives, and which isolate a set of factors that determines transparency in one of these domains. While there is a large overlap between many of these factor sets, there are some predictions that differ among the accounts. In the absence of reliable evidence, it is difficult to decide which factor set explains the most data and holds up to experimental scrutiny. This point will be the focus of the following experimental chapter, which will test some of these predictions in controlled acceptability studies.

The final major research question in (142c) is concerned with the question about the interplay of core syntactic operations with factors that belong to other modules of the grammar. Some interaction accounts require less severe architectural adjustments, while others explicitly call for the sensitivity of syntactic operations to non-structural factors. This last point is considered problematic for the autonomy of syntax (see Brown 2017). In Section 3.4, I have discussed an alternative proposal to what I have called interaction accounts. Brown (2017) proposes a link between acceptability differences in interrogatives and declaratives, re-locating the source of variation in the general semantic compatibility of the verb–adjunct complex instead of being a direct result of the application of extraction, as claimed for example in Truswell (2011). The main advantages of this alternative approach are that semantic effects are not tied to syntactic operations and that it still offers an explanation for the acceptability differences that occur in interrogatives. While there are identical differences in declaratives, they might be inaccessible to intuitive judgments by the overall high acceptability of the construction.

In conclusion, this chapter has shown that there are several approaches to adjuncts islands which identify different factors responsible for the division into transparent and opaque adjuncts. These approaches differ in their assumptions about which factors are relevant for extraction, as well as in their architectural ramifications. In the following experimental chapter, I will take an experimental perspective on the validity of selected predictions from the existing literature and I will also add further data points that have not been discussed in detail before. Several predictions about grammaticality differences in extraction from the existing literature can be confirmed experimentally, but there is substantial experimental support for the Independence Hypothesis.

4 Experimental evidence

4.1 Research questions and chapter outline

For a long time, the discussion of island phenomena was largely theoretical, based on intuitive judgments and rarely verified by a larger pool of unbiased informants. With the steady increase of controlled experimental research in linguistics, island phenomena have received more and more attention. Still, there is a considerable imbalance when it comes to different island types. Whereas other island types, such as *wh*-islands and subject islands, have been studied in some detail, there are comparatively few studies on adjunct islands in general, and even fewer on participial adjunct islands. As shown in Chapter 3, there are notable exceptions, such as the recent studies on participial adjunct islands in Fábregas & Jiménez-Fernández (2016a) for Spanish, Kohrt et al. (2018) and Kohrt et al. (2020) for English, and Brown's (2017) cross-linguistic comparison between English, German, and Norwegian. Related adjunct island constructions in the form of adverbial clauses have been investigated by C. Müller (2017, 2019) in Swedish and English, Sprouse et al. (2012), Chaves & Putnam (2020) and Gibson et al. (2021) in English, and Kush et al. (2018, 2019) in Norwegian and English.

This chapter contributes to the experimental landscape on adjunct islands in English, focusing on subextraction from the BPPA construction. I will pursue two main goals in this chapter: (i) to find out whether there are factors which modulate the strength of the effect of extraction on acceptability, as suggested by the interaction accounts discussed in the previous chapter, or whether there are independent licensing conditions for the adjunct which do not interact with extraction but which show effects in declaratives, as captured by the Independence Hypothesis; and (ii) to expand the empirical basis for factors which seem relevant to extraction from participle adjuncts. The experiments and discussion presented in this chapter are guided by the following research questions:

(1) a. How acceptable is extraction from participial adjuncts compared to a standardized scale of well-formedness?
   b. Which factors influence the acceptability of extraction from the BPPA construction?
   c. Do the experimental results support the Interaction Hypothesis or the Independence Hypothesis?

The first research question in (1a) examines the overall acceptability of sentences where extraction takes place from an adjunct constituent: despite the predictions of the CED, several examples of apparently transparent adjuncts have been discussed in the theoretical literature and are attested in everyday language (see Santorini 2019). In most of the experiments reported here, I am not only interested in the effects that different factors might have on the acceptability of extraction, but also how the acceptability scores for extraction relate to the cardinal well-formedness sentences developed in Gerbrich et al. (2019). This comparison can provide a partial answer to the larger question whether present participle adjuncts behave like canonical strong islands where extraction is generally strongly degraded, or whether they show behavior that is more characteristic of weak or selective islands with more nuanced patterns of acceptability that are not necessarily strongly degraded (Cinque 1990; Szabolcsi & Lohndal 2017; C. Müller 2019).

Research question (1b) investigates the factors that have an effect on the acceptability of the BPPA construction and extraction from it. The leading question is whether factors proposed in the previous literature are responsible for significant acceptability contrasts. I will focus on the influence of event structure in study series 1, the grammatical verb type of the matrix predicate in study series 2, and the difference between a causal and non-causal relation between the two predicates in study series 3.

The research question in (1c) addresses the issue whether locality operations like *wh*-extraction are sensitive to factors such as event structure or verb types in the BPPA construction, or whether there are independent conditions for adjunct licensing and extraction. These different approaches to the architecture of locality operations have been introduced in Chapter 3 as the Interaction Hypothesis and the Independence Hypothesis, respectively. Results where a factor shows different effects in declaratives and interrogatives provide evidence for the Interaction Hypothesis, whereas the Independence Hypothesis predicts that both structures should be affected to the same degree. Statistically, these predictions can be evaluated by the presence or absence of superadditive or subadditive effect structures, which are discussed in more detail in Section 4.4.

I begin this chapter in Section 4.2 with a discussion of the model of acceptability that I assume as the empirical foundation throughout this and the following chapter. Section 4.3 then discusses a set of factors that are relevant to extraction phenomena in general and to adjunct islands in particular. These factors will be the starting point for the experiments reported in this chapter. Section 4.4 lays out the basic methodology for data collection in the experiments. The remainder of this chapter (Sections 4.5 through 4.7) reports on the experiments conducted for this monograph. It is organized into three study series, which focus on a specific factor. Section 4.8 summarizes and concludes this chapter.

4.2 Categorical and factorial models of acceptability

This section discusses two basic models of grammaticality and acceptability: (i) categorical or binary models, which incorporate strict or inviolable grammaticality constraints; and (ii) factorial models which incorporate several, potentially multi-leveled factors and allow for gradual levels of acceptability. Importantly, these models measure two different concepts, namely the competence-based notion of grammaticality, and the performance-based concept of acceptability; see Chomsky (1965) for this distinction. Despite measuring different concepts, there is a connection between the grammaticality of a sentence and the acceptability judgment it receives: grammatical sentences will typically be judged as acceptable, whereas ungrammatical sentences are usually considered to be unacceptable, even though grammaticality is not the only factor determining acceptability (Chomsky 1965: 11).

Island phenomena have played an integral part in generative syntax because they are assumed to reflect inviolable conditions on extraction that are represented in a speaker's competence grammar. A traditional approach to adjunct islands makes strong predictions about the grammaticality of subextractions from such domains: they are ungrammatical because adjuncts are not properly governed, as for example formulated in Huang's (1982) CED in (2), which is formulated as a strict condition on grammaticality.

(2) Condition on Extraction Domain
    A phrase A may be extracted out of a domain B only if B is properly governed.
    (Huang 1982: 505)

In such a binary CED-style model of grammaticality extraction is grammatical only if this structural condition is met; all other cases are ungrammatical and will typically be judged as unacceptable sentences. This is shown schematically in Figure 4.1, where the CED evaluates whether an interrogative sentence meets the criterion of proper government and then determines whether the input sentence is

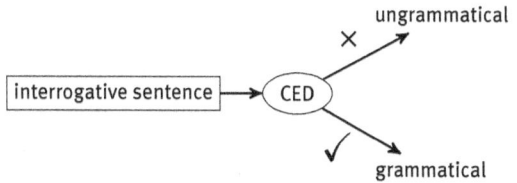

Fig. 4.1: Schematic representation of a categorical model of grammaticality. The violation of a single grammatical constraint like the CED leads to categorical ungrammaticality.

grammatical or not. Such models leave no space for exceptions and blindly apply violation costs which cannot be repaired (Featherston 2011: 315–317). Grammatical constraints like the CED are thus categorical determinants of grammaticality, resulting in a binary distinction between grammatical and ungrammatical sentences.

This binary or categorical model of grammaticality contrasts with the graded levels of acceptability judgments that have been found in countless experimental studies (see Sprouse 2007); there is often no one-to-one mapping from the theoretically determined grammaticality status to the levels of perceived naturalness that participants give in experiments. Gerbrich et al. (2019: 309) observe that there may be as many as 20 degrees of acceptability or well-formedness that speakers can distinguish. Elaborating on the competence–performance distinction, Chomsky (1965) notes that there are other linguistic and extra-linguistic factors which can affect acceptability and thus blur the categorical grammatical–ungrammatical distinction. Acceptability is thus a measure of performance and not competence. In this and the following chapter, I will work under the assumption that the perceived acceptability of subextraction from adjunct islands, as well as the asymmetries seen in such extractions, cannot be reduced to a single linguistic factor or constraint. Rather, there is a set of factors that jointly determine how acceptable a given sentence is. A polyfactorial model of acceptability with a set of grammatical (G), semantic (S), and pragmatic (P) factors and their effect on acceptability is schematically shown in Figure 4.2. This contrasts with theoretical approaches that determine the grammaticality of an extraction by means of a single, often structural, factor.

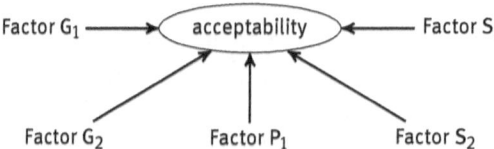

Fig. 4.2: Schematic representation of a polyfactorial model of acceptability. Multiple grammatical (G), semantic (S), and pragmatic (P) factors influence acceptability.

The factors in a polyfactorial model can be (i) additive, meaning that they apply independently of each other and do not influence the magnitude of another factor's effect; or they can be (ii) interactive, in which case one factor has an effect on the strength of another factor. As pointed out in the preceding chapter, many approaches to extraction asymmetries from adjuncts assume that there is a factor, such as aspectual classes (Truswell 2007), which determines how strongly extraction affects acceptability. One of the aims of this chapter is to investigate individual factors and to determine how they affect acceptability and whether they increase or decrease the effect of extraction. Manipulating these factors in isolation allows for an estimation of their respective effect on acceptability and leads to a more comprehensive model of how these factors jointly determine acceptability.

Graded and polyfactorial models of acceptability exist in the generative framework, for example the *Decathlon Model* (Featherston 2008, 2019). This model consists of two components: a Constraint Application module that examines the input and assigns violation costs to it if a constraint is violated. These costs are added up cumulatively for each violation. The second module, Output Selection, selects among the competing structures that have passed through Constraint Application. Since this module is competitive, the structure with the least overall violation cost will not automatically be selected. It is possible that a "suboptimal" contestant makes the cut. Such a model of acceptability explains why attested data, such as examples in corpora, can include tokens that violate a specific grammatical constraint. In categorical models, such occurrences trigger the revision or abandoning of this constraint because it cannot account for this occurrence and is thus empirically inadequate. In contrast, the Decathlon Model allows for such exceptional occurrences and does not require the constraint to be abandoned due to exceptional occurrences (see also Featherston 2011: 308–311).

Similarly, Haegeman et al. (2014) discuss the *Cumulative Effect Hypothesis*, a set of constraints on extraction from subject islands that can be individually violated by extraction. The violation costs then add up to determine the overall acceptability of the structure. This model shares with the Decathlon Model the assumption that acceptability can be traced back to individual constraints which add up incrementally; however, it lacks the competitive component that allows for variation in the observed output data. Some of the experimental results in Greco et al. (2017), which investigates the predictions made by the Cumulative Effect Hypothesis, do not confirm this hypothesis because the factors do not show an incremental and additive pattern.

Both of these models assume that the overall acceptability of a sentence depends on the number and strength of violations that it incurs. Models based on individual violation costs have an advantage in that they offer an explanation for both speaker variation and cross-linguistic variation: the individual violation costs might be weighted slightly different for individual speakers, or may be entirely absent in a given language. Swedish, for example, allows more dependencies into constituents that are considered strong islands in English, which can be interpreted as a parametrization of violation costs (Engdahl 1980; Phillips 2013; Sprouse & Hornstein 2013; C. Müller 2019). Models like the Cumulative Effect Hypothesis and the Decathlon Model are well suited to account for cross-linguistic variation. They are also in principle compatible with both interaction accounts of adjunct islands and with the IH. In interaction accounts, the strength of one factor is determined by the setting of another factor; in contrast, independent factors add up in a linear-additive fashion. This will be discussed in more detail below, including a set of predictions for the possible outcomes of the experiments in this chapter.

4.3 Factors

In this section, I will introduce factors that have an effect on the acceptability of extractions. Some of these are of a very general nature, some apply only to island constructions, and some are specific to adjunct islands. In the experiments reported here, I will for the most part keep these general factors constant, which allows a narrow focus on those factors that are specific to adjunct islands.

4.3.1 General factors relevant to extraction from islands

The literature on extraction from islands includes a variety of different relevant factors; for comprehensive overviews, see Szabolcsi & Dikken (2003), Szabolcsi (2006), Szabolcsi & Lohndal (2017), and Haegeman et al. (2014). Among these general factors, non-syntactic factors like processing occupy a prominent place. For example, Sag et al. (2008) discuss the following factors in connection with the Complex NP Constraint:

(3) a. Distance b. Semantic complexity
    c. Informativity d. Frequency
    e. Similarity f. Finiteness
    g. Contextualization difficulty h. Collocational frequency

Some of these factors have also been discussed in other works on islands, for example the issue of *informativity*, often referred to as *D-linking* (Pesetsky 1987, 2000; Hirose 2003; Onea & Zimmermann 2019; Haegeman et al. 2014). Often, *wh*-questions with a more complex *wh*-phrase are considered to be more acceptable than bare *wh*-pronouns like *who* or *what*, even in non-island constructions (Goodall 2015). This difference has been used as a diagnostic for the strong–weak island distinction (Szabolcsi & Lohndal 2017: 4044, 4057–4059). The relevance of D-linking for subject islands has been discussed, among others, in Jiménez-Fernández (2009: 119–121) and Haegeman et al. (2014: 98–99). As this effect seems to apply across different constructions and independently of whether the extraction site is an island or not, I will not investigate D-linking in detail in the experiments presented here. The relativization conditions in Experiment 1 are an exception because they include the full DP instead of a bare *wh*-pronoun. The general discussion of D-linking leads to the expectation that D-linked *wh*-phrases in *wh*-extractions from islands should slightly increase overall acceptability.

Another factor that carries over to other types of islands is *finiteness* (Szabolcsi 2006; Szabolcsi & Lohndal 2017; Truswell 2011; C. Müller 2019). The general observation is that when extraction takes place from a tensed domain, the sentence is strongly degraded in many languages, including English, but this is not universal; for example, Mainland Scandinavian does not appear to show this effect (C. Müller 2019). Finiteness has long played a role in the discussion of extraction and has received a number of different formulations, such as the *tensed-S condition* of Chomsky (1973: 237–238), the *Propositional Island Constraint* in Chomsky (1977), or in relation to adjunct clauses in G. Müller (1995). I will focus on non-finite adjuncts in the following experiments based on the assumption that finiteness is an established, even if not fully understood, factor that is not exclusive to adjunct islands. To the factors discussed in Sag et al. (2008), at least the following can be added:

(4) a. Dependency type (Van Valin 2005; Sprouse & Hornstein 2013; Abeillé et al. 2020)
 b. Information structure and pragmatic relevance (Erteschik-Shir 1973; Kuno 1987; Goldberg 2006, 2013; Chaves & Putnam 2020)

Filler–gap dependencies come in different varieties, including *wh*-extraction, relativization, topicalization, and others (Sprouse & Hornstein 2013; Phillips 2013; Chaves & Putnam 2020). The majority of the literature on islands is limited to *wh*-extraction, but there is recent work that draws a comparison to relativization (Sprouse et al. 2016; Abeillé et al. 2020). While both of these types of long-distance dependency are grouped together under the general term A'-movement in the generative framework, they show syntactic and semantic differences, as discussed in G. Müller (1995). Relativization can be analyzed in terms of λ-abstraction, whereas *wh*-movement involves existential quantification (G. Müller 1995: 427). Abeillé et al. (2020) investigate the difference between *wh*-extraction and relativization in subject islands and propose that the different patterns of acceptability they find can be explained by the different discourse functions of the two operations, which interact with the information-structural status of the extraction site; see also Liu et al. (2022) for an overview of experiments on different extraction types. A similar position can be found in Role and Reference Grammar (Van Valin 2005: 285). The experiments presented here will focus on *wh*-extraction in order to allow comparisons across experiments more easily. An exception is Experiment 1, which also includes a relativization sub-experiment for comparison.

A more general information-structural factor for extraction is proposed in Goldberg (2006, 2013), who argues that backgrounded constituents strongly resist extraction. Since subjects, adjuncts, and factive complements are often presupposed and thus backgrounded, they resist extraction more strongly than direct objects, which are often new information and thus not backgrounded. The assumption that only potential focus domains allows for extraction has long been discussed in the literature (Erteschik-Shir 1973, 1997; Diesing 1992) and has received more recent attention (Neeleman & Vermeulen 2012; Goldberg 2013; Bianchi & Chesi 2014; Matić 2014). Similarly, Chaves & Putnam (2020) propose that only constituents identified as the "center of attention" in an utterance allow extraction; see also Kuno (1987) and Deane (1991). Information structure and extraction type are two related factors because extraction types differ in their information-structural characteristics and functions (Abeillé et al. 2020; Liu et al. 2022).

4.3.2 Specific factors for adjunct islands

As shown in Chapter 3, the previous literature on adjunct islands has isolated a set of different syntactic, semantic, and pragmatic factors that are assumed to determine the acceptability of subextraction from adjuncts. The following list provides a short overview of the main points, as discussed more extensively in the previous chapter. Many of these factors are either explicitly or implicitly investigated in one of the experiments in this chapter.

Completely isolating these individual factors in an experimental design is challenging: there are several correlations between agentivity, aspectual classes, and grammatical verb type (see Dowty 1991: 607). A factorial design that crosses two or more factors is able to isolate at least some of the individual factors because potential confounding factors are spread evenly across conditions (Sprouse et al. 2012, 2013, 2016; Kush et al. 2018). The implementation of the factorial design and the experimental methodology in this chapter are explained in Section 4.4.

Grammatical verb type of the matrix predicate: Borgonovo & Neeleman (2000) propose that the transparency of a predicative adjunct depends on the grammatical verb type of the embedding verb, formulated in terms of the unaccusativity hypothesis for intransitive predicates (Perlmutter 1978; Burzio 1986; Levin & Rappaport Hovav 1995). Only unaccusatives and reflexive transitives allow subextraction from a predicative adjunct, while unergatives and non-reflexive transitives do not. Reflexive-marking of the adjunct predicate by the matrix predicate is related to L-marking and turns an adjunct transparent for extraction. This factor is investigated in study series 2.

Aspectual classes of the two predicates: Truswell (2007) relates the acceptability of some extractions from adjuncts to the different combinations of aspectual classes of the two predicates. Extraction is only considered grammatical if the matrix predicate is telic and the adjunct atelic. The reason behind this pattern is that the adjunct predicate needs to fill an empty position in the event structure of the matrix predicate to form a complex event. In this approach, the aspectual class of the matrix predicates is predicted to interact with *wh*-extraction. This factor is examined in study series 1.

Agentivity of the two predicates: The influence of agentivity is the main factor proposed in Truswell (2011). In a construction where a participial adjunct predicate modifies another predicate, at most one of the two may be classified as agentive. This is captured in the Single Event Grouping Condition (SEGC), which is motivated by the fact that the predictions from Aktionsart as discussed in Truswell (2007) do not explain why also some combinations of two atelic predicates allow subextraction from the adjunct predicate. The Aktionsart factor is connected to the grammatical verb type of the matrix predicate, as unaccusatives are generally considered non-agentive, whereas unergatives and transitives are usually agentive. Agentivity is not investigated in a dedicated study series, but as it correlates with other factors, some conclusions can be drawn from the results in study series 2 and 3.

Transitivity of the matrix predicate: Brown (2017) reports on experiments with participial adjuncts that find a significant interaction of transitivity with telicity. Telic intransitives allow extraction more readily than atelic intransitives, but there is no effect of telicity in transitives. This result confirms the claim in Borgonovo & Neeleman (2000) that unaccusatives are most acceptable under extraction. Similar results are observed in Fábregas & Jiménez-Fernández (2016a), who find achievements to be the only verb class to allow subextraction from gerund adjunct constructions in Spanish; this can be interpreted as a transitivity effect because Spanish places strong ordering constraints on extractions from such adjunct constructions. Transitivity is investigated in study series 2.

Coherence relations between the two predicates: C. Müller (2019) reports that extraction from adverbial clauses in English is ameliorated if there is a causal relation between the adverbial clause and the matrix predicate. The relevance of coherence relations for linguistic phenomena is also discussed in Kehler (2000, 2002, 2019). The precise implementation of the coherence factor in C. Müller (2019) is in fact a manipulation of telicity of the matrix predicate: achievements and accomplishment matrix predicates are used as coherent conditions and activities as non-coherent conditions. While it is true that the interpretations differ for these predicate groups, this does not reveal much about the role of coherence because C. Müller's (2019) experiments use predicate classes that have been shown to influence acceptability of extraction from the adjunct in other works. Study series 3, especially Experiment 8, investigates two types of matrix predicate that are similar with respect to telicity and agentivity, but which differ in whether the adjunct can be interpreted as a CAUSE or STIMULUS role in the argument structure of the matrix predicate, or only as a depictive secondary predicate.

Syntactic integration of the adjunct predicate: Fabricius-Hansen & Haug (2012a,b) distinguish several types of co-eventive adjuncts, among them those that are syntactically and prosodically integrated into the matrix clause and those that are detached, for example via orthographic separation with a comma; see also the discussion of supplements and the syntactic COMMA feature in Potts (2005). It appears that the degree of syntactic integration is correlated with the transparency of the adjunct, meaning that the higher the degree of integration, the higher the transparency of the adjunct. The BPPA construction shows a high degree of integration, whereas adverbial clauses and detached adjuncts are less integrated. Experiment 3 compares the BPPA construction with free adjuncts, and Experiment 8 investigates adjuncts that can be interpreted as part of the matrix predicate's argument structure.

4.4 Methodology

The basic methodology in the experiments reported below is that of a sentence judgment task (Cowart 1997; Schütze & Sprouse 2013): participants are asked to provide intuitive judgments for individual sentences presented as written stimuli on a numbered, discrete scale of acceptability known as a Likert-scale. Target sentences are created according to a factorial design and distributed across an appropriate number of lists by means of the Latin square design to balance the exposure of participants to experimental stimuli in the target conditions across lexicalizations (Goodall 2021). To avoid list position effects, items are presented in randomized order for each individual participant.

Filler items that are not related to the current experiment are used as distractors; they include reference points for clearly acceptable and unacceptable structures in the form of the standardized cardinal well-formedness sentences developed for English in Gerbrich et al. (2019). The target-to-filler ratio is at least 1:2 in all experiments. Where the standardized items are used, an appropriate number of other filler sentences with varying grades of acceptability is added to the lists. Gerbrich et al. (2019) use five different sets of standardized fillers that represent discrete points on a continuous scale of acceptability; they can roughly be translated into traditional grammaticality judgments as in (5), which shows one of the three items for each level along with the corresponding judgments from Gerbrich et al. (2019: 310). They provide no markings for the A and B levels and refer to both as "grammatical"; the notation with one or two check marks for these levels is adapted from Featherston (2019: 173).

(5) a. ✓✓ A: The patient fooled the dentist by pretending to be in pain.
 b. ✓ B: Before every lesson the teacher must prepare their materials.
 c. ? C: Hannah hates but Linda loves eating popcorn in the cinema.
 d. ?? D: Who did he whisper that had unfairly condemned the prisoner?
 e. * E: Historians wondering what cause is disappear civilization.
   (see Gerbrich et al. 2019: 315)

Importantly, even the worst set of standard fillers has a unique syntactic representation and is not just word salad; for each of the marked levels, the confound of the faulty structure can be clearly identified (Gerbrich et al. 2019: 310–311).

The following measures were taken to ensure the quality of the obtained experimental data: as a basic principle, data from as few participants as possible were removed from the data pool before statistical analysis; participants that merely showed some outlier judgments were not removed. However, three criteria were considered in the removal of participants: (i) participants who reported a first language other than English were systematically removed; this had no negative effect on their payment. (ii) Data sets with more than two missing observations in the target items and participants who did not complete the experiment were removed. (iii) Poor performance on the standardized fillers led to exclusion from the statistical analysis; participants who showed almost random judgments on the standardized fillers were removed because this indicates that they did not actually perform the experiment but rather clicked through the items to complete the experiment as quickly as possible to receive payment. Here I looked at the mean judgments for the five levels of the standardized fillers, each with three tokens: the mean judgments are expected to steadily decline from the A- to the E-standards. Participants that did not show at least a tendency for this decline were removed from the data pool. I did not exclude participants who were biased towards one of the extremes of the scale or when the judgments centered around the middle, as long as the means reflected the predicted gradual decrease in acceptability.

Most of the experiments reported in this chapter use a factorial design that compares declarative base positions to conditions with *wh*-extraction. The second factor varies across experiments and includes, for example, event-semantic properties of the matrix predicate, aspectual marking, or the grammatical verb type of the matrix predicate. This particular setup of a factorial design allows determining whether the second factor modulates the strength of the effect of extraction, i.e. whether one level of the second factor shows a stronger reaction to *wh*-extraction than the other level of this factor. In this way, it is possible to test the theoretical claims in the previous literature and to investigate whether there are factors that decrease the strength of extraction based on specific characteristics of the item. In effect, this is a modification of the factorial design to detect general island effects discussed in Sprouse et al. (2012, 2013, 2016) and Kush et al. (2018) with a few differences: the design does not determine whether BPPA constructions are islands because there is no comparison of extraction from matrix against embedded domains and no comparison between complement against adjunct status of the embedded domain. Rather, the design works under the assumption that BPPA constructions are in general less transparent to subextraction than subcategorized embedded domains. The main point of interest is whether characteristics of the two predicates determine how strong the effect of extraction is, i.e. whether the investigated factors trigger superadditive or subadditive effect structures which are the characteristic predictions of interaction accounts.

There are essentially four possible outcomes of this modified factorial design that are of special interest. These possible outcomes are shown schematically in Figure 4.3. The factor *wh*-extraction (–*wh* & +*wh*) is plotted on the *x*-axis and the different line types show the levels of the second factor, for example the telicity of the matrix predicate in Experiment 2; the *y*-axis shows a hypothetical 5-point Likert scale. The four plots show different effect structures, which I will briefly discuss in turn. I expect that *wh*-extraction always decreases acceptability because it is cognitively demanding (Sprouse et al. 2013; Wagers 2013; Bornkessel-Schlesewsky & Schlesewsky 2009); this is why +*wh* conditions are always lower on the acceptability scale than –*wh* conditions.

(a) *Only extraction effect:* The top left plot shows a situation where there is only an effect of *wh*-extraction without a significant effect for the second factor. In this case, the second factor does not have an effect on acceptability and both levels of the factor react identically to extraction.
(b) *linear-additive effects:* The top right plot differs from the previous one in that both factors show significant effects. In the absence of a significant interaction, the two factors both have an impact on acceptability; the acceptability of the worst condition can be predicted by adding up individual decreases in acceptability of the two factors. Both levels of Factor 2 are affected to the same degree by extraction.

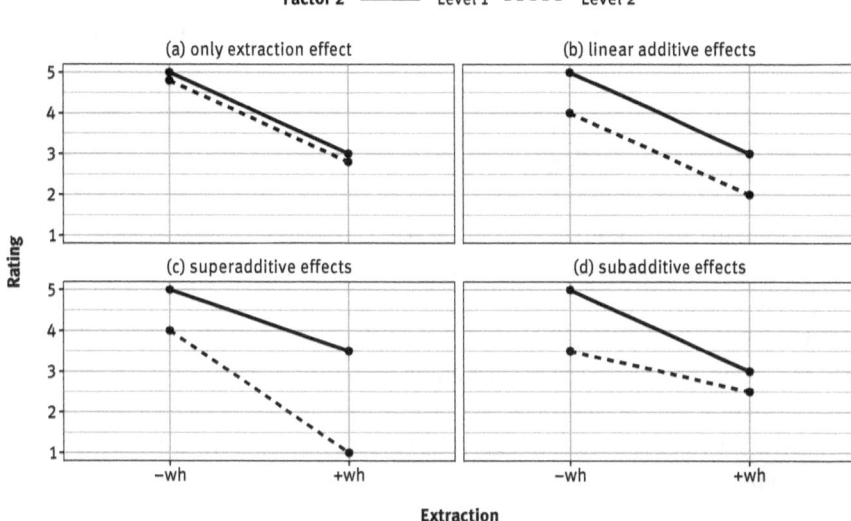

Fig. 4.3: Schematic representation of possible results of a 2 × 2 factorial design with extraction on the x-axis and a second factor shown by different line types.

(c) *Superadditive effects:* The bottom left plot shows a situation where one level of Factor 2 is affected more strongly affected by extraction than the other level. This additional decrease in acceptability cannot be explained by adding up the effects of the two individual factors. Statistically, this results in an interaction between the two factors and instantiates an additional penalty that requires a theoretical explanation. Superadditive effects are characteristic of extractions from islands compared to non-islands.

(d) *Subadditive effects:* The bottom right plot shows a subadditive effect structure that can be interpreted as an island-repair effect: one level of Factor 2 is less affected by the extraction than the other level of the factor. The statistical interaction leads to ratings that are closer under extraction than they are in declaratives. Similar to a superadditive effect, it has to be explained why one level is affected more by the extraction than the other level, especially if this level has an initial advantage in declaratives.

Different theoretical approaches to participial adjunct islands can usually be expressed in a way that fits one of these outcomes. The factorial design used in most of the studies below can thus serve to find experimental support for largely intuition-based grammaticality judgments in the literature and test novel claims about the transparency of adjuncts and the relation to declaratives. Not all previous experiments on adjunct islands draw a comparison to declaratives, so the contrasts observed for interrogatives do not directly speak for or against the validity of an interaction account.

4.5 Study series 1: Event structure

The focus of this first study series is on the event-structural approach to transparent adjuncts in Truswell (2007), who claims that the aspectual classes of the two predicates in a BPPA construction determine whether the adjunct is transparent for extraction or behaves as an island. Truswell proposes the generalization in (6) and the condition on extraction from adjunct predicates in (7):

(6) All transparent secondary predicates must be atelic, and must modify telic predicates. (Truswell 2007: 1369)

(7) Extraction from Adjunct Secondary Predicates:
Extraction of a complement from a secondary predicate is permitted only if the event denoted by the secondary predicate is identified with an event position in the matrix predicate. (Truswell 2007: 1359)

The generalization in (6) and the condition in (7) are both formulated for *wh*-extraction: Truswell assumes that these conditions are not operative in declaratives, resulting in a different pattern of grammaticality in the two constructions (Truswell 2007: 1373–1374). Atelic adjunct predicates are also preferred in declaratives, but the choice of matrix predicate as telic or atelic is irrelevant. Truswell (2007) argues for a semantically determined island-repair effect that reduces the effect of an ungrammatical extraction operation for a specific combination of aspectual classes.

The following experiments will first examine the paradigm in Truswell (2007) to see whether the aspectual classes of matrix and adjunct predicate show the predicted effects in Experiment 1. In addition to declaratives and *wh*-extraction, I also examine relativization from the adjunct. With the exception of Sprouse et al. (2016) and Abeillé et al. (2020), this type of A'-movement has not been systematically discussed in the previous literature, but since many attested examples of transparent adjuncts involve relativization, this construction deserves closer attention (Cattell 1976; Chomsky 1982; Santorini 2019; Chaves & Putnam 2020). In Experiment 2, I will investigate whether aspectual classes impose constraints on the application of *wh*-extraction that are not operative in declaratives; to achieve this, I directly compare declarative baseline conditions with interrogatives. Experiment 3 examines the effect of adjunct integration by comparing the BPPA construction with a type of free adjunct construction that is clearly syntactically detached from the matrix clause by means of orthographic marking.

4.5.1 Experiment 1: Aspectual classes across constructions

This experiment investigates the effect of different combinations of aspectual classes on the acceptability of BPPA constructions in three different sentence structures: the declarative base position, *wh*-extraction from the adjunct, and relativization from the adjunct. By manipulating the telicity of matrix and adjunct predicates, the predictions in Truswell (2007) about the relative differences in declaratives and *wh*-extraction can be experimentally tested; specifically, the interest is in whether the three syntactic forms differ in the presence or absence of effects for telicity in the two predicates.

4.5.1.1 Study design, methods, and participants

This experiment uses a 2 × 2 factorial design with the factors MATRIX TELICITY and ADJUNCT TELICITY, both with the levels *telic* and *atelic*. Additionally, there is a between-subjects factor STRUCTURE with the three levels *declarative*, *wh-extraction*, and *relativization*; this creates three sub-experiments which were run on different participant pools and are analyzed independently. Crossing the two factors MATRIX TELICITY and ADJUNCT TELICITY yields four conditions for each level of the between-subjects factor. Sample items for the three levels of STRUCTURE are shown in (8)–(10). Underscores in the *wh*-extraction and relativization sub-experiments indicate the gap position; they were not shown in the actual experiment.

(8) STRUCTURE: Declarative
    a. Liz got nervous noticing the spider on her arm.   [telic/telic]
    b. Liz got nervous watching a horror movie.   [telic/atelic]
    c. Liz lay in bed noticing the spider on her arm.   [atelic/telic]
    d. Liz lay in bed watching a horror movie.   [atelic/atelic]

(9) STRUCTURE: *wh*-extraction
    a. What did Liz get nervous noticing __ ?   [telic/telic]
    b. What did Liz get nervous watching __ ?   [telic/atelic]
    c. What did Liz lie in bed noticing __ ?   [atelic/telic]
    d. What did Liz lie in bed watching __ ?   [atelic/atelic]

(10) STRUCTURE: Relativization
    a. This is the spider that Liz got nervous noticing __ .   [telic/telic]
    b. This is the movie that Liz got nervous watching __ .   [telic/atelic]
    c. This is the spider that Liz lay in bed noticing __ .   [atelic/telic]
    d. This is the movie that Liz lay in bed watching __ .   [atelic/atelic]

For each of the three structures, the experiment consisted of 16 items, which were distributed across four lists according to the Latin Square design so that each participant judged four lexicalizations per condition. Items were presented together with 32 fillers with varying degrees of grammaticality; the items-to-filler ratio was 1:2. Telic predicates are either achievements or accomplishments, and atelic predicates are activity predicates in the sense of Vendler (1957) and Dowty (1979). Half of the items had an intransitive matrix predicate, the other half transitive matrix predicates with an overt complement. A reduced relative clause reading of the adjunct predicate was avoided for transitive matrix predicates, based on plausibility criteria for the complement DP and the adjunct predicate, e.g. an inanimate complement DP with an agentive predicate in the adjunct. The possibility of a free adjunct reading could not be completely excluded in this experimental setup with written stimuli, but the absence of an orthographic separation with commas or dashes between the matrix clause and the adjunct should make this reading less plausible. This potential ambiguity is the reason Brown (2017) uses auditory stimuli without an intonational break between matrix clause and adjunct.

The three levels of the between-subjects factor STRUCTURE have the following characteristics: the base position is a declarative BPPA construction, which serves as a control condition to see whether the three structures show different effects of telicity. In the *wh*-extraction conditions, there is a filler–gap dependency between the sentence-initial bare *wh*-word *what* and the direct object of the adjunct predicate. Relativization conditions are *that*-relative clauses with clause-external antecedents (Huddleston & Pullum 2002: 1081) in a cleft-like *this is X* construction. This is still a focalizing construction in terms of Liu et al. (2022), so that similar effects as for *wh*-extraction can be expected.

The experiment was conducted as an online acceptability study with written stimuli using the OnExp platform hosted by the University of Tübingen.[16] After a page with questions about personal information like age, first language, and occupation, a short practice phase explained how the experiment works. The study description did not exclusively specify the need for English as a first language to receive payment in order to avoid participants lying about their first language;

---

16 http://www.lingexp.uni-tuebingen.de/OnExp2/

participants who indicated a first language other than English were removed from the results and were not included in the analysis. In the actual experiment, participants saw one sentence at a time in randomized order for each participant together with the fillers. There were no time restrictions for individual answers. Participants were instructed to rate the naturalness of sentences on a 7-point Likert scale, with 1 being "totally unnatural" and 7 being "completely natural". They were instructed to provide quick, intuitive judgments, but also to read the sentences carefully.

A total of 144 participants was recruited via Amazon's Mechanical Turk platform,[17] 48 for each level of STRUCTURE and twelve per list. They were paid for their participation. Before statistical analysis, participants who indicated a first language other than English were removed from the results. For base position, this affected five participants. Two additional participants were excluded due to a technical problem with the OnExp platform that resulted in incomplete data sets. The total number of participants for this sub-experiment was 41. For the *wh*-extraction lists, four participants were excluded from analysis because they indicated a first language other than English. One additional participant was excluded due to a technical problem with OnExp. The total number of participants for this sub-experiment lists was 43. For the Relativization lists, eight participants were excluded because their first language was not English; one additional participant was removed due to an incomplete data set. The total number of participants for this sub-experiment was thus 39.

4.5.1.2 Hypotheses

For this experiment, I investigate the following hypotheses, which are derived from the Aktionsart generalization in (6) proposed in Truswell (2007). Note that Truswell (2007) does not discuss relativization; I assume that the same predictions as for *wh*-extraction hold here because both structures instantiate A'-extraction from an adjunct constituent.

(11) Hypotheses for Experiment 1
    H1a. ADJUNCT TELICITY has a significant effect in declaratives: conditions with atelic adjuncts are significantly more acceptable than conditions with telic adjuncts; see Truswell (2007: 1373).
    H1b. No significant effect of MATRIX TELICITY in declaratives: conditions with telic and atelic matrix predicates are equally acceptable; see Truswell (2007: 1373).

---

[17] https://www.mturk.com

H1c. Under *wh*-extraction and relativization, both MATRIX TELICITY and ADJUNCT TELICITY show significant effects: the condition with a telic matrix and atelic adjunct predicate is significantly more acceptable than the other three conditions; see Truswell (2007: 1369).

Conditions with atelic adjunct predicates should be significantly more acceptable in declaratives than conditions with telic adjuncts (H1a). In declarative sentences, the requirement for an atelic adjunct is taken as a result of the morphological marking of the *-ing*-form, which blocks a telic interpretation of the adjunct predicate and is independent of extraction: "The requirement for an atelic secondary predicate remains in declarative constructions" (Truswell 2007: 1373). If this requirement is satisfied, Truswell states that the aspectual class of the matrix predicate does not affect the grammaticality of the declarative construction: "declaratives with atelic matrix verbs are quite unremarkable" (Truswell 2007: 1373). Thus, there should be no significant effect of MATRIX PREDICATE in declaratives (H1b).

The two extraction structures are expected to show a different effect structure than declaratives: both MATRIX TELICITY and ADJUNCT TELICITY are predicted to show significant main effects (H1c). In these structures, there same effect of ADJUNCT TELICITY is expected, but also a reverse effect of MATRIX PREDICATE, where telic conditions are predicted to be more acceptable than atelic conditions. As a result, the condition with a telic matrix and atelic adjunct predicate should be significantly more acceptable than the other three conditions.[18]

4.5.1.3 Results

The mean ratings plus standard deviations (SDs) for the four conditions in the three structures are shown in Table 4.1. The results are shown graphically in the interaction plot in Figure 4.4.[19] Judgments for declaratives are quite favorable in general with the highest ratings for the [telic/atelic] condition (mean: 5.88, SD: 1.23), but there are differences between the four conditions. Ratings for relativization are lower than those for declaratives and marginally higher than those for *wh*-extraction. The lowest overall judgments are reported for the [atelic/telic] condition with *wh*-extraction (mean: 3.06, SD: 1.61).

---

[18] This experimental design does not directly permit conclusions about the presence or absence of an island-repair effect in case of an interaction; this can only be done in a direct comparison of declarative and extraction structures, which is the objective of Experiment 2 for a subset of the conditions used in this experiment.

[19] All graphs were created in R using the GGPLOT2 (version 3.3-3; Wickham 2016) and GGPUBR (version 0.4.0; Kassambara 2020) packages.

Tab. 4.1: Numerical results for Experiment 1. Mean ratings plus standard deviations (SD) and 95 % confidence intervals (CI) for the four experimental conditions in the three sub-experiments.

Structure	Matrix telicity	Adjunct telicity	Mean	SD	CI$_{95}$
Declarative	telic	telic	5.45	1.28	[5.25;5.64]
	telic	atelic	5.88	1.23	[5.69;6.07]
	atelic	telic	4.85	1.47	[4.62;5.08]
	atelic	atelic	5.47	1.34	[5.26;5.68]
wh-extraction	telic	telic	3.84	1.73	[3.58;4.10]
	telic	atelic	4.37	1.91	[4.09;4.66]
	atelic	telic	3.06	1.61	[2.82;3.30]
	atelic	atelic	3.72	1.78	[3.45;3.98]
Relativization	telic	telic	3.87	1.71	[3.60;4.14]
	telic	atelic	4.68	1.81	[4.39;4.97]
	atelic	telic	3.19	1.55	[2.94;3.43]
	atelic	atelic	3.85	1.74	[3.58;4.13]

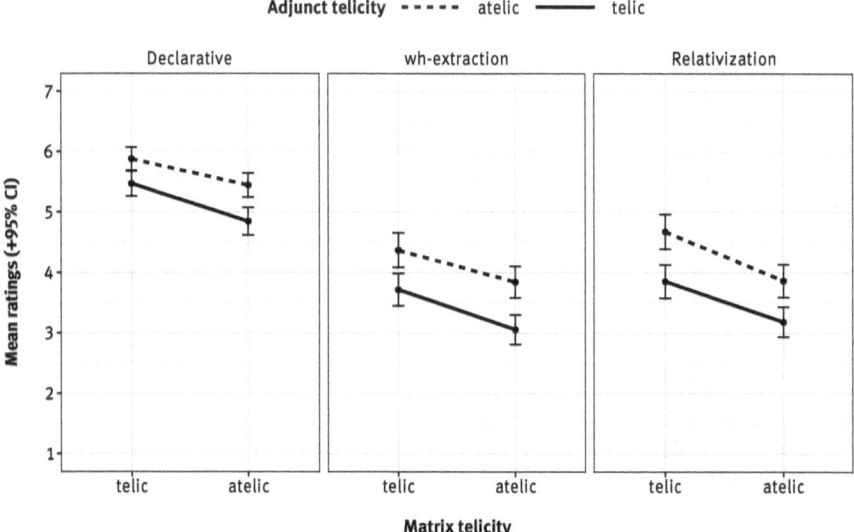

Fig. 4.4: Results of Experiment 1 (mean ratings). The three vertical panels show the levels of the between-subjects factor STRUCTURE (declarative, *wh*-extraction & relativization). Error bars show 95 % confidence intervals.

For statistical analysis, three linear mixed-effects models (LMEMs) were created in the statistical programming language R (version 4.0.2; R Core Team 2020), one for each level of the between-subjects factor STRUCTURE. These and all models in the following experiments are created using the MIXED() function from the AFEX package (version 0.22-2; Singmann et al. 2020), which creates LMEMs using the LMER() function from the LME4 package (version 1.1-21; Bates et al. 2015). As recommended in Singmann & Kellen (2020: 16–17) for random effects with small numbers of levels, the Kenward-Roger method option for estimating degrees of freedom was chosen in the function call (METHOD = 'K'). The MIXED() function uses sum-coding for factors by default. In the three models, MATRIX TELICITY (TELM) and ADJUNCT TELICITY (TELA) are entered as fixed effects because they were manipulated in the experiment; participants (= ID) and ITEM are considered random effects and were included to account for the non-independence of the data (Singmann & Kellen 2020: 5–6). The models are calculated on untransformed ratings, as the random intercepts for participants (ID) are considered to capture individual variations in the use of the Likert scale sufficiently and because raw values can be better localized on the underlying 7-point Likert scale.[20] The fixed effects were re-leveled so that the level which Truswell (2007) predicts to be worse is set as the reference level. Thus, MATRIX TELICITY has the reference level *atelic* and ADJUNCT TELICITY the level *telic*. With the default sum-coding of the MIXED() function, a negative parameter estimate shows that the reference level is less acceptable than the other level.

Following Barr et al. (2013), the models include the maximal random effect structure that led to model convergence in order to include as many sources of variability as possible (see Winter 2020; Singmann & Kellen 2020). In a maximal random effects structure, all factors of the experiment plus their interactions are allowed to vary in their intercepts and slopes by both cluster variables (random effects). Since the experimental design includes within-subjects and within-items factors, random slopes for the fixed effects are recommended for the ITEM random effect (Barr et al. 2013: 257, 260). This also includes the correlations between random effects (see Singmann & Kellen 2020: 18). The following example illustrates the general formula used in these maximal models for two generic factors F1/F2; see Bates et al. (2015) and Winter (2020) for a detailed description of LMEM syntax.

---

[20] Fitting LMEMs on Likert scale data makes the assumption that the ordinal data can be treated as continuous interval data. There is disagreement whether this violation of model assumptions leads to increased Type I error rates. I follow Gibson et al. (2011) and Norman (2010) in assuming that a LMEM analysis for the data reported here is possible; see also the methodological comments in C. Müller (2019: 117).

(12) a. RATING ~ F1 * F2 + (F1 * F2 | ID) + (F1 * F2 | ITEM)
b. Read: the dependent variable RATING is modeled as depending on the main effects and interaction of two factors F1/F2, while allowing random intercepts and slopes for both factors plus interaction and correlations by the cluster variables ID and ITEM

Since the number of parameters to be estimated in these models is quite high, it can happen that the model does not converge successfully. For example, a maximal random effect structure for one cluster variable introduces ten different parameters that need to be estimated by the model; see Winter (2020: 240–241). Issues of non-convergence are still debated in the statistical literature, and there are several suggestions how to handle them. See Jaeger (2009), Matuschek et al. (2017), Eager & Roy (2017), Singmann & Kellen (2020), and Winter (2020) for discussion. Barr et al. (2013: 276) agree that a simplification of the random effects structure is sometimes necessary to reach convergence. In the models reported here, I first tried to fit the maximal random effects structure as in (12a) above. If the model did not converge, I reduced the random effects structure following the methods suggested in Jaeger (2009) and Singmann & Kellen (2020: 18–19). In a first step, I examined the correlation between random effects: if correlations showed "perfect" values (i.e. 0.00 or 1.00), I removed the correlation, signified by '||' in the model syntax. The MIXED() function requires the optional argument 'EXPAND_RE = TRUE' in this case. If the model still showed convergence issues, I removed random effect terms that showed the lowest variance estimates until the model reached convergence. This can be called the "maximal random effects structure justified by the experimental design and supported by the data"; Matuschek et al. (2017) use the term "parsimonious random effects structure". Even though there is no agreed-upon procedure for dealing with non-convergence issues due to complex random effects structures, including varying intercepts and slopes for as many factors as possible that are justified by the experimental design is an important step to capture variability in the data that would otherwise be ignored in the analysis. The function call, parameter estimates, and significance values are reported in Table 4.2 on the following page.[21] Each level of the between-subjects factor STRUCTURE is shown in an individual table.

All three sub-experiments show a similar effect structure: there are significant effects for the factors MATRIX TELICITY and ADJUNCT TELICITY (all $|t| > 2$, $p < .05$),

---

[21] The significance codes used in this chapter are as follows, following standard practice: *** = $p < .001$; ** = $p < .01$; * = $p < .05$; . = $p < .1$. Unmarked p-values are not significant. Parameter estimates and significance statistics for the intercept are omitted as they have no bearing on the interpretation of the results.

Tab. 4.2: Statistical results for Experiment 1. Model syntax, parameter estimates, standard errors (SE), and *t*-statistics for the two factors of the experimental design plus their interaction. Results for the three sub-experiments are shown in separate tables.

Model: mixed(rating~telm*tela+(telm+tela||id)+(telm*tela||item))						
Fixed effects:	Estimate	SE	df	*t*-value	*p*-value	Sig.
Matrix telicity	−.26254	.05620	14.13	−4.672	< .001	***
Adjunct telicity	−.25241	.08127	17.30	−3.106	< .01	**
Matrix telicity × Adjunct telicity	−.03925	.06711	13.95	−.585	.567935	

(a) STRUCTURE: declarative

Model: mixed(rating~telm*tela+(telm+tela||id)+(telm*tela||item))						
Fixed effects:	Estimate	SE	df	*t*-value	*p*-value	Sig.
Matrix telicity	−.30289	.10695	15.80	−2.832	< .05	*
Adjunct telicity	−.36360	.15804	16.44	−2.301	< .05	*
Matrix telicity × Adjunct telicity	−.06827	.06827	12.85	−.786	.4460	

(b) STRUCTURE: *wh*-extraction

Model: mixed(rating~telm*tela+(telm+tela||id)+(telm*tela||item))						
Fixed effects:	Estimate	SE	df	*t*-value	*p*-value	Sig.
Matrix telicity	−.38969	.11101	14.32	−3.510	< .01	**
Adjunct telicity	−.36554	.11094	15.44	−3.295	< .01	**
Matrix telicity × Adjunct telicity	.03052	.09610	12.71	.318	.75595	

(c) STRUCTURE: relativization

but no significant interaction between them (all $|t| < 1$, $p > .1$). In addition, the parameter estimates for both fixed effects are negative, meaning that the change from telic to atelic matrix predicates and the change from atelic to telic adjunct predicates results in lower acceptability. Note that due to sum-coding, the parameter estimates are half the actual size of the numerical differences between conditions in the model. Despite some differences between the sub-experiments, the parameter estimates for the two factors are very similar to each other, suggesting that both factors have roughly equal effects on acceptability. As the parameter estimates for the interaction terms are close to zero and not statistically significant, they are not further analyzed here. The fact that declaratives and interrogatives have a negative estimate for the interaction whereas relativization has a positive estimate would be interesting in the presence of a significant interaction. A negative estimate for the interaction indicates a superadditive effect, a positive one a subadditive effect.

The results of the three sub-experiments lead to the following conclusions about the hypotheses for this experiment: hypothesis (H1a) can be confirmed, as ADJUNCT TELICITY shows a significant effect in the declarative sub-experiment. Conditions with atelic adjunct predicates are significantly more acceptable than conditions with telic adjuncts. However, hypothesis (H1b) cannot be confirmed because MATRIX TELICITY also has a significant effect in declaratives: conditions with atelic matrix predicates are significantly less acceptable than conditions with telic ones. For the two extraction sub-experiments, hypothesis (H1c) is confirmed because both factors show significant main effects. It is also the case that the condition with telic matrix predicates and atelic adjuncts is significantly more acceptable than the other three conditions.

4.5.1.4 Discussion

The main focus of this experiment was on the effects of aspectual classes in the BPPA construction and how well the predictions from Truswell (2007) are reflected in the results. I will discuss four points in this section: (i) the identical effect structures in the three sub-experiments, (ii) the relation to the predictions for declaratives and interrogatives in Truswell (2007), (iii) the advantage of non-categorical models of acceptability to explain the data patterns, and (iv) the architectural conclusions which can be drawn from this experiment.

(i) The results clearly show that there are significant effects of the aspectual classes of the two predicates in the three sub-experiments. In all structures, telic matrix predicates are preferred over atelic ones and atelic adjuncts are more acceptable than telic ones. Since no sub-experiment shows a significant interaction of the two factors, the effect structure is identical in the three experiments: the effects of both factors are linear-additive, which means that they operate independently and do not influence each other. As the three sub-experiments are tested with different participant pools, I will not statistically compare the relative acceptability of the conditions in the three structures. However, the results indicate that the two extraction sub-experiments yield lower acceptability ratings than the declarative. This is not surprising considering the agreement in the literature that processing costs are associated with extraction operations because they are cognitively demanding (Hawkins 1999; Hofmeister & Sag 2010; Hofmeister et al. 2013; Sprouse et al. 2013; Wagers 2013; Sprouse et al. 2016). It also appears that relativization receives marginally better judgments than *wh*-extraction. There are two possible reasons for this: the D-linked *wh*-elements in relativization are more accessible than bare *wh*-pronouns (Sag et al. 2008), and the fact that explicitly mentioning the extracted nominal can disambiguate the structure and make the gap site in complement position of the adjunct predicate semantically more plausible than the potential gap site in complement position to the matrix predicate, which was not overtly filled in all items. Following the observations in Abeillé et al. (2020) and Liu et al. (2022), it is to be expected that judgments for a non-focalizing embedding of relativization such as *I liked the song that John arrived whistling* should receive even more favorable ratings closer to the declarative condition.

(ii) The results of this experiment do not fully confirm the intuitive grammaticality judgments in Truswell (2007). In conditions with *wh*-extraction, the aspectual classes of the two predicates behave as predicted: telic matrix and atelic adjunct predicates are preferred. The results also single out the combination of a telic matrix and an atelic adjunct predicate as the condition that is judged most acceptable by the participants (Truswell 2007: 1363). The negative effect of telic adjuncts in declaratives is likewise predicted in Truswell (2007: 1373). However, the remaining predictions are not supported by the results. Truswell states that declarative sentences with atelic matrix predicates are "quite unremarkable" (Truswell 2007: 1373) as long as the adjunct is atelic. This cannot be confirmed in the results: there is a significant effect of MATRIX TELICITY in declaratives which decreases acceptability for conditions with telic and atelic adjuncts to the same degree, as shown by the non-significant interaction. The same effect structure shows up in the two extraction conditions. This means that the choice of matrix predicate is not irrelevant, as Truswell (2007) assumes, even if only the conditions with atelic adjuncts are considered. These results do not confirm all the predictions for declaratives in Truswell (2007): instead of only one main effect of ADJUNCT TELICITY, both factors have significant main effects. In fact, the pattern observed in declaratives is problematic for the judgments in Truswell (2007) because the condition with two telic predicates receives almost identical mean ratings as the condition with two atelic predicates. If there are only penalties for telic adjuncts but not for atelic matrix predicates, as Truswell (2007) predicts, then it comes as a surprise that these two conditions receive virtually identical mean ratings.

(iii) The results of the interrogative sub-experiment reveal a more intricate pattern of acceptability than Truswell (2007) predicts: instead of one grammatical and three ungrammatical conditions, there is a gradient acceptability decrease which depends on the two factor levels of the two predicates. Atelic matrix predicates and telic adjunct predicates individually lower acceptability; as the parameter estimates for MATRIX and ADJUNCT TELICITY indicate, these effects are roughly of the same size. These non-categorical results show that a categorical model of grammar struggles to deal with fine-grained data (see Featherston 2019: 159); this is not a criticism of categorical judgments, but rather a strong motivation to check theoretical predictions against experimental facts (see Jurka 2010: section 2.2). It could be argued that the three "ungrammatical" conditions fall below a cut-off line that separates unacceptable from acceptable sentences. If this cut-off line lies just below the mean rating for the condition with telic matrix and atelic adjunct predicates, this exactly reproduces the predicted pattern with one grammatical and three ungrammatical conditions. However, this simplification blurs the individual distinctions between the different conditions and thus leads to a loss of valuable data about these contrasts. In reverse, it could be argued that Truswell (2007) does not notice the differences in declaratives with atelic adjuncts because both are highly acceptable. A model of grammar that recognizes gradual levels of acceptability has an advantage in dealing with such subtle contrasts.

(iv) The fact that the same effect structure is found in the three syntactic structures casts doubt on the theoretical conclusions in Truswell (2007), who predicts different patterns for declaratives and interrogatives: recall that his condition on extraction from adjunct predicates in (7) above is formulated as a condition operative only under extraction:

(13)   The fact that corresponding declarative constructions do not obey the restrictions ... indicates that these restrictions arise as a result of *wh*-extraction from the secondary predicate. This makes ([7]), in effect, a generalization about locality, albeit one couched in less strictly phrase-structural terms than usual.   (Truswell 2007: 1374)

In the light of the results for the declarative base position in this experiment compared to the pattern with *wh*-extraction, this conclusion has to be called into question: since the effect structures of declaratives and interrogatives are identical, there is no evidence that extraction is sensitive to the two telicity factors.[22] The results are more compatible with the Independence Hypothesis than with the Interaction Hypothesis because an identical effect structure is observed in all three structures, which indicates that the construction-specific licensing conditions determine acceptability in the declarative, to which are added the operation-specific effects of *wh*-extraction and relativization; these are allowed to differ, as suggested by the ratings for the relativization sub-experiment, which are marginally more favorable than those for *wh*-extraction. Truswell's (2007) claims cannot be fully rejected yet without testing declarative and extraction conditions in one experimental design with the same participants. This is done in the next experiment.

---

22 Similar results are reported for freezing effects in Culicover & Winkler (2018), especially their experiments on extraction from extraposition and Heavy NP Shift (see also Hofmeister et al. 2015; Winkler et al. 2016; Konietzko et al. 2018; Konietzko 2018). Culicover & Winkler show that the shifting and extraposition operations result in less acceptable ratings even in the absence of extraction; the mean acceptability of conditions where both movement of a constituent and subextraction from this constituent happens can be predicted in a linear-additive fashion, adding the individual costs for the operations. Culicover & Winkler (2018: 364) offer an explanation in terms of processing costs, where operations are costly because they affect the probability of the predicted parse for the sentence.

4.5.2 Experiment 2: Event structure in declaratives and interrogatives

This experiment compares a subset of the Aktionsart combinations investigated in Experiment 1 in a direct comparison of declaratives with *wh*-extraction conditions. This comparison between the base position and extraction is crucial in determining whether event-structural characteristics influences the strength of the extraction effect, as claimed by event-structural interaction accounts such as Truswell (2007). Only sentences with atelic adjuncts are used in this experiment because telic adjuncts have a negative effect on acceptability for both declaratives and interrogatives, whereas the telicity of the matrix predicate is taken to only apply in interrogatives (Truswell 2007). The direct comparison of declaratives and interrogatives that only differ in the aspectual class of the matrix predicate allows conclusions about the question whether the aspectual class of the matrix predicate imposes constraints on the application of *wh*-extraction that are not operative in declaratives. This experimental design also allows for a better evaluation of the claim in Truswell (2007) that the preference for a telic matrix predicate in interrogatives is caused by the application of *wh*-extraction.

4.5.2.1 Study design, methods, and participants

This experiment uses a 2 × 2 factorial design with the factors MATRIX TELICITY (levels: *telic* & *atelic*) and STRUCTURE (levels: *–wh* & *+wh*); corresponding to conditions 2 and 4 of Experiment 1. Sixteen target items were distributed across four lists in a Latin Square design so that participants saw four lexicalizations of each condition. Items were mixed with 32 fillers of different degrees of grammaticality; 15 of the fillers are the cardinal well-formedness sentences developed in Gerbrich et al. (2019). They are used to anchor the scale across the spectrum of grammaticality from perfectly natural to strongly degraded. As an additional advantage, they allow for a standardized comparison of the target items to degrees of acceptability that have proven constant across numerous experiments. The study design is shown in (14).

(14) a. Peter got excited reading the newspaper.   [telic/–wh]
      b. What did Peter get excited reading __ ?   [telic/+wh]
      c. Peter sat at the computer reading the newspaper.   [atelic/–wh]
      d. What did Peter sit at the computer reading __ ?   [atelic/+wh]

The telicity of the adjunct predicate was kept constant across target items, which are all atelic activity predicates. Telic matrix predicates are accomplishments or achievements, atelic ones activities in terms of Vendler (1957). With a few adjustments, most items were re-used from Experiment 1.

The experiment was uploaded to the OnExp platform and participants were recruited via Amazon Mechanical Turk. The instructions were identical to those of Experiment 1. Items were shown in randomized order per participant together with the fillers; participants were asked to judge the naturalness of the sentences on a 7-point Likert scale, with 1 being "totally unnatural" and 7 "completely natural".

A total of 48 participants was recruited for this experiment, twelve for each of the four lists. Four participants had to be removed before statistical analysis because they indicated a first language other than English. In addition, one participant had to be removed because of technical problems with the OnExp platform. Four participants were removed because they did not use the scale properly; this was judged by their performance on the standardized fillers according to the methodological notes on participant exclusion in Section 4.4. All in all, responses from 39 participants were included in the statistical analysis.

4.5.2.2 Hypotheses

For this experiment, I assume the following hypotheses based on the predictions in Truswell (2007):

(15) Hypotheses for Experiment 2
 H2a. There is a significant effect of STRUCTURE.
 H2b. MATRIX TELICITY only has an effect for the [+wh] level of STRUCTURE: there should be a significant interaction between the two factors.

Hypothesis (H2a) reflects the fact that there should be an effect of extracting out of an adjunct constituent, leading to a decrease in acceptability, as predicted by the CED and the general cognitive cost of *wh*-extraction (Wagers 2013). As far as the factor MATRIX TELICITY is concerned, this factor should only have an effect in the extraction conditions. In the [–wh] level of STRUCTURE, it should not make a difference (H2b); see Truswell (2007: 1374). Statistically, this leads to the predicted presence of an interaction between these two factors, which would show that the *atelic* level of the factor MATRIX TELICITY reacts more strongly to the extraction than the *telic* level. This is the major claim presented in Truswell (2007): matrix predicates differing in their telicity show different reactions when extraction takes place, while they behave similarly in declaratives.

4.5.2.3 Results

Table 4.3 shows the mean ratings for the four experimental conditions together with the mean ratings for the standard fillers. A graphical representation can be found in Figure 4.5, which also includes the standardized fillers with the labels 'A' through 'E', where A is fully natural and E fully unnatural. They reproduce the expected pattern reported in Gerbrich et al. (2019), and provide upper and lower bounds on the scale (see Featherston 2009: 65–68). All conditions fall within the range of the highest and lowest standardized fillers.

A linear mixed-effects model was created for the untransformed results as described in Experiment 1. MATRIX TELICITY and STRUCTURE are entered as fixed effects, while participants (ID) and ITEMS are used as random effects. The model

Tab. 4.3: Numerical results for Experiment 2. Mean ratings plus standard deviations (SD) and 95 % confidence intervals (CI) for the four experimental conditions and the five levels of the standard fillers.

	Experimental items				Standard fillers			
Matrix telicity	Structure	Mean	SD	CI$_{95}$	A–E	Mean	SD	CI$_{95}$
telic	–wh	6.31	1.06	[6.14;6.48]	A	6.80	0.53	[6.71;6.90]
telic	+wh	4.41	1.84	[4.12;4.70]	B	5.55	1.32	[5.31;5.79]
atelic	–wh	5.54	1.36	[5.32;5.75]	C	3.56	1.34	[3.31;3.80]
atelic	+wh	3.50	1.81	[3.21;3.79]	D	3.09	1.32	[2.84;3.33]
					E	1.56	0.70	[1.44;1.69]

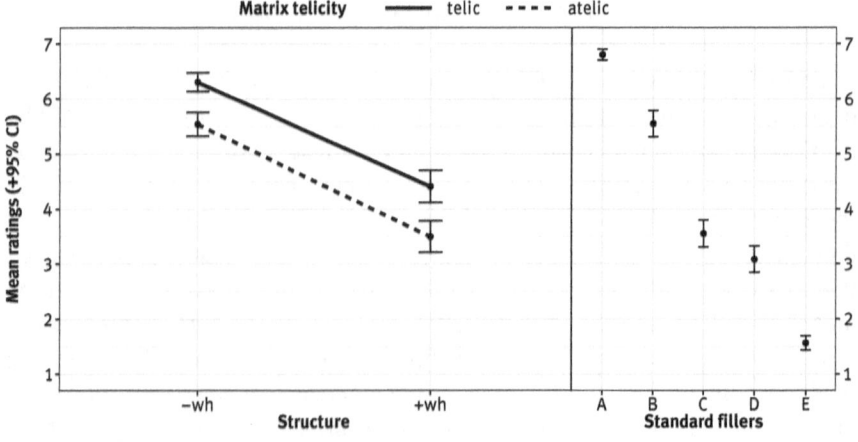

Fig. 4.5: Results of Experiment 2 (mean ratings) compared to standardized fillers. Mean ratings for the five levels of the standardized fillers A–E are shown on the right for comparison. Error bars show 95 % confidence intervals.

includes both fixed effects plus their interaction. The reference level for MATRIX TELICITY was set to *atelic* and to *+wh* for STRUCTURE; negative parameter estimates thus indicate that these levels reduce acceptability. The maximal converging random effects structure includes random slopes for STRUCTURE by participants and random slopes for MATRIX TELICITY and STRUCTURE and their interaction by items without correlations.

The model syntax, parameter estimates, and significance values are reported in Table 4.4. There are significant effects for MATRIX TELICITY ($\beta = -.413, t = -3.712, p < .01$) and STRUCTURE ($\beta = -.995, t = -9.578, p < .001$), but the interaction is not significant ($\beta = -.037, t = -.327, p = .716$). Telic matrix predicates are more acceptable than atelic ones, as the negative estimate for MATRIX TELICITY shows. The decrease in acceptability for *wh*-extraction is more than twice as large as that of an atelic matrix predicate. No evidence is found for a superadditive effect when the adjunct is atelic and extraction takes place, as the estimate for the interaction term is close to zero.

Tab. 4.4: Statistical results for Experiment 2. Model syntax, parameter estimates, standard errors (SE), and *t*-statistics for the two factors of the experimental design plus their interaction.

Model: mixed(rating~telm*struc+(struc||id)+(telm*struc||item))						
Fixed effects:	Estimate	SE	df	*t*-value	*p*-value	Sig.
Matrix telicity	−.41258	.11116	14.74	−3.712	< .01	**
Structure	−.99464	.10385	18.77	−9.578	< .001	***
Matrix telicity × Structure	−.03685	.09909	13.75	−.372	.71567	

The statistical results support the hypothesis that extraction leads to lower acceptability, as predicted in hypothesis (H2a). However, the hypothesis that MATRIX TELICITY affects only the [+wh] level of STRUCTURE (H2b), as predicted in Truswell (2007), cannot be confirmed. The lack of an interaction and the presence of a significant main effect of MATRIX TELICITY shows that both levels of MATRIX TELICITY are equally affected by the extraction. It is thus not the case that *wh*-extraction interacts directly with the aspectual class of the matrix predicate; this result does not provide evidence for the claim in Truswell (2007) about the sensitivity of extraction to aspectual classes. Rather, the differences observed in interrogatives are the same as in the corresponding declaratives.

4.5.2.4 Discussion

These results are interesting in three aspects: (i) the relation to the predictions in Truswell (2007) that extraction is sensitive to the aspectual class of the matrix predicate, (ii) the relation to the research questions for this chapter, and (iii) the acceptability of extraction from BPPA compared to the standardized fillers.

(i) The failure to confirm hypothesis (H2b) is the most interesting and relevant for an evaluation of the predictions in Truswell (2007). The choice of matrix predicate has a significant effect on judgments in both declarative and extraction conditions. While such a behavior is predicted for extraction conditions, it is not for declaratives. The results show that the two factors operate independently: it is not the case that atelic matrix predicates are affected disproportionally by extraction than telic ones. These results show that the factors MATRIX TELICITY and STRUCTURE both affect the unmarked reference condition [telic/−wh] in a linear-additive fashion. There is no evidence of an island-repair effect that depends on the telicity of the matrix predicate; there is also no additional island-effect when the matrix predicate is atelic. As such, the central claim of Truswell (2007) cannot be confirmed. Instead of drawing direct conclusions about the interaction of aspectual classes with the application of filler–gap dependencies across island boundaries, it is necessary to take a step back and think about what causes the observed differences in declaratives. This is exactly what the Independence Hypothesis predicts: the licensing conditions for the adjunct need to be distinguished from the syntactic licensing of the gap inside the adjunct.

(ii) The results of this experiment support some preliminary conclusions regarding the research questions for this chapter: first, the results speak for the Independence Hypothesis rather than the interaction account as formulated in Truswell (2007). Second, the predictions in Truswell (2007) cannot be directly replicated because the telicity of the matrix predicate does have an influence on acceptability. Third, the lexical semantics of the matrix predicate in the form of telicity has an effect on acceptability which is independent of extraction. This result indicates that the acceptability differences in interrogatives are not the result of extraction, as claimed in Truswell (2007: 1374) and that extraction per se need not be sensitive to aspectual classes.

(iii) The mean acceptability ratings for the two [+wh] conditions are not as low as could be expected: a comparison to the standardized fillers from Gerbrich et al. (2019) shows that neither of the two extraction conditions is close to the bottom of the scale. Instead, they receive remarkably high judgments considering that both instantiate a CED-violation. However, there are some differences between them: the extraction condition with telic matrix predicates received judgments that are between the B- and C-standards. With atelic matrix predicates, judgments are on the level of the C-standards, which would receive a single '?' judgment in the conventions of Gerbrich et al. (2019); there is still a considerable contrast to the E-standards, which are considered ungrammatical but still interpretable. Note that the standardized fillers do not show a perfectly declining slope: the C-standards are much closer to the D-standards than to the B-standards. With the present set of standardized fillers, this is a common result, as seen for example in the results from Jäger (2020). The same is reported for other experiments (Andreas Konietzko and Sam Featherston, p. c.). Gerbrich et al. (2019) are aware of this phenomenon and attribute it to a distortion effect when "the well-formedness values of the experimental sentences fall disproportionately often between two specific values" (Gerbrich et al. 2019: 315–316) and participants try to accommodate the target items between levels of the standard fillers. Since the two conditions with atelic matrix predicates align almost perfectly with the B-standards and the C-standards, and the [+wh] condition with telic matrix predicates is in the middle between B and C, this explanation seems plausible. Nothing hinges on the exact placement of target items to fillers, so this is not problematic.

This experiment has shown that Truswell's (2007) claim that the grammaticality pattern of telic and atelic matrix predicates is a result of extraction does not receive experimental support. Rather, it is necessary to find an explanation why the aspectual class of the matrix predicate has an influence on acceptability in both declaratives and interrogatives. The syntactic analysis of the BPPA construction as an instance of depictive secondary predication offers a first step in this direction because not all activities accept depictives equally (Irimia 2012); I will return to this issue in the conclusion to this study series and in Chapter 5.

4.5.3 Experiment 3: Adjunct integration

The BPPA construction shows a potential ambiguity between the intended reading where the adjunct is part of the same intonation unit as the matrix clause and an analysis where the adjunct predicate is phonologically detached from the matrix clause. This distinction between so-called "integrated" and "detached" adjuncts is discussed in Fabricius-Hansen & Haug (2012a: 43–50). They link the different orthographic notation to an underlying difference in the degree of syntactic integration and a resulting phonetic realization in two intonation units; see also the syntactic COMMA feature in Potts (2005). For Behrens et al. (2012: 194), detached adjuncts share with coordinate structures the characteristic that they are not related by a tighter relation than shared topic time. The example in (16a) shows an orthographically integrated adjunct, (16b) an adjunct that is detached by a comma and thus analyzed as a separate intonation unit.

(16) a. Peter entered the room whistling a song. [integrated adjunct]
    b. Peter entered the room, whistling a song. [detached adjunct]

Detached adjuncts of this form can be described as free adjuncts in the sense of Stump (1985). They are conventionally separated from the matrix clause by orthographic means, such as commas or dashes. This indicates that there is an intonational break, which opens a separate intonation phrase and potentially a new clausal domain. On the other hand, integrated adjuncts are not conventionally separated by orthography and do not constitute a separate intonation phrase: they are syntactically and phonologically integrated into the structure of the matrix predicate (Fabricius-Hansen & Haug 2012a).

With detached adjuncts, an interpretation as a single-event structure is less likely than in the integrated adjunct structure because in contrast to depictives, free adjuncts are analyzed as being derived from adverbial clauses (Stump 1985: 4). They are thus separate and subordinate clausal domains; depictives, on the other hand, are usually analyzed as adjuncts within the verbal projection of the matrix clause (McNally 1997; Winkler 1997; Rothstein 2017) and have the potential to be part of the same event structure if the matrix predicate allows it.

In a setup with written stimuli, this can be problematic due to the variation in English between so-called "light" and "heavy" punctuation: the detached reading may arise even in sentences without an orthographic separation because the comma need not be written in a light punctuation style but can still be interpreted (Fabricius-Hansen & Haug 2012a: 45; Huddleston & Pullum 2002: 1727). For example, the integrated adjunct in (16a) can also be interpreted as (16b) with light punctuation, but the detached version (16b) cannot be interpreted as the integrated version (16a). It is possible that participants interpret a target item as a detached adjunct, even if the adjunct is not separated from the matrix clause by a comma. Brown (2017) avoids this potential problem by presenting her stimuli in auditory form, read by a native speaker with a clearly integrated prosody where there is no pause between the matrix clause and the adjunct. This experiment investigates whether participants are sensitive to the presence or absence of a comma and are able to distinguish between these two constructions.

4.5.3.1 Study design, methods, and participants

This experiment uses a 2 × 2 design with the two factors ATTACHMENT (levels: *integrated* & *detached*) and STRUCTURE (levels: –*wh* & +*wh*). The design is shown in (17).

(17) a. Mark died admitting his biggest mistakes. [integrated/–wh]
 b. What did Mark die admitting __ ? [integrated/+wh]
 c. Mike died, admitting his biggest mistakes. [detached/–wh]
 d. What did Mark die, admitting __ ? [detached/+wh]

This experiments uses most of the conditions with telic matrix predicates from Experiment 2 for the integrated adjunct conditions. Some items, especially those with *get*, did not easily allow the detached comma notation and were replaced with suitable telic predicates. Detached adjunct conditions are formed by separating the participle from the matrix clause with a comma. A set of 16 items was created and distributed across four lists according to the Latin square design so that each participant judged four lexicalizations of each condition. The same 32 fillers as in Experiment 2 were used, including the 15 standard fillers from Gerbrich et al. (2019). The total number of sentences to be judged in this experiment was 48.

The experiment was conducted as an online rating study task with written stimuli, in a similar setup than the previous experiments. Items and fillers were presented in randomized order and participants were instructed to judge the naturalness of the sentences on a 7-point scale. There was a two-hour time limit for the entire experiment, but no limit for individual answers.

A total of 48 participants was recruited via Amazon Mechanical Turk; they were paid for participation in the experiment. Three participants were excluded due to a technical problem with OnExp, which resulted in incomplete data sets. The results from three participants were removed due to poor performance on the standardized fillers. Overall, the results from 42 participants were used in the statistical analysis.

4.5.3.2 Hypotheses

In this experiment, I investigate the following hypotheses about the differences between integrated and detached adjuncts:

(18) Hypotheses for Experiment 3
   H3a. There is a significant effect of ATTACHMENT.
   H3b. There is a significant effect of STRUCTURE.
   H3c. There is a significant interaction between ATTACHMENT and STRUCTURE: detached adjuncts are more sensitive to *wh*-extraction than integrated adjuncts.

I expect a significant main effect of ATTACHMENT (H3a). This is due to the fact that the comma indicates two separate events to be processed (Fabricius-Hansen & Haug 2012a: 46). Instead of a complex event structure with the particle analyzed as an adjunct, the detached adjunct condition calls for the processing of two clausal domains with a matrix clause and a subordinate clause. There should also be a significant effect of STRUCTURE (H3b) because extraction incurs processing costs. The crucial question in this experiment is whether integrated and detached adjuncts differ in their sensitivity to extraction: if detached adjuncts are more sensitive to extraction, this should be visible in an interaction between the two factors (H3c). This hypothesis is partially based on the discussion of detached adjuncts in Fabricius-Hansen & Haug (2012a), but is also expected by Dependency Locality Theory (Gibson 1998, 2000) because the filler–gap dependency crosses a separate clausal domain. See also Potts (2005: 133–135) for extraction asymmetries in relative clauses.

4.5.3.3 Results

Mean ratings for the four conditions and the five levels of the standard fillers including standard deviations are given in Table 4.5. Figure 4.6 shows the results graphically compared to the standardized fillers. It can be seen that the best target condition [integrated/−wh] is close to the A-standards and that the worst condition [detached/+wh] is slightly above the C-standards.

A linear mixed-effects model was created with ATTACHMENT (ATTACH) and STRUCTURE (STRUC) as fixed effects plus their interaction, and participants (ID) and ITEM as random effects. Detached conditions are set as the reference level for ATTACHMENT, interrogative conditions for STRUCTURE. The maximal converging random effects structure contains random slopes for both factors including their interaction, without correlations between random slopes and intercepts. The model syntax as well as parameter estimates and significance values are given in Table 4.6. There are highly significant effects of ATTACHMENT ($\beta = -.422, t = -5.215, p < .001$) and STRUCTURE ($\beta = -.814, t = -7.669, p < .001$), but no significant interaction ($\beta = -.107, t = -1.738, p = .104$).

As expected, conditions with detached adjuncts result in significantly lower judgments across the levels of STRUCTURE. The parameter estimate for the interac-

Tab. 4.5: Numerical results for Experiment 3. Mean ratings plus standard deviations (SD) and 95 % confidence intervals (CI) for the four experimental conditions and the five levels of the standard fillers.

Experimental items					Standard fillers			
Attachment	Structure	Mean	SD	CI$_{95}$	A–E	Mean	SD	CI$_{95}$
integrated	−wh	6.50	0.95	[6.36;6.65]	A	6.79	0.57	[6.68;6.89]
integrated	+wh	5.11	1.93	[4.82;5.41]	B	5.80	1.25	[5.58;6.02]
detached	−wh	5.88	1.24	[5.69;6.07]	C	3.57	1.56	[3.30;3.85]
detached	+wh	4.04	1.77	[3.77;4.31]	D	3.16	1.48	[2.90;3.42]
					E	1.56	0.89	[1.41;1.72]

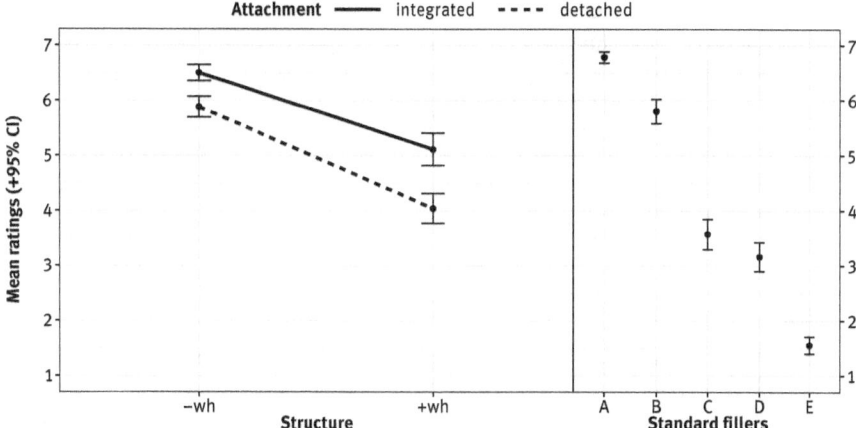

Fig. 4.6: Results of Experiment 3 (mean ratings) compared to standardized fillers. Mean ratings for the five levels of the standardized fillers A–E are shown on the right for comparison. Error bars show 95 % confidence intervals.

Tab. 4.6: Statistical results for Experiment 3. Model syntax, parameter estimates, standard errors (SE), and *t*-statistics for the two factors of the experimental design plus their interaction.

Model: mixed(rating~attach*struc+(attach*struc||id)+(attach*struc||item))						
Fixed effects:	Estimate	SE	df	*t*-value	*p*-value	Sig.
Attachment	−.42243	.08100	27.90	−5.215	< .001	***
Structure	−.81375	.10610	22.36	−7.669	< .001	***
Attachment × Structure	−.10694	.06154	13.87	−1.738	.104	

tion term between the two fixed effects is close to the marginal area $p < .1$, but does not reach significance, especially compared to the highly significant main effects of the other factors with much larger *t*-values; however, it indicates that there is a very small superadditive effect of the interaction term that further decreases the acceptability when both fixed effects are set to the levels expected to decrease acceptability (*detached* and +wh). However, extraction from detached adjuncts is not as low in acceptability as might be expected, considering that extraction takes places across a new intonational domain indicated by the comma notation.

The hypotheses for this experiment are only partially confirmed. There are indeed significant main effects for both ATTACHMENT (H3a) and STRUCTURE (H3b). Conditions with detached adjuncts are significantly less acceptable than conditions with integrated adjuncts. As expected, conditions with *wh*-extraction are less acceptable than the declarative counterparts. However, there is no interaction between the two factors, meaning that the hypothesis about a stronger effect of *wh*-

extraction for detached adjuncts in (H3c) has to be rejected. Again, the effect structure is linear-additive: the acceptability of detached adjuncts with *wh*-extraction from the adjunct can be predicted by adding up the decreases in acceptability for the detached structure and *wh*-extraction. No significant additional penalty applies to detached adjunct predicates. This shows that the degree of syntactic integration of the adjunct predicate into the main clause leads to lower acceptability, but does not modulate the effect of *wh*-extraction.

4.5.3.4 Discussion

In general, the acceptability of the items in this experiment is very high for the two declarative conditions: they both score above the level of the B-standards and can thus be considered fully grammatical. For the two extraction conditions, extractions from integrated adjuncts are almost on the B-level, indicating a fairly acceptable status; extractions from detached adjuncts are roughly on the C-level, which shows some minor degradation but not full-blown ungrammaticality. From a comparison to the results of Experiment 2, it can be seen that detached adjuncts have roughly the same status as conditions with atelic matrix predicates, which also show decreased ratings that are not completely ungrammatical.

The lack of a significant interaction in this experiment is somewhat surprising considering the fact that detached adjuncts should constitute a separate clausal and intonational domain. Still, the clear difference between integrated and detached adjuncts in general shows that the degree of integration between the two predicates makes a significant contribution to acceptability. This contrast shows that participants are sensitive to the two possible readings for the BPPA construction and that the presence or absence of a comma favors one reading over the other. The linear-additive effect structure in this experiment provides further support for the Independence Hypothesis: the differences under *wh*-extraction are a reflection of the same differences in declaratives, where independent decreases in acceptability are caused by the different characteristics of detached adjuncts.

4.5.4 Interim conclusion for study series 1

The experiments in this study series have shown that the aspectual classes of both matrix and adjunct predicate are significant predictors of acceptability for the BPPA construction. They provide partial support for the aspectual condition on extraction proposed in Truswell (2007) but also clearly show that this framework does not explain the entire pattern and that the conclusions about the sensitivity of extraction operations to aspectual classes is not supported by experimental evidence. The main findings in this study series are the following:

(19) a. The aspectual class of both matrix and adjunct predicate has an effect on acceptability.
  b. *wh*-extraction is not sensitive to the aspectual class of the matrix predicate.
  c. The degree of adjunct integration matters but does not influence the strength of the extraction effect.

Experiment 1 shows that atelic matrix predicates and telic adjuncts lead to reduced acceptability. The same linear-additive effect structure is found across three sentence types: (i) base-position declaratives, (ii) sentences with *wh*-extraction from the adjunct, and (iii) sentences with relativization from the adjunct. This identical effect structure shows that Truswell's (2007) generalization that matrix predicates should be telic and adjuncts atelic is partially correct, but that this is not a a result of applying extraction (cf. Truswell 2007: 1374). Another result from this experiment is that the two instances of A'-movements show slightly different levels of acceptability: relativization from the adjunct is marginally more acceptable than *wh*-extraction, but still clearly less acceptable than the declarative base position. This may be due to the different information-structural characteristics of the two extraction operations (Van Valin 2005; Abeillé et al. 2020), or to the fact that relativization involves a D-linked filler (Pesetsky 1987; Haegeman et al. 2014).

Experiment 2 reveals that the aspectual class of the matrix predicate has a significant effect in declaratives. This provides evidence for the fact that Truswell's telicity generalization is not a condition on extraction from the adjunct, but a more general condition on the acceptability of modification by a participle adjunct predicate. The lack of an interaction between the aspectual class of the matrix predicate and *wh*-extraction shows a linear-additive effect structure, so that the differences under extraction are a reflection of the same differences in declaratives. There is no evidence that adjuncts to telic matrix predicates are more transparent than adjuncts to atelic predicates: there is no subadditive island-repair effect or a superadditive additional penalty when the telicity condition is not met.

As already noted in the discussion of Experiment 1, the intuitive judgments in Truswell (2007) are plausible in a categorical model of grammaticality: there are statistically significant differences in the declarative conditions in Experiment 2, but since both are highly acceptable, they will both remain unmarked in a categorical model of grammaticality. It is possible that only conditions which fall below a certain threshold of grammaticality will be marked as ungrammatical. This is compatible with the simple reductionist account discussed in Sprouse et al.

(2013: 25–28): the individual processing costs of an atelic adjunct and extraction can be handled by the cognitive system, but exceed the system's capacity when both are simultaneously present. Such subtle acceptability differences might go unnoticed in intuitive judgments.

A similar situation obtains in Experiment 3, which compared the BPPA construction to detached free adjuncts that constitute a separate intonation domain and thus show a lower degree of syntactic integration with the matrix clause. Detached adjuncts are already less acceptable in declaratives compared to integrated adjuncts. These differences are enough to estimate the differences in *wh*-extraction sentences; there is no super- or subadditive effect requiring an explanation other than the addition of the two independent decreases in acceptability.

The linear-additive effect structures in Experiments 2 and 3 are fully compatible with the Independence Hypothesis. The acceptability of a construction with a participle adjunct predicate depends on the type of matrix predicate, irrespective of whether extraction has taken place or not. There is no evidence to support the specific formulation of the Interaction Hypothesis in Truswell (2007).

One of the questions raised by this first set of experiments is why the aspectual characteristics of the two predicates involved in the BPPA construction have an influence on acceptability. It appears that an explanation why telic adjunct predicates are less acceptable than atelic ones is easier to come by as the reverse situation for matrix predicates: I agree with Truswell (2007: 1373) that telic adjuncts may be independently ruled out because they do not meet the conditions on depictive modification. The decrease in acceptability is probably related to the fact that telic adjunct predicates require aspectual shift when they appear as a present participle: a lexically telic predicate is shifted to an atelic state or activity reading (Kamp & Reyle 1993; Zucchi 1998; Rothstein 2004b; de Swart 2012), leading to the decreased judgments.

In conclusion, while there is a reasonable explanation for the lower acceptability of telic adjuncts, the fact that telic matrix predicates have an advantage over atelic ones does not have such an explanation. The next study series will take a closer look at further characteristics of the matrix predicate that affect acceptability in declaratives and interrogatives.

4.6 Study series 2: Grammatical verb type

This study series takes a closer look at the grammatical verb type of the matrix predicate and its effect on the possibility to extract from the adjunct participle. I assume the distinction between transitive, unergative, and unaccusative predicates as formulated in Perlmutter (1978), Burzio (1986), and Levin & Rappaport Hovav

(1995). As discussed in the theoretical overview in Chapter 3, Borgonovo & Neeleman (2000) argue that the transparency of an adjunct predicate for extraction depends on the characteristics of these verb classes, which is surprising because "extraction out of the adjunct should not be sensitive to properties of the verb" (Borgonovo & Neeleman 2000: 200). This is related to the distinction between strong and weak islands (Cinque 1990; Szabolcsi & Lohndal 2017), which is based on properties of the extracted element, not properties of the embedding domain. In framework of Borgonovo & Neeleman (2000), syntactic reflexivity of the matrix predicate is the decisive factor allowing for extraction. Reflexivity is defined as a co-indexing or coreference relation between arguments of a verb (see Reinhart & Reuland 1993; Reuland 2006). As inherently reflexive predicates, unaccusatives are prime candidates for grammatical extractions; transitive predicates encoding a reflexive predication like *hurt oneself* also allow reflexive-marking and can host transparent adjuncts.

Compared to the approach in Truswell (2007, 2011), the predicted pattern differs slightly because there is no one-to-one mapping between telicity and grammatical verb type, especially for transitives, which can be both telic accomplishments or atelic activities; unergatives and unaccusatives are more predictable with respect to telicity; see the correlations in Dowty (1991: 607). Under the assumption that unaccusative predicates usually encode achievements, the predictions for this class are identical: they should allow *wh*-extraction from the adjunct. For transitive matrix predicates, however, the two approaches differ. Borgonovo & Neeleman (2000) claim that non-reflexive transitives do not allow transparent adjuncts, while Truswell (2007, 2011) observes that accomplishment predicates, which are usually transitive and do not need to involve two coreferring arguments, allow extraction from the adjunct as long as the following conditions are met: the matrix predicate is telic, and the adjunct fills an underspecified cause component in the event structure of the matrix predicate.

This study series employs the same strategy as the previous one: I test different grammatical verb types in declaratives and interrogatives, with the goal of finding out whether one of the verb types is less affected by the extraction than others. Based on the predictions from Borgonovo & Neeleman (2000), this should single out unaccusatives. Note that while Borgonovo & Neeleman (2000) do not discuss the declarative counterparts in detail, they are all unmarked without further differentiation. Similar to Truswell (2007, 2011), their theory intends to explain differences under extraction as a function of the matrix verb type; in declaratives, this effect is not assumed to be operative. They likewise assume that the extraction operation itself is sensitive to grammatical properties of the matrix predicate.

4.6.1 Experiment 4: Transitives, unaccusatives, and unergatives

This experiment isolates the effect that the grammatical verb type of the matrix predicate has on the acceptability of the BPPA construction in declaratives and interrogatives. The distinction between verb types used here is between non-reflexive transitives, unergatives, and unaccusatives. Transitives are distinguished from the other verb types by taking two arguments, often an AGENT and a THEME role, whereas unergatives and unaccusatives are intransitive and take only one argument. These two predicate types differ in the type of single argument they take: unergatives usually take an AGENT subject, unaccusatives a THEME subject (Perlmutter 1978; Burzio 1986; Levin & Rappaport Hovav 1995). This is also taken to reflect a syntactic distinction, with the subject of unergatives being in the specifier position of a verbal projection, and the subject of an unaccusative being in complement position. Theories which assume a split verbal domain typically locate agentive subjects in a different projection layer than the surface subjects of unaccusatives; see Kratzer (1996), Harley (2013), and Alexiadou et al. (2015).

The main points of interest in this experiment are two-fold: first, to see whether unaccusatives show a privileged status under *wh*-extraction; second, to determine whether the application of *wh*-extraction really is sensitive to the type of matrix predicate, as claimed in Borgonovo & Neeleman (2000), or whether the differences in interrogatives can be traced back to those in declaratives. If the verb type approach in Borgonovo & Neeleman (2000) is on the right track, an island-repair effect is expected for unaccusative matrix predicates only, meaning that they are less affected by the extraction than other predicate types.

4.6.1.1 Study design, methods, and participants

In this experiment, I use a 3 × 2 factorial design, with the two factors VERB TYPE and STRUCTURE. VERB TYPE has three levels, corresponding to the three grammatical verb classes under investigation: *unaccusative*, *unergative*, and *transitive*. STRUCTURE has the two levels *–wh* and *+wh*. The study design is shown in (20):

(20) a. Peter arrived whistling a horrible melody.   [unaccusative/–wh]
      b. What did Peter arrive whistling __ ?   [unaccusative/+wh]
      c. Peter danced whistling a horrible melody.   [unergative/–wh]
      d. What did Peter dance whistling __ ?   [unergative/+wh]
      e. Peter annoyed Lisa whistling a horrible melody.   [transitive/–wh]
      f. What did Peter annoy Lisa whistling __ ?   [transitive/+wh]

A set of 24 items was created and distributed across six lists so that each participant saw four lexicalizations for each of the six conditions. Based on the results from Experiment 1, the adjunct predicates are atelic transitive activities so that the adjunct's aspectual class does not interfere with the results. Transitive matrix predicates have either accomplishment or activity readings; as shown in Brown (2017), transitive matrix predicates are insensitive to telicity, so this distinction is not made here. The transitive predicates do not qualify as reflexive predicates since there is a direct object that is distinct from the matrix clause subject. Unaccusative predicates are all achievement predicates, and unergative matrix predicates qualify as activities in the sense of Vendler (1957) and Dowty (1979).

The 24 target items were mixed with 48 fillers including the 15 cardinal well-formedness sentences from Gerbrich et al. (2019), resulting in a total of 72 items per experiment. The experiment was uploaded to the OnExp platform and participant recruitment was carried out via Amazon's Mechanical Turk platform. In this experiment, participants were not only required to be reliable workers on Mechanical Turk, judged by the number of approved tasks, but also a location restriction to the US and UK was imposed. This resulted in a noticeable increase in data quality, as less non-native speakers were recruited, and the number of participants who performed poorly on the standardized fillers was also reduced. Participants were paid for taking the experiment. They saw the sentences in randomized order and were instructed to judge the naturalness of each sentence on a 7-point Likert scale. There was a two-hour time restriction for taking the entire experiment but no restrictions for individual answers.

For this experiment, 63 participants were recruited via Mechanical Turk. One participant was removed before statistical analysis for indicating a first language other than English; one additional participant was removed due to technical problems with the OnExp platform, which resulted in an incomplete data set; also, three participants were not included in the analysis because they performed poorly on the standardized filler items. In total, 58 participants were included in the statistical analysis.

4.6.1.2 Hypotheses

For this experiment, I investigate the following hypotheses in (21), which are derived from the predictions in Borgonovo & Neeleman (2000) and the experimental results reported in Brown (2017) as well as Jurka (2010). Although the relevant experiments in Jurka (2010) are on German subject island data, the contrast between unaccusatives and unergatives for subject islands is very clear: unergatives show a larger degradation under extraction than unaccusatives. I assume that this is also visible for adjunct islands.

(21) Hypotheses for Experiment 4
  H4a. Significant effect of VERB TYPE.
  H4b. Significant effect of STRUCTURE.
  H4c. Significant interaction between VERB TYPE and STRUCTURE.

Manipulation of the matrix predicate is expected to result in different acceptability levels for both declarative and interrogative conditions (H4a), contra the judgments for declaratives in Borgonovo & Neeleman (2000). I expect that there is already an effect of VERB TYPE in declaratives, resulting in lower judgments for unergatives. Experiment 1 shows that atelic matrix predicates are less acceptable than telic ones, so this should also be reflected in this experiment. In the interrogative conditions, unaccusatives are expected to receive the most favorable judgments. Regarding transitives, predictions are more difficult to make, but based on the results from Brown (2017), they should also show degraded ratings, irrespective of whether they are transitive atelic activities or telic accomplishments.

As in the two previous experiments, there should be a clear effect of STRUCTURE (H4b). However, this effect is predicted to affect the three matrix predicates to a different degree: unaccusatives should be less affected by the extraction than unergatives and transitives because they are the only verb type that allows reflexive-marking in the sense of Borgonovo & Neeleman (2000). This difference in the strength of the factor STRUCTURE should thus lead to a statistical interaction between the two factors (H4c).

4.6.1.3 Results

The mean ratings for the six target conditions plus standard deviations and confidence intervals are shown in Table 4.7, together with the mean ratings for the standard fillers. A graphical representation is given in Figure 4.7, which includes the standardized fillers for reference. The positioning of the lines is slightly moved on the x-axis to make the unergative and transitive lines visible; otherwise, they overlap nearly completely. The difference between unaccusatives and the other two conditions is clearly visible, but there is almost no difference between unergatives and transitives. The best experimental condition [unaccusative/–wh] receives judgments between the A and B fillers (mean: 6.10, SD: 1.29), the remaining two declarative conditions are roughly on the level of the B fillers. The condition with extraction from unaccusative matrix predicates [unaccusative/+wh] is judged to be between the B and C level (mean: 4.50, SD: 1.83), while the other two extraction conditions are between C and D. This shows that the three extraction conditions are degraded, but not entirely ungrammatical; following the conventions in Gerbrich et al. (2019), the C level would be marked with a single '?' judgment and the

Tab. 4.7: Numerical results for Experiment 4. Mean ratings plus standard deviations (SD) and 95 % confidence intervals (CI) for the six experimental conditions and the five levels of the standard fillers.

	Experimental items					Standard fillers		
Verb type	Structure	Mean	SD	CI$_{95}$	A–E	Mean	SD	CI$_{95}$
unaccusative	−wh	6.10	1.29	[5.93;6.27]	A	6.89	0.38	[6.83;6.95]
unaccusative	+wh	4.50	1.83	[4.27;4.74]	B	5.79	1.22	[5.61;5.97]
unergative	−wh	5.44	1.49	[5.25;5.64]	C	3.85	1.51	[3.62;4.08]
unergative	+wh	3.53	1.69	[3.31;3.75]	D	3.37	1.39	[3.17;3.58]
transitive	−wh	5.46	1.55	[5.26;5.66]	E	1.64	1.06	[1.48;1.80]
transitive	+wh	3.56	1.73	[3.34;3.78]				

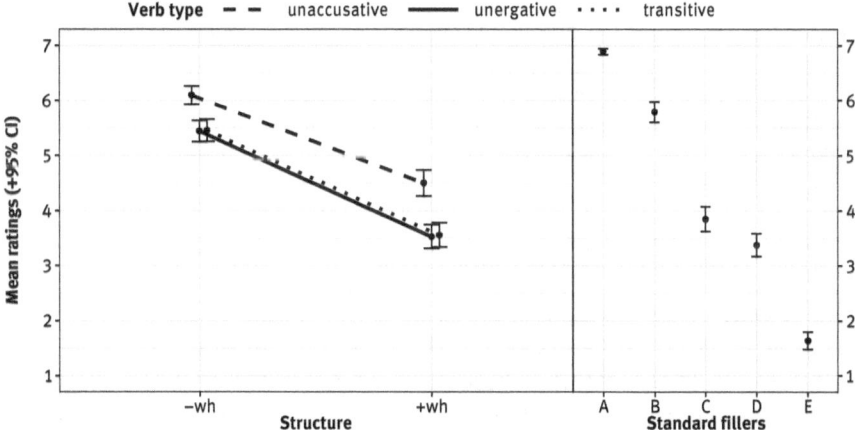

Fig. 4.7: Results of Experiment 4 (mean ratings) compared to standardized fillers. Mean ratings for the five levels of the standardized fillers A–E are shown on the right for comparison. Error bars show 95 % confidence intervals.

D level '??'. A comparable result was obtained in Experiment 2, where extractions from telic matrix predicates were between B and C, while extractions from atelic matrix predicates were on the level of the C standards.

A linear mixed-effects model was created which included VERB TYPE and STRUCTURE as fixed effects and participants (ID) and ITEM as random effects. The random effects structure includes varying slopes for STRUCTURE by participants and varying slopes for both factors plus their interaction, excluding all correlations. For a better analysis of individual contrasts between the three-level VERB TYPE, I applied successive differences contrast coding, and set the unaccusative condition as the reference level: the model then compares the second level of the factor to the reference level and the third level to the second. It is thus possible to make a direct comparison between unaccusatives–transitives and transitives–unergatives. This requires the additional argument 'CHECK_CONTRASTS=F' in the function call. Note that this results in lower t- and p-values for the factor VERB TYPE than with the default sum-coding. The two-level factor STRUCTURE was manually sum-coded. The function call, parameter estimates for fixed effects and interactions, as well as significance values are reported in Table 4.8.

Tab. 4.8: Statistical results for Experiment 4. Model syntax, parameter estimates, standard errors (SE), and t-statistics for the two factors of the experimental design plus their interaction.

Model: mixed(rating~verbtype*struc+(struc||id)+(verbtype*struc||item))						
Fixed effects:	Estimate	SE	df	t-value	p-value	Sig.
Verbtype2-1	−.78232	.19865	22.65	−3.938	< .001	***
Verbtype3-2	−.02903	.21275	22.27	−.136	.892702	
Structure	−1.80894	.13820	36.07	−13.089	< .001	***
Verbtype2-1 × Structure	−.27047	.19671	25.68	−1.375	.181020	
Verbtype3-2 × Structure	−.05267	.20098	25.05	−.262	.795413	

There is a highly significant effect of VERB TYPE in the comparison between unaccusatives and transitives (VERBTYPE2-1: $\beta = -.782$, $t = -.394$, $p < .001$), but not in the comparison between transitives and unergatives (VERBTYPE3-2: $\beta = -.029$, $t = -.136$, $p = .892$). STRUCTURE shows a highly significant effect ($\beta = 1.809$, $t = -13.089$, $p < .001$), but the interactions between STRUCTURE and the levels of VERBTYPE are not significant (both $p > .1$). The overall effect of VERBTYPE, obtained with the ANOVA() function from the LMERTEST package (version 3.1-1; Kuznetsova et al. 2017), is also significant, but there is no overall interaction between the two fixed effects. In contrast to the parameter estimates returned by the model summary, the ANOVA() function evaluates the overall effect of factors and does not provide comparisons between individual levels of factors with more than two levels. The statistical results confirm the first two hypotheses (H4a) and (H4b). Both VERB TYPE and STRUCTURE have a significant effect on acceptability. As predicted, unaccusatives receive the most favorable judgments in interrogatives, but this is also the case in the declarative counterparts. The absence of a significant interaction means that hypothesis (H4c) cannot be confirmed: acceptability differences under extraction are a reflection of the differences in declaratives, with no additional penalty for a specific type of matrix predicate. This poses a serious problem for the account in Borgonovo & Neeleman (2000) because there is no evidence for an island-repair effect for the unaccusative condition or for additional superadditive island effects for the other two verb types. Again, this speaks for independent licensing conditions of the adjunct predicate in line with the Independence Hypothesis.

4.6.1.4 Discussion
This experiment shows that there are differences between the grammatical verb types in both declarative and *wh*-extraction structures and that all three verb types are affected equally by the extraction. There are four points that require closer discussion: (i) the relation of these results to the previous literature, (ii) the behavior of transitives in declaratives, (iii) the lack of an interaction between the two factors, and (iv) the unique behavior of unaccusative predicates.

(i) First, these results partially confirm the predictions made in Borgonovo & Neeleman (2000): extraction from adjuncts to unaccusative matrix predicates is more acceptable than from adjuncts to unergatives and non-reflexive transitives. Similar results are found in Fábregas & Jiménez-Fernández (2016a), Brown (2017), and Kohrt et al. (2018), even though their experiments are formulated in terms of aspectual classes rather than grammatical verb types. As in the previous study series, however, there is no evidence for the proposal that the application of extraction causes these differences. The results here are also problematic to a certain degree for Truswell (2007): his predictions about aspectual classes can be transferred to the unaccusative and unergative conditions, but again the same differences are found in the respective declarative conditions as well. This is similar to the results from Experiment 2, which also failed to find an interaction between the telicity of the matrix predicate and *wh*-extraction. On first sight, the results of this experiment seem to fit with the predictions made in Truswell (2011) about the permissible number of agentive events in an event grouping that allows for subextraction from the participle predicate: this constraint singles out the unaccusative conditions in this experiment because they are the only conditions in which Truswell's Single Event Grouping Condition (SEGC) is satisfied. Both the unergative and transitive conditions contain two agentive predicates and thus violate the SEGC. However, the same problem as with the generalization about aspectual classes arises: the same differences apply to both declaratives and interrogatives, with no interaction between the verb type of the matrix predicate and *wh*-extraction. The verb type that meets the SEGC is no less affected by extraction than the verb types that violate it. Like the generalization about aspectual classes in Truswell (2007), the SEGC might be a condition that is not limited to interrogatives, but has a wider range of application than proposed in Truswell (2011). There is also the issue of achievements that can have agentive readings of the preparatory phase and that still meet unaccusative diagnostics, as noted in Borer (2005: 97–98, fn. 1). Despite Truswell's claim that achievements are characterized by an "obligatorily nonagentive preparatory process" (Truswell 2011: 161), animate subjects regularly invoke this agentive reading, as in (22); see also the remarks on achievements in Ryle (1949: 149–153).

(22) a. Pat reached the summit.
     b. Kim won the race.
       (Borer 2005: 98, fn. 1)

In those cases, the maximum of at most one agentive event per event grouping would be exceeded in the BPPA construction and the extraction should be degraded compared to unaccusative achievements that do not have this agentive interpretation. As such, this experiment shows that there are problems with the interaction accounts in both Borgonovo & Neeleman (2000) and Truswell (2011). Again, this provides evidence for the Independence Hypothesis despite the fact that Borgonovo & Neeleman (2000) and Truswell (2007, 2011) capture important aspects of the extraction conditions.

(ii) The fact that transitive matrix predicates receive judgments that are almost identical to unergatives is surprising, especially in declaratives. Two possible explanations present themselves: (a) conditions with transitives include both activity and accomplishment readings, and (b) their more complex argument structure causes the lower ratings compared to unaccusatives. As shown in (23), transitive conditions include both activities (23a) and accomplishments (23b). Since the former are atelic and the latter telic, this helps explain why transitive conditions in base position show a rating disadvantage compared to the uniformly telic unaccusatives. Experiment 1 and Experiment 2 showed that atelic matrix predicates are significantly less acceptable than telic ones, so this characteristic explains part of the difference.

(23) a. Michael ate tons of chips watching an old movie.   [Item 3]
     b. Mike scratched the car carrying a large suitcase.   [Item 9]

Since Borgonovo & Neeleman (2000) do not consider this distinction and rely on the contrast between reflexive and non-reflexive transitives, the telicity of transitives was not a factor in this experiment. Brown (2017) draws this distinction, and finds that telicity does not have an effect for transitive conditions. For this reason, this distinction did not seem relevant for the present experiment, but this can be seen as one possible explanation for the unexpected behavior in declaratives. Under *wh*-extraction, the judgments on the level of unergatives conform to the proposal in Borgonovo & Neeleman (2000) because transitive predicates are all non-reflexive in this experiment. The second possible explanation is that unaccusatives and transitives differ in complexity: transitives encode a second argument, whereas unaccusative conditions are intransitive. Items with unaccusative and unergative matrix predicates have a shorter overall sentence length than transitives, which could explain the overall lower ratings for transitives. A similar effect has been observed in the studies in Konietzko (2021) and Jurka (2013: 274–279) on German, Polinsky et al. (2013: 292–297) on English, and Polinsky et al. (2013: 301–303) on Russian. Jurka's results show that conditions with two arguments are slightly less acceptable in declarative sentences than single-argument conditions, which show almost identical ratings. Polinsky et al. (2013) report significant effects of transitivity compared to unergatives and unaccusatives in studies on English and Russian. Jurka (2013: 276) briefly notes that the lower judgments for transitive declarative conditions are probably due to the presence of a second argument, which needs to be assigned a θ-role and thus incurs a processing burden. This is directly reflected in decreased acceptability. Polinsky et al. (2013) tentatively interpret their result as a "transitivity penalty" that is operative when the number of arguments increases. The fact that transitives pattern differently from unergatives means that the presence of an external argument is not the reason for these results. It is not obvious whether a syntactic explanation for the behavior of transitives in declaratives is available or whether a processing explanation is needed.

(iii) The third point of interest, the lack of interaction between the two factors investigated in this experiment, leads to a conclusion similar to the one in the previous study series: there is no evidence for an island-repair effect for unaccusative matrix predicates. While the prediction from Borgonovo & Neeleman (2000) can be confirmed that extraction from unaccusatives is more acceptable than from other predicate types, the lack of an interaction leads to the conclusion that VERB TYPE and STRUCTURE are linear-additive and independent effects; extraction is not sensitive to properties of the matrix predicate. There are restrictions on the BPPA construction that are sensitive to the grammatical verb type of the matrix predicate but that are independent of extraction; this is a comparable result to Experiment 2 for the telicity of the matrix predicate. The three predicate types investigated in this experiment thus differ in the availability of modification by a participle predicate. Adjectival depictives show similar behavior: while there are many unergative predicates that easily accept them, there are also some that are degraded. Merging an adjunct may apply freely, but not all results are equally acceptable from a semantic perspective; see Rapoport (2019: 434–435), Irimia (2012), and Brown (2017) for discussion.

(iv) As a last point of interest, I want to discuss why unaccusative matrix predicates receive better judgments in declaratives and interrogatives compared to transitives and unergatives. The consensus in the literature is that the surface subject of unergatives shares properties with the subject of transitives, whereas the surface subject of unaccusatives patterns with the object of transitives (Perlmutter 1978). This difference in interpretation is taken to reflect different underlying argument structures (Chomsky 1995b; Hornstein et al. 2005; Alexiadou et al. 2004), but there is disagreement about the precise layout of the verbal domain. The disagreement centers around the question whether unaccusatives also project a vP layer, or more generally, whether unaccusatives lack a projection that is present in unergatives and transitives. Unergatives have also been analyzed as hidden transitives, for example in Levin & Rappaport Hovav (1995) and Chomsky (1995b: 315–316); evidence for this comes from cognate object constructions and has been prominently discussed in Hale & Keyser (1993, 2002). What the distinction between these three predicate types reveals is that unaccusatives are the only verb type where the participle adjunct is controlled by an argument that is an underlying object. It is unclear why this specific property of unaccusatives seems to have an impact on the availability of an adjunct predicate, as the data suggest. However, the results reported here are compatible with the discussion of subject-oriented depictives in Irimia (2012), who notes that unaccusatives are more accessible for depictives than transitives, and that unergatives take them only under specific conditions, such as the addition of degree modification (Irimia 2012: 206). Together with the possible transitivity penalty discussed above, this could derive the pattern in the data.

In conclusion, this experiment has shown that the verb type of the embedding verb has a similar effect on the acceptability of BPPA constructions in declaratives and interrogatives alike, which presents previous theoretical approaches with a challenge because they fail to offer an explanation for the differences in declaratives and draw conclusions about the application of *wh*-extraction that are not supported by the experimental data. Again, there is evidence for the Independence Hypothesis, which emphasizes the need to examine the licensing conditions for BPPAs in greater detail. One question that this experiment leaves open is whether the lower acceptability of transitive matrix predicates in declaratives compared to unaccusatives is caused by their larger complexity in terms of sentence length. It is possible that this difference obscures a possible interaction between verb type and extraction. In the next experiment, I will investigate whether there is an interaction in sentences with transitive and unaccusative matrix predicates where the unaccusative conditions are matched in sentence complexity.

4.6.2 Experiment 5: Complex unaccusatives and transitives

This experiment investigates in more detail the difference between unaccusative and transitive matrix predicates and the effects of *wh*-extraction from inside an adjunct to those predicate types. Experiment 4 showed that unaccusatives modified by a participial adjunct have an advantage in declaratives and interrogatives; this opens up the question of why sentences with transitives should be less acceptable in declaratives than those with unaccusatives. One possible answer in the discussion of Experiment 4 was that overall sentence length and the additional θ-role encoded in transitives leads to a processing disadvantage compared to the shorter, single-argument unaccusatives (Polinsky et al. 2013; Jurka 2013). From this perspective, it is conceivable that the simpler θ-grid of unaccusatives receives better ratings and that this is simply an effect of sentence length.

This experiment draws a comparison between BPPA sentences with transitive and unaccusative matrix predicates that are more closely matched in complexity and sentence length. While unaccusatives are essentially single-argument verbs, many allow the addition of a PP/DP that encodes a goal or origin; this applies to most cases of change-of-location unaccusatives such as *arrive*, which are classified as verbs of directed motion in terms of Levin (1993). This PP/DP phrase adds a θ-role to the syntactic structure and removes the difference in sentence length between unaccusatives and transitives.[23] By making the unaccusative conditions more complex, they become better minimal pairs to conditions with transitive matrix predicates, which allows more meaningful conclusions about the relative strength of *wh*-extraction from an adjunct predicate. The main goal of this experiment is similar to that of Experiment 4: finding out whether *wh*-extraction shows a stronger effect for one of the two predicate types.

4.6.2.1 Study design, methods, and participants

This experiment uses a 2 × 2 design with the two factors VERB TYPE (levels: *unaccusative* & *transitive*) and STRUCTURE (levels: *–wh* & *+wh*), resulting in four conditions. The design for this experiment is described in (24).

(24) a. Liz came to the meeting humming a song. [unaccusative/–wh]
b. What did Liz come to the meeting humming __ ? [unaccusative/+wh]
c. Liz cleaned her apartment humming a song. [transitive/–wh]
d. What did Liz clean her apartment humming __ ? [transitive/+wh]

Unaccusative predicates are augmented with a PP/DP that specifies a goal or origin. This increases the total number of words in these conditions and results in a more comparable sentence length than in the previous experiment. Since the addition of

---

23 A θ-role like GOAL or SOURCE differs from ones like AGENT and THEME in that the former are more often realized as oblique arguments and often behave like adjuncts.

a PP/DP was not possible for all unaccusatives in Experiment 4, some items were replaced; the unaccusative predicates were selected from those used in Experiment 4 as well as from the studies in Friedmann et al. (2008) and Sullivan et al. (2017). . They can all be assigned to verb classes in Levin (1993) that qualify as unaccusative according to the diagnostics discussed there (more specifically, classes 45, 47, 48, and 51). The addition of a PP does not alter the telicity of unaccusatives as it does with unergative motion predicates (Borgonovo & Neeleman 2000: 200; van Hout 2004: 71–72; Alexiadou et al. 2004: 3). The presence of a PP/DP phrase after the unaccusative matrix verb also serves to exclude the possibility that the *wh*-filler is linked to this position; this disambiguates the gap site for the overall structure. Possibly, this could result in filled-gap effects (Stowe 1986), but as this applies to both predicate types, this effect does not impact the interpretation of the results because the potential confound is spread equally across the relevant conditions (see Kush et al. 2018: 748). The transitive condition items are modeled after accomplishment predicates, but some of them can receive an atelic transitive activity reading; since telicity is not one of the factors investigated here and Brown (2017) has shown that the telic–atelic distinction does not affect transitives, this was not considered to be a problem.

For this experiment, 16 items were created with the four conditions described above and mixed with 32 filler items, including the standardized fillers from Gerbrich et al. (2019); they were distributed across four lists so that each list contained four lexicalizations per condition. Participants performed an online acceptability judgment task with the same methodology as in the previous studies reported here. A total of 48 participants was recruited for this experiment on Amazon's Mechanical Turk platform. Four participant were removed because they performed poorly on the standardized fillers. In total, judgments from 44 participants were included in the statistical analysis.

4.6.2.2 Hypotheses

In this experiment, I investigate the following hypothesis based on the previous experiment:

(25) Hypotheses for Experiment 5
 H5a. There is no overall effect of VERB TYPE.
 H5b. Transitives are more strongly affected by extraction than unaccusatives, resulting in an interaction between VERB TYPE and EXTRACTION.

I expect no overall effect of VERB TYPE since the two predicate types are now more closely matched in complexity, so that no processing disadvantages for the second θ-role in transitives should affect acceptability (H5a); rather, VERB TYPE should only show a significant effect for the [+wh] level of the factor STRUCTURE, resulting in an interaction between the two factors (H5b). If there is an effect of VERB TYPE, then this indicates that transitive matrix predicates are in general less acceptable with a BPPA than unaccusatives, which strengthens the claim that contrasts observed in interrogatives can be traced back to contrasts in declaratives. The crucial assumption is that conditions with transitive matrix predicates are affected more strongly by the extraction than conditions with unaccusatives. This would provide evidence for the interaction account in Borgonovo & Neeleman (2000), which was not found in the previous experiment. If the interaction does not show up when the potential confound of sentence length is controlled for, this increases the challenge this account has to face.

4.6.2.3 Results

Mean ratings plus standard deviations are reported in Table 4.9, together with the mean ratings for the standardized fillers. Figure 4.8 on the following page shows the mean ratings of the target items in a comparison to the standardized fillers. It appears that the two declarative conditions [unaccusative/−wh] and [transitive/−wh] are closer together than in Experiment 4. Compared to the standardized fillers, the results are also similar to the previous experiment.

For statistical analysis, I created a linear mixed-effects model with VERB TYPE and STRUCTURE as fixed effects, and participants and items as random effects. Transitive conditions are selected as the reference level for VERB TYPE, the interrogative conditions for STRUCTURE. The maximal random effects structure that allowed the

Tab. 4.9: Numerical results for Experiment 5. Mean ratings plus standard deviations (SD) and 95 % confidence intervals (CI) for the four experimental conditions and the five levels of the standard fillers.

	Experimental items					Standard fillers		
Verb type	Structure	Mean	SD	CI$_{95}$	A–E	Mean	SD	CI$_{95}$
unaccusative	−wh	6.10	1.26	[5.92;6.29]	A	6.85	0.38	[6.78;6.91]
unaccusative	+wh	4.53	1.46	[4.32;4.75]	B	5.64	1.31	[5.42;5.87]
transitive	−wh	5.77	1.15	[5.60;5.94]	C	3.65	1.47	[3.40;3.90]
transitive	+wh	3.79	1.59	[3.55;4.03]	D	3.30	1.46	[3.05;3.55]
					E	1.71	0.92	[1.55;1.87]

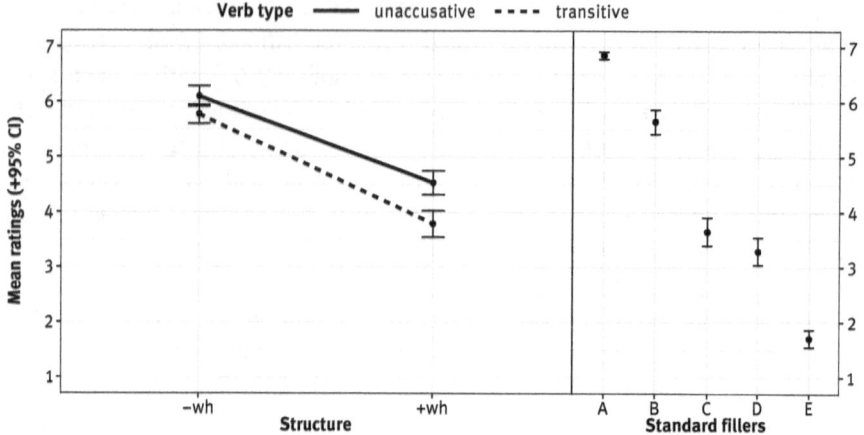

Fig. 4.8: Results of Experiment 5 (mean ratings) compared to standardized fillers. Mean ratings for the five levels of the standardized fillers A–E are shown on the right for comparison. Error bars show 95 % confidence intervals.

Tab. 4.10: Statistical results for Experiment 5. Model syntax, parameter estimates, standard errors (SE), and *t*-statistics for the two factors of the experimental design plus their interaction.

Model: mixed(rating~verbtype*struc+(struc||id)+(verbtype*struc||item))						
Fixed effects:	Estimate	SE	df	*t*-value	*p*-value	Sig.
Verb type	−.26706	.12199	14.65	−2.189	< .05	*
Structure	−.90249	.06877	29.43	−13.124	< .001	***
Verb type × Structure	−.10060	.05420	13.67	−1.856	.0851	.

model to converge included random slopes for STRUCTURE by participants as well as random slopes for both factors including their interaction by items, excluding all correlations. The model syntax, parameter estimates, and significance values are reported in Table 4.10.

There are significant effects of VERB TYPE ($\beta = -.267, t = -2.189, p < .05$) and STRUCTURE ($\beta = -.902, t = -13.124, p < .001$). As in Experiment 4, transitive conditions are less acceptable than unaccusative conditions, despite the complexity matching; this does not confirm hypothesis (H5a). However, the numerical differences between the two predicate types in declaratives and interrogatives are smaller than in Experiment 4, visible in the smaller parameter estimates for VERB TYPE in the relevant comparisons. The interaction between the two fixed effects is not significant ($\beta = -.101, t = -1.856, p = .085$), but has a higher parameter estimate than in previous experiments and a *p*-value < .1, which can be interpreted as marginal. Still, this is not significant enough to confirm hypothesis (H5b).

4.6.2.4 Discussion

The main motivation for this experiment was to investigate whether the lack of an interaction between the grammatical verb type of the matrix predicate and extraction in Experiment 4 was caused by the possible confound of a difference in sentence length between unaccusatives and transitives. The factor VERB TYPE is still significant in this experiment, but the parameter estimate is much smaller than in Experiment 4 for the unaccusative–transitive pair; the two verb types now receive closer ratings than in the previous experiment. Even with this adjustment in sentence length, there is no evidence for a stable interaction. This experiment thus does not provide evidence for the hypothesis that *wh*-extraction has a stronger effect on the acceptability of transitive matrix predicates compared to unaccusatives. It is possible that the interaction does not reach stable significance due to the limitations of the experimental design, but a conservative interpretation of the results leads to the rejection of the hypothesis (H5b) that the two verb types are affected differently by the extraction. This is a problematic result for the interaction account in Borgonovo & Neeleman (2000).

The question is why there is still a significant effect of VERB TYPE in the items matched in complexity. One possible answer is that the adjunct predicates fulfill different roles in terms of coherence relations (see Hobbs 1979; Kehler 2002): for the transitive conditions, the adjunct can provide more specific details about the causal structure of the sentence in the form that the adjunct predicate is the cause of the event in the matrix predicate. However, this is not possible for all items in this experiment. In contrast, with unaccusatives, the adjunct predicate functions like a depictive in describing a temporally overlapping event. There is thus a difference in the elaboration relation in terms of Haug et al. (2012), with a specification relation for most transitive and an expansion relation for unaccusative predicates. Another possibility is that there are processing differences between the second, syntactically selected argument in transitive conditions and the adjunct-like GOAL/SOURCE argument in unaccusative conditions. Regardless of these differences, the two factors of the experimental design operate in a linear-additive fashion and decrease acceptability almost identically for both predicate types.

As in the results of Experiment 2 and Experiment 4, no significant additional penalty can be observed for sentences with matrix predicates that fail to conform to the reflexivity hypothesis in the interaction account of Borgonovo & Neeleman (2000). While their observation that unaccusatives receive better judgments under *wh*-extraction can be confirmed, there is no evidence for a constraint which allows extraction from adjuncts to this predicate type but not others.

4.6.3 Interim conclusion for study series 2

This study series has investigated the predictions of Borgonovo & Neeleman's (2000) interaction account based on the grammatical verb type of the matrix predicate. In interrogatives, transitive, unaccusative, and unergative matrix predicate behave differently, as predicted; the pattern discovered in Experiment 4 confirms the predictions of this account. However, this experiment also reveals that these same contrasts apply to the declarative counterparts as well. The three verb types show the same decrease in acceptability when *wh*-extraction takes place, which is shown by the lack of an interaction in Experiment 4. This was confirmed in Experiment 5, which compared unaccusative matrix predicates that are matched in complexity with transitives, thus removing a potential confound in the items. Still, there is no significant interaction: both predicate types statistically show the same reaction to *wh*-extraction.

This is problematic for the account in Borgonovo & Neeleman (2000) because they rely on the fact that the relative differences between predicate types under extraction differ from those in declaratives, like Truswell (2007). For them, there are no observable differences in the declarative counterparts of interrogatives that show grammaticality contrasts. Similar to the conclusions from study series 1, the predictions for interrogatives can be confirmed, but it has to be pointed out that the conclusions about licensing mechanisms for the gap inside the adjunct are not necessary. What remains to be explained is again the fact that the same effects are operative in declaratives. The Independence Hypothesis naturally accounts for acceptability patterns that interaction approaches struggle with.

4.7 Study series 3: *get*-predicates and achievements

This study series draws a comparison between achievement predicates and a type of matrix predicate that so far has not been discussed in detail in previous approaches to transparent adjuncts. This type consists of a form of the verb *get* followed by an adjective; like many other matrix predicates, it can be modified by a participle adjunct. I will call this class *get-predicates* in the following. The structure is exemplified in (26):

(26) Peter got scared watching a horror movie
      subject get adjective   participle adjunct

The adjective does not need to be a psychological adjective as in (26); others are possible as well:

(27) Peter got fat eating too much fast food.

The *get*-predicate construction shows similarities to the so-called *get*-passive, as in *Peter got arrested* (Huddleston & Pullum 2002: 1429–1430, 1440–1443; Chappell 1980; Haegeman 1985; Wanner 2013). The similarity arises because *get* has this use in passive-like constructions and because many psych-adjectives look like participles of the corresponding psych-verb. However, Quirk et al. (1972: 802–803, §12.3) are reluctant to group *get*-predicates and passives together; rather, they prefer to classify *get* as a "resulting copula" (Quirk et al. 1972: 820–821, §12.32), along with the predicate *become*; see also McIntyre (2005, 2012) for similar discussion. Chappell (1980) also notes this non-passive, inchoative use of the *get*-construction.[24] The major difference to canonical passives is that the *get*-construction is partially ambiguous between an adjectival and a verbal reading: *scared* can be both an adjective and a participle. However, only the adjectival predicate allows modification by degree adverbs (Chappell 1980: 423; see also Wanner 2013: 46). This seems to be the right analysis for *get*-predicates, which freely allow such adverbials (28a), compared to passive constructions involving *get*, which do not (28b).

(28) a. Peter got very/completely/totally scared watching a horror movie.
      b. Peter got *very/*completely/*totally arrested by the police.

The meaning of the non-passive *get*-construction can be paraphrased as in (29), taken from Chappell (1980).

(29) An entity (the subject) begins to be in a new state as the result of some event, usually unspecified.   (Chappell 1980: 423)

In the BPPA construction, the adjunct is an obvious candidate for filling the slot of this unspecified event; this links the semantics of the *get*-construction back to the discussion of underspecified causal event structures in Truswell (2007) and event specification in Haug et al. (2012).

---

[24] A distinction between *get*-predicates and passive constructions is relevant in the framework of Borgonovo & Neeleman (2000), who note that passives fail to host transparent adjuncts because they are not reflexive; in other respects, passives pattern with unaccusative predicates. Aspectual and agentivity characteristics based on Truswell (2007, 2011) predict that passives should be able to host transparent adjuncts because they are usually telic and non-agentive; the data in Borgonovo & Neeleman (2000: 211), however, suggest that passive predicates do not readily accept extraction from a predicative adjunct.

The *get*-predicate construction also has similarities to resultative secondary predicates (see Rothstein 2017), and specifically to those resultatives that are syntactically obligatory, as the resultative in *The joggers ran their Nikes threadbare*; see Carrier & Randall (1992: 173). From an aspectual perspective, *get*-predicates share properties with so-called degree achievements like *cool* or *lengthen* (Dowty 1979; Rothstein 2004b, 2008; Hay et al. 1999; Kennedy & Levin 2008).[25] The culmination is not always entailed in this predicate class, as it can be defeated without resulting in contradiction (30a) and accepts both *in*- and *for*-adverbials (30b).

(30) a. The soup is cooling, but it hasn't cooled. (Kennedy & Levin 2008: 160)
 b. The soup cooled in/for an hour.

Like degree achievements, *get*-predicates accept the progressive (31a) and are compatible with both *for*- and *in*-adverbials (31b), which result in different interpretations. The main difference to degree achievements is that modification with a *for*-adverbial does not measure the process leading up to the culmination, but rather the interval of the resulting state, which leads to a stative interpretation: "When a *for*-phrase is used with a liminal predicate [achievement, AK], the *for*-phrase measures the duration of the state that results after the change, not the duration of the process" (Timberlake 2007: 285–286); see also Beavers & Koontz-Garboden (2020: 18–19).[26]

(31) a. Bill is getting bored.
 b. Bill got bored in/for five minutes.

In the progressive, *get*-predicates are interpreted similarly to other progressive achievements: the culmination is seen as imminent, which is called the "prospective" reading (Truswell 2011, 2019a; Rothstein 2004b). From a decompositional perspective, the meaning of *get*-predicates is close to non-causative changes-of-state, which is compatible with an analysis as a resulting copula: [y BECOME STATE] (Levin & Rappaport Hovav 1995: 24).[27]

---

25 Virtually all literature after Dowty (1979) agrees that degree achievements behave more like accomplishments than achievements, but the term is still widely used (Mittwoch 2019: 42, fn. 8).
26 A reading parallel to that of *for*-adverbials with accomplishments appears to be marginally available, but only under the assumption that there is a gradual progression: *John got more and more bored during the politics lecture, so after 30 minutes he decided to go home*.
27 Dowty's (1979) analysis of the BECOME operator in an interval-based semantics allows for non-punctual changes of state, which is also discussed in Embick's (2004) [FIENT] operator or INCH in Jackendoff (1990).

Degree achievements are not fully lexically specified as either telic or atelic; their telicity is derived from a variety of sources, such as lexical factors, contextual information, or modification that favors one reading over the other (Kennedy & Levin 2008: 160). In the absence of markers indicating an atelic reading, the telic reading is usually the default, especially in the simple past (Jackendoff 1996; Kennedy & Levin 2008: 160). With this default interpretation, *get*-predicates are good candidates for extraction from the adjunct, as they are non-agentive and otherwise fit in the group of unaccusatives (see Dowty's 1991: 607 correlations).

In addition to the underspecified telicity of *get*-predicates, their argument structure differs from that of accomplishments in that they encode a causal relation of the two predicates, similar to many BPPA constructions with accomplishment matrix predicates. In the experiments reported in this study series, I will take a closer look at the effects of grammatical aspect by means of progressive-marking, as well as the possible effects of the matrix predicate's argument structure in the comparison of *get*-predicates with achievement predicates. I will investigate the effect of progressive-marking with *get*-predicates (Experiment 6) and achievements (Experiment 7), and investigate whether these two predicate types differ in their sensitivity to *wh*-extraction (Experiment 8).

4.7.1 Experiment 6: *get*-predicates

The experiments in study series 1 have shown that lexically telic matrix predicates are judged as more acceptable than lexically atelic matrix predicates, which partially confirms Truswell's (2007) generalization about aspectual classes; identical contrasts were found in declaratives and interrogatives, so that the aspectual class of the matrix predicate does not modulate the strength of *wh*-extraction. Building on this insight, this experiment investigates whether a manipulation of outer or grammatical aspect by means of progressive-marking has an effect on the strength of *wh*-extraction for matrix predicates that receive a default telic interpretation.

Specifically, I want to explore whether *get*-predicates in the aspectually neutral simple past (de Swart 2012: 761) and past progressive show different reactions to *wh*-extraction. The distinction between inner or lexical and outer or grammatical aspect has been widely noted in the literature (Comrie 1976; Dowty 1979; Verkuyl 1993, 2005; Sasse 2006; MacDonald 2008; Travis 2010; Filip 2012; de Swart 2012); while the notion of telicity is usually assumed to be an inherent lexical property of the predicate and its arguments (see van Lambalgen & Hamm 2005: 169; Verkuyl 1989, 1993), progressivity is in the domain of outer aspect and applies on top of the lexical aspect of the predicate (Dowty 1979; Kamp & Reyle 1993; Borer 2005; de Swart 2012). One way of viewing the relation between the two aspects is that grammatical aspect acts as an operator on the input from lexical aspect. When embedded in an aspectually marked category, the lexical aspect of the predicate can be shifted to another type (Comrie 1976; Jackendoff 1996: 306, fn. 2; Zucchi 1998; Higginbotham 2004: 332; Sasse 2006: 535; van Lambalgen & Hamm 2005: chapter 11). Consider (32), where the lexically telic predicate *die* in (32a) entails that John is now dead, whereas this entailment is canceled in the progressive in (32b); progressive-marking is one way to obtain an imperfective reading, which entails that the event is not completed. Perfective aspectual marking as in (32c), on the other hand, does not cancel the entailment.

(32) a. John died → he is dead [telic lexical aspect]
 b. John is dying → he is not dead yet [imperfective grammatical aspect]
 c. John has died → he is dead [perfective grammatical aspect]

A grammatical shifting operation for the progressive is, for example, formulated in de Swart (1998), who argues that progressive-marking introduces an operator function PROG that shifts processes P and events E to states S, as in (33); note that de Swart does not assume the Vendlerian four-way distinction of event types and collapses achievements and accomplishments into the class of *events*; see also Mourelatos (1978) and Verkuyl (1989).

(33) PROG: $P \cup E \rightarrow S$ (de Swart 1998: 354)

The PROG operator shifts activities and achievements/accomplishments into stative predicates and removes the implication of a culmination for telic predicates (de Swart 1998: 355). A similar function of the progressive is given in Kamp & Reyle (1993):

(34) Semantic Effect of the Progressive:
 The eventualities described by progressive forms of a verb **v** are of the type which is represented by that part of the schema corresponding to the Aktionsart of **v** which terminates in, but does not include, the culmination point.
 (Kamp & Reyle 1993: 566)

Against claims that the progressive is simply uninformative about whether the culmination is reached or not, Verkuyl (2019: 200) argues that "the Progressive does not underinform about completion, it stands in the way of expressing it", thus denying the possibility that the culmination is reached; see also Dowty (1979: 65) for the same observations about the entailments of accomplishments. When the culmination point is removed in the progressive, the remaining part of accomplishment predicates is the phase preceding the culmination, which is usually a durative activity; for achievements, the progressive behaves differently and augments the event to include an interval that precedes the culmination (Rothstein 2004b: 48; van Lambalgen & Hamm 2005: 172; Arsenijević et al. 2013: 13). The availability of the progressive indicates that there is an accessible process stage in the conceptualization of the situation, even if this is not part of the predicate's event structure (Portner 2011: 1242–1243).

From a processing perspective, the progressive is relevant to the issue of adjunct islands because it has different effects depending on how the input event is modified: Bott (2010) reports no processing disadvantages for aspectual shifting or coercion operations that remove a part of the predicate's event structure, called "subtractive coercion", whereas there are processing disadvantages for operations that add a subevent, called "additive coercion". Since the progressive removes the entailment of the culmination, it can be expected to behave like subtractive coercion and not have a negative processing effect.

The question in this first experiment of this study series is whether the progressive shows the same effect as manipulations of lexical aspect in study series 1, where atelic matrix predicates received significantly lower judgments. From a processing perspective, no reduction in acceptability is expected, but if a culmination point is required to allow extraction (see Truswell 2007; Brown 2017), then there should be a negative effect of the progressive. As *get*-predicates readily accept the progressive, they are a suitable verb type to examine potential contrasts when they are embedded in tenses that are aspectually unmarked or marked.

4.7.1.1 Study design, methods, and participants

This experiment employs a 2×2 factorial design with the two factors PROGRESSIVITY of the matrix predicate (levels: *–prog –* & *+prog*) and STRUCTURE (*–wh* & *+wh*). The design is exemplified in (35).

(35) a. Liz got scared watching a horror movie.   [–prog/–wh]
     b. What did Liz get scared watching __ ?   [–prog/+wh]
     c. Liz was getting scared watching a horror movie.   [+prog/–wh]
     d. What was Liz getting scared watching __ ?   [+prog/+wh]

Manipulating progressivity of the matrix predicate requires additional care in the creation of experimental items because the present participle adjunct bears the same *-ing*-morphology; if they occur in sequence, this is predicted to independently degrade the construction ("doubl-ing", see Ross 1972; Pires & Milsark 2017). In this aspect, *get*-predicates are ideal because the adjective separates matrix and adjunct predicate and this problem does not arise. At the same time, *get*-predicates are clearly intransitive in the presence of the adjective, so no gap site is available after the matrix predicate; this reduces the risk of processing difficulties arising from the disambiguation of potential gap sites (Chaves & Putnam 2020).

The state predicates in the matrix clause include simple adjectives like *nervous* or *mad* as well as participle adjectives such as *excited* or *worried*. Adjunct predicates are transitive atelic activities, as in most previous experiments. A total of 16 experimental items were created and distributed across four lists according to the Latin square design. Each list contained four lexicalizations of each condition. Target items were mixed with 34 fillers of different degrees of grammaticality, including the 15 cardinal well-formedness sentences from Gerbrich et al. (2019). The complete experiment contained 50 sentences.

The experiment was uploaded to the OnExp platform and participant recruitment was carried out via Amazon's Mechanical Turk platform, limited geographically to US and UK residents. Participants were paid for taking part in the experiment. They saw the sentences as written stimuli one at a time in individually randomized order and were instructed to judge the naturalness of each sentence on a 7-point Likert scale. There was a two-hour time restriction to complete the entire experiment but no restrictions for individual answers.

A total of 48 participants was recruited for the experiment via Mechanical Turk. One participant was removed due to technical problems with the OnExp platform which resulted in an incomplete data set; five participants were not included in the analysis because they performed poorly on the standardized filler items. Judgments from 42 participants were included in the statistical analysis.

4.7.1.2 Hypotheses

This experiment investigates the hypotheses in (36), which are based on the results from study series 1 and the predictions about the effect of aspectual shift induced by the progressive (see Zucchi 1998; Bott 2010).

(36) Hypotheses for Experiment 6
    H6a. Significant effect of PROGRESSIVITY.
    H6b. Significant effect of STRUCTURE.
    H6c. No interaction between PROGRESSIVITY and STRUCTURE.

I expect a significant effect of PROGRESSIVITY in this experiment due to the aspectual shift towards an atelic interpretation (H6a). Progressive-marking induces this atelic reading, whereas the output of lexical telicity is not manipulated in the simple past (Higginbotham 2004: 332). This is an instance of subtractive aspect shifting (van Lambalgen & Hamm 2005; Bott 2010), where the culmination part is removed from the event structure of the predicate. While this type of aspect shift does not necessarily incur processing disadvantages, as reported in Bott (2010: 149), Experiment 1 and Experiment 2 showed that conditions with atelic matrix predicates are less acceptable than conditions with telic predicates, both in declaratives and interrogatives. This effect should be visible in both declarative and interrogative conditions, which would further confirm that the telic culmination point is a requirement not only for interrogatives (Truswell 2007), but also for the declarative BPPA construction (Brown 2017). There should also be a significant effect of STRUCTURE due to the extraction from an adjunct constituent and the general cognitive cost of establishing a filler–gap dependency (H6b).

Hypothesis (H6c) predicts that there should be no significant interaction between the two factors. Matrix predicates with an atelic interpretation are less acceptable than those with a telic reading (see Experiment 1 and Experiment 2), regardless of whether *wh*-extraction has taken place or not. Like the aspectual class of the matrix predicate, progressivity should thus be an independent factor that does not interact with extraction. The lack of an interaction would again point in the direction of the Independence Hypothesis.

4.7.1.3 Results

Mean ratings plus standard deviations for the four conditions are shown in Table 4.11 together with the standardized fillers for comparison. The two declarative conditions receive very high acceptability judgments, which are almost on the level of the perfectly acceptable A-standards. Even the worst condition [+prog/+wh] receives judgments which are only slightly below the level of the B-standards.

Tab. 4.11: Numerical results for Experiment 6. Mean ratings plus standard deviations (SD) and 95 % confidence intervals (CI) for the four experimental conditions and the five levels of the standard fillers.

Experimental items					Standard fillers			
Progressivity	Structure	Mean	SD	CI_{95}	A–E	Mean	SD	CI_{95}
−prog	−wh	6.44	0.87	[6.30;6.57]	A	6.75	0.58	[6.65;6.86]
−prog	+wh	5.13	1.47	[4.90;5.35]	B	5.46	1.47	[5.20;5.72]
+prog	−wh	6.29	0.91	[6.15;6.43]	C	3.74	1.51	[3.47;4.01]
+prog	+wh	4.89	1.44	[4.67;5.11]	D	3.24	1.42	[2.99;3.49]
					E	1.68	0.94	[1.52;1.85]

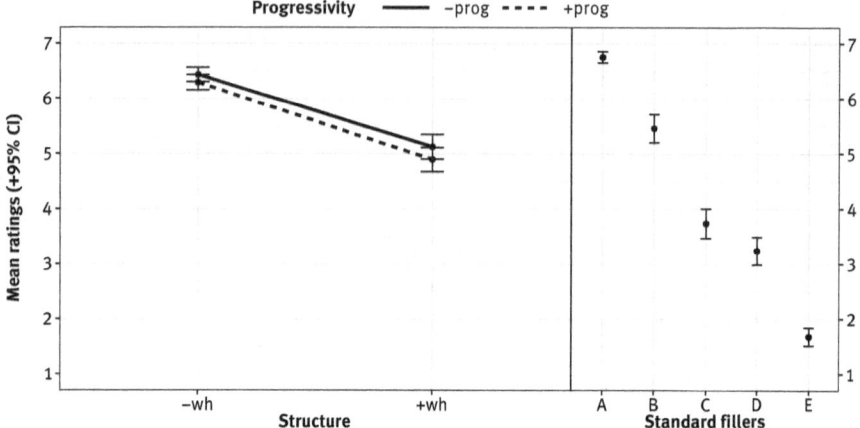

Fig. 4.9: Results of Experiment 6 (mean ratings) compared to standardized fillers. Mean ratings for the five levels of the standardized fillers A–E are shown on the right for comparison. Error bars show 95 % confidence intervals.

The results for the conditions and standardized fillers are shown graphically in Figure 4.9.

For statistical analysis, I constructed a linear mixed-effects model with PROGRESSIVITY and STRUCTURE as fixed effects, and participants and items as random effects. The factors were re-leveled so that +*prog* and +*wh* levels are set as reference levels. The maximal random effects structure that allowed convergence of the model includes random slopes for both factors by participants and for both factors plus interaction by items, excluding correlations. Model syntax, parameter estimates, and significance values are reported in Table 4.12. The results show that there is a marginal effect of PROGRESSIVITY ($\beta = -.101, t = -2.163, p = .051$) which does not reach significance below $p < .05$. In contrast, STRUCTURE is highly significant ($\beta = -.677, t = -6.995, p < .001$). There is no evidence of a significant interaction between the two factors ($\beta = .024, t = -.545, p = .594$).

Tab. 4.12: Statistical results for Experiment 6. Model syntax, parameter estimates, standard errors (SE), and *t*-statistics for the two factors of the experimental design plus their interaction.

Model: mixed(rating~prog*struc+(prog+struc||id)+(prog*struc||item))						
Fixed effects:	Estimate	SE	df	*t*-value	*p*-value	Sig.
Progressivity	−.10090	.04664	12.35	−2.163	.0508	.
Structure	−.67714	.09680	24.11	−6.995	< .001	***
Progressivity × Structure	−.02379	.04365	13.98	−.545	.5943	

In contrast to the predictions for this experiment, there is no significant effect of PROGRESSIVITY (H6a). Progressive-marked *get*-predicates are not significantly less acceptable than those in the simple past, despite the differences in telicity that should result from the aspectual shift induced by the progressive. Extraction from the adjunct predicate results in significantly lower acceptability, seen in the effect of STRUCTURE (H6b). The hypothesis that there is no interaction between the two factors is also confirmed (H6c): progressive-marked *get*-predicates are just as much affected by the extraction as the non-progressive condition, providing further evidence for the Independence Hypothesis.

4.7.1.4 Discussion

Several aspects of these results that deserve closer examination. The first thing to note is that *get*-predicates with a participle adjunct receive nearly perfect ratings in the two declarative conditions; they are close to the A-standards and thus near the upper bound of the scale. The interrogative conditions are also fairly acceptable, with judgments that place them directly below the level of the grammatical B-standards. In the remainder of this discussion, I focus on three points: (i) the fact that progressivity shows no effect, (ii) the relation of *get*-predicates to degree achievements, and (iii) the availability of a paraphrase where the adjunct predicate acts as the subject, which indicates a different argument structure compared to other BPPA constructions. I will argue that the availability of this paraphrase indicates that the participle predicate in BPPA constructions with *get*-predicates is a semantic argument which is expressed as a syntactic adjunct, similar to the AGENT argument in passive *by*-phrases (Grimshaw 1990). The question resulting from this observation is whether this difference in argument structure has an effect on the transparency of BPPA constructions with *get*.

(i) First, as discussed in the introduction to this experiment, the hypothesis about the significantly lower acceptability of atelic, progressive-marked conditions is based on the assumption that atelic matrix predicates are less acceptable than telic ones, which was shown to be the case in Experiment 1 and Experiment 2. Since *get*-predicates allow both telic and atelic readings depending on the grammatical context in which they appear, they are good candidate verbs to examine the effect of aspectual shift in relation to grammatical aspect. One crucial difference between the matrix predicates used in study series 1 and the present experiment is that study series 1 manipulated lexical aspect, whereas Experiment 6 manipulates grammatical aspect. Lexical aspect is concerned with the temporal properties of lexical items plus their arguments, whereas grammatical aspect distinguishes between different viewpoints on a situation, such as the perfective–imperfective distinction (see Comrie 1976; Sasse 2006; Travis 2010). In contrast to the aspectually neutral simple past, progressive-marking modifies the aspectual interpretation of the sentence but does not change the lexical aspect of the predicate itself (see de Swart 2012: 761). This would lead to the explanation that manipulations of outer aspect do not have an effect on the acceptability of a participle adjunct in declaratives and interrogatives, as long as the matrix predicate has a lexically telic interpretation available; additionally, the predicate has to be in principle compatible with the progressive, either by lexicalizing the process part, as seen in accomplishments, or by allowing the augmentation of a preceding process component, which is the case for many achievements. The fact that there is no statistically significant effect of the progressive in this experiment shows that *get*-predicates fulfill the input criteria for progressive-formation (Croft 2012: 152–155). A second possible explanation is that telicity as formulated in Truswell (2007) is not the only relevant factor in determining acceptability because aspectual shift from a telic to an atelic reading does not have an effect on the strength of extraction. Since *get*-predicates are compatible with both readings, this claim cannot be made based on the present results. It has to be pointed out that these results are partially compatible with the intuitions in Truswell (2007): the telic or atelic interpretation of the matrix predicate does not make a difference in declaratives. Both are equally acceptable. The contrast here is in the interrogative conditions, which do not show the expected difference. This is the reverse pattern than in Experiment 2, where Truswell's intuitions predict no differences in declaratives but under extraction. One of the possible conclusions is that the licensing conditions for the adjunct predicate are relevant before the application of outer aspect. If outer aspect is taken as a component that operates on the input from inner aspect (de Swart 2012; Croft 2012) and either modifies the input, as in the progressive, or hands it over unmodified, as in the simple past, this can explain why there is no effect of the progressive: as an unmodified aspectual category, *get*-predicates are able to host the adjunct predicate, and this compatibility is unaffected by subsequent modification of outer aspect.

(ii) A second point about *get*-predicates is that the aspectual interpretation depends to a certain degree on the characteristics of the adjective complement: as frequently pointed out in the discussion of degree achievements like *cool*, *widen*, or *straighten*, the inference of culmination is conditioned by the scale properties of the adjective (Hay et al. 1999; Kennedy & Levin 2002, 2008; Kearns 2007; Piñón 2008). The adjectival scale may be open (like *wide*), closed (like *straight*), or contextually closed (like *cool*). Verbs based on closed-scale adjectives like *straighten* are more readily interpreted as telic because there is a clear endpoint; this is not the case for open-scale de-adjectival verbs like *widen* because there is no clear point when something counts as wide. Sentences with a closed scale may be evaluated according to the endpoint entailed in the adjective, as a measurement how far the progression towards that endpoint has obtained. On the other hand, sentences with an open scale are evaluated according to the gradual progression towards the property denoted by the adjective. Consider the examples in (37): the progressive of *straighten* does not entail that the rope has become straight, but the progressive of *widen* entails that some widening has happened.

(37) a. They are straightening the rope. ≠> They have straightened the rope.
 b. They are widening the road. ⇒ They have widened the road.
 (Kennedy & Levin 2002: 10)

These differences in the entailments are similar to the imperfective paradox distinguishing between activities and accomplishments in Dowty (1979). It shows that the inference of telicity depends on the scalar properties of the adjective. What characterizes the adjectives used in this experiment is that as psychological affect predicates, they are to a certain degree contextually bounded and do not have definite endpoints; at the same time, they can be conceptualized as scalar predicates, which are measured against a scale of having the property described by the adjective. Getting bored in a lecture or getting scared when watching a horror movie does not require that this happens in an instant; rather, a gradual increase in the relevant psychological disposition is possible. The high compatibility with the progressive shows that the matrix predicates in this experiment emphasize the possibility of a scalar property progression along a temporal scale (see Croft 2012: 153–154). The activity denoted by the adjunct predicate in this particular construction causes this increase. Not only does the adjunct predicate provide a discourse-coherent relation between the two predicates, they are also temporally contingent. A similar argument has been made in Brown (2017: 75) about the "amalgamation" of the two predicate scales; the temporal scale of the matrix predicate is subsumed in the temporal scale of the adjunct predicate, which coincides with the prototypical interpretation of depictives (McNally 1997).[28]

(iii) The third and final point is the observation that, in contrast to other predicate types, BPPA constructions with *get*-predicates and a psychological adjective complement can be paraphrased as a psych-predicate structure with a de-adjectival verb; see (38). For ease of reference, I will refer to the BPPA construction (38a) as the inchoative, and to (38b) as the causative version. The causative version is not possible for all psych adjectives, because not all de-adjectival psych verbs are lexicalized in English; for example, there is no verb *to anxious*.

---

[28] While this approach based on temporal scales provides an initial good fit with the data reported in the literature, I will adjust this proposal in Chapter 5 to account for a wider set of data.

(38) a. Peter got scared (watching a horror movie). [inchoative]
 b. Watching a horror movie scared Peter. [causative]

In the construction investigated in this study series, as in (38a), the participle adjunct is entirely optional. The paraphrase in (38b) places the adjunct predicate in subject position and is interpreted as the STIMULUS of the psych-predicate. This sentence pair bears close resemblance to the causative–inchoative alternation (Levin 1993: 27–30). The causative alternation shows similar characteristics in that the causing component is suppressed in the intransitive inchoative alternate, while it is explicit in the transitive causative counterpart. I will not apply the term "causative alternation" to these sentence pairs because the inchoative version is impossible without the mediation of the resulting copula *get*; the term "causative pair" seems appropriate (Levin & Rappaport Hovav 1995: 110). In *get*-predicate pairs, the EXPERIENCER can be either realized as the subject (39a), or the object (39b).

(39) a. Peter got scared [watching a horror movie]. [experiencer subject]
 b. [Watching a horror movie] scared Peter. [experiencer object]

Lakoff (1970: 38–39) points out the following link between *get*-predicates and reflexive inchoatives:

(40) a. John got hurt when he fell down.
 b. John hurt himself when he fell down.
 (Lakoff 1970: 39)

These examples point to the relation between *get*-predicates and transitive reflexive predicates, which allow for transparent adjuncts according to Borgonovo & Neeleman (2000). However, it does not seem very natural to say *Peter scared himself*.

The meaning of the non-passive *get*-construction is essentially the transition to a new state that is caused by an unspecified event (Chappell 1980). As the sentence pairs in (38) and (39) show, the adjunct participle can encode this causing event. It thus occupies a slot in the lexical semantic representation of the matrix predicate. Thus, the causative paraphrase of *get*-predicates can be analyzed as in (41b), whereas the inchoative version in the absence of the BPPA is interpreted as in (41a). The BPPA construction of *get*-predicates has conceptual similarities to passive constructions, where the AGENT is also expressed in a syntactically optional constituent (Grimshaw 1990).

(41) a. Bill got scared. → [y BECOME *STATE*]
 b. Watching a horror movie scared Peter. → [x CAUSE [y BECOME *STATE*]]
   (see Levin & Rappaport Hovav 1995: 24, 75)

Note that the adjunct may also be interpreted as a cause or STIMULUS for other predicates, such as the achievement in (42a), but the causative paraphrase is not possible (42b), in contrast to *get*-predicates. The relevant distinction here is most likely to be found in the contrast between direct and indirect causation, as falling asleep during a lecture does not necessarily mean that the lecture was the direct cause (Copley & Wolff 2014: 50, 54–55).

(42) a. Peter fell asleep listening to a politics lecture.
 b. *Listening to a politics lecture fell Peter asleep.

However, the availability of a causative paraphrase cannot serve as a diagnostic for whether the matrix predicates will allow extraction from the adjunct, as not all predicates reported to allow extraction have a causative pair. Thus, the causative paraphrase does not distinguish between unaccusative verbs of directed motion and unergative manner-of-motion verbs (Levin & Rappaport Hovav 1995); see (43).

(43) a. *Whistling a funny song arrived John.
 b. *Screaming the lyrics danced John.
   (adapted from Truswell 2011: 155)

It is also noteworthy that the participle adjunct in *get*-predicate sentences cannot be easily interpreted as a free adjunct:

(44) a. Peter got scared watching a horror movie.
 b. ?Peter got scared, watching a horror movie.

This shows that the adjunct in this construction depends on the matrix clause in such a way that it cannot occur in a separate intonation or information-structural domain. From the perspective of event integration (Fabricius-Hansen & Haug 2012a), these adjuncts are closer to the matrix predicate than for other matrix predicates, where the free adjunct interpretation works without problems:

(45) a. Mary arrived at the station whistling a funny song.
 b. Mary arrived at the station, whistling a funny song.

Summarizing the discussion, the adjunct predicate in BPPA constructions based on *get*-predicates provides the implicit cause for the change of state encoded in the matrix predicate (Chappell 1980). This contrasts with the depictive interpretation of the adjunct for achievements like *arrive*. The adjunct in sentences with *get*-predicates can be described as a semantic argument that is expressed as a syntactic adjunct, similar to the *by*-phrase in passive constructions; this has been discussed in Grimshaw (1990) under the term "argument-adjunct" (see also Randall 2010; Graf 2015). The availability of a paraphrase where the adjunct serves as the subject of a de-adjectival psych verb supports this view. This makes *get*-predicates a highly interesting class of matrix predicate for the investigation of extraction from participle adjuncts because they behave much like transitive accomplishments as far as their argument structure is concerned, but show an intransitive syntax where a semantic argument is expressed as a syntactic adjunct. As a result, they are similar on the surface to achievement predicates, but differ in their argument structure. For achievements, the adjunct can only be interpreted as a depictive, i.e. a syntactic and semantic adjunct. This raises the question whether this difference in argument structure has an effect on the strength of extraction from the participle adjunct. Before returning to this point in Experiment 8, the next experiment investigates whether there is a different effect of progressivity with achievement matrix predicates such as *arrive*.

4.7.2 Experiment 7: Progressive achievements

In Experiment 6, *get*-predicates did not show any effect of progressive-marking in comparison to simple past conditions in declaratives and interrogatives. Thus, removing the culmination point from the matrix predicate's event structure does not lead to a significant decrease in acceptability, which is in line with Bott's (2010) observations about subtractive event coercion. This result is problematic for approaches to the BPPA construction that formulate a requirement for a culmination point in the event structure of the matrix predicate (Truswell 2007; Brown 2017).[29] In this experiment, I want to examine whether the same situation holds for achievement matrix predicates. Even though achievements have traditionally been considered to be less compatible with the progressive than activities or accomplishments (Vendler 1957), there is consensus that at least a subset of achievements accepts the progressive under a prospective interpretation, i.e. that the culmination

---

[29] It is still possible that lexical aspect is the relevant level and that a manipulation of outer aspect has no effect because BPPA compatibility is checked before outer aspect is introduced.

encoded in the achievement is just about to happen (Mittwoch 1991; Truswell 2011, 2019b; Rothstein 2004b); see (46).

(46) a. The train is arriving at the station → The train is about to arrive at the station. (Rothstein 2004b: 44)
b. He's winning the race → He is about to win the race.
(see Mourelatos 1978: 417)

On this reading, the event structure of progressive achievements is more similar to accomplishments. There is, however, a subset of achievements that strongly resists the progressive, even under the prospective reading, only allowing a so-called "slow-motion" reading that has an event structure more similar to activities (Rothstein 2004b: 56–58); see (47) with two perception verbs that are not very natural in the progressive.

(47) #She is noticing/spotting the eagle. (Mittwoch 1991: 76)

One of the possible explanations for this distinction among achievements with respect to the progressive has been made in terms of events that simply "happen" and are not under the control of the subject they are predicated of (Rothstein 2004b: 52); these are the "purely lucky achievements" in Ryle (1949), which are not associated with a preceding activity. Another explanation can be seen in the input requirements of the progressive, which is not compatible with all types of predicates: whereas activities, accomplishments, semelfactives, non-punctual achievements and probably temporary statives are suitable input predicates for the progressive, permanent states and predicates that only allow a punctual interpretation are not (Croft 2012: 152–155). The issue appears to be whether a predicate that allows a punctual construal, like *arrive*, can be extended with an activity component preceding the culmination. This point is made in Truswell (2007: 1370) but not discussed in later work.

This experiment aims to investigate the effects of the progressive on achievements that can be augmented with a preceding stage, avoiding clearly punctual, accidental predicates like *notice/spot*. One of the main differences in this experiment is that the progressive has the opposite effect than in Experiment 6: there, the progressive removed the culmination part of the event structure, whereas the simple past places the entire event structure prior to the utterance time. This is an instance of subtractive coercion. In the present experiment, the progressive acts as additive coercion, extending the event with a preceding process that is not usually part of the punctual nature of achievements (van Lambalgen & Hamm 2005: 172). Additive coercion, in contrast to other types of aspectual coercion, is reported to be the only one that causes processing difficulty: the "abductive reasoning about missing aspectual information ... is cognitively demanding" (Bott 2010: 135). The main issue to be determined here is what the effect of the progressive is on declarative achievements and whether progressivity has an effect on how strong *wh*-extraction degrades acceptability.

4.7.2.1 Study design, methods, and participants
The study design for this experiment is a 2 × 2 factorial design crossing the two factors PROGRESSIVITY (levels: –*prog* & +*prog*) and STRUCTURE (–*wh* & +*wh*). The design is given in (48).

(48) a. Emma fell asleep listening to a politics lecture. [–prog/–wh]
 b. What did Emma fall asleep listening to? [–prog/+wh]
 c. Emma was falling asleep listening to a politics lecture. [+prog/–wh]
 d. What was Emma falling asleep listening to? [+prog/+wh]

A set of 16 items was created and distributed across four lists according to the Latin square design; each list contained four lexicalizations of each condition. The target items were mixed with 32 distractors, including the standardized filler items from Gerbrich et al. (2019). Achievements that would have led to two sequential *-ing*-forms were avoided, so there are no sentences such as *What was Peter dying thinking about*. Achievements that are reported in the literature to strongly resist the progressive, such as *notice, spot, recognize, realize,* or *appear,* were also avoided. This resulted in the majority of the matrix predicates being verbs of inherently directed motion and other change of state verbs, as in the example item. For each predicate, it was considered possible that a preceding process takes place which results in the culmination encoded in the achievement. Adjunct predicates are again transitive agentive activity verbs.

The four lists were uploaded to the OnExp experimental platform as an online acceptability rating study with written stimuli. The lists were randomized for each individual participant to preclude list position effects. Participants saw one item at a time and responded on a 7-point Likert scale ranging from "completely unnatural" to "fully natural". There was a two-hour time limit to complete the entire experiment, but no limit for individual items.

A total of 48 participants was recruited via Amazon's Mechanical Turk platform, with twelve participants per list; they were paid for taking the experiment. One participant was removed because the data set was incomplete. Seven additional participants were not included in the statistics for poor performance on the standardized fillers. The total number of participants included in the statistical analysis was 40.

4.7.2.2 Hypotheses
In this experiment, I examine the support for the following two hypotheses:

(49) Hypotheses for Experiment 7
 H7a. There is a significant effect of PROGRESSIVITY.
 H7b. There is a subadditive interaction between PROGRESSIVITY and EXTRACTION.

As reported in Bott (2010), adding a subevent that is not normally part of a predicate increases processing difficulty. This should be visible in the results as a negative effect of PROGRESSIVITY (H7a). A punctual achievement has to be enriched with a preceding phase that is not lexically encoded. The use of progressive-marking, however, requires the presence of this preceding process stage (van Lambalgen & Hamm 2005; Croft 2012). Even if achievement predicates are in principle compatible with this added subevent, the construction of this subevent should lower acceptability because the enriched event is more complex to process (Bott 2010).

The second hypothesis (H7b) is that progressive-marking interacts with *wh*-extraction. The possibility of adding a preceding stage to an achievement predicate is seen as an important factor for determining the transparency of the adjunct predicate in Truswell (2007). In the simple past, the necessity of a preceding stage is only realized by the parser when the adjunct predicate is encountered, possibly triggering a re-calculation of the aspectual contour of the sentence. If this subevent is already required as input to the progressive, there are two indications that this stage is needed, not only for hosting the adjunct predicate. This could lead to a facilitation of processing and thus comparatively higher acceptability ratings than in the absence of progressive-marking. The expected effect structure pattern is thus subadditive, with a smaller decrease in acceptability for progressive-marked conditions when *wh*-extraction is applied.

4.7.2.3 Results
Mean ratings for the four conditions and the standardized fillers can be found in Table 4.13 on the following page and are shown graphically in Figure 4.10 on the next page. The numerical results show a decrease in acceptability for both PROGRESSIVITY and STRUCTURE; the mean judgments for the standardized fillers follow the expected pattern, but the C-standards are slightly lower than expected. Condi-

Tab. 4.13: Numerical results for Experiment 7. Mean ratings plus standard deviations (SD) and 95 % confidence intervals (CI) for the four experimental conditions and the five levels of the standard fillers.

	Experimental items					Standard fillers		
Progressivity	Structure	Mean	SD	CI$_{95}$	A–E	Mean	SD	CI$_{95}$
–prog	–wh	6.36	1.02	[6.20;6.52]	A	6.94	0.24	[6.90;6.98]
–prog	+wh	5.20	1.47	[4.97;5.43]	B	5.62	1.27	[5.39;5.85]
+prog	–wh	5.45	1.42	[5.23;5.67]	C	3.61	1.36	[3.36;3.85]
+prog	+wh	4.31	1.59	[4.06;4.56]	D	3.18	1.38	[2.93;3.43]
					E	1.81	0.96	[1.63;1.98]

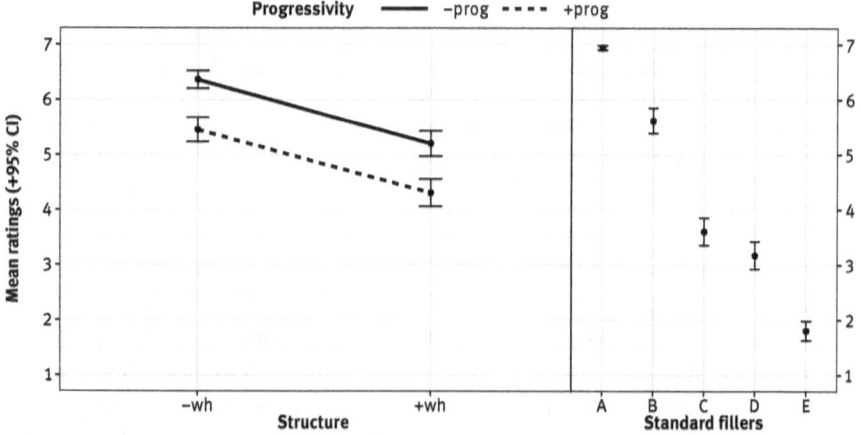

Fig. 4.10: Results of Experiment 7 (mean ratings) compared to standardized fillers. Mean ratings for the five levels of the standardized fillers A–E are shown on the right for comparison. Error bars show 95 % confidence intervals.

tions with progressive-marking and *wh*-extraction received the lowest judgments (mean: 4.31, SD: 1.59), which are still better than the C-standards (mean: 3.61, SD: 1.36). Declarative without progressive-marking received the most favorable judgments (mean: 6.36, SD: 1.02), which are between the A- and B-standards. The A-standards receive ratings close to the upper limit of the scale with little variation (mean: 6.94, SD: 0.24).

A linear mixed-effects model was created using the MIXED() function in R. PROGRESSIVITY and STRUCTURE are included as fixed effects, participants (ID) and items are considered random effects. As in the previous experiment, *+prog* was set as the reference level for PROGRESSIVITY and *+wh* for STRUCTURE. The maximal random effects structure that led to model convergence includes random intercepts and slopes for both fixed effects plus interaction but no correlations. The model syntax, parameter estimates, and significance values are reported in Table 4.14. Both PROGRESSIVITY ($\beta = -.447, t = -8.644, p < .001$) and STRUCTURE ($\beta = -.580, t = -8.348, p < .001$) show highly significant effects, whereas the interaction term between the two factors is almost non-existent ($\beta = -.009, t = -.15, p = .883$).

Tab. 4.14: Statistical results for Experiment 7. Model syntax, parameter estimates, standard errors (SE), and t-statistics for the two factors of the experimental design plus their interaction.

Model: mixed(rating~prog*struc+(prog*struc‖id)+(prog*struc‖item))						
Fixed effects:	Estimate	SE	df	t-value	p-value	Sig.
Progressivity	−.44705	.05172	12.93	−8.644	< .001	***
Structure	−.57969	.06944	18.76	−8.348	< .001	***
Progressivity × Structure	.00885	.05902	14.77	−.150	.883	

The hypothesis in (H7a) that there is a significant effect of PROGRESSIVITY is confirmed. Conditions with progressive achievements are indeed significantly less acceptable than the non-progressive counterparts. This is compatible with the observation in Bott (2010) that additive event coercion as the augmentation of the punctual achievement with a preceding stage affects processing. This higher processing cost leads to a decrease in acceptability in the present experiment. It can also be seen that progressive-marked declaratives are still acceptable, with relatively high judgments (mean: 5.45, SD: 1.42) just below the B-standards (mean: 5.62, SD: 1.27). In contrast, the hypothesis in (H7b) about the interaction between the two factors cannot be confirmed; the variance estimate contributed by the interaction is close to zero. There is no advantage for progressive-marked conditions in interrogatives compared to the simple past conditions, even though the presence of a phase preceding the culmination is already triggered before the adjunct is encountered. It is thus not the case that progressive-marked achievements are less affected by the extraction than achievements in the simple past where no event coercion has taken place.

4.7.2.4 Discussion
The central observations in this experiment are as follows: there is no subadditive effect of extraction when the aspectual coercion is specified earlier in the sentence; neither is there an additional penalty in the form of a superadditive effect when both additive aspectual coercion and extraction take place. In this discussion, I

focus on (i) what the absence of an interaction reveals about the transparency of BPPA constructions with achievement matrix predicates, (ii) further subclasses of achievement predicates, and (iii) the relation to previous experiments.

(i) The lack of a subadditive effect may be explained by the type of measurement implemented in this experiment: acceptability judgments are not able to provide information on online processes going on in sentence processing. There might be further insights that could be gathered from a reading time study on the same experimental items. In the holistic judgment of sentence acceptability, however, such measures are invisible. The lack of a superadditive or subadditive effect shows that the two factors result in independent decreases in acceptability. In this experiment, there is no additional penalty when two memory-intensive operations, aspectual coercion and the FGD, occur in the same sentence. As the FGD spans across the progressive-marked matrix predicate, both operations necessarily occur simultaneously: still, they do not seem to overload the available memory resources of the participants (see Kluender & Kutas 1993; Phillips 2013; Sprouse et al. 2012). The fact that progressive-marked achievements with a participial adjunct show a high level of acceptability indicates that participants did not have major issues in augmenting the event structure of the punctual culmination with a preceding process phase that hosts the adjunct predicate. However, it has to be acknowledged that this augmentation is costly and has an effect on the acceptability of extractions from the adjunct predicate. In comparison with the absence of an effect of PROGRESSIVITY in Experiment 6, these results show that aspectual coercion does have an effect on acceptability, but that this depends on the type of aspectual coercion, which in turn depends on the type of matrix predicate that serves as input to the progressive (Bott 2010; Croft 2012). Predicates that already include a temporally extended process phase show no effect of progressivity because subtractive coercion is less costly than additive coercion in cases where the predicate does not include this process phase (Bott 2010). Even in the absence of a subadditive effect as a case of island-repair, the results here show that the augmentation of the event semantics of achievements does not affect how strongly a sentence is degraded when *wh*-extraction takes place. This is another argument for the Independence Hypothesis; additionally, it indicates that the combined memory loads incurred by these two operations do not overload the parser's available memory resources and thus lead to superadditive effect structures as formulated in more complex reductionist accounts (Sprouse et al. 2013: 28–31). The linear-additive effect structure found in this experiment is still compatible with more basic reductionist accounts that assume cumulative effects leading to unacceptability in the presence of two costly operations (Sprouse et al. 2013: 25–28). In the present results, it seems unlikely that this condition with two simultaneous costly operations is considered unacceptable since the mean ratings for the [+prog/+wh] is still fairly high (mean:

4.31, SD: 1.59), also in comparison to the standardized fillers, where they are clearly above the C-level.

(ii) This experiment has shied away from achievement predicates that are reported in the literature to strongly resist the progressive, such as *notice, spot, appear* (Rothstein 2004b; Croft 2012). One of the open questions in this area is whether the preceding stage of achievement predicates is lexically encoded but not readily accessible, i.e. whether achievements in general and verbs of inherently directed motion in particular are encoded as punctual culminations or whether they include information about the preceding path stage. This option is considered in Krifka (1998):

(50)   For example, *Mary arrived in London* describes an instantaneous change of Mary's position from not being in London to being in London, or *perhaps the final part of this change*. We can express this as saying that it refers to events that are *minimal final events* of movements of Mary to London.
(Krifka 1998: 230, emphasis mine)

This already points to the fact that some punctual achievements refer to a preceding activity, as also pointed out in Truswell (2007) in relation to participial adjuncts for the *arrive–appear* distinction. A similar analysis of achievements is given in Higginbotham (2009); see the two formulations in (51), which both include reference to the path component that precedes the point of arrival.

(51)   a.   Mary arrived in London.
            $\lambda e \exists \lambda e' \in U_E \exists x \in U_H[\text{MOVE}(\text{M}, x, e') \wedge \text{GOAL}(x, \text{L}, e') \wedge \text{FIN}(e, e'') \wedge$
            $\forall e''[\text{FIN}(e'', e') \rightarrow e \leq e'']]$ (Krifka 1998: 230)
       b.   arrive$(x, e) \leftrightarrow (\exists p)[\text{at}(x, p, e) \& (\exists e')$ (e' is a journey by x & (e', e) is a telic pair)]   (Higginbotham 2009: 120)

The question is whether Krifka and Higginbotham would also analyze inherently punctual achievements like *appear* or *notice* in this way or as simple telic pairs excluding a preceding process. It seems warranted to draw a distinction along the lines of those achievements that can be coerced into a progressive reading without severe degradation and those that strongly resist the progressive because they can only be interpreted as punctual (see Rothstein 2004b; Croft 2012). Predicates like *notice* or *appear* are among those predicates which Rothstein (2004b) reports to resist the progressive because they "just happen", so there is no meaning component corresponding to Krifka's (1998) MOVE or Higginbotham's (2009) "journey".

(iii) As a final note on this experiment, it has to be acknowledged that the high acceptability judgments for the two extraction conditions in this experiment are not surprising considering the results of the previous experiments: the achievement predicates used here are perfectly compatible with a participle adjunct in declaratives, as the nearly perfect judgments for the non-progressive declarative condition show. Compare this to the declarative conditions with atelic adjuncts in Experiment 2 and with unergative and transitive matrix predicates in Experiment 4 and Experiment 5, which all show more degraded ratings. Also from the perspective of the interaction accounts in Truswell (2007, 2011) and Borgonovo & Neeleman (2000), the predicates used here are optimal candidates for transparent adjuncts.

This experiment has shown that while there is a significant decrease in acceptability for progressive-marked achievements, this does not affect how strongly these predicates react to extraction from the participle adjunct. The lack of an interaction between the two factors in this experiment again points in the direction that manipulations of outer aspect do not modulate the effect of extraction and that event coercion and extraction operate independently of each other.

4.7.3 Experiment 8: *get*-predicates & achievements

In this experiment, I investigate whether *get*-predicates and achievements are affected differently by *wh*-extraction. The results from previous experiments show that unaccusative achievements and *get*-predicates receive relatively high acceptability judgments. However, as the discussion of Experiment 6 has shown, they differ in their argument structure in that the adjunct predicate to *get*-predicates can express an argument role, which is not possible for achievements; they also have a different event structure and require different aspectual coercion processes when occurring in the progressive. Whereas *get*-predicates already encode a preparatory phase that can be targeted by the progressive, achievements do not and require additive aspectual coercion. These observations lead to the question whether *get*-predicates react differently to extraction than achievements such as *arrive*.

Achievements and *get*-predicates share three characteristics: (i) they both have a default telic reading in the simple past, so they conform to the aspectual condition in Truswell (2007) that the matrix predicate needs to be telic to allow for subextraction from the adjunct (see also Brown 2017); (ii) both predicate types are non-agentive, which means that they pose no problem for the restriction to at most one agentive event in a macro-event structure, as proposed in Truswell (2011); (iii) they are intransitive non-agentive change-of-state predicates, which suggests a syntactic analysis as unaccusative and thus the ability to host transparent adjuncts in terms of Borgonovo & Neeleman (2000). Thus, all of these accounts predict that both predicate types equally allow extraction from the adjunct.

The major difference between them is that *get*-predicates allow for a paraphrase where the adjunct participle appears as a gerund subject of the matrix clause and acts as a STIMULUS or THEME argument of the psych-predicate formed from the adjective in the *get*-construction. This is not possible for most achievements because their argument structure is fully saturated. The inability of the achievements used in this experiment to form causative pairs (Levin 1993) supports this difference in argument structure. Another difference is that the adjunct predicate has a causal relation to the matrix predicate for *get*-predicates, whereas achievements only allow for a depictive manner modification (see Hobbs 1979, 1990; Kehler 2002). This might have an independent effect on both the general acceptability of the two predicates, and the strength of extraction (see C. Müller 2019). A comparison of these predicate classes can shed light on the question whether the different argument structure of the matrix predicate has an influence on the possibility to subextract from the adjunct predicate. This difference is also important for pragmatic approaches to adjunct islands such as Chaves & Putnam (2020), who propose that extraction is only possible when the extracted element qualifies as relevant information to the proposition; adjuncts that express the cause component of the matrix predicate should be more relevant than adjuncts which express circumstantial depictive information. By comparing these two similar predicate types in terms of telicity and agentivity, the questions whether argument structure has an effect on acceptability and whether this difference interacts with extraction from the adjunct can be answered.

4.7.3.1 Study design, methods, and participants

This experiment uses a 2 × 2 design with the factors VERB TYPE (levels: *get-predicate* & *achievement*) and STRUCTURE (–*wh* & +*wh*). The design is shown in (52).

(52)   a.   Bill got bored listening to a politics lecture.   [*get*-predicate/–wh]
         b.   What did Bill get bored listening to __ ?   [*get*-predicate/+wh]
         c.   Bill fell asleep listening to a politics lecture.   [achievement/–wh]
         d.   What did Bill fall asleep listening to __ ?   [achievement/+wh]

For the *get*-predicate conditions, most of the items from Experiment 6 were used again; some were slightly adjusted to create plausible minimal pairs with the achievement conditions. Achievement predicates are non-alternating unaccusatives, e.g. *arrive* instead of *break*; these predicates were taken both from previous experiments and from the non-alternating unaccusatives used in an online study by Friedmann et al. (2008); most predicates are verbs of inherently directed motion in terms of Levin (1993). To avoid garden-path effects with homophone transitive matrix predicates, a location was added to achievements when needed, for example *enter the room* instead of simple *enter*. Within items, conditions are matched in complexity and length.

A set of 16 items was created and distributed across four lists according to the Latin square design so that each participant rated four different lexicalizations of each condition. The target items were presented together with 32 filler items including the standardized fillers from Gerbrich et al. (2019) in the form of an online rating study hosted on the OnExp platform. Participants were recruited via Amazon's Mechanical Turk platform and were paid for their participation. They saw one sentence at a time as written stimuli in individually randomized order and were asked to rate the naturalness of the sentences on a 7-point Likert scale ranging from "totally unnatural" to "completely natural". There was no time limit for individual answers but a two-hour time limit to finish the entire experiment.

Overall, 48 participants took part in this experiment. Data from two participants were removed before statistical analysis due to technical problems with the OnExp platform; two participants were excluded for poor performance on the standardized filler items. Data from 44 participants were included in the statistical analysis.

4.7.3.2 Hypotheses

The central hypothesis in this experiment is that the two matrix predicate types are affected to different degrees by extraction from the adjunct (H8a); this means that there should be an interaction between the factors VERB TYPE and STRUCTURE. Conditions with *get*-predicates should show a weaker effect of extraction because the adjunct can be interpreted as part of the matrix predicate's argument structure whereas it is both a syntactic and semantic adjunct in conditions with achievement matrix predicates.

(53) Hypotheses for Experiment 8
 H8a. VERB TYPE and STRUCTURE show a significant interaction.
 H8b. Achievement conditions are significantly less acceptable than conditions with *get*-predicates.

As the two predicate types also differ in their lexically encoded event structure as well as their argument structure in the form of causal or non-causal readings, this can be seen as another possible source of variation: as shown in the previous two experiments, progressivity leads to a significant decrease in acceptability only with achievement predicates, which do not lexically encode a durative subevent but can be coerced to such a reading. In hypothesis (H8b), I predict that conditions with achievement matrix predicates are less acceptable than condition with *get*-predicates because there the adjunct predicate cannot be interpreted as part of the matrix predicate's argument structure.

4.7.3.3 Results

Raw mean ratings for the four conditions and the standardized fillers are reported in Table 4.15. Both extraction conditions receive relatively favorable and nearly identical judgments. The results for the conditions plus standardized fillers are shown in Figure 4.11. Judgments for the two interrogative conditions are virtually indistinguishable, but there are small numerical differences between the declarative

Tab. 4.15: Numerical results for Experiment 8. Mean ratings plus standard deviations (SD) and 95 % confidence intervals (CI) for the four experimental conditions and the five levels of the standard fillers.

	Experimental items					Standard fillers		
Verb type	Structure	Mean	SD	CI$_{95}$	A–E	Mean	SD	CI$_{95}$
get-predicate	−wh	5.87	1.31	[5.68;6.06]	A	6.83	0.56	[6.74;6.93]
get-predicate	+wh	4.68	1.56	[4.45;4.92]	B	5.58	1.34	[5.35;5.81]
achievement	−wh	6.24	1.21	[6.07;6.42]	C	3.52	1.59	[3.25;3.80]
achievement	+wh	4.61	1.72	[4.35;4.86]	D	3.05	1.41	[2.80;3.29]
					E	1.58	0.81	[1.44;1.72]

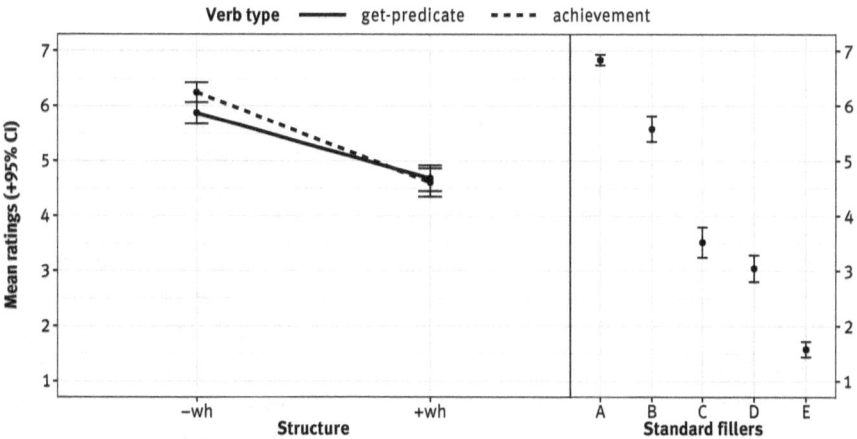

Fig. 4.11: Results of Experiment 8 (mean ratings) compared to standardized fillers. Mean ratings for the five levels of the standardized fillers A–E are shown on the right for comparison. Error bars show 95 % confidence intervals.

conditions; however, the confidence intervals overlap slightly. Again, the declarative conditions fall between the A and B levels of the standardized fillers, indicating a high degree of acceptability; interrogatives are clearly above the C-standards, which in this experiment are very close to the D level.

A linear mixed-effects model was fit over the data using the MIXED() function in R. VERB TYPE and STRUCTURE are included as fixed effects, participants (ID) and ITEMS as random effects. For VERB TYPE, achievements were set as the reference level as they are predicted to be less acceptable than *get*-predicates; +*wh* was selected as the reference level for STRUCTURE. The maximal random effects structure that allowed the model to converge includes random slopes for STRUCTURE by participants, and random slopes for both factors including their interaction by items, including correlations in both random effects. Model syntax, parameter estimates, as well as significance values are given in Table 4.16.

Tab. 4.16: Statistical results for Experiment 8. Model syntax, parameter estimates, standard errors (SE), and *t*-statistics for the two factors of the experimental design plus their interaction.

Model: mixed(rating~verbtype*struc+(struc|id)+(verbtype*struc|item))						
Fixed effects:	Estimate	SE	df	*t*-value	*p*-value	Sig.
Verb type	.06821	.11913	14.23	.573	.5759	
Structure	−.70690	.08476	21.65	−8.340	< .001	***
Verb type × Structure	.11733	.05955	13.19	1.970	.0702	.

There is no significant effect of VERB TYPE ($\beta = .068, t = .573, p = .576$), showing that both verb types receive similar results; in contrast, there is a highly significant effect of STRUCTURE ($\beta = -.707, t = -8.340, p < .001$). The interaction between the two factors is marginal but does not reach stable significance ($\beta = .117, t = 1.970, p = .070$). Against the predictions of hypothesis (H8b), the parameter estimate for VERB TYPE is positive, indicating that achievements are overall slightly more acceptable than *get*-predicates; however, the effect is not significant so that there are no reliable differences between the predicate types.

The statistical results do not confirm hypothesis (H8a). There is no significant interaction between VERB TYPE and STRUCTURE. This means that the two predicate types are affected to the same degree by extraction from the participle predicate, regardless of whether it can be interpreted as part of the matrix predicate's argument structure or not. In addition, there was no significant effect of VERB TYPE, so there are no reliable differences between the two predicates types, neither in declaratives nor in interrogatives; this does not confirm hypothesis (H8b). There appears to be a slight difference in the declarative conditions, and the variance estimate for the interaction is among the largest reported in this chapter. Still, the small benefit that *get*-predicates have over achievements when extraction takes place does not reach the threshold for a statistically significant interaction.

4.7.3.4 Discussion

In the following paragraphs, I want to discuss the following points: (i) the question of why there is no difference between achievements and *get*-predicates despite their argument-structural differences, (ii) what these results indicate about the relevance of semantically selected and unselected adjuncts, and (iii) whether the marginal interaction can be explained in terms of differences in the pragmatic relevance of the adjunct predicate.

(i) As noted above, both *get*-predicates and achievements are "ideal" matrix predicates for subextraction from the BPPA in terms of Truswell (2007, 2011): they are generally telic and non-agentive, so that the conditions of both generalizations are met. In addition, the achievement predicates qualify as unaccusatives, which conforms to the verb type generalization in Borgonovo & Neeleman (2000). Both extraction conditions are largely acceptable, as the comparison to the standardized fillers shows; both are between the B and C level, and are can thus be marked with a '?' in the conventions of Gerbrich et al. (2019). The lack of a reliable effect of VERB TYPE is surprising, considering that the two predicate types differ in two important aspects: first, the non-availability of a causative paraphrase for achievements which indicates a difference in argument structure and second, the different interpretations of the adjunct as a cause for *get*-predicates and a depictive for achievements. It would be expected that these differences show up in the acceptability judgments as a main effect of VERB TYPE, even in the absence of the predicted interaction. At first sight, this speaks against coherence-based approaches to adjunct islands, as long as other conditions such as aspectual classes or verb type are met. The results allow only some preliminary conclusions about this issue and rather point to the fact that other factors are more important.

(ii) Psychological adjectives as complements to *get*-type predicates are also discussed in C. Müller (2019: 23–27), who distinguishes between selected and unselected adverbial clauses.[30] She notes that for *get*-predicates, it is unclear whether an adverbial clause is an argument or an adjunct; the adverbial clause is syntactically optional but the STIMULUS role that can be encoded as an adverbial clause

---

[30] Recall that C. Müller (2019) operationalizes discourse coherence relation differences as the telic–atelic distinction. In some cases, discourse coherence and aspectual classes coincide because aspectual classes differ in the type of coherence relation they can form together with the adjunct predicate.

is entailed by the predicate. This is not the case for adverbial clauses modifying other types of matrix predicates, like achievements: there the adjunct is optional and not entailed, hence a clear syntactic and semantic adjunct (see Graf 2015). C. Müller concludes that this difference in argument structure is not relevant to the transparency of the adjunct, at least in Swedish. Compare the following sentences with topicalization from a conditional clause modifying a *get*-predicate (54a) and a temporal adverbial clause modifying an unaccusative predicate (54b), both cited in C. Müller (2019: 23, 26):

(54) a. [*Den här duken*]$_i$ *blir jag arg* [*om du spiller på* —$_i$]
 the here tablecloth become I angry if you spill on
 'I get angry if you spill on that tablecloth' (Teleman et al. 1999: 424)
 b. *Sportspegeln*$_i$ *somnar jag* [*när jag ser* —$_i$]
 sports program.the fall.asleep I when I watch
 'I fall asleep when I watch the sports program' (Anward 1982: 74)

While it can be argued that the conditional clause in (54a) is entailed as the STIMULUS argument of the matrix predicate *get angry*, the temporal adverbial clause is not entailed by the achievement matrix predicate *fall asleep*. Both adverbial clauses are syntactically optional, but differ in their relation to the argument structure of the matrix predicate. Yet both extractions are equally grammatical according to the judgments in C. Müller (2019).[31] Thus, it appears that a position in the argument structure of the matrix predicate is not a decisive factor in determining the transparency of the adjunct. The results reported in this experiment support C. Müller's conclusion: not only does the difference in argument structure not have an influence on how strong the effect of *wh*-extraction is, it does not lead to any reliable differences between these predicate types.

 (iii) The missing contrast between *get*-predicates and achievements is somewhat surprising in a relevance-based approach such as Chaves & Putnam (2020), who note that adverbial clauses modifying a *get*-predicate in a causal relation instantiate "prototypical states of affairs" (Chaves & Putnam 2020: 91); this does not equally apply to adjuncts modifying achievements, which can also describe plausible events, but here the two predicates stand in a less immediate relation to each other because the adjunct is not evoked in the background frame of the matrix predicate. In Chaves & Putnam's (2020) framework, it would also be predicted that more relevant constituents are easier to extract than less relevant, not-at-

---

[31] The English translation also allows a conditional reading for the *when*-clause; this would allow a causal coherence relation, even though the adverbial clause is not semantically entailed.

issue material. The numerical results for the target conditions and the marginal significance of the interaction in the statistical results do point in this direction, even if they do not reach full significance. In the declarative conditions, there are numerical differences between *get*-predicates (mean: 5.87, SD: 1.31) and achievements (mean: 6.24, SD: 1.21), whereas there are almost no differences in the interrogative conditions. With the contrast coding between the verb types set to achievements as the reference level, the positive sign of the interaction coefficient in the final model indicates that *get*-predicates are slightly less affected by the extraction than achievements, which is in line with the predictions form Chaves & Putnam (2020); but the advantage of *get*-predicates over achievements in their reaction to extraction is not strong enough to show up in the statistical results. The conclusions are the same as for the role of coherence relations in C. Müller (2019): in the absence of clear statistical evidence, the null hypothesis that there are no differences prevails.

This experiment examined the differences between two telic, intransitive predicate types: achievements and *get*-predicates. Against the predictions, the argument structure differences did not show up reliably in the results. This points to the conclusion that other factors are more important for the transparency of the adjunct, such as the grammatical verb type and the aspectual configurations, which have been investigated in study series 1 and 2. While both predicate types investigated in this experiment are in principle compatible with the predictions from Truswell (2007, 2011) and Borgonovo & Neeleman (2000), this experiment again fails to provide support for an interaction account: there is no reliable interaction of argument structure status with *wh*-extraction. Rather, the results point in the direction of the Independence Hypothesis. Under the assumption that the Independence Hypothesis is on the right track, then the question is still open which factors are involved in licensing the adjunct predicate.

4.7.4 Interim conclusion for study series 3

The experiments in this study series have revealed a number of interesting points that deserve discussion. First, they show *wh*-extraction conditions that are quite acceptable and lead to mean judgments that are consistently above the C-level of the standardized fillers and almost on the level of the B-standards in Experiment 6. From a CED-perspective, these ratings are surprisingly good and indicate that present participle adjunct predicates are not absolute islands to extraction.

The results of Experiment 6 show that a manipulation of outer aspect in the form of progressive-marking does not affect the transparency of adjuncts *get*-predicates, which is unexpected in a purely aspectual approach to adjunct islands such as Truswell (2007). The results rather suggest that a telic endpoint is not required to allow extraction from the adjunct. In contrast to *get*-predicates, Experiment 7 shows that progressive-marked achievements are significantly less acceptable than achievements in the simple past, but that this difference is identical in declaratives and interrogatives. One major difference between *get*-predicates and achievements is that the adjunct can be identified with the causal component in the argument structure of *get*-predicates, whereas they are purely depictive with achievements. This difference was the motivation for Experiment 8, which compared *get*-predicates with achievements and found no statistically reliable difference between them. This suggests that the potential argument structure difference does not modulate how strongly these predicate types react to *wh*-extraction.

Especially the results of Experiment 8 reveal several insights: there are no reliable differences between adjunct predicates that function as a causal component in the argument structure of the matrix predicate and adjuncts that can only be interpreted as depictives, i.e. temporally overlapping events. Even if the participle predicate can be considered as a semantically selected argument mapped to a syntactic adjunct, there are no differences to participles that are both syntactic and semantic adjuncts. This situation is in fact quite similar to the discussion in Truswell (2007): the argument there is that extraction from the adjunct is grammatical if the adjunct fills an open position in the event structure of the matrix predicate. This includes both causal positions and depictives, as long as the matrix predicate can be construed with a stage preceding the culmination of achievements. Both predicate types in Experiment 8 appear to fulfill this condition and do not force a multiple-event reading. Evidence for the presence of a preceding stage comes from the relative high acceptability of the progressive-marked forms, even for achievements in Experiment 7; despite the fact that there is a significant effect of PROGRESSIVITY, the conditions are still acceptable. An additional conclusion is that degree achievements, here in the form of *get*-predicates, pattern more with accomplishments than non-alternating achievements (Rothstein 2004b) because they allow a causal interpretation of the adjunct predicate (Truswell 2007: 1367).

The results of Experiment 6 and 7 show that the acceptability of extraction from an adjunct to a *get*-predicate or achievement depends on how acceptable the matrix predicate is with progressive-marking. Since there is no interaction of progressive-marking with extraction for these two predicate types, the possibility of aspectual coercion determines the level of acceptability for extraction conditions. The predicate classes tested in these two experiments both work reasonably well with the progressive, but to different degrees. The subclasses of achievements in Truswell (2019b: 7) show different interpretations of the progressive: purely punctual achievements resist the progressive, semelfactives force an iterated reading, and 'other' achievements have a prospective interpretation which indicates the possibility of augmentation with a preceding stage (see also Truswell 2011: 59). The predicates used in Experiment 7 fall into the third subclass because they accept the progressive with the relevant prospective reading.

The experiments in this study series show that the acceptability of extraction from a participle adjunct is partly determined by the compatibility with the progressive, even though this cannot be the only factor because activities/unergatives readily allow the progressive but are independently less acceptable with adjunct predicates compared to achievements/unaccusatives. For the group of telic or at least scalar, non-agentive matrix predicates, the conclusion can be drawn that the accessibility of a process component has an effect on overall acceptability, also in declaratives. By hypothesis, judgments for predicates that require additive aspectual coercion, such as purely punctual achievements and permanent states, should be even less acceptable in the progressive, with corresponding effects for interrogatives. It appears that the generalization in Truswell (2007, 2011) about the accessibility of a preceding phase for achievement predicates is on the right track. Whereas achievements and *get*-predicates show different reactions to the progressive, they behave virtually uniform in declaratives and interrogatives alike. Both predicate types also receive higher judgments compared to the standardized fillers than unergatives or transitives (Experiment 4 and Experiment 5) or constructions with an atelic matrix predicate (Experiment 2), presumably because they are more easily compatible with the participle adjunct predicate.

4.8 General discussion and conclusion

In the concluding section, I want to return to the research questions from the beginning of this chapter in Section 4.8.1 and then comment on the relation of this chapter to the island debate in more general terms in Section 4.8.2. Section 4.8.3 summarizes the factors investigated in this chapter and outlines observations for moving the debate forward, which will be the main topic of Chapter 5.

4.8.1 Conclusions for the research questions

The research questions from the beginning of this chapter are repeated for convenience in (55); I will summarize the conclusions from the individual experiments in turn.

(55) a. How acceptable is extraction from participial adjuncts compared to a standardized scale of well-formedness?

b. Which factors influence the acceptability of extraction from the BPPA construction?
c. Do the experimental results support the Interaction Hypothesis or the Independence Hypothesis?

Research question (55a): Except for Experiment 1, all experiments in this chapter use the standardized filler items from Gerbrich et al. (2019) to determine how acceptable extraction from the BPPA construction is on an anchored scale of well-formedness. The answer is clear: extraction is surprisingly acceptable. Even conditions that are judged ungrammatical in the literature (e.g. Truswell 2007; Borgonovo & Neeleman 2000) receive ratings which are never much worse than the C-level of the standardized fillers, which corresponds to a '?' judgment following Gerbrich et al. (2019). In the best cases, judgments for extraction conditions are almost on the fairly acceptable B-level, as in Experiment 6. The comparison to the standardized fillers also shows that there are considerable acceptability differences between different declarative conditions, which is typically not predicted in interaction accounts. Most declarative conditions fall into the range between the A- and B-levels and can thus count as unmarked, acceptable sentences. Still, there are statistically significant differences between them that are also reflected in interrogatives; such contrasts may elude introspective judgments, leading to the lack of judgment contrasts in the literature. These results indicate that even BPPA constructions that the literature considers bad candidates for extraction, such as sentences with atelic or transitive matrix predicates, allow it to some degree and are not entirely opaque. Especially the strict predictions by the CED about the ungrammaticality of such extractions need to be reconsidered in the light of this evidence about the relatively high acceptability of interrogative BPPA constructions.

Research question (55b): Section 4.3.2 listed six factors for transparent adjuncts that have been discussed in the previous literature. The experimental results reported here allow the following conclusions about these factors:

(i) *Grammatical verb type of the matrix predicate*
There are clear acceptability contrasts for different types of matrix predicate; the experiments in study series 2 show that unaccusatives have a clear advantage over unergative and transitive predicates (Experiment 4). This advantage, which is also present in the declarative counterparts, can also be observed when the unaccusative is augmented with a second argument to match the sentence length with transitives (Experiment 5). The present results replicate the pattern predicted for interrogatives in Borgonovo & Neeleman (2000), but also reveal the same contrasts in declaratives, which is problematic for their ap-

proach: there are clear distinctions between different types of matrix predicate, but they do not affect how strongly the sentence reacts to extraction.

(ii) *Aspectual classes of the two predicates*
Similar to the grammatical verb type of the matrix predicate, there are clear Aktionsart effects for both matrix and adjunct predicate (Experiments 1 & 2). The requirements on aspectual classes are reversed for the two predicates: telic matrix predicates are more acceptable than atelic ones and atelic adjuncts are more acceptable than telic ones. While this is an exact replication of the pattern predicted in Truswell (2007) for *wh*-extraction, the identical contrasts in declaratives show that the account faces serious problems in its conclusions about possible semantic constraints on extraction.

(iii) *Agentivity of the two predicates*
While agentivity was not directly investigated in these experiments, some preliminary conclusions are possible: Experiment 4 compared three types of matrix predicate that differ in agentivity. Unaccusatives are non-agentive, unergatives and transitives are agentive. There is evidence for the effect predicted in Truswell (2011) that conditions with two agentive events (unergative/ transitive + agentive adjunct predicate) are significantly less acceptable than conditions with at most one agentive event (unaccusative + agentive adjunct). But the fact that this same contrast is also found in declaratives shows that Truswell (2011) wrongly considers agentivity to be a factor determining transparency of the adjunct; there is no evidence for a semantically formulated constraint on extraction or a semantic filter on the output of extraction. It is not easy to say whether the effects found in study series 2 can be reduced to agentivity alone or whether the syntactic configuration of the different predicate types is more relevant.

(iv) *Transitivity of the matrix predicates*
Transitivity has a clear effect, as shown in Experiments 4 and 5; the transitive disadvantage remains when compared to unaccusatives with a locative/goal PP. This indicates that transitivity may depend on more than just taking two arguments (Hopper & Thompson 1980; Dowty 1991). A transitivity penalty that is independent of aspectual class has been observed in Brown (2017) and differentiates the predictions from Borgonovo & Neeleman (2000) and Truswell (2007, 2011); I will return to this point in the following chapter.

(v) *Coherence relations between the two predicates*
Coherence relations are not a primary subject of this chapter, but the results from Experiment 8 are relevant here: this experiment compares adjuncts that can be interpreted causally with predicates that only have a depictive secondary predicate interpretation. They thus differ in the type of coherence relation. As the results show, there are no reliable differences between these

two adjunct interpretations. It is, however, not entirely clear whether there is a contrast between coherent and non-coherent constructions in this experiment; see C. Müller (2019). Adjunct predicates can be interpreted as coherently related to the matrix predicate if they fill an unspecified event position such as the cause, or if they modify a subevent of the matrix predicate such as the phase preceding the culmination; see Haug et al. (2012) for this difference between event specification and event expansion.

(vi) *Syntactic integration of the adjunct predicate*
Experiment 3 shows that there is an effect of the degree syntactic integration in a comparison between the BPPA construction and free adjuncts. As in the remaining experiments, however, there is no evidence for an additional superadditive decrease in acceptability of interrogatives for these adjunct types.

These conclusions show that different factors have a measurable influence on the acceptability of extraction from an adjunct and that no single component is likely to offer a comprehensive explanation for the entire pattern observed in the literature. The most relevant result of the experiments reported here is the necessity of a principled explanation for the acceptability differences in declaratives. There is no evidence for a factor that licenses extraction without also showing an effect in declaratives; from an architectural perspective, this is a welcome result because it allows a division of labor between semantic licensing conditions for the adjunct and the syntactic licensing of the adjunct-internal gap, as first proposed in Brown (2015, 2017).

Research question (55c): This research question can be addressed by examining the effect structure patterns across the different experiments reported here. At the beginning of this chapter, I discussed four possible outcomes for the experiments that are of interest: (a) only an effect of extraction, (b) linear-additive effects, (c) superadditive effects, and (d) subadditive effects; see the overview in Figure 4.3 on p. 165. Superadditive and subadditive effects structures count as support for the Interaction Hypothesis, whereas only an effect of extraction and linear-additive effects support the Independence Hypothesis. For the most part, the experiments show a linear-additive effect structure, meaning that the two factors under investigation result in independent effects on acceptability without one factor determining the strength of the other. Notable exceptions are Experiments 6 and 8, which showed only an effect of extraction but not of the second factor; also, Experiments 5 and 8 showed marginally significant interactions. The results can thus be interpreted as follows: there is no clear evidence for the interaction accounts in Borgonovo & Neeleman (2000) or Truswell (2007). Instead, the results point towards the validity of the Independence Hypothesis: it appears that the syntactic and semantic licensing conditions for the adjunct predicate are independent of the effect of extraction. The architectural conclusions drawn by the interaction accounts are not supported by these results because they are formulated on the assumption of an interaction. This means that a closer investigation of these licensing conditions is required, which will be pursued in the following chapter.

4.8.2 The relation to the islands debate

In this section, I want to take a broader perspective and examine how the experimental results in this chapter relate to the more general debate on extraction from island domains. This discussion will focus on the relation to different general approaches to island effects, and the distinction between strong and weak islands. Approaches to islands can be grouped into three major types; Phillips (2013) and Newmeyer (2016) distinguish between (i) grammatical or competence-based approaches, (ii) so-called "reductionist" or performance-based approaches, and (iii) grounded or hybrid accounts. Each type of approach makes different claims about the underlying reasons for why extractions from specific constituents are perceived as more severely degraded compared to others. Grammatical approaches explain the strong acceptability decrease seen in extraction from islands as violations of a constraint; this type of approach is pervasive in the generative tradition, where constraints on syntactic operations have been formulated as early as Chomsky (1964) and Ross (1967). Performance approaches such as Kluender & Kutas (1993) claim that the simultaneous processing of a complex structure and the formation of a filler–gap dependency result in an additional acceptability decrease that cannot be attributed to the sum of the individual processing costs. Grounded accounts such as Berwick & Weinberg (1984) or Hawkins (1999, 2004) can be seen as a combination of these two types of approaches because they formulate constraints that are seen as grammaticalized processing disadvantages.[32] The experiments in this chapter were not designed to provide evidence for or against these approaches. I have focused on acceptability variations that are specific to the BPPA construction rather than on a more general comparison of this island type to other island types or non-islands. A detailed investigation of these construction-internal variations can still reveal insights about the more general discussion of islands, particularly

---

[32] See also Progovac (2015: chapter 5) for an evolutionary perspective on island constraints; in principle, all domains are considered islands by default, and the possibility for movement only became available for complements at a later stage. For a similar argument of the default island status from a learning perspective, see also Culicover (1999).

because extraction from the BPPA construction has been considered as evidence against the plausibility of syntactic constraints (Truswell 2007, 2011).

As shown throughout the experiments reported in this chapter, there is no evidence that extraction is sensitive to one of the factors investigated here. Aspectual classes, verb types, and argument structure differences do show different levels of acceptability, but they do not strengthen or weaken the effect of extraction. The major challenge for previous accounts of acceptable extractions from adjuncts is that the same contrasts are observed in declaratives. This is left unexplained in interaction accounts such as Borgonovo & Neeleman (2000) and Truswell (2007, 2011), but also puzzling for syntactic gap-licensing approaches such as Boeckx (2003), Oseki (2015), or Narita (2014), who assume that adjuncts can obviate island constraints through Agree-relations or because they are embedded in active phases. The island status of the BPPA constructions investigated in this chapter does not depend on aspectual class or verb type. For a comprehensive explanation of the acceptability contrasts observed in the present set of experiments, it is necessary to consider the factors that cause the contrasts in declaratives. This is the underlying assumption of the Independence Hypothesis, which emphasizes the importance of conditions on the adjunct predicate that already apply to the declaratives.

As far as processing approaches to islands are concerned, the conclusions from the offline studies presented in this chapter have little to say about the online processes going on during sentence comprehension. Acceptability judgments are at best able to indicate that there are processing difficulties in a sentence, resulting in lower acceptability. Sprouse et al. (2013) describe two versions of processing-based explanations for island effects that differ in the complexity of the assumptions they make. A simple processing-based account predicts a linear-additive effect for memory-intensive tasks like processing an embedded domain and the formation of filler–gap dependencies. Each processing burden causes independent acceptability decreases which in combination may be severe enough to result in an unacceptable sentence. More complex processing accounts such as Kluender & Kutas (1993) involve an additional penalty in the form of a capacity overload when too many memory-intensive processes occur simultaneously. This corresponds to the presence of a superadditive decrease in acceptability. The results reported in this chapter are compatible with the simple processing account because no superadditive effect structures are found. Lower acceptability ratings for interrogatives are expected throughout, and the negative effect of a marked BPPA construction can be formulated to accommodate a processing-based explanation.

As discussed at the beginning of this chapter, such models can also be formulated in grammatical terms, notably the Decathlon Model (Featherston 2008, 2019) and the Cumulative Effect Hypothesis (Haegeman et al. 2014). Among the advantages of such models is that individual violation costs can stem from different modules and do not need to be equally strong. For example, the different acceptability judgments in the declarative conditions in this chapter could be the results of semantic mismatches in the formation of the verb–adjunct predicate complex in terms of their event-structural characteristics. The details of this aspect will be discussed in Chapter 5, Section 5.3. On the other hand, the decrease in acceptability in the presence of extraction could receive either a grammatical explanation in terms of a structural constraint like the CED or a processing-based explanation as a reflection of the high processing demand of holding a filler in active memory (Wagers 2013; Sprouse et al. 2013: 25–26).

Adjuncts are usually considered as prototypical cases of strong islands (Szabolcsi & Lohndal 2017; Abrusán 2014), but this consensus has been called into question repeatedly: for example, Truswell (2011: 17) concludes his literature overview with the statement that adjuncts seem to behave more like weak islands than strong islands because not all extractions are ungrammatical. The strong–weak distinction is usually formulated based on characteristics of the extracted element: "Strong islands are domains that are closed for every type of element, while weak islands are only closed for some elements" (Abrusán 2014: 2). Cinque (1990) distinguishes between weak islands that allow for PP and DP gaps and strong islands that allow at most DP gaps, but not all extraction types. There are two issues with applying the term *weak island* to the BPPA construction: (i) acceptability appears to depend on the type and characteristics of the embedding predicate instead of the extractee; and (ii) the same differences in declaratives are not explained. The first point indicates that BPPA constructions instantiate a sort of *bridge verb* phenomenon (see Erteschik-Shir 1973; Truswell 2011; Goldberg 2013; Chaves & Putnam 2020); keeping the extractee constant in the present experiments shows that there are significant effects depending on the choice of matrix predicate. Similar observations from adverbial clauses lead C. Müller (2019: 190) to extend the definition of weak islands to also include properties of the embedding predicate and the coherence relation between the two. However, a bridge verb account fails to explain the behavior in declaratives, where the same contrasts are found. The insight that bridge-verb phenomena can also arise in non-extraction contexts is found as early as Kuno (1987), who relates acceptability to pragmatic factors such as relevance. The experimental results in this chapter are in principle compatible with a pragmatic account of acceptability differences in declarative and interrogative BPPA constructions along the line of Kuno (1987) or Chaves & Putnam (2020), but require the assumption that pragmatic infelicity can also have an effect on acceptability judgments in declaratives. All in all, the experimental evidence gathered in this chapter does not offer clear arguments for or against grammatical or processing approaches to islands. However, the fact that there are no significant superadditive or subadditive effects points to the conclusion that there is no evidence for a capacity overload when extraction takes place from a verb–adjunct predicate complex that is in a sense "suboptimal". Likewise, there is no evidence for additional grammatical constraints that distinguish between extraction from one type of BPPA and other types. In Chapter 2, I have discussed the licensing conditions for depictive secondary predicates and constraints on the formation of complex events. As I will show in the following chapter, such conditions can account for a large part of the data pattern observed in this chapter.

4.8.3 Summary of factors

The experiments reported in this chapter reveal the relevance of the factors in (56), which are partially predicted by the existing literature on adjunct islands. In contrast to most previous accounts, however, these factors are not specific to interrogatives and thus do not require architectural adjustments to the application of *wh*-extraction. In the following chapter, I will propose a factorial model for extraction from the BPPA construction that takes these factors into account.

(56) Factors which decrease acceptability in the BPPA construction:
    a. Telic adjunct predicates (Truswell 2007)
    b. Atelic matrix predicates, especially unergatives (Truswell 2007; Borgonovo & Neeleman 2000)
    c. Transitive matrix predicates (Brown 2017; Borgonovo & Neeleman 2000)
    d. Orthographically detached adjuncts (Fabricius-Hansen & Haug 2012a)
    e. Progressive-marked achievement predicates (Bott 2010)

As noted in Truswell (2007, 2011), the lower acceptability of telic adjunct predicates in factor (56a) is probably related to the progressive morphology, which is not perfectly compatible with telic predicates; this effect is thus independent of extraction. A similar situation holds for progressive-marked achievement matrix predicates, seen in factor (56e), which require cognitively costly additive aspectual coercion in the progressive (Bott 2010). The factors in (56b–c) isolate unaccusative matrix predicates as "ideal" as far as the distinction into unaccusatives, unergatives, and transitive predicates is concerned since they are both intransitive and predominantly telic. The group of *get*-predicates investigated in study series 3 also fits into this characterization because they are intransitive and interpreted as telic in the simple past. Additionally, there is a penalty for orthographically detached adjuncts (56d). These factors isolate the following characteristics of matrix predicates that are most acceptable in declarative and interrogative BPPA constructions:

(57) Characteristics of unmarked matrix predicates:
   a. Intransitive matrix predicates
   b. Telic or degree achievement matrix predicates

As the results of the experiments show, these characteristics do not affect the size of the effect incurred by extraction from the adjunct: extraction has the same effect on BPPA constructions with telic intransitive and atelic transitive matrix predicates, but the different predicate types already lead to acceptability contrasts in declaratives. In the following chapter, I will develop a factorial approach to acceptability criteria for the BPPA construction that combines several independent factors. As this chapter has provided robust evidence in favor of the Independence Hypothesis, the focus will be on patterns in declaratives, since they show the same sensitivity to the investigated factors as interrogatives. Therefore, the main goal of the following chapter will be to develop acceptability criteria for the BPPA construction that capture the patterns in the present experiments and further contrasts observed in the literature. It will be shown that there is a certain overlap between the resulting criteria and existing licensing theories for depictives.

5 A factorial acceptability model for present participle adjuncts

The previous chapter investigated the question if there are factors that determine whether an adjunct predicate allows extraction, or whether the investigated factors show effects that are unrelated to extraction. In this chapter, I will put the experimental results into perspective with two goals in mind: (i) capturing the most important judgment contrasts reported in previous approaches, and (ii) accounting for the effects of the investigated factors that are independent of sentence form.

Two main insights are offered in this chapter: (i) there is good experimental evidence that acceptability contrasts in interrogatives are related to similar contrasts in declaratives, as first noticed by Brown (2015, 2016, 2017) and formulated here as the Independence Hypothesis (IH): the reduced acceptability that is caused by the application of extraction is independent of reduced acceptability that is caused by syntactic and semantic factors which are already operative in declaratives; (ii) there are several factors which determine acceptability in the BPPA construction independently of extraction and which cannot be reduced to a single factor such as event structure or verb type classification. As the experimental results clearly show that extraction is not sensitive to the factors investigated, the effects shown by these factors cannot be formulated with reference to conditions or constraints on extraction. This chapter is thus guided by the following research question:

(1)   How can the acceptability contrasts reported in the literature and observed in the experimental chapter be captured without appealing to conditions on extraction?

I will propose a Factorial Acceptability Model (FAM) for the BPPA construction that captures both the relation between declarative and interrogative BPPAs, as well as the factors which lead to acceptability variations in declaratives. These factors are formulated as three generalizations: acceptability is higher if a generalization is met and lower otherwise. Acceptability is measured in a linear-additive fashion, such that each generalization has an independent effect on acceptability, depending on whether it is satisfied or not.

In a way, these acceptability decreases are similar to the *violation costs* in the graded models of acceptability discussed at the beginning of Chapter 4, namely the Decathlon Model (Featherston 2008, 2019) and the Cumulative Effect Hypothesis (Haegeman et al. 2014). There is, however, a crucial difference between these models and the one I propose in this chapter: I do not assume that the proposed generalizations are necessarily part of the speaker's competence grammar; rather, they are descriptions of the semantic compatibility and syntactic complexity of a BPPA construction that are related to how easily the structure can be processed. In the discussion of acceptability variations, I will prefer the term *effect* rather than *violation* for two reasons: (i) an effect may arise for various reasons that include formal grammatical principles (i.e. competence) as well as phenomena related to plausibility and processing (i.e. performance); and (ii) an effect may be either positive or negative, whereas a violation always results in a negative effect. See also Sprouse & Hornstein (2013: 2, fn. 4) for a similar distinction in the discussion of island violations and island effects. The factorial model I propose is schematically represented in Figure 5.1. It is divided into two stages:

(i) The acceptability of the declarative BPPA construction is calculated based on the characteristics of the two predicates, which include the semantic compatibility of the two predicates as well as the syntactic complexity of the sentence.
(ii) The independent application of extraction decreases acceptability in interrogatives due to the cognitive cost associated with establishing and resolving a filler–gap dependency.

The effects that result from the individual factors in declaratives add up in an incremental, linear-additive fashion, resulting in a graded pattern of acceptability; see also Keller (2000) for a similar model for graded acceptability patterns. This model makes the crucial assumption that the size of the negative effect of extraction is not influenced or modulated by the factors which play a role in the declarative: formulated oversimplistically, extraction operates blindly on the declarative input.

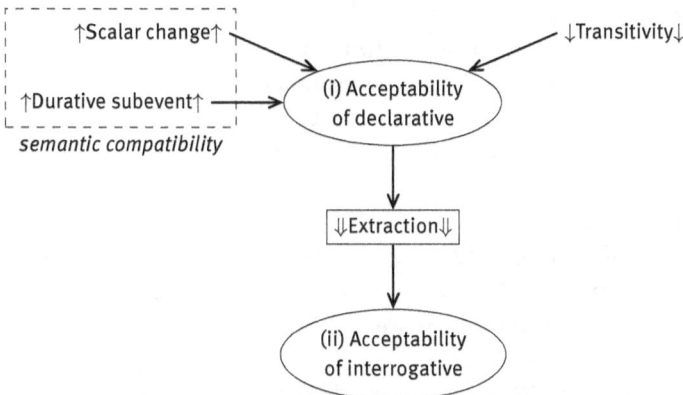

Fig. 5.1: Factorial Acceptability Model for the BPPA construction, showing the factors which determine acceptability in declaratives and the independent effect of extraction.

The factors which influence acceptability in the declarative can be conceptualized as the result of an increased processing effort that leads to lower acceptability. In effect, this makes the proposed factorial model a processing model for the BPPA construction, where syntactic and semantic factors jointly determine how easy or difficult a given BPPA construction is processed; see Featherston (2019: 159) and Culicover & Winkler (2018: 380) for similar proposals about the relation of processing complexity and relative acceptability judgments. The effects of semantic and syntactic factors on processing that are independent of whether extraction takes place or not is directly captured in the independence of the two stages of the FAM, in accordance with the Independence Hypothesis.

In Section 5.1, I will offer a summary of the main findings from the experimental Chapter 4 with the goal of motivating the two stages of the factorial model. Section 5.2 will then discuss the relevant factors for acceptability in the BPPA construction and propose three generalizations which influence the semantic compatibility between the two predicates and the syntactic complexity of the construction. In Section 5.3, I will show that the proposed factorial model provides a principled explanation for the data patterns in the literature, and also for contrasts that are difficult to capture in previous approaches. Section 5.4 notes some potential challenges that the model faces, and Section 5.5 shows how the factorial approach can be extended to related adjunct constructions. Section 5.6 concludes this chapter.

5.1 Main experimental findings

The experimental results have shown that the acceptability contrasts which are observed in interrogatives can be traced back to identical contrasts in declaratives. It is thus not the case that properties of the matrix predicate determine how strongly extraction decreases acceptability. This is the position adopted, for example, in Borgonovo & Neeleman (2000) and Truswell (2007, 2011); in Chapter 3, I formulated this as the Interaction Hypothesis in (2).

(2) Interaction Hypothesis:
     Properties of the matrix and adjunct predicates determine the strength of the effect of *wh*-extraction, for example their aspectual classes, argument structure, or the semantic relation between the two predicates.

Rather, the experimental results support Brown's (2017) proposal about the independence of conditions for gap-licensing and adjunct-licensing, which I have formulated as the Independence Hypothesis in (3).

(3) Independence Hypothesis (IH):
   The syntactic and semantic licensing conditions on the adjunct predicate are independent of the effects of extraction from the adjunct.

The IH disassociates the effects of extracting from an adjunct and the factors that determine the acceptability of the underlying declarative proposition; this means that the judgment differences observed, for example, for the telic–atelic distinction in Truswell (2007) do not need to be formulated as a universal constraint on the application of extraction. Rather, it is an effect that applies independently of extraction. Likewise, the SEGC formulated in Truswell (2011) is not necessarily part of locality theory, but it may very well show independent effects across different sentence forms. There is a growing body of research in this direction, for example the processing-based explanation of freezing effects in Culicover & Winkler (2018) and parasitic gap phenomena in Culicover & Winkler (2022), the pragmatic explanation of island effects in Chaves & Putnam (2020), or the discourse-function approach to different extraction types in Abeillé et al. (2020) and Liu et al. (2022). The shared goal of this line of research and the key idea behind the IH is that many extraction asymmetries that have been hotly debated over the decades since Ross (1967) are not the result of grammatical principles, but rather of more general principles that are not directly related to extraction.

Under the assumption of the IH, the next task is to examine more closely the factors that lead to acceptability differences in the BPPA construction regardless of whether extraction takes place or not. The experimental designs in the previous chapter included factors that are proposed in the theoretical literature, such as telicity or verb type, and other factors that were considered relevant for acceptability, such as argument structure and progressivity. As shown at the end of Chapter 4, telic intransitive predicates and degree achievements in the form of *get*-predicates are the most acceptable matrix predicates in declarative BPPA constructions, which carries over to the interrogative conditions. The preference for intransitive matrix predicates was shown in study series 2, where intransitives are rated significantly better than transitives. For intransitive predicates, telic predicates are judged as more acceptable than atelic ones; see Experiments 1 and 2. An evaluation of these sets of experiments replicates the findings in Brown (2017). However, the results from study series 3 on progressive-marking indicate that the encoding of a telic endpoint may not be required for all predicate types; this also depends on whether the predicate already encodes a durative subevent that can be targeted by the progressive, as with *get*-predicates, or whether additive aspectual shift has to be applied, which is the case for achievements; see Zucchi (1998) and Bott (2010). Progressive-marking also has ramifications on a potential telicity requirement as formulated in Brown (2017) because "the Progressive does not underinform about completion", but rather "stands in the way of expressing it" (Verkuyl 2019: 200). I will show below that there are cases where telicity does not make the right predictions, but where a more general notion of change that does not entail a culmination (see Rappaport Hovav & Levin 2010) is more appropriate. The experimental results also show that the potential argument structure status of the adjunct predicate does not have an effect on acceptability and the strength of extraction (Experiment 8). This points in the direction originally pursued in Truswell (2007) about the integration of the adjunct predicate into the matrix predicate's event structure, which is possible for both predicate types investigated in this experiment even though a causal connection is established for *get*-predicates but not for achievements.

In the next section, I will break down the factorial model into its component parts and motivate the proposed factors with the experimental evidence from Chapter 4 and observations in the literature. In addition to the IH, I will propose three generalizations for the acceptability of declarative and interrogative BPPA constructions, which are integrated into the factorial model sketched above.

5.2 Deriving the factorial acceptability model

Previous approaches to extraction from participle adjuncts typically distill one factor that determines the strength of degradation when extraction takes place from the adjunct: the "good" level of the factor shows a smaller degradation in the presence of extraction than the "bad" level. These factors include a telicity or culmination requirement for the matrix predicate (Truswell 2007; Brown 2017), syntactic reflexivity (Borgonovo & Neeleman 2000), or a limitation in the number of agentive events in the complex event structure (Truswell 2011). In this section, I will develop a factorial acceptability model for declarative and interrogative BPPA constructions in the form of generalizations which cover the data patterns in the literature that have been shown to hold up experimentally, and those cases that have proved to be puzzling in previous approaches.

5.2.1 Independence

This factorial model is proposed in the context of the Independence Hypothesis in (3): the following generalizations are to be understood as more general factors which determine acceptability in the BPPA construction, independently of extraction. This has been consistently shown throughout the experiments reported in Chapter 4 and is also attractive from a theoretical perspective. The independence of extraction from other factors that affect acceptability in the BPPA construction is thus the first key component of this factorial approach. The effect of the IH is that the acceptability of the declarative BPPA construction is calculated before the application of extraction, based on construction-specific criteria to be proposed in the following sections. In other words, the overall acceptability of the underlying (declarative) proposition is predicted to account for the acceptability pattern in extraction structures; a similar position about the importance of the general (pragmatic) felicity of underlying declaratives can be found in Chaves & Putnam (2020) and dates back at least to Kuno (1987).[33] Figure 5.2 shows how extraction connects the two stages of the factorial model: extraction contributes an independent negative effect on acceptability, which is visualized by the downward arrows '↓'. In this and the following partial representations of the factorial model, I will highlight the current factor under discussion in bold typeface.

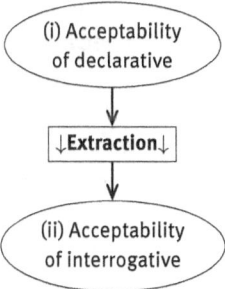

Fig. 5.2: Factorial Acceptability Model (extraction): extraction lowers acceptability, but is independent of factors which apply to the underlying declarative.

The argument that establishing a filler–gap dependency has a negative effect on acceptability is frequently made in the literature; it is cognitively demanding to hold a filler in memory and integrate it in an appropriate gap site (Gibson 1998, 2000; Bornkessel-Schlesewsky & Schlesewsky 2009; Sprouse et al. 2013; Wagers 2013; Chaves & Putnam 2020). Also, interrogatives are semantically more complex than declaratives: the latter are propositions, whereas the former are often considered to be sets of alternative propositions, which means that the processing of interrogatives is more demanding than that of simple propositions (Hofmeister & Sag 2010: 383). Different types of extraction, such as relativization or topicalization, may show larger or smaller cognitive demands and thus affect acceptability to dif-

---

[33] The discussion of the so-called *Restricted Answers Puzzle* in Truswell (2011: 30–31) in relation to prepositional adjuncts already points at the fact that good questions can only be formed from good assertions, i.e. that *wh*-extraction from a marked structure can only result in stronger markedness.

ferent degrees (Abeillé et al. 2020). Possible reasons for such a non-uniform effect on acceptability include the relative frequency of the extraction construction, and the ease of mapping a structure to the intended meaning (Culicover & Jackendoff 2005) and its intended discourse function (Abeillé et al. 2020).

In a next step, it is necessary to find generalizations that allow predictions about which types of matrix verb will be most compatible with a participle adjunct predicate. I will follow Brown (2017) and Rapoport (2019) in the assumption that adjunction of verbal adjuncts is not constrained by syntactic conditions, but that the acceptability of adjunction depends on semantic criteria, i.e. how well the two predicates fit together (see also Truswell 2007, 2011). The discussion in this chapter will focus on characteristics of the matrix predicate. Chapter 2 and the results of Experiment 1 have shown that there are also conditions on the adjunct predicate: depictive secondary predicates are constrained by the SLP–ILP distinction as well as conditions on meaning components in terms of Rappaport Hovav & Levin (2010) and Talmy (2000); also, telic adjuncts are less acceptable, probably because of an interaction with the progressive morphology (Truswell 2007: 1373). As a result, atelic activities are the most acceptable type of adjunct predicate, whereas telic predicates and statives are marked; additionally, if subextraction is to happen from the adjunct, this trivially imposes the requirement that the adjunct needs to be transitive. I will not explicitly discuss telic adjunct predicates and rather concentrate on BPPA constructions with atelic adjuncts (e.g. *arrive whistling* instead of *arrive noticing*).

The experimental results in Chapter 4 have shown that the predictions formulated for extraction in Borgonovo & Neeleman (2000) and Truswell (2007, 2011) are valid generalizations, even though they should carry over to declaratives, as formulated in the IH. The contrasts in declaratives may have been missed in the previous literature because the declarative conditions generally receive high acceptability judgments. A characterization of unmarked matrix predicates should therefore take these contrasts into account. The patterns from Truswell (2007) for the effects of aspectual classes and Borgonovo & Neeleman (2000) for the verb type of the matrix verb are reproduced in (4) and (5).

(4) a. *What did John work whistling? [atelic matrix predicate]
    b. What did John arrive whistling? [telic matrix predicate]
    (see Truswell 2007: 1369)

(5) a. *What$_i$ did John dance [imagining t$_i$]? [unergative]
    b. *What$_i$ did John finish the portrait [covered in t$_i$]? [transitive]
    c. What$_i$ did John come back [addicted to t$_i$]? [unaccusative]
    (Borgonovo & Neeleman 2000: 199–200)

The differences between telic or unaccusative and atelic or unergative predicates suggests that telicity is indeed a relevant factor, as proposed in Truswell (2007); however, the reported ungrammaticality of (5b) and the high acceptability of *get*-predicates in study series 3 indicate that this is not the entire story.

I will propose three generalizations about characteristics of the matrix predicate that lead to high acceptability in the declarative BPPA construction. The first two of these generalizations determine the semantic compatibility between the two predicates, whereas the third generalization is related to syntactic complexity and higher processing burdens. Extraction then operates on this input and incurs the cognitive costs associated with the formation of filler–gap dependencies (Sprouse et al. 2013; Wagers 2013). These generalizations serve as components of the factorial model. In the following sections, I will define and motivate these generalizations based on the experimental results from Chapter 4 and additional contrasts discussed in the literature.

5.2.2 Durativity

The first generalization I propose is that the semantic compatibility and thus acceptability of declarative BPPA constructions is higher when the matrix predicate encodes a durative subevent. This is formulated in the DG in (6):

(6) Durativity Generalization (DG):
The semantic compatibility between the matrix and adjunct predicate in the BPPA construction is higher if the matrix predicate encodes a durative subevent, either by means of lexical encoding or via event template augmentation.

The DG alone does not offer a comprehensive explanation for the acceptability differences in (4) and (5), but accounts for further contrasts discussed in the previous literature which were not explicitly addressed in the preceding chapter. These contrasts include differences between permanent and temporary states (see Maienborn 2019), as in (7), as well as the fact that not all achievement predicates allow extraction, seen in (8).

(7) a. *Which of your magic hats do you know Georgian [wearing t]?
(Truswell 2007: 1362)
b. What did John lie around [reading __] all day? (Truswell 2011: 155)

(8) a. *What did John appear whistling?
  b. *What$_j$ did John$_i$ [notice his brother] [looking through t$_j$]$_i$?
   (Truswell 2007: 1370)

Permanent statives as in (7a) are not normally compatible with secondary predicates because "there is a conflict set up between the temporary state involved in a depictive and the enduring state involved in many statives" (Himmelmann & Schultze-Berndt 2005: 100); in contrast, states that are interpreted as temporary allow depictives (7b). Similarly, there is a group of achievement predicates that is ungrammatical in interrogatives such as in (8), which contrasts with the grammatical extractions for achievements reported in (4b) and (5c).

The property that captures the differences in (7) is related to whether the predicate encodes a durative subevent. Permanent states hold as property ascriptions, making subintervals irrelevant for interpretation; it has been argued that these predicates do not have an event variable (Maienborn 2019; Rappaport Hovav 2008: 16–17, fn. 3). Temporary states, however, are evaluated at intervals during which the property either holds or does not hold. The further division of states is not new: Bach (1986: 6) differentiates between dynamic and static states, the SLP–ILP contrast of Carlson (1977) provides a similar division, and Maienborn (2005, 2019) draws a lexical semantic distinction between states. There is thus good reason to draw this distinction and incorporate it into the factorial model.

For the achievement cases in (8), Rothstein (2004b: 52) proposes that such purely punctual predicates cannot be augmented by a preceding phase that leads to the culmination; they simply encode the punctual transition between two opposite states. Achievements like *arrive* or *die*, on the other hand, can be extended to include a preceding phase. A clear manifestation of these differences between the two stative and achievement groups is seen in the possibility of progressive-marking of the matrix predicate, which is possible for (7b), but not the other examples in (7a) and (8). Permanent states (9a) and punctual achievements (9c) are incompatible with the progressive, whereas temporary states (9b) and extendable achievements (9d) allow it; the punctual achievement in (9c) can only receive a slow-motion reading (Rothstein 2004b; Croft 2012: 152–155).

(9) a. *I am knowing Georgian.   [permanent state]
  b. John is lying around all day.   [temporary state]
  c. *John is noticing his brother.   [punctual achievement]
  d. John is arriving at the party.   [extendable achievement]

Crucially, the types of achievement in (4b) and (5c) are among those that allow the progressive in a prospective reading, where the culmination is interpreted as being

5.2 Deriving the factorial acceptability model — 255

imminent, or "can be anticipated in advance" (Mittwoch 1991: 76); see also Dowty (1979: 136–137) and Rothstein (2004a,b). Such an interpretation is similar to that of accomplishments, where the progressive highlights the activity process before the culmination (Rothstein 2004b: 48). However, the progressive for achievements focuses on the imminent culmination instead of the process component (Mittwoch 1991: 76). Parsons (1990: 24) also observes that many typical achievements like *win* or *reach* occur colloquially in the progressive and can thus be considered to encode a "development portion" similar to accomplishments. The limited availability of the prospective reading of the progressive for achievements is captured by the subtypes of achievements in Truswell (2019b: 7) between "points" and "other achievements": only the latter, but not the former allow the progressive with a prospective reading. Truswell (2019b) also includes semelfactives in the group of achievements; in the progressive, semelfactives are interpreted as iterative and cannot be interpreted as an ongoing activity or an imminent culmination (see Truswell 2019b: 7). This fits with the analysis of semelfactives as "cyclic" achievements in Croft (2012: 60); Talmy (2000: 68) uses the term "full cycle", indicating an automatic resetting. In the following discussion, I will follow Truswell (2019b) and use the term "point predicates" rather than "purely punctual achievements". The term "achievement" will be reserved for those achievements which can be augmented by a preceding stage and accept the progressive in a prospective reading, i.e. Truswell's (2019b) 'other achievements'. Point predicates trigger a so-called slow-motion reading in the progressive, which is compositionally different from the prospective reading: its interpretation is closer to the progressive form of activities (Rothstein 2004b: 56–58). Following Verkuyl (1993), I suggest that there is a lexical difference between purely punctual achievements like *appear/notice* and cases like *arrive/enter*: the latter allow a shifting operation to an interpretation that is more similar to accomplishments. Such a reading is only possible for punctual achievements in an appropriate context that allows coercion to this reading (see Section 5.4 below). Therefore, the durativity generalization in (6) predicts that permanent states and point predicates should be less compatible in the BPPA construction; temporary states, activities, accomplishments, and achievements with a prospective reading of the progressive are predicted to be more compatible. When the DG is not met, compatibility is lower, resulting in decreased acceptability in declaratives.

The Durativity Generalization is based both on the data in (7) and (8), and captures the proposal in Truswell (2007) that the BPPA either supplies a causal component for accomplishments that is connected to the durative subevent preceding the culmination, or a preparatory phase for achievements. In both cases, the subevent that is modified by the BPPA has a durative character. The same applies to *get*-predicates, which behave similarly to accomplishments. However, for achievements, this durative subevent is not normally lexically encoded and has to be introduced by event template augmentation, which adds this subevent. A first test for high compatibility and thus higher acceptability in the BPPA construction is the possibility of the matrix predicate to occur in the progressive with a non-slow-motion reading. This is, for example, seen in (9a,c), which resist the progressive more strongly than (9b,d).

Experimental evidence for durativity is found in the experiments reported in study series 3, where *get*-predicates and achievements differ in the effect of progressive-marking: *get*-predicates are not affected by progressive-marking because they lexically encode the durative subevent that is targeted by the progressive; the culmination point is not relevant here. On the other hand, achievements show a negative effect of the progressive, which is visible in degraded acceptability for progressive-marked conditions. Achievements require additive event coercion because they do not lexically encode a durative subevent, and this coercion operation is cognitively costly. These different effects of the progressive for *get*-predicates and achievements are not surprising and have been reported in the literature, for example in Bott (2010), who reports different effects of subtractive and additive event coercion on reading times. Additional support for the DG comes from the results of Experiment 8, which failed to show significant acceptability differences between *get*-predicates and achievements in declaratives and interrogatives. There was also no difference in how strong *wh*-extraction degrades these two predicate types. Both types are compatible with a durative subevent and thus meet the DG.

The group of *get*-predicates is flexible with respect to durativity: the change-of-state can be conceptualized as punctual or extended. As illustrated in (10), durative and punctual adverbial clauses influence the interpretation of the *get*-predicate in the matrix clause: adverbial clauses with a durative activity predicate induce a durative reading of the change-of-state (10a), whereas adverbial clauses with punctual achievement predicates prefer a punctual reading (10b).

(10) a. Peter got scared when he watched a horror movie. [durative adverbial]
     b. Peter got scared when he entered the dark forest. [punctual adverbial]

The temporal characteristics of an adjunct predicate thus interact with the temporal interpretation of aspectually flexible matrix predicates and can specify their interpretation. In the BPPA construction, the adjunct predicate is ideally an atelic activity, which presumably induces a durative interpretation of the adjunct predicate, analog to the adverbial clause in (10a); this offers an explanation why matrix predicates which either lexically encode a durative subevent or can be shifted to a durative reading are more acceptable than predicates which resist durative subevents.

5.2 Deriving the factorial acceptability model

Table 5.1 shows the status of different verb types in relation to the DG; except for permanent states and point predicates, all verb classes encode a durative subevent, which is either supplied by the lexical semantic properties of the predicate, or by aspectual coercion. The main test for durativity is the possibility of progressive-marking in a non-slow-motion reading, as shown in the third column of Table 5.1. The last column indicates the respective interpretation of the progressive: permanent states require a coercion of the ILP to a SLP, so that the progressive describes an interval during which the property holds; this mismatch between lexical meaning and syntactic environment leads to reduced acceptability. Point predicates in the progressive coerce an activity-like slow-motion reading, with likewise reduced acceptability (Rothstein 2004b). Progressive achievements are interpreted as prospective, meaning that the culmination is imminent (Rothstein 2004b; Truswell 2011, 2019b). The remaining verb classes, activities, accomplishments, temporary states, and *get*-predicates, are interpreted as ongoing, which is the default interpretation of the progressive (Kamp & Reyle 1993).

Tab. 5.1: Verb classes and the durativity generalization.

Verb class	DG	Progressivity test	Reading
permanent states	not satisfied	*John is knowing French.	coercion to SLP
points	not satisfied	*John is noticing his brother.	slow-motion
activities	satisfied	John is walking.	ongoing
accomplishments	satisfied	John is drawing a circle.	ongoing
achievements	satisfied	John is arriving.	prospective
temporary states	satisfied	John is lying in bed.	ongoing
get-predicates	satisfied	John is getting scared.	ongoing

Figure 5.3 visualizes the positive effect of the DG on the acceptability of the declarative BPPA construction. Upward arrows indicate that those matrix verbs which encode a durative subevent will lead to higher acceptability in the BPPA construction compared to verbs that do not or can not encode such a subevent.

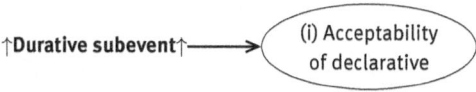

Fig. 5.3: Factorial Acceptability Model (durativity). Acceptability of the declarative is higher if the matrix predicate encodes a durative subevent.

5.2.3 Scalar change

The DG, however, cannot be the whole story because it is too permissive: it does not account for the differences in (4) and (5), all of which allow the progressive and therefore encode a durative subevent or can be augmented to do so. The most problematic verb type are activities, where the literature and the experimental results from Chapter 4 agree that they are less acceptable in BPPA constructions; see Experiments 2, 4, and 5. As the second generalization, I propose that BPPA compatibility is increased when the matrix predicate encodes a meaning that can be measured against a prominent scale, similar to measuring-out effects in Tenny (1987, 1994, 1995).

(11) Scalar Change Generalization (SCG):
The semantic compatibility between the matrix and adjunct predicate in the BPPA construction is higher if the event described by the matrix predicate can be measured against a prominent scale, such as temporal intervals, incremental themes, paths, and property scales.

To account for the lower acceptability of activity matrix predicates in the BPPA construction, it is necessary to examine what distinguishes them from achievements, accomplishments, and *get*-predicates. The problem is that the difference to other verb types cannot be reduced to telicity alone, as this would lead to unclear predictions about *get*-predicates and contrasts such as between (12) and (13), where the addition of an object improves both the declarative and the interrogative. This addition does not turn the sentence telic, since both (12a) and (13a) take the same temporal adverbial; the slightly marked judgment for (12a) reflects the results of Experiments 4 and 5.

(12) a. ?John worked drinking lots of coffee (for/*in three hours).
b. *What did John work drinking lots of __ ?

(13) a. John worked on his thesis drinking lots of coffee (for/*in three hours).
b. ?What did John work on his thesis drinking lots of __ ?

Traditionally, all dynamic (i.e. non-stative) predicates are analyzed as events that encode some kind of change meaning component (Dowty 1979). Predicate types differ, however, in the type of change that they encode: what achievements, accomplishments, and *get*-predicates have in common is that they encode a scalar or gradual change component, as opposed to bare activities without an incremental theme object, which encode non-scalar change (Rappaport Hovav 2008, 2014;

Rappaport Hovav & Levin 2010). The concept of scalar change is defined as follows in Rappaport Hovav (2008):

(14) A scalar change is one which involves an ordered set of changes in a particular direction of the values of a single attribute and so can be characterized as movement in a particular direction along the scale.

(Rappaport Hovav 2008: 17)

The distinction between scalar and non-scalar change requires some additional explanation: verbs that encode scalar change can be clearly measured against a prominent scale, for example time, paths, properties, or extents. Motion verbs with a prominent path scale are typical examples, and the analogy of a path component carries over to other domains as well, such as properties (Krifka 1998: 228–230). On the other hand, there are verbs that encode other types of complex changes that cannot be reduced to one single prominent scale (see Rappaport Hovav 2008: 17; Rappaport Hovav & Levin 2010). Activities like *work* or *walk* in (15a) do not encode a single prominent scale on their own; the achievements in (15b) and the accomplishments in (15c), on the other hand, do. Isolated activity predicates often encode complex changes, such as the individual movements making up a walking event, but these changes do not happen along one prominent scale.

(15) a. *work, walk, read* and other activities [–prominent scale]
 b. *arrive, break, fall* and other achievements [+prominent scale]
 c. *finish, build, drive crazy* and other accomplishments
 [+prominent scale]

The sentences in (16) exemplify verbs with such a scalar change meaning; typical instances of scalar change are paths (16a), incremental themes (16b), and property scales (16c). In both cases, the progression of the event can be measured against properties of these prominent scalar structures. This means that there is a point on the path scale between the origin and the station that measures 50 % of the total path; likewise, the event of eating three apples is two-thirds over when Susan has consumed two apples. Tenny (1995) and Krifka (1998) refer to this as "mapping to (sub)events". At any arbitrary point during which the event is going on, the progression along the relevant scale can be measured, as shown schematically in (17).

(16) a. Peter walked to the station. [path scale]
 b. Susan ate three apples. [incremental theme]
 c. Mary heated the water. [property scale]

(17) a. Distance to station: 500 m → 398 m → 210.5 m → 5 m → 0 m
 b. Apples consumed: 0 → 0.75 → 1.3 → 2.1 → 3
 c. Temperature of water: 22 °C → 36 °C → 61 °C → 89 °C

Note that sub-parts of the path scale cannot be directly accessed in the default interpretation of achievements because they encode two-point scales which by definition do not have relevant intermediate parts; see (18). Compare this to (19), where the point on the path scale that marks 50 % is easily accessible. This is a further argument for the relevance of a durative interpretation, which requires coercion of achievements to include a process preceding the culmination (Rothstein 2004b). Rappaport Hovav & Levin (2010: 31) point out that the notion of scalar change is "not equivalent to gradable change", which is the reason that *arrive* in (18) resists a gradual modifier like *halfway*.

(18) Jane arrived (*halfway) to the US. (Erteschik-Shir & Rapoport 2005)

(19) Peter walked halfway to the station.

Tenny (1995) captures the distinction between verbs with and without prominent scales as follows: verbs are fundamentally divided into those that never measure out an event, verbs that always do so, and verbs that do not measure out in their basic sense but which can do so when a measuring scale is added by a non-verbal argument. Tenny exemplifies this difference with manner-of-motion verbs like *walk*, which are non-measuring-out in their basic sense, but which can receive a measuring-out reading if another constituent introduces a relevant scale against which the progress can be measured. Just as the nature of the object has an influence on telicity, as in the atelic *eat bagels* against the telic *eat a bagel*, the scale encoded by the verb can be modified by additional material in the sentence. In these cases, the measuring-out effect is contributed by an argument which turns the default non-measuring-out reading into an optional measuring-out reading. This is seen in (20), where the addition of a goal PP introduces a prominent scale that is not encoded in the verb; the prominent scale is now the path between an unknown origin and the station; see also Beavers (2013), who argues that the implicit goal in sentences like (20a) leads to an atelic interpretation.

(20) a. John walked. [−prominent scale]
 b. John walked to the station. [+prominent scale]

Lukassek et al. (2017) show experimentally that a large group of motion verbs are aspectually underspecified in this way and receive their aspectual interpretation compositionally with telic or atelic PPs. Tenny (1995) focuses on optional measuring-out effects with manner-of-motion activity predicates, but the same effects carry over to other activity predicates, as shown in (21). Adding a complement measures out the events described and provides a measuring scale. As shown in (22), this does not necessarily entail telicity because the results can still be compatible with both *in-* and *for*-adverbials; the atelic readings are generally improved in a conative reading, as in (22b) and (22d), where the completion can be explicitly denied.

(21) a. John read (a book).
　　 b. Mary painted (a picture).
　　 c. Peter cooked (dinner).

(22) a. John read a book in two hours. #He never finished it.
　　 b. John read (in) a book for two hours. He never finished it.
　　 c. Peter cooked dinner in two hours. #Then he gave up and ordered Chinese.
　　 d. Peter cooked dinner for two hours. Then he gave up and ordered Chinese.

A fundamental question is whether this means that there are predicates that measure an event but do not necessarily measure out the event in the sense that completion is entailed, resulting in a telic interpretation. This seems to be the case, as there are sentences which encode a prominent scale that measures the progression of the event, but which are still atelic: for accomplishments, it does not matter whether the result is telic or atelic: there is a prominent scale in both the telic *draw a circle* and the atelic *draw circles*. This captures the experimental results reported in Brown (2017: 123–125), who finds no effect of telicity for transitive predicates. Tenny (1994: 15) notes that measuring-out has two components: a measuring scale and a temporal bound. The SCG refers only to the measuring scale but not to temporal delimitation; as this delimitation is a necessary condition of measuring-out, the requirements of the SCG do not correspond completely to Tenny's (1987; 1994; 1995) measuring-out concept.

Dowty (1979: 168–169) discusses a similar contrast between the change seen in activities and accomplishments, which is related to subintervals and existential quantification: whereas the changes in activities can be evaluated at every subinterval, changes in accomplishments are evaluated in relation to the culmination point. Dowty characterizes the difference as follows:

> Activities, of the motional sort at least, are characterized by a change in physical properties over time. But we also characterized accomplishments and achievements by a change of

> state over time, so what is the difference in the two classes? It would seem to be the difference between a "definite" and an "indefinite" change of state. The activity *the ball moves* is *true of any interval in which the ball changes its location to any degree at all*, and thus may be simultaneously true of an interval and various subintervals of that interval. The accomplishments *the ball moves six feet, the ball moves to the bottom of the slope* are *true when a change of location of a particular specified location has taken place*, and thus are true of a single interval, but not of any subintervals or superinterval of that interval.
>
> (Dowty 1979: 168, emphasis mine)

The definition of motion activities involves existential quantification over places, which introduces indefiniteness; thus, any change away from a location p makes the verb *move* true, regardless of the direction. In effect, truth conditions for motion activities can be evaluated at every subinterval of the event. Accomplishments and achievements, on the other hand, do not quantify over places and evaluate truth conditions for the entire interval of the event as a relation between the moving entity x and a location p; truth values can only be evaluated for the entire interval, but not for subintervals; see Dowty (1979: 168–170) for the formalizations. This distinction between types of change is one of the underlying reasons for the imperfective paradox and the entailments of the progressive for activities and accomplishments, shown in (23).

(23) a. John was pushing a cart. ⇒ John pushed a cart.   [activity]
      b. John was drawing a circle. ⇏ John drew a circle. [accomplishment]
      (see Dowty 1979: 133)

This difference in the nature of the change meaning component distinguishes between activities on the one hand and achievements, accomplishments, and *get*-predicates on the other hand. Only the latter involve a prominent scale that measures the progression of the event. Therefore, the SCG in (11) serves as a further semantic compatibility criterion in the BPPA construction which further restricts the group of unmarked matrix predicates in this construction. It distinguishes predicates like permanent states and activities from predicates that encode a scalar change component; permanent states by definition do not encode any kind of change and are inherent properties (Mittwoch 2019). Among non-stative predicates, activities are singled out as being the only predicate type that does not encode a prominent scale; rather, they involve complex changes that cannot be reduced to one prominent scalar structure (Rappaport Hovav & Levin 2010). Achievements, accomplishments, and *get*-predicates, on the other hand, can be measured against a path or property scale and thus qualify as definite change in the sense of Dowty (1979) or directed change in Levin & Rappaport Hovav (1995). It is important to note that scalar change is not identical to telicity because it is possible that the scale is unbounded and thus cannot identify a natural endpoint. Telicity is a special form of temporally bounded scalar change, but scalar change can also be encoded in atelic predicates. Not only *get*-predicates, but also other scale-based predicates fall in this latter group: prototypical scalar predicates such as incremental theme accomplishments can be turned into atelic predicates, even though the underlying scale is not eliminated. This can be seen in different measuring-out effects contributed by plural subject and object arguments, which are then compatible with durative adverbials; see the examples in (24) and (25), as well as Verkuyl (1993) for discussion.[34]

(24) a. *John discovered that quaint little village for years.
     b. Tourists discovered that quaint little village for years.
        (Dowty 1979: 63)

(25) a. *John built a house for years.
     b. John built houses for years.

Non-permanent statives such as posture verbs are intuitively problematic in this respect, but considering stasis as a type of change is not without precedent (see Talmy 2000: 218), and they can be measured against a temporal scale. See also the analysis of verbs like *stay/remain* in Jackendoff (1996: 328), which differ from permanent states in having a more complex event structure. A scalar meaning component can also offer an explanation for the reported grammaticality of extractions from resultative accomplishments as in (26) because resultatives can be analyzed as "scale-denoting expressions" (Fleischhauer 2016: 86).

(26) What did John drive Mary crazy whistling __ ?

The combined predictions from the DG and the SCG are shown in Table 5.2 on the following page. As there are two generalizations and each verb class may fail to meet either generalization, this predicts three levels of semantic compatibility in the BPPA construction: compatibility is low when both generalizations are not satisfied, intermediate if only one is not satisfied, and high if both are satisfied. This threefold division of semantic compatibility makes novel predictions about

---

[34] Kennedy (2012: 113–120) argues that incremental theme verbs differ from de-adjectival degree achievements in that the measure of change is not encoded in the verb but rather in properties of the nominal argument; as this is also the case with manner-of-motion predicates, where the measure scale is contributed by locational arguments, the precise source of the measure does not seem to be crucial in an evaluation of the SCG.

the relative acceptability of declarative BPPA constructions, which are further discussed in Section 5.3.

Tab. 5.2: Verb classes and the durativity/scalar change generalizations.

Verb class	DG	SCG	Compatibility
permanent states	not satisfied	not satisfied	low
points	not satisfied	satisfied	intermediate
activities	satisfied	not satisfied	intermediate
accomplishments	satisfied	satisfied	high
achievements	satisfied	satisfied	high
temporary states	satisfied	satisfied	high
get-predicates	satisfied	satisfied	high

In Figure 5.4, the positive influence of a scalar change meaning component encoded in the matrix predicate is added to the factorial model; the semantic compatibility of the BPPA construction is determined by these two factors and affects acceptability in the declarative. Both generalizations are in principle independent of each other, as scalar change does not depend on durativity and vice versa. The next section adds another factor to the present model that is not related to semantic compatibility, but rather to the overall syntactic complexity of the construction.

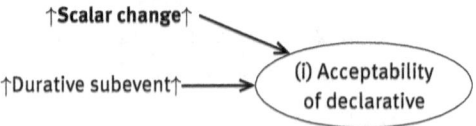

Fig. 5.4: Factorial Acceptability Model (durativity & scalar change). Acceptability of the declarative is higher if the matrix predicate encodes scalar change.

5.2.4 Transitivity

The last generalization for the acceptability of declarative BPPA constructions differentiates between the numbers of arguments that are directly selected by the matrix predicate. A further generalization is required because the DG and the SCG are still too permissive for transitive predicates. Therefore, I propose the TG in (27), which states that matrix predicates which select only one referentially distinct argument are more acceptable in the BPPA construction.

(27) Transitivity Generalization (TG):
BPPA constructions are more acceptable if the matrix predicate directly selects only one referentially distinct argument.

BPPA constructions with transitive matrix predicate are the most controversial group in the previous literature on extraction from adjuncts. Borgonovo & Neeleman (2000) distinguish between reflexive and non-reflexive transitives, and only the former allow extraction from the adjunct; Truswell (2007, 2011) claims that as long as the transitive predicate is an accomplishment and the adjunct can be interpreted as the cause, extraction is licensed; finally, Brown's (2017) gap-licensing approach predicts that a large set of transitives should be able to allow extraction. As shown in the experiments in Brown (2017) and the results of Experiment 4 in Chapter 4, transitives are less acceptable in declaratives and interrogatives, on par with unergatives. Experiment 5 showed that this is not simply an effect of sentence length, as transitives are still less acceptable than unaccusatives with a locational phrase. This suggests that the second argument is responsible for the lower acceptability.

As formulated in the TG in (27), I propose that the acceptability of the BPPA construction is sensitive to the number of arguments that are directly selected by the matrix predicate. Under direct selection, I understand θ-marking of the second argument by the matrix predicate. I will focus on three types of BPPA construction with two nominal arguments: transitives with two referentially distinct arguments (28a), reflexive transitives (28b), and resultative BPPA constructions (28c), as discussed at the end of Chapter 2.

(28) a. John hurt Bill [trying to fix the roof]. [transitive]
 b. John hurt himself [trying to fix the roof]. [reflexive]
 c. John drove Mary crazy [talking about his sacking]. [resultative]
 (Borgonovo & Neeleman 2000: 200, 211)

The TG makes the following predictions about the influence on acceptability of these three types: transitives like (28a) receive a transitivity penalty because the matrix predicate directly selects and θ-marks two referentially distinct nominal arguments; reflexive transitives as in (28b) may incur a smaller transitivity penalty because the two arguments selected by the matrix predicate are co-referential in accordance with Binding Principle A (Chomsky 1981); resultative BPPA constructions are expected to incur a small transitivity penalty or none at all because the second argument is not selected by the matrix predicate and receives its θ-role as part of the resultative secondary predication structure (Rapoport 1993a; Winkler 1997; Rothstein 2017; Hu 2018).

All examples in (28) are interpreted as telic accomplishments. The predictions of the TG are thus independent of telicity and apply to transitive accomplishments (29a) and activities (29b) alike. In these cases, both the DG and the SCG are satisfied, as the sentences encode a durative subevent and can be measured against a prominent scale defined by the object. Compared to reflexive transitives and resultative BPPAs, these sentences are predicted to be less acceptable by the TG.

(29)   a.   John painted a picture whistling a funny song.   [accomplishment]
         b.   John painted pictures whistling a funny song.   [activity]

In the light of this discussion, I propose that there is a three-way distinction in the BPPA construction that depends on two properties: (i) how many arguments are licensed by the main verb; (ii) what type of second argument is licensed. This can be expressed in the following hierarchy for transitives in (30), where '>' stands for "more acceptable" because the transitivity penalty is smaller.

(30)   Transitivity hierarchy in the BPPA construction:
        intransitive > resultative/reflexive > transitive

It is also possible to apply a more fine-grained approach to transitivity, as for example in Hopper & Thompson (1980), who develop a set of properties that distinguish between degrees of transitivity; transitivity is not understood there as the encoding of one or more arguments, but rather as a property based on concepts like aspect, agentivity, affectedness, and individuation.

The TG differs from the other two generalizations: whereas the DG is an event-structural notion and the SCG refers to the lexical semantics of the matrix predicate, the TG can be formulated in core-syntactic terms such as selection, syntactic category, and direct or indirect θ-marking. I follow Jurka (2010, 2013), Polinsky et al. (2013), and Culicover & Winkler (2022) in analyzing the effect of transitivity on acceptability as related to the increased processing effort required of the parser. Konietzko (2021) also notes the increased complexity of transitive predicates compared to other verb types and draws similar conclusions about the advantage of one-place predicates over two-place predicates.

Table 5.3 illustrates the possibility of a transitivity penalty for different types of matrix predicate. First, not all verb classes have a variant where the verb selects two distinct arguments, so that the TG does not apply in these cases; this is illustrated in the third and fourth columns with simple declarative sentences. For verb classes which have a variant that selects two distinct arguments, the TG assigns a transitivity penalty accordingly in the BPPA construction. Permanent states, points, and activities are already at a disadvantage because they fail to satisfy either the DG, the SCG, or both. The crucial verb class with respect to transitivity are accomplishments, which have a transitive variant, but can also be expressed as resultative or reflexive structures. I will reserve the term "transitive" for those cases where the main verb directly selects two referentially distinct nominals; see Hopper & Thompson (1980: 277–278) for the argument that reflexives occupy an intermediate position on their transitivity scale between sentences with one or two arguments.

Tab. 5.3: Verb classes and transitivity. Where applicable, variants with two distinct arguments are less acceptable in the BPPA construction than variants with one distinct argument.

Verb class	Transitivity penalty	One distinct argument	Two distinct arguments
permanent states	possible	John is bald.	John knows French.
points	possible	John appeared.	John noticed his brother.
activities	possible	John walked.	John painted pictures.
accomplishments*	possible	John drove Mary crazy./ John hurt himself.	John painted a picture.
achievements	no	John arrived.	—
temporary states	no	John lay on the sofa.	—
get-predicates	no	John got scared.	—

*Variants with one distinct argument include resultative and reflexive accomplishments.

Figure 5.5 adds the effect of transitivity to the factorial model. The DG and the SCG determine the semantic compatibility of the matrix and adjunct predicates, and the TG adds a further penalty depending on the number of arguments which the matrix predicate directly selects. This is the final representation of the components of the Factorial Acceptability Model in declarative BPPA constructions, which will be slightly refined and connected to the effect of extraction in the next section.

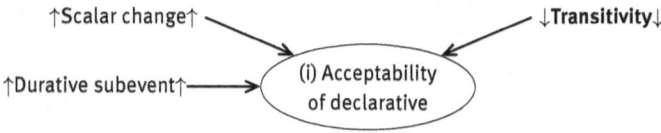

Fig. 5.5: Factorial Acceptability Model (durativity, scalar change & transitivity). Acceptability of the declarative is lower if the matrix predicate is transitive.

5.2.5 Description of the final model

The last three sections motivated three generalizations about the acceptability of declarative BPPA constructions. In this section, I will provide a description of the final model: the Durativity Generalization and the Scalar Change Generalization will determine the semantic compatibility between the two predicates, the Transitivity Generalization optionally adds a transitivity penalty for matrix predicates which select more than one referentially distinct argument, and extraction adds a further decrease in acceptability for interrogatives. This model covers the grammaticality contrasts reported for extraction in the literature, and also captures the result from the experiments reported in Chapter 4 that extraction is not sensitive to the factors under investigation.

In a first step, I will focus on the predictions from the semantic compatibility criteria formulated in the DG and SCG with respect to different verb classes. As both the DG and the SCG have two possible values, this results in four verb clusters which cannot be reduced to aspectual classes or grammatical verb types alone. The conclusion that depictive modification is not entirely dependent on either concept has already been suggested in Irimia (2012). Table 5.4 shows how different verb classes are distinguished by their scale and durativity properties.

Tab. 5.4: Semantic compatibility for different verb classes.

Scalar change	Durativity	
	not satisfied	satisfied
not satisfied	permanent states	activities
satisfied	points	*achievements, accomplishments temporary states, get-predicates*

The verb classes which satisfy both the DG and the SCG are highlighted in italics: they show the highest relative semantic compatibility between the two predicates and are thus more acceptable in the BPPA construction than the other verb classes. Permanent states and activities do not encode a prominent scalar change meaning component and thus do not satisfy the SCG; permanent states and points do not encode a durative subevent and thus fail to satisfy the DG. The verb classes that satisfy both the DG and the SCG are achievements, accomplishments, temporary states, and *get*-predicates. The examples in (31) illustrate the predictions for BPPA compatibility based on the DG and the SCG. Permanent states (31a) have two negative values for the compatibility generalizations and are thus marked as '??'; point predicates (31b) and activities (31c) receive one negative value and are slightly less marked as '?'; achievements (31d), accomplishments (31e), temporary states (31f), and *get*-predicates (31g) receive positive values for both generalizations and are thus unmarked. The verb types in (31d–g) are predicted to be most acceptable in the BPPA construction based on the DG and the SCG.

(31) a. ??John knows French wearing his magic hat. [permanent state]
 b. ?John noticed his brother whistling a funny song. [point]
 c. ?John ran whistling a funny song. [activity]
 d. John arrived whistling a funny song. [achievement]
 e. John drove Mary crazy whistling a funny song. [accomplishment]
 f. John lay in bed watching a horror movie. [temporary state]
 g. John got scared watching a horror movie. [*get*-predicate]

The effect of semantic compatibility on acceptability is here understood as a result of the processing effort for the parser: processing is easiest if the two predicates in the BPPA construction show a high degree of semantic compatibility by satisfying both the DG and the SCG. Lower semantic compatibility requires a larger processing effort of the parser and results in lower acceptability. There seems to be no need to formulate strict licensing constraints on the BPPA construction: none of the sentences in (31) are fully ungrammatical, but they are not equally acceptable. Such graded patterns of acceptability can be adequately described by semantic compatibility factors as proposed in the DG and the SCG.

Acceptability of declarative BPPAs is further affected by transitivity, which is only relevant for those verb classes that can encode a second argument. Examples are given in (32) for permanent states, points, activities, and accomplishments.

(32) a. John knows French. [permanent state]
 b. John noticed his brother. [point]
 c. John painted pictures. [activity]
 d. John ran a marathon. [accomplishment]

Table 5.5 on the next page summarizes the predictions from the DG and SCG, which determine the semantic compatibility of the BPPA construction; the TG can add the processing-related transitivity penalty when the verb selects more than one argument. Accomplishments can circumvent a transitivity penalty if they encode a resultative construction where the non-subject argument is licensed by the resultative predicate, or a reflexive predicate with an anaphor that is coreferential with the subject.

The generalizations about BPPA acceptability proposed here show similarities to the general licensing conditions on depictives discussed in Chapter 2, and to

Tab. 5.5: Overview of predictions in the factorial acceptability model.

Verb class	Durativity	Scalar change	Semantic compatibility	Transitivity penalty
permanent states	not satisfied	not satisfied	low	possible
points	not satisfied	satisfied	intermediate	possible
activities	satisfied	not satisfied	intermediate	possible
accomplishments	satisfied	satisfied	high	possible
achievements	satisfied	satisfied	high	no
temporary states	satisfied	satisfied	high	no
get-predicates	satisfied	satisfied	high	no

two proposals about the compatibility of depictives that depend on the type of verb they modify. These are the accessibility hierarchy for SODs in Irimia (2012), shown in (33), and the DAC formulated for OODs in Farrell (2019); see (34).

(33)   Accessibility hierarchy for SODs:
       unaccusative > transitive > unergative (> more accessible)
                                                              (Irimia 2012: 206)

(34)   Depictive Aspectuality Constraint:
       For Object-Oriented depictives, the verb-object-depictive complex must be aspectually compatible with durativity and telicity.   (Farrell 2019: 109)

Irimia's (2012) hierarchy captures the fact that unaccusative predicates are more accessible for depictive modification than transitives, which are in turn more accessible than unergatives. Translated into event-structural terms, achievements and manner-of-motion verbs with a goal PP are more accessible than accomplishments and bare activity predicates. This provides a good initial fit with the DG and the SCG. Farrell's (2019) DAC, even though formulated only for OODs, is nearly identical to the combined predictions of the two generalizations. The only difference is that the DAC requires telicity instead of scalar change, like Brown's (2017) culmination requirement. A crucial characteristic of the DAC is that durativity and telicity need not both be encoded in the matrix predicate, but can also be supplied by properties of the secondary predicate. I will show below that this carries over to some BPPA examples that are difficult to capture when only looking at the matrix predicate.

From an architectural perspective, the generalizations proposed in this section lead to the following factorial model: a BPPA is liberally merged to the matrix predication, and acceptability is determined by checking whether the two verbal predicates conform to the DG and the SCG and can establish a suitable overlap relation. If they fail to meet one or both of the generalizations, acceptability decreases. Acceptability is further decreased according to the TG, depending on how many referentially distinct arguments are directly selected by the matrix predicate. In Chapter 4, Section 4.2, I discussed the difference between a categorical CED-style approach to grammaticality and a factorial model for acceptability that incorporates several and potentially independent factors. I argue that a factorial model is better capable of explaining nuanced acceptability differences than a categorical model that evaluates only one factor. Based on the Independence Hypothesis and the generalizations in the preceding sections, I propose the factorial model in Figure 5.6 for the overall acceptability of the BPPA construction in declaratives and interrogatives.

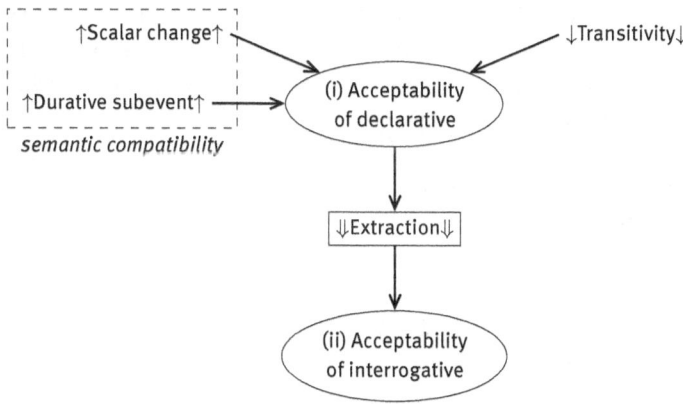

Fig. 5.6: Factorial Acceptability Model for the BPPA construction (final model).

The semantic compatibility factors DURATIVE SUBEVENT, SCALAR CHANGE, as well as the syntactic complexity factor TRANSITIVITY show an effect on acceptability in the declarative; the syntactic factor EXTRACTION mediates between the declarative and interrogative sentence form and causes a decrease in acceptability. The arrows on the factors indicate the effect they have: the encoding of a durative subevent and scalar change increase semantic compatibility and thus acceptability, whereas transitivity has a negative effect on acceptability in declaratives. This factorial model differentiates between semantic compatibility and syntactic complexity criteria for the BPPA construction on the one hand, and the additional cost of extraction from the adjunct predicate on the other. Since the acceptability of the input for extraction is calculated before extraction applies, the effect of extraction is not modulated by the semantic compatibility and syntactic complexity criteria. This emphasizes the predictions of the IH.

It is in principle possible to assign these factors a quantified effect size, and to differentiate between the precise weight they have compared to the other factors. However, as the factors were manipulated with different populations in the experiments, this is not implemented here. The only weighting that can be reliably made is that extraction shows a much stronger negative effect on acceptability than the factors which determine acceptability in declaratives; this is indicated by the double downward arrows '⇓' for EXTRACTION. In order to formulate a quantified model with predictive factors, the effects of the individual factors need to be isolated and compared with each other. The overview of the factors with respect to different verb types in the FAM in Table 5.5 can be taken as a starting point.

I have suggested above that the decreases in acceptability which are observed in the experimental results and predicted by the factorial model can be conceptualized as processing costs that have an impact on how easy or hard it is for the parser to process the sentence. To be more concrete, the FAM predicts that processing is harder when the matrix predicate does not encode a durative subevent or scalar change, and that further processing costs are assigned if the verb is transitive. Sentences which are harder to process are expected to be less acceptable than sentences which do not present the parser with difficulties (Culicover & Winkler 2018; Featherston 2019). This is the reason the factors of the factorial model are formulated as generalizations and not as constraints.[35] A formalization of the generalization in terms of constraints that are part of the speaker's competence grammar would require a more articulated syntactic representation that allows for the systematic encoding of lexical semantic information such as telicity, durativity, and scale properties of individual verbs. Such rich syntactic structures are, among others, proposed in Borer (2005), Ramchand (2008), and MacDonald (2008). The generalizations proposed in this chapter could then be formalized as conditions on semantic feature matching. For example, Miyamoto (2012) presents an account of transparent adjuncts in Japanese that makes use of syntactically encoded lexical semantic information to license extraction under certain conditions. I have refrained from such a formalization due to the conceptualization of the generalizations as performance-related effects rather than competence-based constraints.[36]

I leave for future research the possibility that the proposed factors can be understood as characteristics which affect the pragmatic relevance of the adjunct

---

[35] This is also the main conceptual difference to cumulative constraint application models of island effects like the Cumulative Effect Hypothesis in Haegeman et al. (2014), noted at the beginning of this chapter. I thank an anonymous reviewer for suggesting a clarification of the similarities and differences of such models to the one proposed in this chapter.

[36] This point was raised by an anonymous reviewer.

predicate relative to the matrix predicate, as proposed in the semantic–pragmatic approach to most island effects in Chaves & Putnam (2020).

It is possible that there are additional factors which determine acceptability in declaratives; this includes properties of the adjunct predicate as well as further issues which I will raise below in Section 5.4. Here I have focused on BPPA constructions with transitive activity adjunct predicates because they select an object that can be extracted, and because they are most easily compatible with the progressive morphology. I also expect that there are further distinctions for the extraction factor. I have concentrated on the acceptability criteria for the declarative BPPA construction and not on the properties of extraction. Factors that apply to extraction in general, such as D-linking, are expected to show effects that are not unique to islands or the BPPA construction (Sag et al. 2008; Haegeman et al. 2014); likewise, different types of extraction, such as relativization or topicalization, may show smaller or larger effects compared to *wh*-extraction (see Sprouse et al. 2016; Abeillé et al. 2020). I leave this point for further research; what I have shown here is that *wh*-extraction from present participle adjuncts can be unexpectedly acceptable when the right conditions are met in the underlying declarative. In the next section, I turn to additional predictions and advantages of the proposed model.

5.3 Predictions and advantages of the factorial model

The notion of general conditions that affect the acceptability of the BPPA construction as set out in the preceding section enables a more flexible way to approach the sets of examples that are difficult to capture in previous approaches. The three generalizations do not single out one specific verb type as ideal for extraction, but result in a continuum of acceptability which depends on how many generalizations are satisfied by a predicate; the more generalizations a verb fails to satisfy, the lower the acceptability of the BPPA construction will be. In this section, I will lay out some cases where the factorial model has an advantage over previous analyses. The discussion is based on contrasts in interrogatives because the intuitions are clearer than for declaratives; following the IH, the same contrasts are expected to hold in declaratives. I will discuss the following points: (i) the empirical coverage of the factorial model compared to previous approaches, (ii) the compatibility with a CED-style approach to the lower transparency of adjuncts compared to complements, (iii) the effects of directional phrases with activity matrix predicates, (iv) conceptual differences to the independence approach in Brown (2017), and (v) the possibility to capture the DG and the SCG in one unified generalization.

5.3.1 Empirical coverage

The three generalizations proposed in the context of the factorial model capture the major contrasts discussed in the existing literature: they derive the effects of aspectual classes proposed in Truswell (2007) as well as the effects of grammatical verb types in Borgonovo & Neeleman (2000). Achievement predicates emerge as one of the most acceptable types of matrix predicates, as predicted in Truswell (2007), but a subset of accomplishments, certain states, and reflexive predicates (Borgonovo & Neeleman 2000) can also yield high acceptability. Instead of reducing this pattern to one central factor, the factorial model is the result of several factors; this allows for more fine-grained patterns of acceptability in declaratives and interrogatives. The DG also provides a straightforward explanation for the contrast between point predicates like *appear* or *notice* and extendable achievements like *arrive*, seen in (35). This contrast is difficult to capture in an approach that is only based on a telicity requirement.

(35) a. What did John *appear/√arrive whistling __ ?
      b. *What$_j$ did John$_i$ [notice his brother] [looking through t$_j$]$_i$?
          (Truswell 2007: 1356, 1370)

Truswell (2007) observes that point predicates may be distinguished from other achievements in the possibility to add a preceding stage, but does not draw the connection to aspectual coercion from a punctual achievement to an accomplishment reading, which is not possible for all achievements (Rothstein 2004b); Truswell (2007) also does not consider the distinction between permanent (36a) and temporary states (36b), which show a similar contrast, but cannot be explained in terms of telicity or agentivity.

(36) a. *What was John blond whistling __ ?   [permanent state]
      b. What did John lie in bed reading __ ?   [temporary state]

The SCG offers an explanation for the acceptable extractions in (37), where a locative particle like *around/about* is added to an activity main verb. In the absence of such particles, extraction is unacceptable with activities, as seen in (38) and the results of Experiments 4 and 5.

(37) a. What did John lie around [reading __] all day?
      b. What was John walking about [whistling __]?
          (Truswell 2011: 155)

(38) *What did John walk whistling __ ?

For Truswell (2011), such contrasts can only be explained in terms of agentivity and not in terms of aspectual classes alone. As already noted in Brown (2017), there are cases where transparency does not depend on agentivity, as other factors also show an effect; see (39), where the addition of an object improves extraction. The addition of the object also disambiguates the gap site; see Section 5.4.3 below.

(39) a. *What does John dance screaming?
      b. What did John dance the YMCA screaming?
      (see Brown 2017: 54–55)

Truswell (2011) discusses the example in (40) as additional support for his agentivity approach; the extraction is grammatical because *sit* is non-agentive and the maximum number of agentive events is not exceeded.

(40) Which chair did John eat his breakfast [sitting on __]? (Truswell 2011: 155)

The SCG captures the effects of locative particles and the grammatical extraction in (40) as follows: locative particles add a scalar path component to the meaning of the predicate, so that the manner-of-motion predicate *walk* is interpreted as a verb of directed motion, the progression of which can be measured against a prominent scale (see Borgonovo & Neeleman 2000; Horrocks & Stavrou 2007). Only in the presence of an explicit scale are manner-of-motion verbs similar to other scale-based verbs like incremental-theme verbs or change-of-state verbs; in their bare form, they are aspectually underspecified (Tenny 1995; Lukassek et al. 2017). The extraction in (40) is acceptable because the matrix predicate encodes a scalar component in the object *his breakfast*: the progression of the eating event can be measured against the incremental theme object. Brown's (2017) counterexample to the agentivity approach in (39) can be explained similarly: the incremental theme object provides the possibility for reference to a scale that improves the sentence, in accordance with the SCG.

In the context of this discussion, consider the attested example in (41a), which has a progressive-marked accomplishment main predicate. This sentence is problematic for previous approaches: (i) it speaks against the agentivity proposal in Truswell (2011) because both predicates are agentive; (ii) and it is not compatible with the culmination requirement in Brown (2017) because the matrix predicate can be interpreted as atelic, for example when adverbs like *continuously* or *always* are added (41b).

(41) a. a scenario that government agencies are spending billions of dollars preparing for (Santorini 2019)
b. This is a scenario that government agencies are continuously/always spending billions of dollars preparing for.

Encoding a scalar change structure in the matrix predicate provides a straightforward answer why *get*-predicates with psychological adjectival complements are highly acceptable in declaratives and only slightly degraded in interrogatives. They inherently encode scalar transitions, with the type, points, and ordering relation of the scale depending on the meaning of the adjective as well as contextual information (Hay et al. 1999; Kennedy & Levin 2002, 2008; Kennedy 2012). One of the puzzles in Experiment 6 was the lack of a difference between *get*-predicates in the simple past and the progressive, irrespective of extraction. As a possible solution, I offered that acceptability in declarative and interrogative BPPA constructions is determined before the application of outer aspect in the form of progressivity and that it could be lexical telicity that is required in an aspectual approach to BPPAs. The DG and SCG offer a new evaluation of the data form Experiment 6: *get*-predicates always encode scalar change, and it does not matter whether a final or complete state is reached, as in the simple past, or whether there is simply progression along a property trajectory, as in the past progressive. The SCG makes predictions that cannot be explained entirely by the aspectual classification in Truswell (2007); reference to a scale does not depend on telicity, but telicity always encodes a scale (Fleischhauer 2016: 89).

A novel prediction made by the factorial model is that there is a further division among the matrix predicates which do not meet the DG or SCG, or both: predicates that do not meet both generalizations should be less acceptable than predicates which only fail to meet one of the two generalizations. Intuitively, this seems to be the case, as the examples in (42) indicate.

(42) a. *What was John blond whistling __ ? [–durative, –scale]
b. ??What did John appear whistling __ ? [–durative, +scale]
c. ??What did John work whistling __ ? [+durative, –scale]
d. What did John arrive whistling __ ? [+durative, +scale]

Permanent states as in (42a) do not encode a durative subevent or a prominent scalar change, failing both generalizations. Punctual achievements as in (42b) fail the DG but meet the SCG; the reverse holds for activities as in (42c), which encode a durative subevent but no prominent scalar change. The reason for these apparent contrasts seems to be related to the amount of coercion that is required to make the matrix predicate compatible with the requirements of the BPPA construction:

it is probably less demanding of the parser to re-conceptualize an appearing event as temporally extended or add a scalar change structure to activity predicates than it is to impose temporal bounds and a scalar structure to a permanent state. There are cases where permanent states (ILP) like *be blond* or *be rich* can be interpreted as a temporary or context-dependent property (SLP), but this requires considerable adjustments to the default interpretation; see Maienborn (2004). The proposed factorial model has the advantage over previous approaches that such nuanced patterns in declarative and interrogative BPPA constructions fall out naturally from the multiple factors which influence acceptability in the declaratives, plus the independent effect of extraction.

5.3.2 Compatibility with CED-style locality conditions

In principle, the factorial model is compatible with a CED-style approach to the lower transparency of adjuncts compared to complements. It is possible that extraction from an adjunct incurs a higher processing burden on the parser than extraction from a complement position, i.e. that there is an island effect. The experiments in Chapter 4 did not draw a direct comparison between adjuncts and non-adjuncts, but other experimental studies, such as Sprouse et al. (2012) and Sprouse et al. (2016), indicate that *wh*-extraction from adjuncts in the form of adverbial clauses do show island effects.[37] What the experiments reveal is that there are no island-internal factors which further modulate the strength of the effect of extraction. This insight stands in contrast to interaction accounts which identify such factors, often non-structural ones, as an explanation for the counterexamples to the CED in the form of apparently grammatical extractions from adjuncts. The results of Chapter 4 show that these counterexamples can be explained by construction-specific semantic compatibility and complexity factors that are not connected to the application of extraction. It is thus possible to retain a CED-style condition which states that extraction from adjuncts is harder and thus less acceptable than extraction from complements. The contribution of the factorial model to the discussion of counterexamples to the CED is that the effect of extraction can be applied without taking into account adjunct-internal factors that influence acceptability in the declarative.

Some interrogative BPPA constructions can be surprisingly acceptable, especially compared to other types of adjuncts. Compare the extraction from an

---

[37] There are, however, also studies revealing that other types of extraction, such as relativization, do not show such an effect, indicating that adjunct island effects do not appear to be cross-constructionally active; see Abeillé et al. (2020) and Liu et al. (2022).

adverbial clause in (43a) to extraction from a BPPA construction with an achievement matrix predicate in (43b), or a *get*-predicate in (43c):

(43) a. *Who did Susan watch TV [while talking to __]? (Phillips 2013: 67)
 b. What did John die [whistling __]? (Truswell 2011: 30)
 c. What did Peter get scared [watching __]?

Strong degradations like in (43a) have served as motivations for the CED whereas acceptable extractions as in (43b,c) are arguments against the validity of the CED. In a non-categorical model of grammar such as the Decathlon Model (Featherston 2008, 2019), extraction from adjuncts would not need to be formulated as a strict and inviolable constraint that leads to ungrammaticality. Such an approach also offers the possibility to distinguish between different types of adjuncts that show smaller and greater effects of extraction. The factorial model is also more flexible than a categorical model of grammaticality because it leaves open the possibility that different extraction types show different effect sizes, so that for example relativization lowers acceptability less than *wh*-extraction (Abeillé et al. 2020). This could be expanded to a model for extraction from adjuncts that takes both properties of the adjunct construction and properties of the extraction into account. Further factors such as tense-marking in the adjunct predicate (C. Müller 2019), D-linking (Pesetsky 1987; Haegeman et al. 2014), and others (Sag et al. 2008; Hofmeister & Sag 2010) can also be added.

5.3.3 Activities with directional phrases

One of the predictions made by the factorial model is that there should be a positive effect of prepositional phrases in motion verb constructions such as in (44) because they add a path component and thus help to satisfy the SCG. This effect is similar to that of directional particles noted for the examples in (37) above. In the absence of a directional specification, the activity matrix predicate in (44a) is interpreted as atelic, encoding a non-scalar change (Rappaport Hovav & Levin 2010).[38] When the activity predicate is augmented with a locative or directional PP, as in (44b–d), an overt scale is added and extraction seems to improve.

---

[38] See Smith (1997: 135–137) for the effects of PP and particle extensions to basic aspectual classes; the effects of path components to manner-of-motion predicates is also noted in Hoekstra & Mulder (1990), Levin & Rappaport Hovav (1995), and Erteschik-Shir & Rapoport (2005).

(44) a. *What did John walk whistling __ ? [no PP]
 b. What did John walk in the park whistling __ ? [atelic locative PP]
 c. What did John walk away from the park whistling __ ?
  [atelic directional PP]
 d. What did John walk to the park whistling __ ? [telic directional PP]

In analogy to the verbal domain, prepositions can be classified as unbounded/atelic or bounded/telic; see Jackendoff (1996: 309), Zwarts (2005, 2008) and den Dikken (2010a,b) for discussion of the different types of prepositions. In (44b), the unbounded locative preposition *in* defines a location where the activity takes place; it could be argued that even an atelic locative/non-directional PP provides a scale of directed change.[39] Examples with directional PPs as in (44c,d) are a bit clearer because they obviously encode a scalar path component. Note that (44c) is still interpreted as unbounded because the preposition *towards* does not entail a culmination and focuses on the traversed path; in contrast, (44d) is interpreted as bounded but also includes a prominent path component. In effect, the only unacceptable extraction seems to be (44a) without any prepositional element.

From the perspective of approaches which are formulated in terms of agentivity (Truswell 2011) and telicity (Truswell 2007; Brown 2017), these examples are problematic. They are a challenge to an agentivity-based approach because all the matrix predicates in (44) should be classified as agentive, thus violating Truswell's (2011) SEGC; even if (44b) is assigned a non-agentive interpretation because there is no specified goal and thus lack of intentionality (McIntyre 2004; Truswell 2011), this does not explain why (44c,d) are at least equally good if not better since they are harder to force into a non-agentive reading. Like the high acceptability of degree achievements, even in the non-culminated progressive, the effect of these different prepositions points out a weak spot in approaches that require the matrix predicate to encode a culmination point, as proposed in Truswell (2007) and Brown (2017). The differences between the data pattern in (44) and the predictions of agentivity and culmination approaches are shown in Table 5.6 on the next page.

Agentivity and culmination approaches have different reasons for considering (44b) grammatical: if the walking is just taking place in the park without a specific goal, it can be interpreted as non-agentive, respecting the SEGC (Truswell 2011). If the preposition *in* is interpreted as a directional instead of a locational P, this satisfies the requirement for telicity in culmination approaches (Truswell 2007;

---

[39] As pointed out in den Dikken (2010b), *in* can also be interpreted as directional with certain verbs that are not informationally heavy, such as *waltz*; I focus on the locational meaning here.

Tab. 5.6: Effects of telic/atelic PPs on acceptability in (44) and predictions from agentivity and culmination approaches.

PP type	Acceptability pattern in (44)	Agentivity approaches	Culmination approaches
(44a) no PP	*	*	*
(44b) atelic locative PP	✓	*/✓	*/✓
(44c) atelic directional PP	✓	*	*
(44d) telic directional PP	✓	*	✓

Brown 2017). Under the present proposal, these interpretations are not immediately relevant, as both the directional and locational interpretation allow for the encoding of a scalar path structure. Boundedness is not exclusive to verbal aspect, but can also be observed in the nominal and prepositional domain; see den Dikken (2010b) and Champollion (2017). This explains why the overall boundedness or unboundedness of a sentence will be determined by the choice of verb, its arguments, and the spatial reference. A broad notion of scalar change structures, which includes scales such as paths, property, and temporal scales captures the data patterns revealed in the experimental chapter, and also offers an explanation for examples from the previous literature that are difficult to capture.

But why should the presence or absence of a directional element have an effect on the acceptability of declarative BPPA constructions? I suggest that this is related to the interpretations associated with the adjunct predicate; there are cases like (45a) where a participle specifies the manner of motion. In contrast, the adjunct in (45c) does not describe a specific manner of motion, but modifies the walking event as a whole. The marked status of examples like (45b), as shown in Experiment 4, could be caused by the unsuccessful attempt of the parser to interpret the adjunct as a manner modifier; but since walking and whistling are not part of the same semantic domain (motion vs. articulation), this could cause re-analysis as a depictive event-modifier that incurs processing effort.

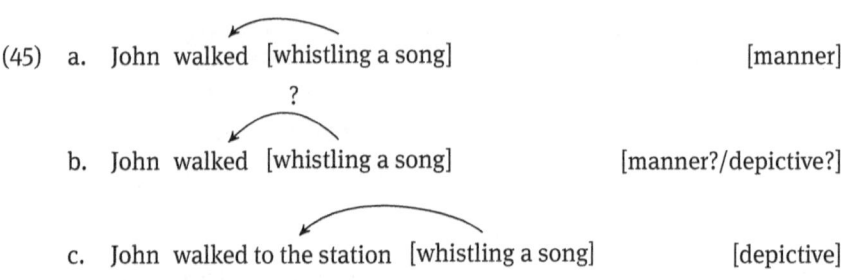

(45) a. John walked [whistling a song] [manner]

b. John walked [whistling a song] [manner?/depictive?]

c. John walked to the station [whistling a song] [depictive]

The distinction between a manner and depictive interpretation of the adjunct predicate corresponds to the difference between event specification and event expansion in Haug et al. (2012); see the discussion in Chapter 2, Section 2.3.2. The formulae in (46) show that (45a) and (45c) receive a straightforward interpretation in terms of specification (46a) and expansion (46c), respectively. (46b) shows the attempted interpretation of *whistling a song* as a manner of motion specification, which is pragmatically odd because of the semantic domain mismatch. The participle fails to be identified with the "manner" linking event.

(46) a. $\lambda e.[e_a e' \mid \text{walk}(e), \text{manner}(e_a), e_a \leq e, \tau(e) \circ \tau(e_a), \text{limp}(e_a)]$
b. #$\lambda e.[e_a e' \mid \text{walk}(e), \text{manner}(e_a), e_a \leq e, \tau(e) \circ \tau(e'),$
   $\text{whistle\_song}(e'), e' = ?]$
c. $\lambda t.[ee'e^* \mid \text{walk\_to\_station}(e), e \leq e^*, \tau(e) \subseteq t, \text{whistle\_song}(e')$
   $\& \tau(e) \circ \tau(e') \& e' \leq e^*]$
   (adapted from Haug et al. 2012)

The semantic analysis in (46b) needs to be modified to an interpretation along the lines of (46c) to resolve this mismatch. It is not obvious which factors lead the parser to chose between attempting a specification or expansion analysis and whether one or the other is the default analysis that is tried first. This also connects to the discussion of background frames or scripts in Chaves & Putnam (2020): a manner modification of a motion predicate as in (45a) is a straightforward relation between the two predicates, and the same can be said about depictive modification of a motion event towards a goal in (45c), where the depictive provides additional information about how the event unfolds. The frame evoked by the bare motion predicate in (45b) may be too impoverished or unclear to allow a clear determination of what exactly is modified, as argued here with reference to event specification or event expansion relations. I leave the details of such a potential explanation of the data pattern for further research.

5.3.4 Differences to adjunct licensing in Brown (2017)

The main difference of the present proposal to that in Brown (2017) is that the depictive overlap relation between the two predicates can be established in the absence of a culmination point in the event structure of the matrix predicate. Brown's concept of scale amalgamation is intriguing because it shares much with the present proposal. For Brown (2017), the culmination of the matrix predicate is properly included in the interval of the adjunct predicate, which acts as a background eventuality. This proper inclusion allows the adjunct predicate to continue after the culmination point of the matrix predicate (Brown 2017: 74–75). Instead of proper inclusion of the matrix predicate's culmination point within the interval of the adjunct predicate, the generalizations proposed in this chapter lead to an overlap relation between two non-punctual, durative events. This is similar to the overlap for depictive secondary predicates, as proposed in Geuder (2004) and Irimia (2012). The result is that there are two events which are temporally independent but which share an overlapping interval without requiring strict co-extensiveness. This similarity to depictive interpretation also offers an explanation why the adjunct predicate in the BPPA construction shows similar sensitivities to the verb type of the matrix predicate as in the depictive construction.

This analysis has the advantage that it captures the independence of the two predicates, but works in both directions. For Brown (2017), the adjunct predicate can hold before and after the culmination point of the matrix predicate; since the focus for matrix predicate is on the culmination and not a process leading up to this, it is difficult to capture the independence of the matrix predicate. Analyzing achievement predicates as culminations that terminate a gradual progression, however, suggests that a part of the progression may have been happening before the event described in the adjunct holds. Take *arrive* as an example, which is considered by Krifka (1998: 230) as describing the final part of a series of gradual progressions towards a goal point.

(47) Mary arrived at the station whistling a song.

This sentence entails that Mary traveled to the station and that she was whistling at the moment of arrival, but not during the entire trip. After all, *arrive* profiles only the final part of the trip. The result is a loose overlap relation between the trip and the whistling, allowing a variety of different realizations depending on when either of the two predicates holds precisely (see Irimia 2012).

The nature of the overlap relation is stricter when the two predicates stand in a causal relation: here it is required that the adjunct predicate is co-extensive with the durative subevent that leads to the culmination. The scalar progression of the matrix predicate then depends on the occurrence of the adjunct predicate:

(48) Peter drove Mary crazy whistling an annoying song.

Instead of telicity, the focus of the factorial model is on the encoding of scalar change encoded in the matrix predicate; this allows an explanation for the effects of different kinds of scale-inducing elements such as path particles, telic and atelic prepositions, as well as the behavior of predicates that allow both bounded and unbounded readings. See also Rappaport Hovav (2008), Gawron (2005, 2009),

Champollion (2017), and Beavers & Koontz-Garboden (2020) for similar proposals about scales that are not limited to temporal intervals.

In addition to these differences in the requirements for adjunct licensing, the factorial model explicitly takes into account the processing burden incurred by the formation of a filler–gap dependency and the ensuing decreases in acceptability. For Brown (2017), there are two types of extraction: syntactically well-formed extractions from an adjunct to non-phasal VP, and syntactically ill-formed extractions from an adjunct to phasal vP. She does not explicitly take into account that even well-formed extractions incur processing costs that are reflected in slightly reduced acceptability; see Sprouse et al. (2013), Wagers (2013), as well as Chaves & Putnam (2020: 15) and references therein.

Finally, the generalizations about semantic compatibility and syntactic complexity are not necessarily understood in the same way as Brown's (2017) licensing conditions on the adjunct. I have noted at the beginning of this chapter that I do not make the assumption that the generalizations are necessarily part of the speaker's competence grammar, thus drawing a distinction to the concept of constraints as used, for example, in constraint satisfaction models. Rather, the generalizations are conceptualized as factors that determine ease of processing in the BPPA construction. Brown (2017) argues that when an adjunct is not semantically licensed in its merge position, coercion needs to apply, which results in a negative effect on acceptability. My argument goes in the same direction, but without the appeal to strict licensing conditions that need to be repaired if they are not satisfied. The question whether the licensing conditions on depictive secondary predicates discussed in the literature, which overlap considerably with the DG, are also rather an effect of increased processing effort or a case of a licensing condition is another issue that I leave for future research.

5.3.5 A connection between durativity and scalar change

It may be possible to collapse the DG and SCG into one unified generalization that captures both the durative and scalar change characteristics. This would entail limiting the change meaning components that are most compatible in the BPPA construction to what I will call non-trivial scalar change structures. A trivial change happens in point predicates like *appear*, which have only a two-point scale with an instantaneous change from one state to another ($\neg p \rightarrow p$). In contrast, a non-trivial scalar change involves intermediate points on the scale. Tenny (1995) draws the same distinction between measuring-out effects: there are cases where measuring-out applies across an extended temporal interval, and cases where measuring-out occurs instantaneously without temporal spread. The distinction is modeled along the traditional Vendlerian split between punctual achievements without temporal spread and accomplishments, where change has temporal spread. See the examples in (49), which show the punctual interpretation of the achievement *die* and the incremental theme accomplishment *melt* and their properties in terms of temporal spread of the measuring-out effect.

(49)   a.   John died.   [instantaneous, no temporal spread]
       b.   John melted the butter.   [extended, temporal spread]
          (Tenny 1995: 44, 53)

The distinction between trivial and non-trivial scalar change is shown schematically in Figure 5.7, where Figure 5.7a on the left side corresponds to the instantaneous change in (49a), and Figure 5.7b on the right to the extended change event in (49b). Trivial scalar change involves a binary contrast between two states $\neg p$ and p; there is no temporal spread of the change across intervals. In contrast, non-trivial scalar change is depicted as a function from time to property degrees; the duration of the change event is determined by the slope of the function, so that the change can either happen in a short interval, or a long one. Beavers (2012: 48–49) and Beavers & Koontz-Garboden (2020: 40) draw a similar mereological distinction between atomic, simplex, and complex objects, which can be transferred to scales; scales like paths are simplex rather than atomic because they involve at least two points. This function of times to points on a scale can be directly transferred to all kinds of predicates encoding a scale: incremental themes, paths, and change-of-state verbs.

The key difference between these two types of change is that non-trivial scalar change is more complex because there are a variety of "degrees of *p*-ness" between

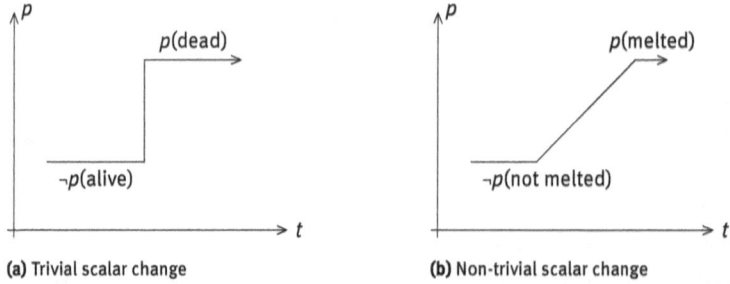

(a) Trivial scalar change   (b) Non-trivial scalar change

Fig. 5.7: Schematic representation of trivial and non-trivial scalar change; trivial scalar changes happen instantly without temporal spread, the scale has only two values on the property scale *p*. Non-trivial scalar change takes place over an interval and has multiple accessible values on the property scale *p*.

the two states described by ¬p and p. In the example (49b), this corresponds to the following states: at the beginning, no part of the butter qualifies as melted (¬p); then there is the interval during which more and more of the butter is melted until no solid butter is left (p). Importantly, the degree of scalar change can be evaluated at subintervals, which is not possible for trivial scalar change: there are only two relevant values, and the change between these cannot be captured at intervals. Achievements that typically encode trivial scalar change, such as *arrive* or *die*, can be coerced into a non-trivial reading by means such as the progressive and possibly modification by a durative adjunct predicate; in effect, this changes the slope of the change function so that the achievement is interpreted as having temporal spread. Take the example in (50), where the adverb and the adverbial indicate that the punctual transition of dying is conceptualized as stretched over a longer duration instead of happening instantaneously.

(50) John slowly died over the course of several days.

As the distinction between *arrive* and *appear* and evidence from perception verbs indicates, this may not be possible for all achievements with equal success. As noted in Rothstein (2004b), almost all achievements can occur in the progressive, which indicates temporal spread, but with different readings. The slow-motion reading for points behaves more like the progressive of activities, whereas extendable achievements in the progressive are more similar to accomplishments. Jackendoff (1996: 312) proposes that the slope of the function and thus the distinction between trivial and non-trivial scalar change is at least in part determined pragmatically and thus not exclusively a lexical phenomenon; thus, it is possible to interpret the lexically trivial scalar change encoded in *die* as temporally extended. The same applies to verbs like *appear* and perception verbs, which can also be coerced into a non-punctual interpretation, but with greater difficulty. See also Verkuyl (2019: 192–195) for an analysis of aspectual properties of different verb classes in terms of functions that map times to property degrees. I will leave the details of these distinctions for further research.

This discussion shows that there is a connection between the precise nature of the scale encoded in an event that involves change and the temporal properties of the event. It is therefore not unlikely that the DG and the SCG can be unified. I give a tentative formulation of such a possible unified semantic compatibility generalization for durativity and scalar change in (51) and leave the details of this extension for future research.

(51) Unified generalization for semantic compatibility (tentative):
The semantic compatibility between the predicates in the BPPA construction is higher when the matrix predicate encodes non-trivial scalar change.

This formulation may have an advantage over the separate DG and SCG in the analysis of the low semantic compatibility with permanent state matrix predicates; the low compatibility of this verb class with respect to the DG rests on the assumption that permanent states do not encode an event variable and that there is thus no reference to subevents; permanent states are temporally persistent, but do not count as durative in the sense of the DG. The unified semantic compatibility generalization in (51) could be better suited to explain the behavior of permanent states. On the other hand, the flexibility of two conceptually independent generalizations allows for a more fine-grained continuum of compatibility with at least three levels, which can be further extended if other factors are considered to contribute to compatibility.

5.4 Potential challenges

In this section, I discuss potential challenges to the factorial model proposed in the previous section. So far, the model incorporates three factors which determine acceptability in declarative BPPA constructions plus the independent effect of extraction. It is possible that there are other relevant factors which lead to more fine-grained distinctions. I do not claim that the factorial model provides an exhaustive approach to the BPPA construction; however, the three generalizations provide a suitable description of the most important data patterns observed in the previous literature and the experimental chapter. I discuss the following potential challenges: (i) possible interpretation requirements on the adjunct with accomplishment matrix predicates, (ii) accomplishment readings of perception verbs, (iii) gap site ambiguity with unergative matrix predicates, (iv) possible lexical differences between point predicates like *show up* and *appear*, (v) linearization problems for V–V sequences, and (vi) informativity differences between bare activities and achievements.

5.4.1 Event specification or event expansion

A first possible challenge for the factorial model in the form proposed in Section 5.2.5 concerns the interpretations of the adjunct with accomplishment matrix predicates. Truswell (2007, 2011) proposes that the adjunct predicate needs to be interpreted as the cause of the matrix predicate to allow extraction. Thus, the extraction from the causal adjunct in (52) is considered grammatical. As shown in (53a), the adjunct does not need to specify a causal component; it can also be interpreted as a depictive. The experiments in Chapter 4 did not explicitly examine this distinction, but it is possible that extractions from non-causal adjuncts with accomplishment matrix predicates are less acceptable (53b) than extractions from causal adjuncts (52b).

(52) a. John drove Mary crazy whistling hornpipes.
 b. What did John drive Mary crazy [whistling __]?
 (Truswell 2011: 32)

(53) a. John$_i$ fixed the car whistling a happy tune$_i$. (Farrell 2019: 100)
 b. (?) What did John fix the car [whistling __]?

The IH predicts that the same contrast should apply in the declaratives, meaning that (53a) is slightly less acceptable than (52a). A further complication for these different types of accomplishments is the difference between the resultative accomplishment in (52) and the transitive accomplishment in (53), which I argued to be a relevant distinction. The contrast, however, appears to remain with a causal BPPA modifying a non-resultative accomplishment, as in (54):

(54) a. John enraged his neighbours whistling hornpipes.
 b. What did John enrage his neighbours [whistling t]?
 (Truswell 2007: 1357)

In the interpretation framework for complex events proposed in Bary & Haug (2011) and Haug et al. (2012), the interpretations of causal and depictive adjunct predicates arise through two different mechanisms: event specification for causal adjuncts and event expansion for depictive adjuncts. If there really is an acceptability difference between (52a) and (53a) that is mirrored in the interrogatives, this can be expressed as an additional generalization for BPPA constructions with accomplishment predicates; a tentative formulation of such a generalization is given in (55):

(55) Event Specification Generalization (tentative):
 BPPA constructions with accomplishment matrix predicates are more acceptable when the adjunct stands in an *event specification* rather than *event expansion* relation to the matrix predicate.

Intuitively, this generalization is not unwarranted, as there are predicate types which have an accomplishment interpretation where a depictive, non-causal interpretation of the adjunct may be possible but is pragmatically odd, as in (56).

(56) John got scared watching a horror movie.
    a. The movie scared John.
    b. #The movie had nothing to do with John getting scared.

Cases like these support the intuition that a causal interpretation of the adjunct is preferred with accomplishment matrix predicates, and that this preference is independent of extraction. The tentative generalization in (55) could thus be added as a further component of the factorial model proposed in this chapter.

The tentative Event Specification Generalization for accomplishment matrix predicates could in fact be interpreted as evidence for the semantic–pragmatic explanation of many island effects based on relevance criteria, as proposed in Chaves & Putnam (2020): an adjunct predicate that stands in a causal relation to the matrix predicate is more relevant to the main proposition compared to an unrelated activity and should thus allow extraction more easily.

5.4.2 Perception verbs

The prediction made by the DG is that verbs like *appear* and most perception verbs should be degraded in the BPPA construction compared to structures with more suitable matrix predicates. It is true that perception verbs resist progressive formation more strongly than other verb types, which indicates that additive event coercion to include a process component is harder for this verb class. There are cases where an appropriate context can provide clues for the existence of such a process component that allows an interpretation that is very close to accomplishments. This is shown in the following:

(57) a. After hours of proofreading, John finally spotted the typo in his essay.
    b. After a sleepless night of trial and error, Jane realized that she forgot a closing bracket in her code.
    c. Spending most of the afternoon with preparations, the orchestra appeared on stage for the concert.

In these cases, it is reasonable to assume that the perception event is the result caused by the preceding activity: it is interpreted as an accomplishment. This differs from the typical interpretation of *spot/notice* as purely punctual predicates that simply "happen" (see Rothstein 2004b: 52). Nevertheless, it is still difficult to construct a BPPA sentence with these verbs as main predicates, which indicates that there is a considerable degree of coercion necessary to get the required readings.

(58) a. #John finally spotted the typo proofreading his essay.
b. #Jane realized she forgot a closing bracket checking her code.
c. #The orchestra appeared on stage spending most of the afternoon with preparations.

There is something inherently odd about these sentences and the available paraphrases are not always that for depictive constructions; typically, an appropriate paraphrase involves a causal or temporal anterior reading of the BPPA, showing that these constructions are more likely adverbial clauses than depictives. Under the assumption that depictives are closer to complement status than adverbial clauses (Simpson 2005), this can explain the oddness of the reduced adverbial clause readings.

An open question concerns the interplay of matrix and adjunct predicate: it could be possible that the durative subevent required by the DG is actually contributed by the adjunct predicate. Evidence for this comes from the fact that the event encoded in the adjunct predicate needs to be atelic or durative, regardless of whether the matrix predicate is an achievement or an accomplishment. For accomplishments, the durative subevent is already lexically encoded; with achievements, this is not the case, but a durative subevent can be added by means of progressive-marking, an instance of additive aspectual coercion. In the BPPA construction, there is a depictive-like overlap relation between the two predicates, and the durative adjunct predicate could be the reason an achievement matrix predicate is shifted towards a durative interpretation leading up to the lexically encoded culmination. I leave this matter open here, but the contribution of durative meaning seems to work similar to the analysis of the Depictive Aspectuality Constraint in Farrell (2019), where both the main verb and the depictive can contribute the necessary ingredients for aspectual licensing of the depictive.

5.4.3 Gap site ambiguity

A major problem with many types of matrix predicates is that they can be used either transitively or intransitively, meaning that the object does not need to be encoded overtly. Often, the semantics of the verb will determine possible objects via s-selection (Boeckx 2008b). This applies especially to unergatives, as in (59).

(59) a. John danced (a waltz).
b. Mary ate (pizza).
c. Peter drew (a painting).

In extraction from the BPPA construction, this introduces gap site ambiguity, as the matrix object gap site cannot be entirely excluded. Chaves & Putnam (2020: 15) argue that the slightest possibility of a transitive interpretation is typically preferred by the parser, even if this results in implausible sentences; see also Staub (2007). This erroneous linking of the filler to the matrix object position, even if no object is present in the structure, is most likely one of the reasons why extractions like (60) improve in the presence of a matrix object because this disambiguates the gap site:

(60) What does John dance *(the YMCA) screaming?   (see Brown 2017: 54–55)

Brown (2017) considers (60) to be a counterexample to Truswell's (2011) agentivity condition because the addition of the object increases the acceptability of extraction without modifying the agentive interpretation of *dance*. This contrast is elusive in an agentivity-based framework but receives a natural explanation in the model proposed here by means of the SCG: the matrix object introduces a prominent scale against which the progress of the event can be measured.

The examples in (61) illustrate the gap site ambiguity problem in BPPA constructions with unergative main verbs: in (61a), the filler can associate with both optional gap sites, which are indicated by parentheses. As both *dance* and *scream* have intransitive uses, this means that the filler can be associated with both gap sites without violating selectional requirements of the second gap site. In contrast, when the adjunct predicate is obligatorily transitive, as in (61b), the potential gap site in complement position of the matrix predicate is excluded because this would leave the complement gap of the adjunct without a filler.

(61) a. What$_{i/j}$ did John dance (_$_i$) screaming (_$_j$)?   [two optional gaps]
b. What$_i$ did John dance (_) proclaiming _$_i$?
                                               [optional + obligatory gap]

However, this means that the true gap site which does not violate lexical selection is only encountered at the very end of the sentence; until then, the parser will still try to integrate the filler in complement position of the matrix predicate (Chaves & Putnam 2020: 15); see also Clifton & Frazier (1989) for different gap-filling strategies based on lexical expectations. This means that even though the verb *dance* may have a much higher frequency of its intransitive use, the presence of the filler will push the parser into analyzing it as transitive; when the true gap site is in complement position to the adjunct predicate, this requires a re-analysis of the parse, which incurs processing costs. Thus, the example in (60) receives a processing explanation: the parser knows that the first possible gap site cannot be the true one because it is already filled; the filler will be held in memory until the next potential gap site appears. This situation could be described as a reversed filled-gap effect along the original observations in Stowe (1986). A similar effect can be observed with other optionally transitive unergatives, as in (62), where (62b) is a plausible answer to (62a) and no extraction from the intransitive depictive is necessary.

(62) a. What did John walk whistling?
    b. John walked the dog whistling.

The improvement of extraction when the matrix predicate has an overt complement is surprising under a parasitic gap account of examples like (60): if the filler is semantically compatible with both potential gap sites, as is the case in this specific examples, then it should be possible to have a parasitic gap construction here, where the gap in the adjunct is licensed by the presence of a gap in the matrix clause that does not c-command the parasitic gap (Engdahl 1983; Culicover 2001). Removing the parasitic gap construction by adding the complement to the matrix predicate should thus make the extraction worse instead of better; I leave the details of the relation to parasitic gaps for further research.

Support for the improvement of unambiguous gap sites comes from the results of Experiment 1, which included relativization as an alternative extraction operation to *wh*-extraction. In relativization, the complement of the adjunct predicate is given explicitly: this disambiguates the gap site based on plausibility criteria. See the differences in gap sites in (63). In a *wh*-question with an unspecific *wh*-pronoun (63a), the filler can in principle be integrated at the complement position for both predicates; the true gap site is only encountered when the adjunct predicate is processed because the adjunct predicate is obligatorily transitive. In contrast, the relativization in (63b), the gap site is clear because a dress is not a suitable complement of *dance*, due to lexical subcategorization; thus, the only available gap site is in complement position of the adjunct. Since the integration of the filler is lexically implausible, the parser will hold the filler in working memory until a suitable gap site is encountered which is syntactically possible and semantically plausible.

(63) a. What$_{i/j}$ did Martha dance (__$_i$) wearing (__$_j$)?
    b. This is [the dress]$_i$ that Martha danced (__) wearing (__$_i$).

The factorial model presented in this chapter does not directly account for these processing effects. However, they can be added to the model as further factors without substantial revisions; it is also possible that durativity, scalar change, and transitivity correlate with processing factors such as the gap disambiguating mechanism and lexical biases about transitivity which help to determine the true gap site. I leave this extension for further study.

5.4.4 The cases of *show up* and *appear*

A potential counterexample to the DG comes from intuitively different acceptability judgments for predicates that have in common their punctual interpretation. The two predicates in (64) exemplify this contrast:

(64) a. Peter appeared $^?$(at the party) whistling a funny song.
b. Peter showed up (at the party) whistling a funny song.
(Paula Menéndez Benito, p. c.)

Whereas the presence of the PP *at the party* seems to be required to remove the slight oddness in (64a), the semantically nearly identical predicate like *show up* in (64b) appears to be completely fine in this construction in the absence of the PP. While these two predicates are semantically very similar, they differ syntactically in that *show up* is a particle verb and has a resultative flair to it; it also has an idiomatic chartacter. This provides further indication that resultative and/or idiomatic matrix predicates such as *drive crazy* deserve further investigation. I suggest that these differences can account for the different effect of the PP.

A complicating factor with *appear* is that it is ambiguous between a directed verb of motion, as in *appear at the party*, and a perception verb like *seem*; this is an entirely different syntactic structure, which requires an infinitival copular construction to be grammatical with the present participle complement (65).

(65) *Peter appeared$_{seem}$ ~~to be~~ whistling a funny song.

The special case of *appear* could thus not only be related to a missing path component, but also to this lexical ambiguity which could require the parser to re-analyze the sentence. A re-analysis of the reading that is required by the syntactic form of the sentence is another instance of processing complexity that can have an effect on overall acceptability. If the *seem*-reading is not discarded, the result will be unacceptable even in the absence of extraction. One question that is raised by this discussion concerns the role of frequency of the respective readings. Sam Featherston (p. c.) suggests that the raising verb interpretation of *appear*, similar to *seem*, might be more frequent than the directed motion reading in the sense of *arrive*. The relevance of frequency for acceptability is widely noted in the literature, e.g. Sag et al. (2008) and Hofmeister & Sag (2010), and it is not unreasonable to transfer this to the relative frequency of two readings of the same verb form. I will have to leave the role of frequency to future research.

5.4.5 V–V linearization

An issue that may be independent of the BPPA construction and the discussion of adjunct islands is that the combination of some matrix predicates with a participle adjunct predicate results in configurations that pose a problem for linearization. This happens when the matrix predicate is intransitive and the BPPA immediately follows the matrix predicate. Especially for unergatives (66a), this seems to degrade acceptability (judgments by Sam Featherston, p. c.). Unaccusatives do not seem to be affected in the same way (66c). Both predicate types, however, are considerably worse when the matrix predicate is in the progressive, so that two *-ing*-marked predicates are in sequence (66b,d).

(66) a. ??John [$_{VP}$ walked] [$_{VP}$ whistling a song].
  b. *John was [$_{VP}$ walking] [$_{VP}$ whistling a song].
  c. Peter [$_{VP}$ arrived] [$_{VP}$ whistling a song].
  d. ?Peter [$_{VP}$ was arriving] [$_{VP}$ whistling a song].

The fact that two consecutive constituents of the same category are problematic for optimal interface conditions during Spell-Out is discussed at length in Richards (2010), who proposes that the linearization algorithm is sensitive to category information and other characteristics of constituents. This is captured in the *Distinctness* condition on linearization:

(67) *Distinctness*:
  If a linearization statement <α, α> is generated, the derivation crashes.
  (Richards 2010: 5)

This means that if two nodes that are too similar, linearization does not succeed; in languages like English, the same phrase structure category is enough to violate Distinctness. Thus, two sequential VPs fail to be linearized when they are in the same Spell-Out domain (Richards 2010: 5). This explains why (66a) is intuitively slightly degraded, and why the even less distinct (66b,d) are even worse; the latter fall under the so-called "doubl-ing" constraint (Ross 1972; Pires & Milsark 2017). However, an explanation along these lines leaves open why the same effect appears to be absent for unaccusative matrix predicates (66c). Richards (2010: 4) considers only transitive *v*P as a strong phase triggering Spell-Out, whereas intransitive *v*P is not a strong phase. This may be a reason why the transitive BPPA constructions in (68) do not show similar effects because the conditions for distinctness are met.

(68) a. John walked the dog whistling a song.
b. John was walking the dog whistling a song.

A possible consequence of the intransitive–transitive distinction is that Spell-Out in the intransitive case has to include the adjunct predicate, leading to a linearization problem with two sequential and non-distinct VPs, whereas in transitive sentences the matrix and adjunct VP are in different Spell-Out domains. The difference for unergative and unaccusative predicates noted in (66) above may also be related to the phase-based timing of Spell-Out. If, however, unergatives are hidden transitives, as claimed in Levin & Rappaport Hovav (1995) or Chomsky (1995b: 315–316), this is problematic for an explanation along these lines.

One possibility to avoid Distinctness violations is to add structure (Richards 2010: 54). This may be an alternative explanation for the apparent amelioration of intransitive activities with particles, such as the contrast in (69), which I explained in terms of the presence vs. absence of a scalar path structure.

(69) John walked $^?$(around) whistling a song.

If there is a preference for separating the main verb from the verb heading the adjunct predicate, this should apply cross-linguistically. Fábregas & Jiménez-Fernández (2016a), however, observe the reverse situation in Spanish: here, the two verbs need to be immediately adjacent in linear order for the extraction to be grammatical, which is clearly shown in their data. Since achievements are the only type of main verb that is judged as acceptable in their extraction study, a direct comparison to English is problematic: as shown in (66c) and (70), the VP–VP sequence seems acceptable for unaccusatives in English.

(70) David arrived (at the station) whistling a song.

Thus, it is relevant to look at the effects of intervening material in the Spanish declaratives and examine whether there is a similar difference in the presence or absence of such material. Compare the declaratives in (71) with achievement (71a) and activity (71b) main verbs.

(71) a. *María llegó   (a casa) silbando la   Marsellesa.*
       María arrived-3SG at home whistling the Marseillaise
       'María arrived (at home) whistling the Marseillaise.'
    b. *El   tonel rodaba   (por el   monte) perdiendo aceite.*
       The barrel rolled-3SG by the mount   losing   oil
       'The barrel rolled (down the hill) losing oil.'
       (see Fábregas & Jiménez-Fernández 2016a: 1312)

If declaratives show a similar negative effect of the goal phrase as interrogatives, then this is evidence for a more general condition that is unrelated extraction; the situation is further complicated by the fact that unergatives with goal phrases show unaccusative characteristics, at least in English (Levin & Rappaport Hovav 1995; Borgonovo & Neeleman 2000: 200). In the discussion of the Spanish data, it has to be noted that Talmy (2000: 224) draws a distinction between gerunds that immediately follow the main verb, as in (71) without the directional phrases, and sentence-final gerunds after directional phrases. The former form a tighter relation with the event of the main verb, whereas the latter are analyzed as subordinate gerundives with a less tight bond. It is thus possible that the adjacency requirement formulated in Fábregas & Jiménez-Fernández (2016a) is a consequence of the syntactic status of the gerund and the possibilities for complex event interpretations.

The different sensitivity of unergatives and unaccusatives to a VP–VP sequence could also be related to a prosodic difference: it has been noted that sentences with unergative verbs receive stress on the verb by default, whereas for unaccusatives the main stress is on the subject (Chafe 1974; Sasse 1987; Zubizarreta & Vergnaud 2006; Irwin 2011, 2012). Under the assumption that the verb in the adjunct predicate always receives stress, this results in two consecutive stressed words for unergative sentences (72a,b), but not for unaccusative sentences (72c).

(72) a. John wálked $^?$(to the station) whístling a song.
    b. Susan wórked $^?$(on her dissertation) whístling a song.
    c. Dávid arrived (at the station) whístling a song.

This provides an explanation for the contrast of bare unaccusatives and unergatives, but does not carry over directly to *get*-predicates and resultative accomplishments, shown in (73). There, the sequence of the stressed resultative and the verb of the adjunct predicate does not seem problematic.

(73) a. John drove Mary crázy whístling a song.
    b. Peter got scáred wátching a horror movie.

It cannot be ruled out that there is a difference in the stress of the adjunct predicate for the constructions in (72) and (73). The BPPA in sentences like (73) could receive secondary stress instead of primary stress, marked by a grave accent (`) instead of the acute (´) on the respective syllables. This seems to work out for *get*-predicates and other resultatives, but not for unergatives:

(74)   a.   #John wórked whìstling a song.
       b.   John drove Mary crázy whìstling a song.

The prosodic characteristics of the BPPA construction, especially in relation to the alternative interpretation as a free adjunct, have not been studied in sufficient detail to draw principled conclusions, so I leave the details of these potential contrasts for further study.

5.4.6 Informativity

The preference for a path or other scale component may not be specific to the BPPA construction, but apply to unergatives more generally. As noted by Sam Featherston (p. c.), some unergatives are odd in isolation and ameliorated by a scale component. See the contrasts in (75) with two different types of unergative, a manner-of-motion predicate in (75a) and a simple activity predicate in (75b).

(75)   a.   John walked #(to the park).   (Sam Featherston, p. c.)
       b.   Susan worked #(on her dissertation).

In both cases, the sentence seems odd in the absence of the postverbal material because they are not very informative.[40] A manner-of-motion predicate like *walk* in (75a) always entails a certain path, and is only informative in isolation to contrast it with other manners-of-motion, such as jogging or running. The activity predicate *work* in (75b), on the other hand, seems less dependent in isolation on the incremental theme object. Considering these apparent contrasts, the predictions from the SCG may be even more general in nature than assumed in the factorial model, and it is a reasonable question whether the intuitive contrasts in (75) apply to more cases. A follow-up question is whether a path or scale component has similar effects for unaccusatives, or whether they can stand in isolation; see (76). The isolated unergative construction with a definite or indefinite subject in (76a)

---

40 This could be an alternative explanation for the pattern of unergatives with telic and atelic goal phrases discussed for (44) on p. 279.

seems worse compared to the unaccusative construction in (76b). However, adding a locative preposition to the unergative, as shown in (76c), considerably ameliorates the sentence; this may be connected to the fact that unergatives with locative PPs behave like unaccusatives (Levin & Rappaport Hovav 1995; Borgonovo & Neeleman 2000), presumably because (76b,c) represent thetic judgments whereas (76a) should be analyzed as categorical (Kuroda 1972; Irwin 2020).

(76) a. #John/??A man walked.
  b. John/A man arrived.
  c. John/A man walked in.

The difference in (76) is not only one between unergatives and unaccusatives, but also between the lexical meaning encoded in these predicates. Both are predicates related to motion, but only *arrive* and similar predicates encode the path component in the verb from an unspecified location to the deictic center or a location specified by a PP like *at the station*; *walk* and other manner-of-motion-verbs, on the other hand, encode only the manner and not the path (see Talmy 2000; Levin & Rappaport Hovav 2019). It would be expected that a path or scale component is optional for unaccusatives like *arrive*, but may be required for manner-of-motion predicates to make them informative.

From the perspective of background frames in the semantic-pragmatic approach to island effects in Chaves & Putnam (2020), it could also be argued that the frame evoked by a bare unergative like *work* or *walk* implies that there is something being worked on or a goal or path of the walking event, so that it is pragmatically odd not to express this event component. It is tempting to explain the effects of the SCG in terms of the thetic–categorical distinction because this would easily explain the ameliorating effects of added path components like directional PPs or particles like *around*; it could be argued that the matrix clause represents a thetic judgment, i.e. a presentational or existential proposition, and that the adjunct predicate turns the sentence into a categorical judgment where the adjunct is predicated of the subject in the matrix clause. However, the apparent positive effects of other scale-inducing elements like incremental themes in (75b) suggest that this is not possible without allowing sentences like *Susan worked on her dissertation* a thetic judgment interpretation. I leave the details for future research.

5.5 Similarities to past participle adjuncts

The empirical focus here has been on present participle adjunct predicates, but other types of adjunct predicate also need to be considered for a comprehensive analysis of transparent adjuncts, such as adverbial clauses or adjunct constructions with past participles. Past participle adjuncts show distinct aspectual properties compared to present participles: they are typically stative and non-agentive instead of agentive activities. There are several examples of transparent past participles in the literature, such as those given in (77).

(77) a. What did John come home [covered in __] yesterday?
b. What did the chef$_i$ serve the meat$_j$ [wrapped in __]$_{i/j}$ [?]
(Truswell 2011: 167, fn. 17)

The SOD reading in (77b) is probably excluded by plausibility criteria in this particular example, but seems possible or even preferred in sentences like (78):

(78) The chef$_i$ served the meat$_j$ covered in sweat$_{i/j}$.

For Truswell (2011), the transparency of past participles receives a straightforward explanation: because of their stative and non-agentive properties, they always meet the restriction to at most one agentive event as formulated in the SEGC. It does not matter whether the matrix predicate is non-agentive (77a) or agentive (77b) because the maximum number of agentive events for the formation of a single event grouping will not be exceeded (Truswell 2011: 167, fn. 17).

In contrast to this liberal perspective, Borgonovo & Neeleman (2000) observe grammaticality differences for extraction from past participle adjuncts which, like present participles, depend on the type of matrix predicate. Extraction from participles modifying unergatives (79a) and non-reflexive transitives (79b) are ungrammatical, whereas the extraction is grammatical with unaccusative matrix predicates (79c,d).

(79) a. *What$_i$ did John dance [dressed as t$_i$]?
b. *What$_i$ did John finish the portrait [covered in t$_i$]?
c. What$_i$ did John come back [addicted to t$_i$]?
d. What$_i$ did John leave [satisfied with t$_i$]?
(Borgonovo & Neeleman 2000: 199–200, 203)

In the absence of controlled experimental evidence, it is difficult to decide which judgments are correct, especially since (77b) and (79b) are very similar. However, the difference between (77a) and (79a) suggests that even non-agentive past participle adjuncts are sensitive to factors that cannot be captured by an agentivity restriction; the addition of an object in (80a) or a path component in (80b) improves the extraction considerably. Whether this is caused by the presence of a prominent scale, as proposed in the SCG, or a disambiguation of the gap site is a different question, but it is clear that agentivity does not explain this contrast.

(80) a. What did John dance the tango [dressed as __]?
b. What did John dance into the room [dressed as __]?

The example in (79d) deserves closer attention because it can receive a causative reading of the adjunct predicate, which is not usually possible with unaccusative matrix predicates; in this respect, it has to be noted that *leave* can be interpreted as agentive in this case, making it look more like an accomplishment.

Like depictives, past participles are often used as adjectives (Huddleston & Pullum 2002: 77–79); since in this use they encode a state that holds after an event, they qualify as stage-level predicates and are thus not independently excluded as depictives. However, like BPPAs, they are complex in the sense of Himmelmann & Schultze-Berndt (2005) because they are not single lexemes and have internal argument and event structures. All the above examples show past participles derived from telic predicates; they are most commonly interpreted in the so-called "target state" reading (see Rapp 2000; Pancheva 2003; Borik & Gehrke 2019). Past participles based on atelic predicates are significantly less acceptable, as in (81).

(81) a. *John arrived at the station danced.
b. *John left the party whistled.

This analysis allows tracing back the grammaticality differences observed in Borgonovo & Neeleman (2000) to the general accessibility of main verbs to depictive modification, meaning that unaccusatives will generally be highly accessible, followed by transitives and finally unergatives, which are not very accessible for depictives (see Irimia 2012). The predictions of the FAM can account for the reported judgment pattern in (79) and the improvement of unergative matrix predicates when a scale-inducing object or path is added, as in (80). In addition to the conditions on the adjunct predicate itself, similar to present participles, the properties of the matrix predicate seem to have a similar influence. Again, an approach to extraction from adjuncts formulated in terms of several independent factors explains many of the empirical observations. The precise influence of the matrix predicate type for past participle adjuncts is beyond the scope of the present discussion and is left for further research.

5.6 Chapter conclusion

In this chapter, I have proposed a factorial model for the grammaticality judgment patterns for participial adjunct islands in the literature and the experimental chapter of the present work. This factorial approach strongly distinguishes between the acceptability decreases caused by the application of extraction operations and the factors that determine how acceptable declarative BPPA constructions are. I have formulated three generalizations which influence acceptability in the declaratives. BPPA constructions with activity adjunct predicates are most acceptable when the matrix encodes a durative subevent and a prominent scale, such as a path or property; additionally, the number of arguments directly selected by the matrix predicates influences acceptability. Following models of acceptability such as the Decathlon Model (Featherston 2008, 2019) and the Cumulative Effect Hypothesis (Haegeman et al. 2014), the failure to satisfy one or more of these generalizations incrementally lowers acceptability, which can be formulated as the effect of increased processing effort. The factorial model implements the Independence Hypothesis through a separation into two stages: first the acceptability of the declarative BPPA construction is determined by the proposed generalizations and extraction further lowers acceptability in the second stage.

The discussion in this chapter has shown that the Independence Hypothesis and the proposed generalizations make adequate predictions about the general data patterns in the literature as well as the results of the experiments reported in Chapter 4. The generalizations also offer an explanation for contrasts that are more difficult to capture in previous approaches.

6 Conclusion and outlook

This monograph has investigated the factors that have an effect on the acceptability of extraction from present participle adjuncts in English. The discussion centered around the research question as formulated in Chapter 1, repeated here in (1):

(1)　How strong is the relation between acceptability contrasts in interrogative and declarative BPPA constructions? Are there factors that affect acceptability independently of extraction?

In Chapter 1, I introduced the phenomenon of apparently grammatical extractions from adjunct constituents, which the CED (Huang 1982) predicts to be ungrammatical; it was shown that such extractions are not limited to constructed examples from the theoretical literature, but are also attested in natural language examples. Chapter 2 focused on a syntactic analysis of the BPPA construction. I have shown that BPPAs show many similarities to depictive secondary predicates, and that a large part of the grammaticality pattern reported for extraction from such adjuncts in the literature can be explained by syntactic and semantic licensing conditions on depictives. I have also discussed the semantic contribution of the adjunct to the main predication by examining theories for the interpretation of complex events and the meaning restrictions in such constructions. In Chapter 3, I provided an overview of the existing literature on extraction from adjunct islands, grouped into three major types of approaches: (i) pure syntactic gap-licensing accounts which aim at an explanation for grammatical extractions from adjunct islands; (ii) interaction accounts, which claim that extraction from an adjunct must be licensed by factors that are often not captured in core-syntactic terms and are thus problematic for the independence of syntax; and (iii) an independence approach which distinguishes conditions on adjunct-internal gap-licensing from the syntactic and semantic licensing conditions on the adjunct itself. Such an approach is conceptually appealing because it provides an explanation for a larger pattern of acceptability that also includes differences in declaratives. The main aim of Chapter 4 was two-fold: first, to find out whether there is principled evidence for interaction or independence accounts, and second, which factors show a significant influence on the acceptability of extraction. I have shown throughout that there is robust evidence in favor of independence approaches because all experiments found reliable connections between acceptability differences in declaratives and interrogatives alike. I have also shown that the factors isolated in previous interaction accounts such as Borgonovo & Neeleman (2000) or Truswell (2007) are on the right track, but ignore the fact that these factors affect acceptability independently of extraction. The resulting theory of locality can be considerably simpler than in these two approaches. Based on these experimental insights, Chapter 5 developed a Factorial Acceptability Model for the BPPA construction that takes acceptability differences in declaratives seriously. The result is a two-stage model where syntactic and semantic factors affect acceptability in declarative BPPA constructions and extraction operates on this input. Acceptability in declaratives is determined by a set of semantic compatibility and syntactic complexity generalizations which lead to lower acceptability when they are not met; these generalizations act as soft constraints that can be violated at a certain cost rather than categorical and inviolable constraints, such as the CED. The acceptability of interrogative BPPA constructions is the sum of the negative effects resulting from the failure to meet one or more of the proposed generalizations plus the independent effect of extraction. Locality operations need not be sensitive to non-syntactic factors.

The main insight of the foregoing discussion is that the extraction operation alone is not responsible for the grammaticality contrasts reported in the literature for interrogatives; rather, these contrasts are the result of identical contrasts which are operative in the corresponding declaratives. These insights confirm the proposal for independent licensing conditions on the adjunct predicate and adjunct-internal gaps as proposed in Brown (2017); I have formulated this as the Independence Hypothesis, which receives strong empirical support from the experimental results reported in Chapter 4. The confirmation of the Independence Hypothesis is a welcome result because this means that locality operations need not be sensitive to non-structural factors such as aspectual classes or agentivity. The central research question in (1) can thus be answered as follows: the relation between acceptability contrasts in interrogative and declarative BPPA constructions is very strong. The observation of acceptability differences in declaratives, even if they remain undetected in intuitive judgments due to their overall high acceptability, casts doubt on the post-extraction semantic filter proposed in Truswell (2011). In fact, the reverse situation obtains: any acceptability differences resulting from semantic factors like aspectual classes and event structure apply before extraction. Importantly, this pre-extraction determination of acceptability does not interact with the application of locality operations, contra Truswell (2007, 2011).

One of the contrasts between the factorial model and previous approaches is that there is no single factor that determines acceptability: rather, there are multiple and partially independent factors that result in a gradual continuum of acceptability. For example, for intransitive matrix predicates, it is not simply their aspectual class, agentivity characteristics, or reflexivity that determines acceptability in the BPPA construction, but the encoding of a durative subevent and a prominent scalar change meaning component.

There are three arguments that lead to these conclusions: (i) the existence of verb classes such as *get*-predicates that speak against a culmination requirement because they do not explicitly encode a telic endpoint and still yield highly acceptable experimental results; (ii) the fact that progressive-marking, which removes the entailment of a culmination, does not degrade the structures beyond what is expected from the effects of additive event coercion (Bott 2010); and (iii) the empirical coverage of the predictions from the factorial model, which capture the experimental results in Chapter 4 as well as contrasts in the literature which are difficult to explain purely in terms of agentivity (Truswell 2011) or the requirement for a culmination (Truswell 2007; Brown 2017).

The experimental results in Chapter 4 partially provide support for claims in the literature: it was shown that telic matrix predicates are indeed more acceptable than atelic ones, as proposed in Truswell (2007), and that unaccusatives have an advantage over unergatives and non-reflexive transitives, which is the central claim of Borgonovo & Neeleman (2000). However, both of these accounts face three major challenges: they assume (i) that these factors are not fully operative in declaratives, (ii) that the grammaticality of extraction is sensitive to these distinctions, and (iii) that BPPA constructions with different matrix predicates are affected to different degrees by extraction operations. These types of approaches require adjustments to locality theory. In contrast, the experiments in Chapter 4 have shown that identical contrasts can be observed in declaratives; this indicates that locality operations can be blind to such distinctions, but that the overall acceptability of the BPPA construction is sensitive to such differences. The acceptability differences in declaratives fall victim to categorical judgments often used in the literature (see Featherston 2019: 158–159) because even the least acceptable declarative BPPA constructions are "good enough" to occur, as clearly shown by a comparison to the standardized scale of well-formedness from Gerbrich et al. (2019). Thus, the consistent comparison of declaratives and interrogatives, as implemented in Experiments 2 through 8, reveals more information than a focus on relative contrasts in interrogatives alone.

The findings in the experiments reported here and the proposed Factorial Acceptability Model tie in with recent work on the role of grammatical (i.e. competence) principles in extraction asymmetries and related phenomena. Experimental investigations on the so-called *Freezing Principle* from Wexler & Culicover (1980) has shown that the effects of this grammatical principle can be explained by independent effects of processing complexity; this renders the Freezing Principle unnecessary and simplifies the grammar by shifting explanations for a phenomenon to independently motivated aspects like processing complexity; see also Sag et al. (2008) and Hofmeister & Sag (2010). Further examples of this line of work are found in Hofmeister et al. (2015), Winkler et al. (2016), Konietzko et al. (2018), Culicover & Winkler (2018), and Culicover et al. (2022); see also Culicover & Winkler (2022) for a similar explanation of the parasitic gap phenomenon. In relation to the question whether island effects should be captured by grammatical principles such as the traditional island constraints, Chaves & Putnam (2020, 2022) argue that the vast majority of the empirical evidence speaks against the requirement to formalize the observed effects as syntactic constraints.

Culicover et al. (2022) capture these observations about the conceptual necessity of syntactic constraints on extraction in the *Radical Unacceptability Hypothesis* (RUH), which reduces judgment asymmetries in extraction phenomena to underlying differences in processing complexity:

(2) Radical Unacceptability Hypothesis (RUH):
[A]ll judgments of reduced acceptability in cases of otherwise well-formed (i.e., locally well-formed) extractions are due to processing complexity, not syntactic constraints. (Culicover et al. 2022: 2)

Following the gap-licensing accounts discussed in Chapter 3, it seems possible that extraction from a BPPA can indeed be locally well-formed, so that the judgment asymmetries observed there are not a result of a grammatical principle, such as a sensitivity to the telic–atelic distinction, but rather an effect of processing complexity differences resulting from the factors discussed in the preceding chapter. As some extractions from BPPAs are less acceptable than others, this can be explained with an underlying difference in processing complexity, conforming to the RUH. The experimental results presented in Chapter 4 and the FAM proposed in Chapter 5 align well with this line of research, and the more detailed connections to the RUH deserve closer attention. In contrast to most interaction accounts discussed in Chapter 3, the FAM does not introduce grammatical constraints on extraction, based on the observation that the effects are not exclusive to extraction. It also captures a certain degree of gradience by including several factors rather than postulating a binary condition on extraction (Chaves & Putnam 2022). Instead of increasing the formal theoretical machinery governing extraction, the FAM aims at disentangling the set of factors that lead to judgment differences that have been shown to be unrelated to whether extraction takes place or not; in the light of the RUH and proposals along this line, this is a theoretically attractive option.

There are several issues which deserve closer investigation in future research: first, the contrasts that are predicted by the factorial model which have not been explicitly investigated in the experiments reported here. This includes the differences between point predicates like *appear* and extendable achievements like *arrive* as well as the contrasts between different types of transitive matrix predicates. Especially the difference between resultative accomplishments (3), reflexive (4a), and non-reflexive transitives (4b) deserves further examination in the light of the Transitivity Generalization.

(3)   What did John drive Mary crazy [whistling t]?   (Truswell 2007: 1357)

(4) a. What$_i$ did John hurt himself [trying to fix t$_i$]?
    b. *What$_i$ did John hurt Bill [trying to fix t$_i$]?
    (Borgonovo & Neeleman 2000: 200)

A second point for further study is how high the acceptability of interrogative BPPA constructions can be pushed, for example with explicit *wh*-phrases as a form of D-linking (Sag et al. 2008). Also, the relative strength of the effects of different types of extraction operations are of further interest; it is possible that relative clause formation from the adjunct leads to a smaller effect compared to *wh*-extraction. This could be related to D-linking in relativization, the declarative character of relativization, differences in relative frequency and semantic complexity, or the information-structural requirements of different extraction types (Abeillé et al. 2020). From this perspective, the potential acceptability differences between the three sentence forms in (5) and the question whether there are similar judgment patterns for different types of matrix predicates are relevant questions for a more complete picture of participle adjunct constructions.

(5) a. John arrived [whistling a funny song].   [declarative]
    b. What$_i$ did John arrive [whistling ―$_i$]?   [interrogative]
    c. I liked [the song]$_i$ John arrived [whistling ―$_i$].   [relativization]

Finally, the importance of the syntax–pragmatics interface in relation to extraction from adjuncts and other island types is a highly fruitful avenue for further research. This includes the roles of a licensing context, which has been shown to remove island effects for clausal adjuncts in Gibson et al. (2021) and can license other non-canonical word orders (Hörnig et al. 2019). Also, the prosodic realization of the adjunct requires further study because deaccentuation of the matrix predicate, for example by means of pronominalization, could make the adjunct pragmatically more dominant than the matrix clause.

Borgonovo & Neeleman (2000: 219) optimistically claimed that "[t]he problem of transparent adjuncts is now solved". It is true that the understanding of factors which influence the acceptability of extraction from adjunct constituents has increased considerably since the early observations about transparent adjuncts in Cattell (1976) or Chomsky (1982) and the formulation of the CED in Huang (1982). However, there still remain elusive cases and contrasts that are not yet explained in a satisfactory way. The experimental results in Chapter 4 have made it clear that extraction from the BPPA construction can be fairly acceptable under the right conditions; especially in comparison with the cardinal well-formedness sentences from Gerbrich et al. (2019), it is clear that extraction from a BPPA is surprisingly acceptable in the light of the CED. None of the extraction conditions reported Chapter 4 result in clearly unacceptable sentences. As it stands, the factorial model captures several crucial contrasts discussed for adjunct islands, but it is likely that further factors play a role; I will leave these for future research. What I have shown in this monograph is that the acceptability differences in interrogative BPPA constructions can be explained by an approach that does not require drastic changes to the theory of locality but which is still sensitive to the effects of non-syntactic factors on acceptability.

References

Abeillé, Anne, Barbara Hemforth, Elodie Winckel & Edward Gibson. 2020. Extraction from subjects: Differences in acceptability depend on the discourse function of the construction. *Cognition* 204. Article 104293. https://doi.org/10.1016/j.cognition.2020.104293.
Abrusán, Márta. 2014. *Weak island semantics*. Oxford: Oxford University Press.
Abrusán, Márta. 2019. Semantic anomaly, pragmatic infelicity, and ungrammaticality. *Annual Review of Linguistics* 5. 329–351.
Acedo-Matellán, Víctor. 2016. *The morphosyntax of transitions: A case study in Latin and other languages*. Oxford: Oxford University Press.
Ackema, Peter. 2015. Arguments and adjuncts. In Tibor Kiss & Artemis Alexiadou (eds.), *Syntax – Theory and analysis: An international handbook*, vol. 1, 246–274. Berlin, Munich & Boston: Mouton de Gruyter.
Adger, David. 2018. The autonomy of syntax. In Norbert Hornstein, Howard Lasnik, Pritty Patel-Grosz & Charles Yang (eds.), *Syntactic structures after 60 years: The impact of the Chomskyan revolution in linguistics*, 153–175. Berlin & Boston: Mouton de Gruyter.
Åfarli, Tor A. 2010. Adjunction and 3D phrase structure: A study of Norwegian adverbials. In Nomi Erteschik-Shir & Lisa Rochman (eds.), *The sound patterns of syntax*, 9–32. Oxford: Oxford University Press.
Alexiadou, Artemis, Elena Anagnostopoulou & Martin Everaert. 2004. Introduction. In Artemis Alexiadou, Elena Anagnostopoulou & Martin Everaert (eds.), *The unaccusative puzzle: Explorations of the syntax-lexicon interface*, 1–21. Oxford: Oxford University Press.
Alexiadou, Artemis, Elena Anagnostopoulou & Florian Schäfer. 2015. *External arguments in transitivity alternations: A layering approach*. Oxford: Oxford University Press.
Anward, Jan. 1982. Basic Swedish. In Elisabet Engdahl & Eva Ejerhed (eds.), *Readings on unbounded dependencies in Scandinavian languages*, 47–75. Stockholm: Almqvist & Wiksell.
Arsenijević, Boban, Berit Gehrke & Rafael Marín. 2013. The (de)composition of event predicates. In Boban Arsenijević, Berit Gehrke & Rafael Marín (eds.), *Studies in the decomposition of event predicates*, 1–26. Dordrecht: Springer.
Aske, John. 1989. Path predicates in English and Spanish: A closer look. In *Proceedings of the Berkeley Linguistics Society (BLS)*, vol. 15, 1–14.
Bach, Emmon. 1986. The algebra of events. *Linguistics & Philosophy* 9(1). 5–16.
Baker, Mark Cleland. 1988. *Incorporation: A theory of grammatical function changing*. Chicago: University of Chicago Press.
Barr, Dale J., Roger Levy, Christoph Scheepers & Harry J. Tily. 2013. Random effects structure for confirmatory hypothesis testing: Keep it maximal. *Journal of Memory and Language* 68(3). 255–278.
Bary, Corien & Dag T. T. Haug. 2011. Temporal anaphora across and inside sentences: The function of participles. *Semantics & Pragmatics* 4. 1–56.
Bates, Douglas, Martin Mächler, Benjamin M. Bolker & Steven C. Walker. 2015. Fitting linear mixed-effects models using lme4. *Journal of Statistical Software* 67(1). 1–48.
Beavers, John. 2012. Lexical aspect and multiple incremental themes. In Violeta Demonte & Louise McNally (eds.), *Telicity, change, and state: A cross-categorial view of event structure*, 23–59. Oxford: Oxford University Press.
Beavers, John. 2013. Aspectual classes and scales of change. *Linguistics* 51(4). 681–706.

Beavers, John & Andrew Koontz-Garboden. 2020. *The roots of verbal meaning*. Oxford: Oxford University Press.

Beavers, John, Beth Levin & Shiao Wei Tham. 2010. The typology of motion expressions revisited. *Journal of Linguistics* 46. 331–377.

Behrens, Bergljot, Cathrine Fabricius-Hansen & Kåre Solfjeld. 2012. Competing structures: The discourse perspective. In Cathrine Fabricius-Hansen & Dag T. T. Haug (eds.), *Big events, small clauses: The grammar of elaboration*, 179–225. Berlin & Boston: de Gruyter.

Berwick, Robert C. & Amy S. Weinberg. 1984. *The grammatical basis of linguistic performance*. Cambridge, MA: MIT Press.

Bianchi, Valentina & Cristiano Chesi. 2014. Subject islands, reconstruction, and the flow of the computation. *Linguistic Inquiry* 45(4). 525–569.

Boeckx, Cedric. 2003. *Islands and chains: Resumption as stranding*. Amsterdam & Philadelphia: John Benjamins.

Boeckx, Cedric. 2008a. *Aspects of the syntax of agreement*. New York, NY: Routledge.

Boeckx, Cedric. 2008b. *Bare syntax*. Oxford: Oxford University Press.

Boeckx, Cedric. 2012. *Syntactic islands*. Cambridge: Cambridge University Press.

Boeckx, Cedric. 2015. *Elementary syntactic structures: Prospects of a feature-free syntax*. Cambridge: Cambridge University Press.

Bolinger, Dwight. 1972. *Degree words*. The Hague & Paris: Mouton.

Borer, Hagit. 2005. *Structuring sense, vol. 2: The normal course of events*. Oxford: Oxford University Press.

Borgonovo, Claudia & Ad Neeleman. 2000. Transparent adjuncts. *Canadian Journal of Linguistics/La Revue Canadienne de Linguistique* 45(3/4). 199–224.

Borik, Olga & Berit Gehrke. 2019. Participles: Form, use and meaning. *Glossa* 4(1). 1–27.

Bornkessel-Schlesewsky, Ina & Matthias Schlesewsky. 2009. *Processing syntax and morphology: A neurocognitive perspective*. Oxford: Oxford University Press.

Bott, Oliver. 2010. *The processing of events*. Amsterdam & Philadelphia: John Benjamins.

Brown, Jessica M. M. 2015. Apparently semantically-motivated extraction in an autonomous syntax. *Cambridge occasional papers in linguistics* 8. 6–23.

Brown, Jessica M. M. 2016. Blackholes and subextraction from adjuncts in English and Norwegian. In *Proceedings of the Chicago Linguistic Society (CLS)*, vol. 51, 67–81.

Brown, Jessica M. M. 2017. *Heads and adjuncts: An experimental study of subextraction from participials and coordination in English, German and Norwegian*. Cambridge: University of Cambridge dissertation.

Burzio, Luigi. 1986. *Italian syntax*. Dordrecht: D. Reidel.

Carlson, Gregory. 1977. *Reference to kinds in English*. Amherst, MA: University of Massachusetts dissertation.

Carrier, Jill & Janet H. Randall. 1992. The argument structure and syntactic structure of resultatives. *Linguistic Inquiry* 23(2). 173–234.

Cattell, Ray. 1976. Constraints on movement rules. *Language* 52(1). 18–50.

Chafe, Wallace L. 1974. Language and consciousness. *Language* 50(1). 111–133.

Chafe, Wallace L. 1976. Givenness, contrastiveness, definiteness, subjects, topics, and point of view. In Charles Li (ed.), *Subject and topic*, 25–56. London & New York: Academic Press.

Champollion, Lucas. 2017. *Parts of a whole: Distributivity as a bridge between aspect and measurement*. Oxford: Oxford University Press.

Chappell, Hilary. 1980. Is the get-passive adversative? *Papers in Linguistics* 13(3). 411–452.

Chaves, Rui P. 2013. An expectation-based account of subject islands and parasitism. *Journal of Linguistics* 49(2). 285–327.

Chaves, Rui P. & Jeruen E. Dery. 2019. Frequency effects in subject islands. *Journal of Linguistics* 55(3). 475–521.

Chaves, Rui P. & Michael T. Putnam. 2020. *Unbounded dependency constructions: Theoretical and experimental perspectives.* Oxford: Oxford University Press.

Chaves, Rui P. & Michael T. Putnam. 2022. Islands, expressiveness, and the theory/formalism confusion. *Theoretical Linguistics* 48(3–4). 219–231.

Chesi, Cristiano. 2015. On the directionality of phrase structure building. *Journal of Psycholinguistic Research* 44. 65–89.

Chomsky, Noam. 1957. *Syntactic structures.* The Hague: Mouton.

Chomsky, Noam. 1964. *Current issues in linguistic theory.* The Hague: Mouton.

Chomsky, Noam. 1965. *Aspects of the theory of syntax.* Cambridge, MA: MIT Press.

Chomsky, Noam. 1973. Conditions on transformations. In Stephen R. Anderson & Paul Kiparsky (eds.), *A Festschrift for Morris Halle*, 232–286. New York, NY: Holt, Rinehart & Winston.

Chomsky, Noam. 1977. On wh-movement. In Peter W. Culicover, Thomas Wasow & Adrian Akmajian (eds.), *Formal syntax*, 71–133. New York, San Francisco & London: Academic Press.

Chomsky, Noam. 1981. *Lectures on government and binding: The Pisa lectures.* Dordrecht: Foris.

Chomsky, Noam. 1982. *Some concepts and consequences of the theory of government and binding.* Cambridge, MA & London: MIT Press.

Chomsky, Noam. 1986a. *Barriers.* Cambridge, MA & London: MIT Press.

Chomsky, Noam. 1986b. *Knowledge of language: Its nature, origin, and use.* New York, NY: Praeger.

Chomsky, Noam. 1993. A minimalist program for linguistic theory. In Kenneth L. Hale, Samuel Jay Keyser & Sylvain Bromberger (eds.), *The view from Building 20: Essays in linguistics in honor of Sylvain Bromberger*, 1–52. Cambridge, MA: MIT Press.

Chomsky, Noam. 1995a. Bare phrase structure. In Héctor Campos & Paula Marie Kempchinsky (eds.), *Evolution and revolution in linguistic theory*, 51–109. Washington, DC: Georgetown University Press.

Chomsky, Noam. 1995b. *The minimalist program.* Cambridge, MA & London: MIT Press.

Chomsky, Noam. 2001. Derivation by phase. In Michael Kenstowicz (ed.), *Ken Hale: A life in language*, 1–52. Cambridge, MA: MIT Press.

Chomsky, Noam. 2004. Beyond explanatory adequacy. In Adriana Belletti (ed.), *Structures and beyond*, 104–131. Oxford: Oxford University Press.

Chomsky, Noam. 2008. On phases. In Robert Freidin, Carlos P. Otero & Maria Luisa Zubizarreta (eds.), *Foundational issues in linguistic theory: Essays in honor of Jean-Roger Vergnaud*, 133–166. Cambridge, MA & London: MIT Press.

Chomsky, Noam. 2013. Problems of projection. *Lingua* 130. 33–49.

Chomsky, Noam. 2015. Problems of projection: Extensions. In Elisa Di Domenico, Cornelia Hamann & Simona Metteini (eds.), *Structures, strategies, and beyond: Studies in honour of Adriana Belletti*, 3–16. Amsterdam & Philadelphia: John Benjamins.

Cinque, Guglielmo. 1990. *Types of A'-dependencies.* Cambridge, MA & London: MIT Press.

Citko, Barbara. 2005. On the nature of merge: External merge, internal merge, and parallel merge. *Linguistic Inquiry* 36(4). 475–496.

Citko, Barbara. 2011a. Multidominance. In Cedric Boeckx (ed.), *The Oxford handbook of linguistic minimalism*, 119–142. Oxford: Oxford University Press.

Citko, Barbara. 2011b. *Symmetry in syntax: Merge, move, and labels*. Cambridge: Cambridge University Press.
Clifton, Charles, Jr. & Lyn Frazier. 1989. Comprehending sentences with long-distance dependencies. In Michael Tanenhaus & Gregory Carlson (eds.), *Linguistic structure in language processing*, 273–317. Dordrecht: Kluwer.
Comrie, Bernard. 1976. *Aspect: An introduction to the study of verbal aspect and related problems*. Cambridge: Cambridge University Press.
Copley, Bridget & Phillip Wolff. 2014. Theories of causation should inform linguistic theory and vice versa. In Bridget Copley & Fabienne Martin (eds.), *Causation in grammatical structures*, 11–57. Oxford: Oxford University Press.
Corver, Norbert. 2006. Subextraction. In Martin Everaert & Henk van Riemsdijk (eds.), *The Blackwell companion to syntax*, vol. 4, 566–600. Malden, MA & Oxford: Blackwell.
Cowart, Wayne. 1997. *Experimental syntax: Applying objective methods to sentence judgments*. Thousand Oaks, CA: SAGE.
Croft, William. 2012. *Verbs: Aspect and causal structure*. Oxford: Oxford University Press.
Croft, William, Jóhanna Barðdal, Willem Hollmann, Violeta Sotirova & Chiaki Taoka. 2010. Revisiting Talmy's typological classification of complex event constructions. In Hans C. Boas (ed.), *Contrastive studies in construction grammar*, 201–235. Amsterdam & Philadelphia: John Benjamins.
Culicover, Peter W. 1999. *Syntactic nuts: Hard cases, syntactic theory, and language acquisition*. Oxford: Oxford University Press.
Culicover, Peter W. 2001. Parasitic gaps: A history. In Peter W. Culicover & Paul M. Postal (eds.), *Parasitic gaps*, 3–68. Cambridge, MA: MIT Press.
Culicover, Peter W. & Ray Jackendoff. 2005. *Simpler syntax*. Oxford: Oxford University Press.
Culicover, Peter W., Giuseppe Varaschin & Susanne Winkler. 2022. The radical unacceptability hypothesis: Accounting for unacceptability without universal constraints. *Languages* 7(2). Article 96. https://doi.org/10.3390/languages7020096.
Culicover, Peter W. & Susanne Winkler. 2018. Freezing: Between grammar and processing. In Jutta M. Hartmann, Marion Jäger, Andreas Kehl, Andreas Konietzko & Susanne Winkler (eds.), *Freezing: Theoretical approaches and empirical domains*, 353–386. Berlin & New York: Mouton de Gruyter.
Culicover, Peter W. & Susanne Winkler. 2022. Parasitic gaps aren't parasitic, or, the case of the uninvited guest. *The Linguistic Review* 39(1). 1–35.
Danks, David. 2009. The psychology of causal perception and reasoning. In Helen Beebee, Christopher Hitchcock & Peter Menzies (eds.), *The Oxford handbook of causation*, 447–470. Oxford: Oxford University Press.
Davidson, Donald. 1967. The logical form of action sentences. In Nicholas Rescher (ed.), *The logic of decision and action*, 81–120. Pittsburgh: University of Pittsburgh Press.
Deane, Paul D. 1991. Limits to attention: A cognitive theory of island phenomena. *Cognitive Linguistics* 2(2). 1–63.
Deane, Paul D. 1992. *Grammar in mind and brain: Explorations in cognitive syntax*. Berlin: Mouton de Gruyter.
Demonte, Violeta. 1988. Remarks on secondary predicates: C-command, extraction, and reanalysis. *The Linguistic Review* 6. 1–39.
Demonte, Violeta. 1992. Temporal and aspectual constraints on predicative adjective phrases. In Héctor Campos & Fernando Martínez-Gil (eds.), *Current studies in Spanish linguistics*, 165–200. Washington, DC: Georgetown University Press.

Diesing, Molly. 1992. *Indefinites*. Cambridge, MA: MIT Press.
den Dikken, Marcel. 2010a. Directions from the GET-GO: On the syntax of manner-of-motion verbs in directional constructions. *Catalan Journal of Linguistics* 9. 23–53.
den Dikken, Marcel. 2010b. On the functional structure of locative and directional PPs. In Guglielmo Cinque & Luigi Rizzi (eds.), *Mapping spatial PPs*, 74–126. Oxford: Oxford University Press.
den Dikken, Marcel. 2018. *Dependency and directionality*. Cambridge: Cambridge University Press.
Dowty, David R. 1979. *Word meaning and Montague grammar: The semantics of verbs and times in generative semantics and in Montague's PTQ*. Dordrecht: Reidel.
Dowty, David R. 1991. Thematic proto-roles and argument selection. *Language* 67(3). 547–619.
Eager, Christopher & Joseph Roy. 2017. Mixed effects models are sometimes terrible. Manuscript, University of Illinois.
Embick, David. 2004. On the structure of resultative participles in English. *Linguistic Inquiry* 35(3). 355–392.
Emonds, Joseph. 2009. Valuing V features and N features: What adjuncts tell us about case, agreement, and syntax in general. In José M. Brucart, Anna Gavarró & Jaume Solà (eds.), *Merging features: Computation, interpretation, and acquisition*, 194–214. Oxford University Press.
Engdahl, Elisabet. 1980. *The syntax and semantics of questions in Swedish*. Amherst, MA: University of Massachusetts dissertation.
Engdahl, Elisabet. 1983. Parasitic gaps. *Linguistics & Philosophy* 6(1). 5–34.
Epstein, Samuel David, Hisatsugu Kitahara & Daniel Seely. 2012. Structure building that can't be. In Myriam Uribe-Etxebarria & Vidal Valmala (eds.), *Ways of structure building*, 253–270. Oxford: Oxford University Press.
Ernst, Thomas. 2002. *The syntax of adjuncts*. Cambridge: Cambridge University Press.
Ernst, Thomas. 2022. The adjunct condition and the nature of adjuncts. *The Linguistic Review* 39(1). 85–128.
Erteschik-Shir, Nomi. 1973. *On the nature of island constraints*. Cambridge, MA: Massachusetts Institute of Technology dissertation.
Erteschik-Shir, Nomi. 1997. *The dynamics of focus structure*. Cambridge: Cambridge University Press.
Erteschik-Shir, Nomi. 2007. *Information structure: The syntax–discourse interface*. Oxford: Oxford University Press.
Erteschik-Shir, Nomi & Shalom Lappin. 1979. Dominance and the functional explanation of island phenomena. *Theoretical Linguistics* 6. 41–86.
Erteschik-Shir, Nomi & Tova R. Rapoport. 2005. Path predicates. In Nomi Erteschik-Shir & Tova R. Rapoport (eds.), *The syntax of aspect: Deriving thematic and aspectual interpretation*, 65–86. Oxford: Oxford University Press.
Fábregas, Antonio & Ángel L. Jiménez-Fernández. 2016a. Extraction from gerunds and the internal syntax of verbs. *Linguistics* 54(6). 1307–1354.
Fábregas, Antonio & Ángel L. Jiménez-Fernández. 2016b. Extraction out of adjectival secondary predicates in English and Spanish: A nanosyntactic account. *Questions and Answers in Linguistics* 3(2). 41–56.
Fabricius-Hansen, Cathrine & Dag T. T. Haug. 2012a. Co-eventive adjuncts: Main issues and clarifications. In Cathrine Fabricius-Hansen & Dag T. T. Haug (eds.), *Big events, small clauses: The grammar of elaboration*, 21–54. Berlin & Boston: de Gruyter.

Fabricius-Hansen, Cathrine & Dag T. T. Haug. 2012b. Introduction. In Cathrine Fabricius-Hansen & Dag T. T. Haug (eds.), *Big events, small clauses: The grammar of elaboration*, 1–17. Berlin & Boston: de Gruyter.
Farrell, Jake Andrew. 2019. Depictive secondary predication and the correlates of inner aspect. *University of Pennsylvania Working Papers in Linguistics* 25(1). 99–108.
Featherston, Sam. 2008. The decathlon model of empirical syntax. In Stephan Kepser & Marga Reis (eds.), *Linguistic evidence: Empirical, theoretical and computational perspectives*, Berlin: Mouton de Gruyter.
Featherston, Sam. 2009. A scale for measuring well-formedness: Why syntax needs boiling and freezing points. In Sam Featherston & Susanne Winkler (eds.), *The fruits of empirical linguistics, vol. 1: Process*, 47–74. Berlin: de Gruyter.
Featherston, Sam. 2011. Three types of exceptions: And all of them rule-based. In Horst J. Simon & Heike Wiese (eds.), *Expecting the unexpected: Exceptions in grammar*, 291–323. Berlin & New York: Mouton de Gruyter.
Featherston, Sam. 2019. The decathlon model. In András Kertész, Edith Moravcsik & Csilla Rákosi (eds.), *Current approaches to syntax: A comparative handbook*, 155–186. Berlin & Boston: Mouton de Gruyter.
Filip, Hana. 2012. Lexical aspect. In Robert I. Binnick (ed.), *The Oxford handbook of tense and aspect*, 721–751. Oxford: Oxford University Press.
Fleischhauer, Jens. 2016. *Degree gradation of verbs*. Düsseldorf: Düsseldorf University Press.
Fodor, Janet Dean. 1978. Parsing strategies and constraints on transformations. *Linguistic Inquiry* 9(3). 427–476.
Fortmann, Christian. 2015. Present participle depictive predicates. In Christian Fortmann, Anja Lübbe & Irene Rapp (eds.), *Situationsargumente im Nominalbereich*, 219–258. Berlin & Boston: de Gruyter.
Friedmann, Naama, Gina Taranto, Lewis P. Shapiro & David A. Swinney. 2008. The leaf fell (the leaf): The online processing of unaccusatives. *Linguistic Inquiry* 39(3). 355–377.
Gawron, Jean Mark. 2005. Generalized paths. In *Proceedings of Semantics and Linguistic Theory (SALT)*, vol. 15, 309–326.
Gawron, Jean Mark. 2009. The lexical semantics of extent verbs. Manuscript, San Diego State University.
Gehrke, Berit. 2019. Event kinds. In Robert Truswell (ed.), *The Oxford handbook of event structure*, 205–233. Oxford: Oxford University Press.
Gerbrich, Hannah, Vivian Schreier & Sam Featherston. 2019. Standard items for English judgment studies: Syntax and semantics. In Sam Featherston, Robin Hörnig, Sophie von Wietersheim & Susanne Winkler (eds.), *Experiments in focus: Information structure and semantic processing*, 305–328. Boston & Berlin: de Gruyter.
Geuder, Wilhelm. 2000. *Oriented adverbs: Issues in the lexical semantics of event adverbs*. Tübingen: Universität Tübingen dissertation.
Geuder, Wilhelm. 2004. Depictives and transparent adverbs. In Jennifer R. Austin, Stefan Engelberg & Gisa Rauh (eds.), *Adverbials: The interplay between meaning, context, and syntactic structure*, 131–166. Amsterdam & Philadelphia: John Benjamins.
Gibson, Edward. 1998. Linguistic complexity: Locality of syntactic dependencies. *Cognition* 68. 1–76.
Gibson, Edward. 2000. The dependency locality theory: A distance-based theory of linguistic complexity. In Alec Marantz, Yasushi Miyashita & Wayne O'Neil (eds.), *Image, language, brain*, 95–126. Cambridge, MA: MIT Press.

Gibson, Edward, Barbara Hemforth, Elodie Winckel & Anne Abeillé. 2021. Acceptability of extraction out of adjuncts depends on discourse factors. Paper presented at the CUNY conference on human sentence processing.

Gibson, Edward, Steve Piantadosi & Kristina Fedorenko. 2011. Using Mechanical Turk to obtain and analyze English acceptability judgments. *Language and Linguistics Compass* 5(8). 509–524.

Goldberg, Adele E. 2006. *Constructions at work: The nature of generalization in language.* Oxford: Oxford University Press.

Goldberg, Adele E. 2013. Backgrounded constituents cannot be "extracted". In Jon Sprouse & Norbert Hornstein (eds.), *Experimental syntax and island effects*, 221–238. Cambridge: Cambridge University Press.

Goodall, Grant. 2015. The D-linking effect on extraction from islands and non-islands. *Frontiers in Psychology* 5. Article 1493. https://doi.org/10.3389/fpsyg.2014.01493.

Goodall, Grant. 2021. Sentence acceptability experiments: What, how, and why. In Grant Goodall (ed.), *The Cambridge handbook of experimental syntax*, 7–38. Cambridge: Cambridge University Press.

Graf, Thomas. 2015. The syntactic algebra of adjuncts. In *Proceedings of the Chicago Linguistic Society (CLS)*, vol. 49, 101–113.

Greco, Ciro, Marco Marelli & Liliane Haegeman. 2017. External syntax and the Cumulative Effect in subject sub-extraction: An experimental evaluation. *The Linguistic Review* 34(3). 479–531.

Grice, Paul Herbert. 1975. Logic and conversation. In Peter Cole & Jerry L. Morgan (eds.), *Syntax and Semantics 3: Speech acts*, 41–58. New York, NY: Academic Press.

Grimshaw, Jane. 1990. *Argument structure.* Cambridge, MA & London: MIT Press.

Haegeman, Liliane. 1985. The 'get'-passive and Burzio's generalization. *Lingua* 66. 53–77.

Haegeman, Liliane. 2010. The internal syntax of adverbial clauses. *Lingua* 120. 628–648.

Haegeman, Liliane. 2012. *The cartography of syntactic structures 8: Adverbial clauses, main clause phenomena, and the composition of the left periphery.* Oxford: Oxford University Press.

Haegeman, Liliane, Ángel L. Jiménez-Fernández & Andrew Radford. 2014. Deconstructing the subject condition in terms of cumulative constraint violation. *The Linguistic Review* 31(1). 73–150.

Hale, Kenneth L. & Samuel Jay Keyser. 1993. On argument structure and the lexical expression of semantic relations. In Kenneth L. Hale, Samuel Jay Keyser & Sylvain Bromberger (eds.), *The view from Building 20: Essays in linguistics in honor of Sylvain Bromberger*, 53–109. Cambridge, MA: MIT Press.

Hale, Kenneth L. & Samuel Jay Keyser. 2002. *Prolegomenon to a theory of argument structure.* Cambridge, MA & London: MIT Press.

Hale, Kenneth L. & Samuel Jay Keyser. 2005. Aspect and the syntax of argument structure. In Nomi Erteschik-Shir & Tova R. Rapoport (eds.), *The syntax of aspect: Deriving thematic and aspectual interpretation*, 11–41. Oxford: Oxford University Press.

Halliday, Michael A. K. 1967a. Notes on transitivity and theme in English, part 1. *Journal of Linguistics* 3(1). 37–81.

Halliday, Michael A. K. 1967b. Notes on transitivity and theme in English, part 2. *Journal of Linguistics* 3(2). 199–244.

Harley, Heidi. 2005. How do verbs get their names? Denominal verbs, manner incorporation, and the ontology of verb roots in English. In Nomi Erteschik-Shir & Tova R. Rapoport (eds.), *The syntax of aspect: Deriving thematic and aspectual interpretation*, 42–64. Oxford: Oxford University Press.

Harley, Heidi. 2013. External arguments and the mirror principle: On the distinctness of Voice and v. *Lingua* 125. 34–57.

Haspelmath, Martin. 1995. The converb as a cross-linguistically valid category. In Martin Haspelmath & Ekkehard König (eds.), *Converbs in cross-linguistic perspective: Structure and meaning of adverbial verb forms – Adverbial participles, gerunds*, 1–55. Berlin & New York: Mouton de Gruyter.

Hatav, Galia. 2020. Verb phrase secondary predication: Biblical Hebrew as a case study. *Linguistics* 58(2). 363–378.

Haug, Dag T. T., Cathrine Fabricius-Hansen, Bergljot Behrens & Hans Petter Helland. 2012. Open adjuncts: Degrees of integration. In Cathrine Fabricius-Hansen & Dag T. T. Haug (eds.), *Big events, small clauses: The grammar of elaboration*, 131–178. Berlin & Boston: de Gruyter.

Hawkins, John A. 1999. Processing complexity and filler–gap dependencies across grammars. *Language* 75(2). 244–285.

Hawkins, John A. 2004. *Efficiency and complexity in grammars*. Oxford: Oxford University Press.

Hay, Jennifer, Christopher Kennedy & Beth Levin. 1999. Scalar structure underlies telicity in "degree achievements". In *Proceedings of Semantics and Linguistic Theory (SALT)*, vol. 9, 127–144.

Helland, Hans Petter & Anneliese Pitz. 2012. Open adjuncts: Participial syntax. In Cathrine Fabricius-Hansen & Dag T. T. Haug (eds.), *Big events, small clauses: The grammar of elaboration*, 93–130. Berlin & Boston: de Gruyter.

Hengeveld, Kees. 1998. Adverbial clauses in the languages of Europe. In Johan van der Auwera (ed.), *Adverbial constructions in the languages of Europe*, 335–419. Berlin & New York: Mouton de Gruyter.

Higginbotham, James. 2004. The English progressive. In Jacqueline Guéron & Jacqueline Lecarme (eds.), *The syntax of time*, 329–358. Cambridge, MA & London: MIT Press.

Higginbotham, James. 2009. *Tense, aspect, and indexicality*. Oxford: Oxford University Press.

Himmelmann, Nikolaus P. & Eva Schultze-Berndt. 2005. Issues in the syntax and semantics of participant-oriented adjuncts: An introduction. In Nikolaus P. Himmelmann & Eva Schultze-Berndt (eds.), *Secondary predication and adverbial modification: The typology of depictives*, 1–67. Oxford: Oxford University Press.

Hirose, Tomio. 2003. The syntax of D-linking. *Linguistic Inquiry* 34(3). 499–506.

Hobbs, Jerry R. 1979. Coherence and coreference. *Cognitive Science* 3. 67–90.

Hobbs, Jerry R. 1990. *Literature and cognition*. Stanford, CA: CSLI.

Hoekstra, Teun & René Mulder. 1990. Unergatives as copular verbs: Locational and existential predication. *The Linguistic Review* 7. 1–79.

Hofmeister, Philip, Peter W. Culicover & Susanne Winkler. 2015. Effects of processing on the acceptability of "frozen" extraposed constituents. *Syntax* 18(4). 464–483.

Hofmeister, Philip & Ivan A. Sag. 2010. Cognitive constraints and island effects. *Language* 86(2). 366–415.

Hofmeister, Philip, Laura Staum Casasanto & Ivan A. Sag. 2013. Islands in the grammar? Standards of evidence. In Jon Sprouse & Norbert Hornstein (eds.), *Experimental syntax and island effects*, 42–63. Cambridge: Cambridge University Press.

Hole, Daniel. 2015. Arguments and adjuncts. In Tibor Kiss & Artemis Alexiadou (eds.), *Syntax – Theory and analysis: An international handbook*, vol. 2, 1285–1320. Berlin, Munich & Boston: Mouton de Gruyter.

Hopper, Paul J. & Sandra A. Thompson. 1980. Transitivity in grammar and discourse. *Language* 56(2). 251–299.

Hörnig, Robin, Sam Featherston, Sophie von Wietersheim & Susanne Winkler. 2019. Markedness in context: An approach to licensing. In Sam Featherston, Robin Hörnig, Sophie von Wietersheim & Susanne Winkler (eds.), *Experiments in focus: Information structure and semantic processing* (Linguistische Arbeiten 571), 1–15. Boston & Berlin: de Gruyter.

Hornstein, Norbert. 2009. *A theory of syntax: Minimal operations and universal grammar*. Cambridge: Cambridge University Press.

Hornstein, Norbert & Jairo Nunes. 2008. Adjunction, labeling, and bare phrase structure. *Biolinguistics* 2(1). 57–86.

Hornstein, Norbert, Jairo Nunes & Kleanthes K. Grohmann. 2005. *Understanding minimalism*. Cambridge: Cambridge University Press.

Horrocks, Geoffrey & Melita Stavrou. 2007. Grammaticalized aspect and spatio-temporal culmination. *Lingua* 117. 605–644.

van Hout, Angeliek. 2004. Unaccusativity as telicity checking. In Artemis Alexiadou, Elena Anagnostopoulou & Martin Everaert (eds.), *The unaccusative puzzle: Explorations of the syntax-lexicon interface*, 60–83. Oxford: Oxford University Press.

Hu, Xuhui. 2018. *Encoding events: Functional structure and variation*. Oxford: Oxford University Press.

Huang, Cheng-Teh James. 1982. *Logical relations in Chinese and the theory of grammar*. Cambridge, MA: Massachusetts Institute of Technology dissertation.

Huddleston, Rodney & Geoffrey K. Pullum. 2002. *The Cambridge grammar of the English language*. Cambridge: Cambridge University Press.

Hunter, Timothy Andrew. 2011. *Syntactic effects of conjunctivist semantics: Unifying movement and adjunction*. Amsterdam & Philadelphia: John Benjamins.

Irimia, Monica-Alexandrina. 2012. *Secondary predicates*. Toronto: University of Toronto dissertation.

Irwin, Patricia. 2011. Intransitive sentences, argument structure, and the syntax-prosody interface. In *Proceedings of the West Coast Conference on Formal Linguistics (WCCFL)*, vol. 28, 275–284.

Irwin, Patricia. 2012. *Unaccusativity at the interfaces*. New York, NY: New York University dissertation.

Irwin, Patricia. 2018. Existential unaccusativity and new discourse referents. *Glossa* 3(1). Article 24. https://doi.org/10.5334/gjgl.283.

Irwin, Patricia. 2020. Unaccusativity and theticity. In Werner Abraham, Elisabeth Leiss & Yasuhiro Fujinawa (eds.), *Thetics and categoricals*, 199–222. Amsterdam & Philadelphia: John Benjamins.

Jackendoff, Ray. 1990. *Semantic structures*. Cambridge, MA: MIT Press.

Jackendoff, Ray. 1996. The proper treatment of measuring out, telicity, and perhaps even quantification in English. *Natural Language & Linguistic Theory* 14(2). 305–354.

Jaeger, T. Florian. 2009. Random effect: Should I stay or should I go? Accessed 2022-10-28. https://hlplab.wordpress.com/2009/05/14/random-effect-structure/.

Jäger, Marion. 2020. *Focus particles and extraction: An experimental investigation of German and English focus particles in constructions with leftward association*. Tübingen: Universitätsbibliothek Tübingen.

Jiménez-Fernández, Ángel L. 2009. On the composite nature of subject islands: A phase-based approach. *SKY Journal of Linguistics* 22. 91–138.

Jin, Dawei. 2015. Coherence relation and clause linkage: Towards a discourse approach to adjunct islands in Chinese. *Studies in Language* 39(2). 424–458.

Johnson, Kyle. 2003. Towards an etiology of adjunct islands. *Nordlyd* 31(1). 187–215.

Jurka, Johannes. 2010. *The importance of being a complement: CED-effects revisited*. College Park, MD: University of Maryland dissertation.

Jurka, Johannes. 2013. Subject islands in German revisited. In Jon Sprouse & Norbert Hornstein (eds.), *Experimental syntax and island effects*, 265–285. Cambridge: Cambridge University Press.

Kamp, Hans & Uwe Reyle. 1993. *From discourse to logic: Introduction to modeltheoretic semantics of natural language, formal logic and discourse representation theory*. Dordrecht: Springer.

Kassambara, Alboukadel. 2020. ggpubr: 'ggplot2' based publication ready plots. R package version 0.4.0. https://cran.r-project.org/package=ggpubr.

Kearns, Kate. 2007. Telic senses of deadjectival verbs. *Lingua* 117. 26–66.

Kehler, Andrew. 2000. Coherence and the resolution of ellipsis. *Linguistics & Philosophy* 23. 553–575.

Kehler, Andrew. 2002. *Coherence, reference, and the theory of grammar*. Stanford, CA: CSLI Publications.

Kehler, Andrew. 2019. Coherence relations. In Robert Truswell (ed.), *The Oxford handbook of event structure*, 583–604. Oxford: Oxford University Press.

Keller, Frank. 2000. *Gradience in grammar: Experimental and computational aspects of degrees of grammaticality*. Edinburgh: University of Edinburgh dissertation.

Kennedy, Christopher. 2012. The composition of incremental change. In Violeta Demonte & Louise McNally (eds.), *Telicity, change, and state: A cross-categorial view of event structure*, 103–121. Oxford: Oxford University Press.

Kennedy, Christopher & Beth Levin. 2002. Telicity corresponds to degree of change. Handout, Topics in the grammar of scalar expressions, University of California Los Angeles.

Kennedy, Christopher & Beth Levin. 2008. Measure of change: The adjectival core of degree achievements. In Louise McNally & Christopher Kennedy (eds.), *Adjectives and adverbs: Syntax, semantics, and discourse*, 156–182. Oxford: Oxford University Press.

Kennedy, Christopher & Louise McNally. 2005. Scale structure and the semantic typology of gradable predicates. *Language* 81(2). 345–381.

Kluender, Robert & Marta Kutas. 1993. Subjacency as a processing phenomenon. *Language and Cognitive Processes* 8(4). 573–633.

Kohrt, Annika, Trey Sorensen & Dustin A. Chacón. 2018. The real-time status of semantic exceptions to the adjunct island constraint. Manuscript, University of Minnesota.

Kohrt, Annika, Trey Sorensen, Peter O'Neill & Dustin A. Chacón. 2020. Inactive gap formation: An ERP study on the processing of extraction from adjunct clauses. In *Proceedings of the Linguistic Society of America (LSA)*, vol. 5 1, 807–821.

Konietzko, Andreas. 2018. Heavy NP shift in context: On the interaction of information structure and subextraction from shifted constituents. In Jutta M. Hartmann, Marion Jäger, Andreas Kehl, Andreas Konietzko & Susanne Winkler (eds.), *Freezing: Theoretical approaches and empirical domains*, 387–402. Berlin & Boston: Mouton de Gruyter.

Konietzko, Andreas. 2021. PP extraction from subject islands in German. Manuscript, University of Tübingen. Accepted for publication in *Glossa*.

Konietzko, Andreas, Susanne Winkler & Peter W. Culicover. 2018. Heavy NP shift does not cause freezing. *Canadian Journal of Linguistics/La Revue Canadienne de Linguistique* 63(3). 454–464.

König, Ekkehard. 1995. The meaning of converb constructions. In Martin Haspelmath & Ekkehard König (eds.), *Converbs in cross-linguistic perspective: Structure and meaning of adverbial verb forms – Adverbial participles, gerunds*, 57–95. Berlin & New York: Mouton de Gruyter.

Kortmann, Bernd. 1995. Adverbial participial clauses in English. In Martin Haspelmath & Ekkehard König (eds.), *Converbs in cross-linguistic perspective: Structure and meaning of adverbial verb forms – Adverbial participles, gerunds*, 189–237. Berlin & New York: Mouton de Gruyter.

Koster, Jan. 1987. *Domains and dynasties: The radical autonomy of syntax*. Dordrecht & Providence: Foris.

Kratzer, Angelika. 1995. Stage-level and individual-level predicates. In Gregory Carlson & Francis Jeffry Pelletier (eds.), *The generic book*, 125–175. Chicago & London: University of Chicago Press.

Kratzer, Angelika. 1996. Severing the external argument from its verb. In Johan Rooryck & Laurie Zaring (eds.), *Phrase structure and the lexicon*, 109–137. Dordrecht: Kluwer.

Kratzer, Angelika. 2005. Building resultatives. In Claudia Maienborn & Angelika Wöllstein (eds.), *Event arguments: Foundations and applications*, 177–212. Tübingen: Niemeyer.

Krifka, Manfred. 1998. The origins of telicity. In Susan Rothstein (ed.), *Events and grammar*, 197–235. Dordrecht, Boston & London: Kluwer.

Kuno, Susumu. 1987. *Functional syntax: Anaphora, discourse and empathy*. Chicago & London: The University of Chicago Press.

Kuroda, Sige-Yuki. 1972. The categorical and the thetic judgment. *Foundations of Language* 9(2). 152–185.

Kush, Dave, Terje Lohndal & Jon Sprouse. 2018. Investigating variation in island effects: A case study of Norwegian wh-extraction. *Natural Language & Linguistic Theory* 36(3). 743–779.

Kush, Dave, Terje Lohndal & Jon Sprouse. 2019. On the island sensitivity of topicalization in Norwegian: An experimental investigation. *Language* 95(3). 393–420.

Kuznetsova, Alexandra, Per B. Brockoff & Rune H. B. Christensen. 2017. lmerTest package: Tests in linear mixed effects models. *Journal of Statistical Software* 82(13). 1–26.

Lakoff, George. 1970. *Irregularity in syntax*. New York, NY: Holt, Rinehart & Winston.

van Lambalgen, Michiel & Fritz Hamm. 2005. *The proper treatment of events*. Malden, MA: Blackwell.

Lambrecht, Knud. 1994. *Information structure and sentence form: Topic, focus, and the mental representations of discourse referents*. Cambridge: Cambridge University Press.

Lasnik, Howard & Mamuro Saito. 1984. On the nature of proper government. *Linguistic Inquiry* 15(2). 235–289.

Lebeaux, David S. 1988. *Language acquisition and the form of the grammar*. Amherst, MA: University of Massachusetts dissertation.

Levin, Beth. 1993. *English verb classes and alternations: A preliminary investigation*. Chicago & London: The University of Chicago Press.

Levin, Beth & Malka Rappaport Hovav. 1995. *Unaccusativity: At the syntax-lexical semantics interface*. Cambridge, MA: MIT Press.

Levin, Beth & Malka Rappaport Hovav. 2013. Lexicalized meaning and manner/result complementarity. In Boban Arsenijević, Berit Gehrke & Rafael Marín (eds.), *Studies in the decomposition of event predicates*, 49–70. Dordrecht: Springer.

Levin, Beth & Malka Rappaport Hovav. 2014. Manner and result: The view from 'clean'. In Rob Pensalfini, Myfany Turpin & Diana Guillemin (eds.), *Language description informed by theory*, 337–357. Amsterdam & Philadelphia: John Benjamins.

Levin, Beth & Malka Rappaport Hovav. 2019. Lexicalization patterns. In Robert Truswell (ed.), *The Oxford handbook of event structure*, 395–425. Oxford: Oxford University Press.

Liu, Yingtong, Elodie Winckel, Anne Abeillé, Barbara Hemforth & Edward Gibson. 2022. Structural, functional, and processing perspectives on linguistic island effects. *Annual Review of Linguistics* 8. 495–525.

Lukassek, Julia, Anna Prysłopska, Robin Hörnig & Claudia Maienborn. 2017. The semantic processing of motion verbs: Coercion or underspecification? *Journal of Psycholinguistic Research* 46. 805–825.

MacDonald, Jonathan E. 2008. *The syntactic nature of inner aspect: A minimalist perspective*. Amsterdam & Philadelphia: John Benjamins.

MacDonald, Jonathan E. 2009. Inner aspect and phases. In Kleanthes K. Grohmann (ed.), *Explorations of phase theory: Features and arguments*, 207–229. Berlin & New York: Mouton de Gruyter.

Maienborn, Claudia. 2004. A pragmatic explanation of the stage level/individual level contrast in combination with locatives. In *Proceedings of the Western Conference on Linguistics (WECOL)*, vol. 15, 158–170.

Maienborn, Claudia. 2005. On the limits of the Davidsonian approach: The case of copular sentences. *Theoretical Linguistics* 31. 275–316.

Maienborn, Claudia. 2019. Events and states. In Robert Truswell (ed.), *The Oxford handbook of event structure*, 50–89. Oxford: Oxford University Press.

Manzini, Maria Rita. 1992. *Locality: A theory and some of its empirical consequences*. Cambridge, MA & London: MIT Press.

Mateu, Jaume & Víctor Acedo-Matellán. 2012. The manner/result complementarity revisited: A syntactic approach. In María Cristina Cuervo & Yves Roberge (eds.), *The end of argument structure?*, 209–228. Bingley: Emerald.

Matić, Dejan. 2014. Questions and syntactic islands in Tundra Yukaghir. In Rik van Gijn, Jeremy Hammond, Dejan Matić, Saskia van Putten & Ana Vailacy Galucio (eds.), *Information structure and reference tracking in complex sentences*, 127–161. Amsterdam & Philadelphia: John Benjamins.

Matuschek, Hannes, Reinhold Kliegl, Shravan Vasishth, Harald Baayen & Douglas Bates. 2017. Balancing Type I error and power in linear mixed models. *Journal of Memory and Language* 94. 305–315.

McIntyre, Andrew. 2004. Event paths, conflation, argument structure, and VP shells. *Linguistics* 42(3). 523–571.

McIntyre, Andrew. 2005. The semantic and syntactic decomposition of get: An interaction between verb meaning and particle placement. *Journal of Semantics* 22(4). 401–438.

McIntyre, Andrew. 2012. The BECOME=CAUSE hypothesis and the polysemy of 'get'. *Linguistics* 50(6). 1251–1287.

McNally, Louise. 1994. Adjunct predicates and the individual/stage distinction. In *Proceedings of the West Coast Conference on Formal Linguistics (WCCFL)*, vol. 12, 561–576.

McNally, Louise. 1997. *A semantics for the English existential construction*. New York, NY: Garland.

Merchant, Jason. 2001. *The syntax of silence: Sluicing, islands, and the theory of ellipsis*. Oxford: Oxford University Press.

Miller, Gerorge A. & Noam Chomsky. 1963. Finitary models of language users. In R. Duncan Luce, Robert R. Bush & Eugene Galanter (eds.), *Handbook of mathematical psychology*, vol. 2, 419–491. New York, NY: Wiley.

Mittwoch, Anita. 1991. In defence of Vendler's achievements. *Journal of Belgian Linguistics* 6(1). 71–84.

Mittwoch, Anita. 2019. Aspectual classes. In Robert Truswell (ed.), *The Oxford handbook of event structure*, 31–49. Oxford: Oxford University Press.

Miyamoto, Yoichi. 2012. On transparent adjuncts in Japanese. In Myriam Uribe-Etxebarria & Vidal Valmala (eds.), *Ways of structure building*, 330–365. Oxford: Oxford University Press.

Moens, Marc & Mark Steedman. 1988. Temporal ontology and temporal reference. *Computational Linguistics* 14(2). 15–28.

Mourelatos, Alexander P. D. 1978. Events, processes, and states. *Linguistics & Philosophy* 2. 415–434.

Müller, Christiane. 2017. Extraction from adjunct islands in Swedish. *Norsk Lingvistik Tidsskrift* 35. 67–85.

Müller, Christiane. 2019. *Permeable islands: A contrastive study of Swedish and English adjunct clause extractions*. Lund: Centre for Languages and Literature, Lund University.

Müller, Gereon. 1995. *A-bar syntax: A study in movement types*. Berlin & New York: Mouton de Gruyter.

Müller, Gereon. 2010. On deriving CED effects from the PIC. *Linguistic Inquiry* 41(1). 35–82.

Müller, Gereon. 2011. *Constraints on displacement: A phase-based approach*. Amsterdam & Philadelphia: John Benjamins.

Müller, Sonja. 2011. *Extraktionsinseln: Zu ihrer Syntax, Semantik und Informationsstruktur*. Trier: Wissenschaftlicher Verlag Trier.

Narita, Hiroki. 2014. *Endocentric structuring of projection-free syntax*. Amsterdam & Philadelphia: John Benjamins.

Nedjalkov, Igor' V. 1998. Converbs in the languages of Europe. In Johan van der Auwera (ed.), *Adverbial constructions in the languages of Europe*, 421–455. Berlin & New York: Mouton de Gruyter.

Neeleman, Ad & Reiko Vermeulen. 2012. The syntactic expression of information structure. In Ad Neeleman & Reiko Vermeulen (eds.), *The syntax of topic, focus, and contrast: An interface-based approach*, 1–38. Berlin & Boston: Mouton de Gruyter.

Newmeyer, Frederick J. 2016. Nonsyntactic explanations of island constraints. *Annual Review of Linguistics* 2. 187–210.

Norman, Geoff. 2010. Likert scales, levels of measurement and the "laws" of statistics. *Advances in Health Science Education* 15. 625–632.

Nunes, Jairo & Juan Uriagereka. 2000. Cyclicity and extraction domains. *Syntax* 3(1). 20–43.

Nyvad, Anne Mette, Christiane Müller & Ken Ramshøj Christensen. 2022. Too good to be true? The non-uniformity of extraction from adjunct clauses in English. *Languages* 7(4). Article 244. https://doi.org/10.3390/languages7040244.

Onea, Edgar & Malte Zimmermann. 2019. Questions in discourse: An overview. In Klaus von Heusinger, Malte Zimmermann & Edgar Onea (eds.), *Questions in discourse, vol. 1: Semantics*, 5–117. Leiden & Boston: Brill.

Oseki, Yohei. 2015. Eliminating pair-merge. In *Proceedings of the West Coast Conference on Formal Linguistics (WCCFL)*, vol. 32, 303–312.

Pancheva, Roumyana. 2003. The aspectual makeup of perfect participles and the interpretations of the perfect. In Artemis Alexiadou, Monika Rathert & Arnim von Stechow (eds.), *Perfect explorations*, 277–306. Berlin & New York: Mouton de Gruyter.
París, Luis Alberto. 2003. *Grammatical encoding of event relations: Gerund phrases in Spanish*. New York, NY: State University of New York dissertation.
Parsons, Terence. 1990. *Events in the semantics of English: A study in subatomic events*. Cambridge, MA & London: MIT Press.
Perlmutter, David M. 1978. Impersonal passives and the unaccusative hypothesis. In *Proceedings of the Berkeley Linguistics Society (BLS)*, vol. 38, 157–189.
Pesetsky, David. 1987. Wh-in situ: Movement and unselective binding. In Eric Reuland & Alice G. B. ter Meulen (eds.), *The representation of (in)definiteness*, 98–129. Cambridge, MA: MIT Press.
Pesetsky, David. 2000. *Phrasal movement and its kin*. Cambridge, MA & London: MIT Press.
Phillips, Colin. 2013. On the nature of island constraints I: Language processing and reductionist accounts. In Jon Sprouse & Norbert Hornstein (eds.), *Experimental syntax and island effects*, 64–108. Cambridge: Cambridge University Press.
Piñón, Christopher. 2008. Aspectual composition with degrees. In Louise McNally & Christopher Kennedy (eds.), *Adjectives and adverbs: Syntax, semantics, and discourse*, 183–219. Oxford: Oxford University Press.
Pires, Acrisio & Gary Milsark. 2017. Gerundive nominalizations. In Martin Everaert & Henk van Riemsdijk (eds.), *The Wiley Blackwell companion to syntax*, vol. 3. 2nd edn., 1784–1808. Hoboken, NJ: Wiley.
Polinsky, Maria, Carlos G. Gallo, Peter Graff, Ekaterina Kravtchenko, Adam Milton Morgan & Anne Sturgeon. 2013. Subject islands are different. In Jon Sprouse & Norbert Hornstein (eds.), *Experimental syntax and island effects*, 286–309. Cambridge: Cambridge University Press.
Pollard, Carl & Ivan A. Sag. 1994. *Head-Driven Phrase Structure Grammar*. Chicago: University of Chicago Press.
Portner, Paul. 2011. Perfect and progressive. In Klaus von Heusinger, Claudia Maienborn & Paul Portner (eds.), *Semantics: An international handbook of natural language meaning*, vol. 2, 1217–1261. Berlin & Boston: Mouton de Gruyter.
Potts, Christopher. 2005. *The logic of conventional implicatures*. Oxford: Oxford University Press.
Progovac, Ljiljana. 2015. *Evolutionary syntax*. Oxford: Oxford University Press.
Pylkkänen, Liina. 2008. *Introducing arguments*. Cambridge, MA & London: MIT Press.
Quirk, Randolph, Sidney Greenbaum, Geoffrey Leech & Jan Svartvik. 1 972. *A grammar of contemporary English*. London: Longman.
R Core Team. 2020. *R: A language and environment for statistical computing*. Vienna, Austria: R Foundation for Statistical Computing. www.r-project.org/. Version 4.0.2.
Rackowski, Andrea & Norvin Richards. 2005. Phase edge and extraction: A Tagalog case study. *Linguistic Inquiry* 36(4). 565–599.
Ramchand, Gillian Catriona. 2008. *Verb meaning and the lexicon: A first phase s yntax*. Cambridge: Cambridge University Press.
Randall, Janet H. 2010. *Linking: The geometry of argument structure*. Dordrecht: Springer.
Rapoport, Tova R. 1993a. Stage and adjunct predicates: Licensing and structure in secondary predication constructions. In Eric Reuland & Werner Abraham (eds.), *Knowledge and language, vol. 2: Lexical and conceptual structure*, 157–182. Dordrecht, Boston & London: Kluwer.

Rapoport, Tova R. 1993b. Verbs in depictives and resultatives. In James Pustejovsky (ed.), *Semantics and the lexicon*, 163–184. Dordrecht: Kluwer.
Rapoport, Tova R. 1999. Structure, aspect, and the predicate. *Language* 75(4). 653–677.
Rapoport, Tova R. 2019. Secondary predication. In Robert Truswell (ed.), *The Oxford handbook of event structure*, 426–455. Oxford: Oxford University Press.
Rapp, Irene. 2000. The attributive past participle: Structure and temporal interpretation. In Caroline Féry & Wolfgang Sternefeld (eds.), *Audiatur vox sapientiae: A Festschrift for Arnim von Stechow*, 392–409. Berlin: Akademie Verlag.
Rappaport Hovav, Malka. 2008. Lexicalized meaning and the internal temporal structure of events. In Susan Rothstein (ed.), *Theoretical and crosslinguistic approaches to the semantics of aspect*, 13–42. Amsterdam & Philadelphia: John Benjamins.
Rappaport Hovav, Malka. 2014. Building scalar changes. In Artemis Alexiadou, Hagit Borer & Florian Schäfer (eds.), *The syntax of roots and the roots of syntax*, 259–281. Oxford: Oxford University Press.
Rappaport Hovav, Malka & Beth Levin. 1998. Building verb meanings. In Miriam Butt & Wilhelm Geuder (eds.), *The projection of arguments: Lexical and compositional factors*, 97–134. Stanford, CA: CSLI Publications.
Rappaport Hovav, Malka & Beth Levin. 2001. An event structure account of English resultatives. *Language* 77(4). 766–797.
Rappaport Hovav, Malka & Beth Levin. 2010. Reflections on manner/result complementarity. In Malka Rappaport Hovav, Edit Doron & Ivy Sichel (eds.), *Lexical semantics, syntax, and event structure*, 21–38. Oxford: Oxford University Press.
Reinhart, Tanya. 2002. The theta system: An overview. *Theoretical Linguistics* 28. 229–290.
Reinhart, Tanya. 2016. The theta system: Syntactic realization of verbal concepts. In Martin Everaert, Marijana Marelj & Eric Reuland (eds.), *Concepts, syntax, and their interface: The theta system*, 1–111. Cambridge, MA & London: MIT Press.
Reinhart, Tanya & Eric Reuland. 1993. Reflexivity. *Linguistic Inquiry* 24(4). 657–720.
Reinhart, Tanya & Tal Siloni. 2005. The lexicon–syntax parameter: Reflexivization and other arity operations. *Linguistic Inquiry* 36(3). 389–436.
Reuland, Eric. 2006. Binding theory: Terms and concepts. In Martin Everaert & Henk van Riemsdijk (eds.), *The Blackwell companion to syntax*, vol. 1, 260–283. Malden, MA & Oxford: Blackwell.
Richards, Norvin. 2010. *Uttering trees*. Cambridge, MA & London: MIT Press.
van Riemsdijk, Henk. 2006. Grafts follow from merge. In Mara Frascarelli (ed.), *Phases of interpretation*, 17–44. Berlin: Mouton de Gruyter.
Ritter, Elizabeth & Sara Thomas Rosen. 1998. Delimiting events in syntax. In Miriam Butt & Wilhelm Geuder (eds.), *The projection of arguments: Lexical and compositional factors*, 135–164. Stanford, CA: CSLI Publications.
Ritter, Elizabeth & Sara Thomas Rosen. 2000. Event structure and ergativity. In Carol Tenny & James Pustejovsky (eds.), *Events as grammatical objects: The converging perspectives of lexical semantics and syntax*, 187–238. Stanford, CA: CSLI Publications.
Roberts, Craige. 1996. Information structure in discourse: Towards an integrated formal theory of pragmatics. *OSU Working Papers in Linguistics* 49. 91–136.
Ross, John Robert. 1967. *Constraints on variables in syntax*. Cambridge, MA: Massachusetts Institute of Technology dissertation.
Ross, John Robert. 1969. Guess who? In *Proceedings of the Chicago Linguistic Society (CLS)*, vol. 5, 252–286.

Ross, John Robert. 1972. Doubl-ing. *Linguistic Inquiry* 3(1). 61–86.
Rothstein, Susan. 1985. *The syntactic forms of predication*. Cambridge, MA: Massachusetts Institute of Technology dissertation.
Rothstein, Susan. 2003. Secondary predication and aspectual structure. In Ewald Lang, Claudia Maienborn & Cathrine Fabricius-Hansen (eds.), *Modifying adjuncts*, 553–590. Berlin: Mouton de Gruyter.
Rothstein, Susan. 2004a. Derived accomplishments and lexical aspect. In Jacqueline Guéron & Jacqueline Lecarme (eds.), *The syntax of time*, 539–553. Cambridge, MA: MIT Press.
Rothstein, Susan. 2004b. *Structuring events: A study in the semantics of lexical aspect*. Malden, MA: Blackwell.
Rothstein, Susan. 2006. Secondary predication. In Martin Everaert & Henk van Riemsdijk (eds.), *The Blackwell companion to syntax*, vol. 4, 209–233. Malden, MA & Oxford: Blackwell.
Rothstein, Susan. 2008. Two puzzles for a theory of lexical aspect: Semelfactives and degree achievements. In Johannes Dölling, Tatjana Heyde-Zybatow & Martin Schäfer (eds.), *Event structures in linguistic form and interpretation*, 175–197. Berlin & New York: de Gruyter.
Rothstein, Susan. 2017. Secondary predication. In Martin Everaert & Henk van Riemsdijk (eds.), *The Wiley Blackwell companion to syntax*, vol. 6. 2nd edn., 3872–3901. Hoboken, NJ: Wiley.
Ryle, Gilbert. 1949. *The concept of mind*. London: Hutchinson.
Sag, Ivan A., Philip Hofmeister & Neal Snider. 2008. Processing Complexity in Subjacency Violations: The Complex Noun Phrase Constraint. Manuscript, Stanford University.
Santorini, Beatrice. 2019. (Un?)expected movement. Accessed 2022-10-28. https://www.ling.upenn.edu/~beatrice/examples/movement.html.
Sasse, Hans-Jürgen. 1987. The thetic/categorical distinction revisited. *Linguistics* 25(3). 511–580.
Sasse, Hans-Jürgen. 2006. Aspect and Aktionsart. In Keith Brown (ed.), *Encyclopedia of language and linguistics*, vol. 1. 2nd edn., 535–538. Oxford: Elsevier.
Schank, Robert C. & Robert P. Abelson. 1977. *Scripts, plans, goals and understanding: An inquiry into human knowledge structures*. Hillsdale, NJ: Lawrence Erlbaum.
Schultze-Berndt, Eva & Nikolaus P. Himmelmann. 2004. Depictive secondary predicates in crosslinguistic perspective. *Linguistic Typology* 8(1). 59–131.
Schütze, Carson T. & Jon Sprouse. 2013. Judgment data. In Robert J. Podesva & Devyani Sharma (eds.), *Research methods in linguistics*, 27–50. Cambridge: Cambridge University Press.
Shafiei, Nazila & Thomas Graf. 2020. The subregular complexity of syntactic islands. In *Proceedings of the Society for Computation in Linguistics (SCiL)*, vol. 3, 272–281.
Sheehan, Michelle. 2013. The resuscitation of CED. In *Proceedings of the North East Linguistic Society (NELS)*, vol. 40(2), 135–150.
Simpson, Jane. 1983. Resultatives. In Beth Levin, Malka Rappaport & Annie Zaenen (eds.), *Papers in Lexical-Functional Grammar*, 143–157. Bloomington, IN: Indiana University Linguistics Club.
Simpson, Jane. 2005. Depictives in English and Walpiri. In Nikolaus P. Himmelmann & Eva Schultze-Berndt (eds.), *Secondary predication and adverbial modification: The typology of depictives*, 69–106. Oxford: Oxford University Press.
Singmann, Henrik, Benjamin M. Bolker, Jake Westfall, Frederik Aust & Mattan S. Ben-Shachar. 2020. afex: Analysis of factorial experiments. R package version 0.22-2. https://cran.r-project.org/package=afex.

Singmann, Henrik & David Kellen. 2020. An introduction to mixed models for experimental psychology. In Daniel Spieler & Eric Schumacher (eds.), *New methods in cognitive psychology*, 4–31. New York & London: Routledge.
Sloman, Steven. 2005. *Causal models: How people think about the world and its alternatives*. Oxford: Oxford University Press.
Smith, Carlota S. 1997. *The parameter of aspect*. 2nd edn. Dordrecht: Kluwer.
Sprouse, Jon. 2007. Continuous acceptability, categorical grammaticality, and experimental syntax. *Biolinguistics* 1. 123–134.
Sprouse, Jon, Ivano Caponigro, Ciro Greco & Carlo Cecchetto. 2016. Experimental syntax and the variation of island effects in English and Italian. *Natural Language & Linguistic Theory* 34. 307–344.
Sprouse, Jon & Norbert Hornstein. 2013. Experimental syntax and island effects: Toward a comprehensive theory of islands. In Jon Sprouse & Norbert Hornstein (eds.), *Experimental syntax and island effects*, 1–17. Cambridge: Cambridge University Press.
Sprouse, Jon, Matthew W. Wagers & Colin Phillips. 2012. A test of the relation between working-memory capacity and syntactic island effects. *Language* 88(1). 82–123.
Sprouse, Jon, Matthew W. Wagers & Colin Phillips. 2013. Deriving competing predictions from grammatical approaches and reductionist approaches to island effects. In Jon Sprouse & Norbert Hornstein (eds.), *Experimental syntax and island effects*, 21–41. Cambridge: Cambridge University Press.
Stalnaker, Robert. 2002. Common ground. *Linguistics & Philosophy* 25(5-6). 701–721.
Stalnaker, Robert. 2014. *Context*. Oxford: Oxford University Press.
Staub, Adrian. 2007. The parser doesn't ignore intransitivity, after all. *Journal of Experimental Psychology* 33(3). 550–569.
Stepanov, Arthur. 2001. Late adjunction and minimalist phrase structure. *Syntax* 4(2). 94–125.
Stepanov, Arthur. 2007. The end of CED? Minimalism and extraction domains. *Syntax and Semantics* 10(1). 80–126.
Stowe, Laurie A. 1986. Parsing wh-constructions: Evidence for on-line gap location. *Language and Cognitive Processes* 1(3). 227–245.
Stump, Gregory T. 1985. *The semantic variability of absolute constructions*. Dordrecht, Boston & Lancaster: Reidel.
Sullivan, Natalie, Matthew Walenski, Tracy Love & Lewis P. Shapiro. 2017. The curious case of processing unaccusative verbs in aphasia. *Aphasiology* 31(10). 1205–1225.
de Swart, Henriëtte. 1998. Aspect shift and coercion. *Natural Language & Linguistic Theory* 16(2). 347–385.
de Swart, Henriëtte. 2012. Verbal aspect. In Robert I. Binnick (ed.), *The Oxford handbook of tense and aspect*, 752–780. Oxford: Oxford University Press.
Szabolcsi, Anna. 2006. Strong vs. weak islands. In Martin Everaert & Henk van Riemsdijk (eds.), *The Blackwell companion to syntax*, vol. 4, 479–531. Malden, MA & Oxford: Blackwell.
Szabolcsi, Anna & Marcel den Dikken. 2003. Islands. In Lisa Cheng & Rint Sybesma (eds.), *The second GLOT International state-of-the-article book: The latest in linguistics*, 213–240. Berlin & New York: Mouton de Gruyter.
Szabolcsi, Anna & Terje Lohndal. 2017. Strong vs. weak islands. In Martin Everaert & Henk van Riemsdijk (eds.), *The Wiley Blackwell companion to syntax*, vol. 7. 2nd edn., 4042–4092. Hoboken, NJ: Wiley.

Talmy, Leonard. 1985. Lexicalization patterns: Semantic structure in lexical forms. In Timothy Shopen (ed.), *Language typology and syntactic description, vol. 3: Grammatical categories and the lexicon*, 57–149. Cambridge: Cambridge University Press.

Talmy, Leonard. 1991. Path to realization: A typology of event conflation. In *Proceedings of the Berkeley Linguistics Society (BLS)*, vol. 17, 480–519.

Talmy, Leonard. 2000. *Towards a cognitive semantics, vol. 2: Typology and process in concept structuring*. Cambridge, MA & London: MIT Press.

Teleman, Ulf, Staffan Hellberg & Erik Andersson. 1999. *Svenska akademiens grammatik*, vol. 4. Stockholm: Svenska akademien.

Tenny, Carol. 1987. *Grammaticalizing aspect and affectedness*. Cambridge, MA: Massachusetts Institute of Technology dissertation.

Tenny, Carol. 1994. *Aspectual roles and the syntax-semantics interface*. Dordrecht: Kluwer.

Tenny, Carol. 1995. How motion verbs are special: The interaction of semantic and pragmatic information in aspectual verb meanings. *Pragmatics & Cognition* 3(1). 31–73.

Timberlake, Alan. 2007. Aspect, tense, mood. In Timothy Shopen (ed.), *Language typology and syntactic description, vol. 3: Grammatical categories and the lexicon*. 2nd edn., 280–333. Cambridge: Cambridge University Press.

Travis, Lisa deMena. 2010. *Inner aspect: The articulation of VP*. Dordrecht: Springer.

Truswell, Robert. 2007. Extraction from adjuncts and the structure of events. *Lingua* 117. 1355–1377.

Truswell, Robert. 2008. Preposition-stranding, passivisation, and extraction from adjuncts in Germanic. In Jeroen van Craenenbroeck & Johan Rooryck (eds.), *Linguistic variation yearbook*, vol. 8, 131–178. Amsterdam: John Benjamins.

Truswell, Robert. 2011. *Events, phrases, and questions*. Oxford: Oxford University Press.

Truswell, Robert. 2019a. Event composition and event individuation. In Robert Truswell (ed.), *The Oxford handbook of event structure*, 90–122. Oxford: Oxford University Press.

Truswell, Robert. 2019b. Introduction. In Robert Truswell (ed.), *The Oxford handbook of event structure*, 1–28. Oxford: Oxford University Press.

Van Valin, Robert D., Jr. 2005. *Exploring the syntax-semantics interface*. Cambridge: Cambridge University Press.

Vendler, Zeno. 1957. Verbs and times. *The Philosophical Review* 66(2). 143–160.

Verkuyl, Henk J. 1989. Aspectual classes and aspectual composition. *Linguistics & Philosophy* 12. 39–94.

Verkuyl, Henk J. 1993. *A theory of aspectuality: The interaction between temporal and atemporal structure*. Cambridge: Cambridge University Press.

Verkuyl, Henk J. 2005. Aspectual composition: Surveying the ingredients. In Henk J. Verkuyl, Henriëtte de Swart & Angeliek van Hout (eds.), *Perspectives on aspect*, 19–39. Dordrecht: Springer.

Verkuyl, Henk J. 2019. Event structure without naïve physics. In Robert Truswell (ed.), *The Oxford handbook of event structure*, 171–204. Oxford: Oxford University Press.

Wagers, Matthew W. 2013. Memory mechanisms for wh-dependency formation and their implications for islandhood. In Jon Sprouse & Norbert Hornstein (eds.), *Experimental syntax and island effects*, 161–185. Cambridge: Cambridge University Press.

Wanner, Anja. 2013. The get-passive at the intersection of get and the passive. In Artemis Alexiadou & Florian Schäfer (eds.), *Non-canonical passives*, 43–61. Amsterdam & Philadelphia: John Benjamins.

Wechsler, Stephen. 2005. Resultatives under the 'Event Argument Homomorphism' model of telicity. In Nomi Erteschik-Shir & Tova R. Rapoport (eds.), *The syntax of aspect: Deriving thematic and aspectual interpretation*, 255–273. Oxford: Oxford University Press.

Weisser, Philipp. 2015. *Derived coordination: A minimalist perspective on clause chains, converbs and asymmetric coordination*. Berlin & Boston: de Gruyter.

Wexler, Kenneth & Peter W. Culicover. 1980. *Formal principles of language acquisition*. Cambridge, MA: MIT Press.

Wickham, Hadley. 2016. *ggplot2: Elegant graphics for data analysis*. New York, NY: Springer.

Williams, Edwin. 1980. Predication. *Linguistic Inquiry* 11(1). 203–238.

Williams, Edwin. 1983. Against small clauses. *Linguistic Inquiry* 14(2). 287–308.

Winkler, Susanne. 1997. *Focus and secondary predication*. Berlin & New York: Mouton de Gruyter.

Winkler, Susanne, Janina Radó & Marian Gutscher. 2016. What determines "freezing" effects in was-für split constructions? In Sam Featherston & Yannik Versley (eds.), *Quantitative approaches to grammar and grammatical change: Perspectives from Germanic*, 207–232. Berlin & Boston: Mouton de Gruyter.

Winter, Bodo. 2020. *Statistics for linguists: An introduction using R*. New York & London: Routledge.

Ylikoski, Jussi. 2003. Defining non-finites: Action nominals, converbs and infinitives. *SKY Journal of Linguistics* 16. 185–237.

Zubizarreta, Maria Luisa & Jean-Roger Vergnaud. 2006. Phrasal stress and syntax. In Martin Everaert & Henk van Riemsdijk (eds.), *The Blackwell companion to syntax*, vol. 3, 522–568. Malden, MA & Oxford: Blackwell.

Zucchi, Sandro. 1998. Aspect shift. In Susan Rothstein (ed.), *Events and grammar*, 349–370. Dordrecht: Kluwer.

Zwarts, Joost. 2005. Prepositional aspect and the algebra of paths. *Linguistics & Philosophy* 28(6). 739–779.

Zwarts, Joost. 2008. Aspects of a typology of direction. In Susan Rothstein (ed.), *Theoretical and crosslinguistic approaches to the semantics of aspect*, 79–105. Amsterdam & Philadelphia: John Benjamins.

Index

acceptability judgment 2, 9, 12, 13, 65, 128–129, 132, 145, 153, 156, 162, 176, 237, 238, 242, 247, 270, 273, 302
accomplishment 51, 89, 90, 99, 113, 117, 122, 124, 144, 220, 265, 284, 286–289
achievement 11, 51–52, 89, 90, 98, 100, 113, 122, 131, 136, 206, 211, 220, 227, 234, 236, 253–254, 274, 289
– degree achievement 51, 147, 149, 208–209, 216, 236, 279
– extendable 92, 108, 221, 254, 255, 274, 282, 285
– purely punctual/point 51, 92, 108, 114, 146, 221, 227, 254, 255, 274, 276, 283–285, 288
activity 11, 51, 56, 89, 99, 100, 105, 107, 113, 117, 124–125, 136, 144, 258, 276
adjunction 67–69, 109, 143
– early vs. late 73, 141
– high vs. low 35, 71–72, 139–141
adverbial clause 5, 7, 19, 21, 44, 76, 97, 129–130, 134–135, 139, 142, 148, 153, 184, 233, 243, 256, 278, 289
– reduced 20–23, 29
agentivity 86, 95, 100–103, 106, 107, 134, 144–145, 161, 197–198, 228, 239, 275, 279, 302
agreement 68, 70, 75–76, 141
argument structure 29, 37, 49, 61, 64, 70, 80, 81, 83–85, 137, 138, 162, 198, 200, 209, 220, 228–236, 250, 264
argument-adjunct distinction 2, 18, 84, 112–113, 120, 123, 127, 164, 233, 236, 277
aspect
– grammatical 209–211, 215, 216, 235, 276
– lexical 209–210, 215–216
aspectual class 6, 13, 17, 19, 22, 50, 64, 87, 99, 118–119, 125, 136, 137, 161, 188–189, 239, 252, 274, 302, 304
aspectual shifting 190, 210, 212, 216, 223, 249

background *see* information structure
barrier 21, 65, 77, 82, 84
binding 69, 265

bridge verb 131, 243

case 72–74, 76
causality 18, 21, 22, 25, 34, 37, 38, 89, 98, 101, 112, 130, 131, 133–137, 161, 209, 219, 229, 230, 234, 236, 282, 287, 288
causative alternation 51, 217–218
CED *see* Condition on Extraction Domain
chain formation 97, 109
coercion 103, 257, 276, 283, 289
– aspectual 143–144, 150, 211, 220, 221, 225–226, 228, 237, 244, 255–256, 260, 274, 288, 289, 303
coherence *see* discourse coherence relation
competence-performance distinction 1, 13, 155, 156, 241, 246, 247, 303
complex event 38, 41–44, 91, 97, 100, 101, 123, 161, 287
complex predicate 52, 58, 60, 80, 81, 96
complexity
– semantic 40, 251, 305
– syntactic 7, 12, 26, 46, 199, 201, 247, 271, 277, 302
Conceptual Structure 70
Condition on Extraction Domain 2–4, 64, 71, 75, 109, 112, 155, 182, 238, 277–278, 305
constraints
– semantic 64, 72, 93, 96, 98, 100, 102, 104, 106, 177, 239
– syntactic 64, 155–157, 241, 244, 247, 249, 252, 272, 277, 278, 303, 304
context 22, 25–26, 51, 127, 148, 288, 305
converb 23–26
coordination 25, 139, 143, 183
coreference 83, 191, 269
cross-linguistic variation 24, 28, 43, 44, 46, 111, 124, 135, 145, 157
cyclicity 73

D-linking 158–159, 175, 189, 273, 278, 305
declarative 9, 42, 65, 83, 86, 93, 98, 99, 104–106, 113–115, 123, 128, 132, 136, 138, 145, 147, 153, 165, 166, 170, 176, 178, 189,

191, 197, 215, 231, 235, 238, 240, 242, 247, 248, 251, 268
dependency *see* filler–gap dependency
Dependency Locality Theory 103, 186
depictive *see* secondary predicate
directional phrase 82, 278–280, 295
discourse coherence relation 7, 22, 35, 36, 39, 97, 134–137, 161–162, 205, 233, 235, 239
discourse function 8, 102, 134, 159, 249
discourse referent 7, 12, 103, 128, 264, 265, 271

effect structure 154, 164–165, 170, 175, 177, 240
– linear-additive effect 10, 12, 164, 174, 175, 177, 181, 182, 188–190, 199, 205, 226, 240, 242, 243, 247
– subadditive effect 165, 223, 240
– superadditive effect 8, 165, 187, 226, 240, 242
enablement 98
event expansion 38–39, 70, 281, 286–288
event grouping 39, 100–101, 130, 197, 198, 298
event specification 36–38, 70, 280–281, 286–288
event structure 11, 29, 49, 50, 61, 92, 122, 123, 161, 184, 228, 236, 302
– boundedness 55, 89, 95, 107, 142, 261, 263, 279, 280, 282
– culmination 102, 142, 144, 147, 208, 210, 254, 261, 281, 289
– durativity 11, 54, 55, 114, 121, 253–256, 260, 271, 276, 285, 289, 302
extraction 8, 14, 42, 56, 69, 132, 170, 203, 232, 238, 241, 242, 245, 247, 251, 268, 271, 272, 277
– clefting 8, 168
– relativization 4, 8, 159, 166, 168, 170, 175, 189, 251, 273, 277, 278, 291, 305
– topicalization 234, 251, 273
– wh-extraction 6, 8, 64, 164, 167, 176, 178, 179, 189, 305

Factorial Acceptability Model 12, 270, 302, 303
factorial design 163–166

feature checking 139, 141
feature sharing 69, 70
filled-gap effect 202, 291
filler–gap dependency 1–2, 14, 68, 74, 75, 159, 226, 247, 251, *see also* extraction
finiteness 5, 7, 20, 23, 72, 130, 131, 135, 159
Finnish 24
focus *see* information structure
frame–satellite typology 42–44, 98, 119
free adjunct 24, 35, 48, 113, 145, 168, 184, 190, 219, 296
freezing 177, 249, 303
frequency 252, 290, 292–293, 305

German 25–26, 46–48, 145, 199
grammaticality judgment 1, 3, 5, 64, 65, 86, 99, 155–156, 163, 189, 303

idiomatic interpretation 58, 60, 292
incorporation 80–81
incremental theme 11, 54, 106, 107, 144, 149, 258, 259, 261, 263, 275, 284, 296, 297
indefinite 20, 296
Independence Hypothesis 10, 138, 150, 153, 249, 302
– support for 146, 177, 182, 188, 190, 198, 205, 206, 215, 226, 235, 240, 245, 302
information structure 8, 112, 116, 127, 138, 159–160, 305
– background 126, 131, 160
– focus 27, 52, 116–117, 126–127, 160
– topic 111, 126, 127, 133
interface 109, 110, 137, 293, 305
interpretation 17–19, 99, 106
interval 31–33, 35, 106, 208, 211
intervention effects 75, 76
intonation unit 35, 183–184, 187, 188, 219
island effect 2, 8, 164, 165, 241, 247, 249, 277
island repair 110, 144, 165, 166, 170, 182, 192, 196, 199, 226, 305

labeling 68, 69
lexical semantics 36, 38, 41, 43, 124, 128, 209, 218, 255, 256, 289
licensing conditions 9, 64, 65, 138, 142, 149, 150, 240, 241, 302
linearization 110, 293–295

locality 9, 63, 64, 88, 93, 94, 96, 138, 249, 301, 303
Logical Form 109–110

manner 18, 25, 37, 38, 102, 116, 280
Manner–Result Complementarity 40–42, 98
Merge 67–69, 71, 141, 270
motion verb 42, 44, 82, 86, 116, 127, 149, 201, 227, 259, 260, 262, 270, 278–279, 281, 296
multidominance 68

Norwegian 145
numeration 72

operator 109–110, 142, 210
optionality 17, 70, 112, 118, 127, 234
overlap 32–34, 36, 48, 53, 90, 101, 113, 270, 282, 289

parasitic gap 75, 249, 291, 303
particle 6, 95, 101, 107, 149, 274, 275, 278
passive 73, 207, 218
past participle 7, 49, 83, 297–299
path 278–279
perception verb 11, 42, 92, 93, 107, 146, 221, 285, 288–289, 292
performance see competence–performance distinction
phase 72, 73, 110, 139–141, 294
phi-features 69, 74
Phonetic Form 110–111
plausibility 51, 76, 81, 103–104, 148, 234, 247, 291
pragmatic constraints 64, 128
pragmatics 38, 76, 126, 132, 148, 243, 305
preposition stranding 102, 111
prepositional adjuncts 22, 71, 97, 99, 139
processing 51, 103, 158, 175, 201, 211, 223, 241, 242, 247, 266, 269, 272, 283
– processing complexity 12, 248, 272, 277, 303, 304
progressive 42, 92, 107, 208–210, 215, 228, 236, 252, 256, 288
projection 71, 121
prosody 184, 295–296, 305

psychological adjective 206, 212, 217, 233, 276
purpose clause 71, 97, 98

reanalysis 80–81
reflexivity 12, 60, 83–85, 96, 114, 191, 218, 265, 267, 269, 302, 304
relativization see extraction
relevance 126–129, 132, 133, 229, 234, 272, 281, 288
result phrase 119, 124
resultative see secondary predicate
Romance languages 43

salience 127
scalar change 11, 45, 49, 95, 107, 149, 258–263, 271, 276, 283, 285, 302
scale 55, 106
– path 90, 95, 107, 114, 117, 122, 123, 149, 227, 259, 260, 262, 282, 284, 296, 297
– property 123, 147, 149, 217, 262, 276
– temporal 142, 143, 149, 217, 263
secondary predicate 16, 27–29
– depictive 27–35, 78, 89, 120, 205, 236, 252, 280–281, 289, 301
– licensing condition 48
– licensing conditions 17, 153, 283, 301
– resultative 27, 52, 57–60, 208, 263, 265, 269, 287
selectional restrictions 50, 59, 70, 290
semantic compatibility 10, 11, 81, 247, 252, 262, 263, 268, 271, 277, 286, 302
semantic mismatch 16, 146, 243
semantic selection 18, 38, 58, 70, 233, 236, 289–291
semelfactive 54, 106, 107, 255
sluicing 110, 111
Spanish 43, 44, 79–81, 112–113, 116, 118–120, 294
Spell-Out 69–71, 141, 293
split intransitivity see verb type
stative 11, 50, 89, 99, 113, 122, 124–125, 147, 253–254
– permanent 50, 254, 276, 286
– temporary 50, 107, 147, 254
strong/weak islands 2, 4, 6, 20, 74, 75, 137, 154, 157, 158, 191, 241, 243

subcategorization 59, 72, 109, 164
subevent 38, 53, 88, 89, 91, 255
subextraction 14, 79, 84, 102, 112, 233, 252
subject island 153, 157, 159, 193
subordination 5, 20, 21, 23
Swedish 135–136, 157, 234
syntactic integration 109, 134, 135, 162, 183, 188, 190, 240, 244
syntactic selection 58, 120, 127, 205, 264–266

telicity 5, 8, 14, 19, 52, 54, 89, 91, 93, 94, 99, 101, 121, 135, 144–146, 166, 170, 173, 176, 179, 191, 209, 213, 215–216, 228, 239, 244, 249, 258, 262, 276, 303
theta-role 17, 27, 57, 58, 74, 82, 84, 116, 199, 201, 265
theticity 20, 297
topicalization *see* extraction
Transfer 69, 71
transitive *see* verb type
transitivity 11, 75, 145, 161, 220, 239, 264–266, 271, 289
– transitivity penalty 199, 239, 265–269

unaccusative *see* verb type
underspecification 37, 39, 88, 91, 260, 275
unergative *see* verb type

verb type 5, 8, 41, 50, 78, 82, 96, 160, 191, 192, 194, 205, 238, 244, 252, 274, 303
– intransitive 12, 19, 82, 115, 149, 212, 228, 245
– transitive 19, 82–83, 86, 96, 114, 149, 191, 194, 198–199, 201
– unaccusative 41, 82, 85, 115, 191, 192, 197, 199–201, 238, 244
– unergative 6, 41, 53, 82, 85, 87, 106, 115, 192, 199, 289
violation 2, 13, 150, 157, 241, 246

weak island *see* strong/weak islands
wh-extraction *see* extraction
wh-in-situ 111
wh-island 79, 153
working memory 1, 77, 226, 242, 243, 251, 291

www.ingramcontent.com/pod-product-compliance
Lightning Source LLC
Chambersburg PA
CBHW020220170426
43201CB00007B/272